CISTERCIAN FATHERS SERIES: NUMBER FIFTY

THE LIFE
OF
BEATRICE OF NAZARETH

Frontispiece: Cistercian Antiphonary executed at Nazareth in 1244 by Sisters Christine and Agnes, under the supervision of Beatrice, who may well have drawn in the initial capital. The antiphonary is preserved in the archives of the Cistercian Abbey of Bornem, near Antwerp, Belgium. Used with permission.

On folio 182 v is written: Anno domini M.CC.XLIIII scriptus et notatus est liber iste finitus autem in crastino Ambrosii anni M.CC.XLV. Quisquem viderit eum orent pro scriptrice (Agnes) et notatrice (Christina) quae laboraverunt in eo. [This book was written and the music noted in the year of Our Lord 1244, but finished on the day after the feast of St Ambrose 1245. Let anyone who shall look at it pray for the scribe (Agnes) and the musical noter (Christina), who worked on it.]

On folio 186, is written: Finito libro sit laus et gloria Christo. Liber Sanctae Mariae de Nazareth. Quiscumque abstulit, anathema sit. [Praise and glory to Christ at the completion of this book. A book <the property> of St Mary of Nazareth <Abbey>. Let anyone who purloins it be anathema.]

CISTERCIAN FATHERS SERIES: NUMBER FIFTY

THE LIFE OF
BEATRICE OF NAZARETH,
1200 - 1268

Translated and annotated by

Roger De Ganck

assisted by

John Baptist Hasbrouck OCSO

Cistercian Publications
Kalamazoo, Michigan
1991

The editors of Cistercian Publications express their appreciation to the Ruusbroecgenootschap and Dr Paul Verdeyen, SJ, its director, and to his predecessor, Dr Joseph Alaerts, SJ, for allowing them to reproduce the Latin text published in their *Vita Beatricis. De autobiografie van de Z. Beatrijs van Tienen O. Cist. 1200-1268 in de Latijnse bewerking van de anonieme biechtvader der abdij van Nazareth te Lier*. Voor het eerst volledig en kritisch uitgegeven door L. REYPENS. *Studiën en tekstuitgaven van Ons Geestelijk Erf* XV. Antwerpen: Ruusbroecgenootschap, 1964, and to the Abbess and community of The Abbey of O.L. Vr. van Nazareth, for the cover illustration and for permission to reproduce it.

Beatrice van Tienen, 1200-1268

Volume One of a series of three:

The Life of Beatrice of Nazareth, (Cistercian Fathers Series, Number 50)
Beatrice of Nazareth in Her Context, (Cistercian Studies Series, Number 121)
Towards Unification with God, (Cistercian Studies Series, Number 122)

The work of Cistercian Publications is made possible in part
by support from Western Michigan University to
The Institute of Cistercian Studies.

Library of Congress Cataloguing-in-Publication Data

Vita Beatricis. English & Latin.
  Beatrice of Nazareth : a thirteenth century biography / translated
by Roger De Ganck.
     p. cm. -- (Beatrice of Nazareth / by Roger De Ganck ; v. 1)
Cistercian Fathers series ; no. 50)
    Latin text and English translation of: Vita Beatricis.
    Includes bibliographical references.
    ISBN 0-87907-450-7. -- ISBN 0-87907-650-X (pbk.)
    1. Beatrijs, van Tienen, ca. 1200-1268. 2. Nuns--Belgium-
-Flanders--Biography--Early works to 1800. 3. Mystics--Belgium-
-Flanders--Biography--Early works to 1800.   I. Ganck, Roger De,
1908-   . II. Title. III. Series. IV. Series: Ganck, Roger De,
1908-   Beatrice of Nazareth ; v. 1.
    BX4705.B25868G36 vol. 1
    271'.97 s--dc20
    [271'.97]   89-27869
    [B]   CIP

Cover design by Alice Duthie-Clark
Typography by Karen Jazayeri-Nejad
Printed in the United States of America

TO

THE MEMORY

OF

CELINA MARTENS

1875-1928

TABLE OF CONTENTS

PREFACE

BEATRICE OF NAZARETH[1] is little known outside the Low Countries (Belgium and the Netherlands). This is not surprising when one realizes that even in Belgium, her own country, she came to light only recently. It was not until the furor of the French Revolution and the dust of the Napoleonic wars had finally settled that scholars could begin their painstaking labors of tracing back, collecting, and publishing their discoveries, including the writings of Beatrice.

Beatrice wrote a small treatise entitled *Seven Manieren van Minne* (*Seven Experiences of Loving*), first critically edited in 1926.[2] A biography had to wait until 1964 when Leonce Reypens published his critical edition of the *Vita*.[3]

What follows is, first of all, a presentation of Beatrice herself, *viz.* her *curriculum vitae*, then a chapter about the extant manuscripts of her Life, her biographer, his credibility and methodology, and the disappearance of her original autobiography. Since only four manuscripts of the *Vita* are known, the Latin text of Dr Reypens' critical edition has been reproduced for the sake of English-speaking scholars. With the text at hand, the reader can conveniently locate citations according to the paragraphs and the pages of the critical Latin edition. References to this edition, given within parentheses, indicate first the paragraph, and then the first line of any citation, even if it covers several lines. When referred to in a footnote, the preceding term *Vita* indicates the biographer's work itself according to Dr Reypen's edition. Facing the Latin text is an English translation. The latter has been kept close to the former in order to acquaint a twentieth-century reader with the way a biog-

---

1. At a time when family names were only in the process of formation, monks and nuns were usually identified by their community; within their community they were sometimes distinguished from others with the same first name by referring to their birthplace. To avoid confusion, it seems best to keep calling her Beatrice of Nazareth.

2. Leonce Reypens and Joseph Van Mierlo, *Beatrijs van Nazareth, Seven Manieren van Minne*, critisch uitgegeven (Leuven, 1926). Henceforth cited: R-VM, *Seven Manieren.*

3. Leonce Reypens, *Vita Beatricis. De Autobiografie van de Z. Beatrijs van Tienen O. Cist., 1200-1268.* Studiën en tekstuitgaven van Ons Geestelijk Erf 15 (Antwerp, 1964). Henceforth cited: *Vita.* When reference is made to what Dr Reypens says in his publication, he is quoted as: Reypens, *Vita,* followed by the page number.

raphy was written in the thirteenth century. The translator is aware that the *Life* often seems stilted, verbose, and occasionally awkward. This has been done deliberately in an attempt to give some idea of the unfortunate Latin style of the biographer. Those who read Latin will be aware that, even so, the English is less precious than the original.

The biography or *Vita* of Beatrice is based on her autobiography, covered by her journal from 1215 till about 1236. What the biographer says about her before she was fifteen should therefore be read with a grain of salt.[4] The *Vita* is exceptionally long, and two volumes of commentary have been published separately in the Cistercian Studies Series (CS121, CS122). In these two volumes—which might advisably be read first—a serious effort has been made to place Beatrice and her spirituality in the context of her time. Without this her biography may easily be incorrectly understood or even misinterpreted. Although she lived from 1200 till 1268, she shows no trace of scholastic influence. It was in the last second half of the thirteenth century that the Dominicans Thomas Acquinas (d.1274) and Albert the Great (d.1280), and the Franciscans Bonaventure (d.1274) and John Duns Scotus (d.1308), shifted scholastic philosophy and theology from Platonic to Aristotelian thought.[5]

My own English translation of Beatrice's *Vita* seemed too defective to be presented to English-speaking readers, which is not surprising since English is not my native tongue. The Very Reverend John Baptist Hasbrouck of Guadalupe Abbey, Lafayette, Oregon, had the kindness and dedication to rewrite the English translation. To him I express my sincere gratitude. I appealed also to Dr Robert Burns, SJ, Professor of Latin at the University of California at Los Angeles; to Dr Karen Carlton, Professor of English at California State University at Arcata; to Mrs Marylee Rohde and Mrs Joan Stroud both of Eureka; and to Mrs Therese Walrath-Mughannam of Santa Rosa. With all this much

---

4. That Beatrice did some of the self-castigations mentioned in Chapters Four to Seven of the first Book of her biography is not in doubt. However, the biographer seems to have sought inspiration in the first book of the biography of Arnulph (1180-1228), a laybrother of Villers, a Cistercian abbey some forty kilometers south of Brussels. Arnulph was notorious for his extraordinary self-torture. The descriptions of Beatrice's self-castigations, some in nearly the same words, can be found in Arnulph's biography (*AA SS* June 7: 612,17 - 616,39). Beatrice herself could have heard about or read the account of Arnulph's feats, although we have no direct evidence she did.

5. For an overview of scholasticism, see Fr. Copleston, *A History of Philosophy,* vol. 2, sixth edition (Westminster, Maryland, 1958).

appreciated help I feel confident in accepting the responsibility for the English translation of Beatrice's *Vita*.

Both thanks and appreciation are expressed to Dr Paul Verdeyen, SJ, director of the Centrum Ruusbroecgenootschap in Antwerp, and to his predecessor, Dr. Joseph Alaerts, SJ, for allowing us to reproduce, without critical apparatus, the text of the *Vita Beatricis* edited by Dr Léonce Reypens (Antwerp, 1964), and the *Seven Manieren Van Minne* (Leuven, 1926). I was also fortunate to receive through the kindness of Dr Paul Wackers of the University of Nijmegen, a copy of the unpublished dissertation of Dr Herman Vekeman, now professor at the University of Cologne: *Seven Manieren van Minne. Lexicografisch Onderzoek*, two volumes (Leuven, 1967). My thanks are no less due to my, now late, abbot, the Rt Reverend Bartholomew De Strijcker of Westmalle, Belgium, for giving the *licentia* for this publication and for his support in the form of a grant. I am grateful to Sister Myriam Dardenne and Sister Kathy DaVico of Redwoods Monastery for many patient hours of editorial assistance. Last, but not least, my gratitude goes to Dr Rozanne Elder, whose gentle, expert, intelligent, and patient editorship has never failed, even in the most trying circumstances.

Roger De Ganck

Redwoods Monastery
Whitethorn, California

CHAPTER ONE

BEATRICE'S *CURRICULUM VITAE*

A LTHOUGH BEATRICE'S BIOGRAPHY, like most medieval *Vitae*, does not mention the year of her birth, the year 1200 can be supplied without great difficulty.[1] She was born in the town of Tienen (8,4), some twenty kilometers east of Leuven. Her parents were middle class,[2] which meant well-to-do,[3] but not wealthy as has sometimes been asserted.[4] It may be safely assumed that Beatrice was the youngest[5] of her parents' six children.

Beatrice, we are assured, was a bright girl who at the age of five could recite David's psalter by heart, without error and in the right order (19,63). Her mother gave her her earliest education in *disciplinis*

---

1. R. De Ganck, 'Chronological Data in the Lives of Ida of Nivelles and Beatrice of Nazareth', *OGE* 57 (1983) 14-28.

2. *Parentibus mediocribus sortita* (8,7). Some more *mulieres religiosae* belonged to this class: Mary of Oignies: *mediocribus orta parentibus* (*AA SS* June 4: 639); Ida of Nivelles: *mediocribus orta parentibus*, C. Henriquez, *Quinque prudentes virgines* [henceforth cited as *Quinque*] (Antwerp, 1630) 199; Ida Lewis: *mediocri prosapia provenisse* (*AA SS* October 13: 169). In fact, Ida's parents belonged to the impoverished rural nobility. See Antoon Steenwegen, *OGE* 57 (1983) 117. The name of her family and also of the little town, now known as Gorsleeuw, was 'de Lewis' in Latin. Since Lewis sounds more familiar in English than Gorsleeuw, the former has been given preference.

3. Herbert Grundmann, *Religiöse Bewegungen im Mittelalter* (Berlin, 1935, rpt Hildesheim, 1961) 192, n. 42. Henceforth cited as *Religiöse Bewegungen*.

4. Simone Roisin, *L'Hagiographie cistercienne dans le diocèse de Liège au XIIIe siècle* (Leuven-Brussels, 1947: henceforth cited: *L'Hagiographie*, 61. Ernest McDonnell, *The Beguines and Beghards in Medieval Culture. With special emphasis on the Belgian Scene*, [henceforth *The Beguines*], (New Brunswick, NJ, 1954) 110. Even Grundmann, *Religiöse Bewegungen*, was of the opinion that Beatrice's father was rich: 'er war ein sehr reicher Bürger'. This opinion is based on the questionable assertion that Bartholomew founded three cistercian monasteries for nuns. (8,12). The community of Bloemendaal did not think that he was rich (47,64). I have treated this question in 'The Three Foundations of Bartholomew of Tienen', *Cîteaux* 37 (1986) 49-75.

5. Reypens, *Vita* 47, n.2.

scolaribus (21,27)[6] and intended to send her to school young.[7] When Beatrice was in her seventh year, however, her mother died and her father sent her to live with a group of beguines in a nearby town called Zoutleeuw, 'that she might make progress in the virtues' (20,11). At the same time her intellectual education was entrusted to teachers in the same town,[8] who taught her the liberal arts (21,27). When she had studied for more than a year in this co-educational school[9] her father called her home. After an interval, he yielded to her desire for monastic life, and took her to Florival or Bloemendaal, a monastery of Cistercian nuns, for which he, a layman, was acting as general manager (38,43). In all likelihood this meant that he was the collector of the rents and fiscal revenues.

Beatrice was quite young,[10] about ten,[11] when she became an oblate[12]

6. The expression *in disciplinis scolaribus*, to go to school, or to study can have different meanings. See Ursmer Berlière, 'Écoles claustrales au Moyen Age', *Académie Royale de la Belgique. Bulletin de la Classe des Lettres et des Sciences morales et politiques, Brussels*, 12 (1921) 550-72; 552.

7. Reypens, *Vita* 23, n.3.

8. Dr Reypens has shown that the opinion that she might have gone to school in Leuven cannot be maintained without more proof. See Reypens, 'Nieuws over Beatrijs van Nazareth. Ging Beatrijs school te Leuven?', *OGE* 26 (1952) 54-60.

9. Beatrice's teacher was a man (21,34) and the biographer's moralizing disgression (22,45) on the flirting among the students indicates a co-educational school. Henri Pirenne describes the multiplication of non-monastic schools in the burgeoning towns of that time in Brabant and even more so in Flanders. See his 'L'Instruction des marchants au Moyen Age', *Annales d'Histoire économique et sociale* 1 (1927), rpt in his *Histoire de l' Occident Médiéval* (Bruges, 1951) 551-70.

10. The biographer was a man of his time when it came to designate the stages of life. Beatrice is said to be an infant till she reached the age of seven (20,4). At fifteen she became an adolescent (31,39; 45,3). In fact, there was no uniform computation in regard to the stages of one's life. William of St Thierry in his *De natura et dignitatae amoris* (written toward 1120) distinguished four stages: *puer* (child), *juvenis* (adolescent), *vir* (adult), and *senex* (elder). In his later treatise *De natura corporis et animae* he again has four stages: adolescence running till 25/30; youth till 35/40; maturity 55/60 and finally the elderly. See Ludo Milis, 'Guillaume de St. Thierry. Son origine, sa formation et ses premières expériences monastiques', in *Saint-Thierry. Une abbaye du VIe au XXe siècle* (Saint-Thierry, 1979) 261-79; 267-69 [English translation in *William Abbot of Saint Thierry*, Cistercian Studies Series, 94 (Kalamazoo, 1987) 9-33; 26-27]. Here he discusses also the computations put forward by Stanislas Ceglar in his *William of St. Thierry...* (dissertation, Washington D.C., 1971) and his references to Varron and Isidore of Seville for whom youth runs respectively till 55/60 years of age. Some authors, keeping four stages, attribute

at Bloemendaal to pursue her education.[13] When she passed her fifteenth

---

to each stage twenty or sixteen years. See David Herlihy, *The Social History of Italy and Western Europe. 700-1500* (London, 1979) 353. Milis pointed out that the Middle Ages appreciated and respected older, more mature people, while adolescents and 'youths' of thirty-five or more were considered to suffer still from inconstancy. This is precisely the point Beatrice's biographer intends to make; in opposition to the butterfly-shallowness of girls her age, Beatrice stood out by her earnestness (*gravitas*) and constancy (18,31). The classification of these stages is no solid basis for calculating exact dates. It is not a contradiction to read in Beatrice's biography that when she went to Rameya in the second half of 1216 she is said to be a *juvencula*, youth, while the one-year older Ida is called *femina*, a woman (50,39). Here Beatrice is compared not with flirting girls but with somebody also in the category of *juvenculae*, but more advanced in maturity than Beatrice was in 1216. It was thanks to Ida that Beatrice in that same year made a decisive advance in her spiritual growth.

11. Ten years is too young to enter religious life according to our standards, which are quite different from those of Beatrice's time. To give examples from Beatrice's home country, the duchy of Brabant, Alice of Schaarbeek was seven years old when she entered Ter Kameren near Brussels (*AA SS* June 2: 477); Ida Lewis, thirteen when she joined the community of Rameya (*AA SS* Oct. 13: 109); Lutgard, before she became a Cistercian at twenty-four, had entered a Benedictine community near her hometown of St Trond when she was twelve (*AA SS* June 4: 191); Catherine went to Vrouwenpark when eight years old (*AA SS* May 1: 538). For similar examples (outside Brabant) in Caesarius of Heisterbach's *Dialogus miraculorum*, see McDonnell, *The Beguines*, 87. Ida of Nivelles was nine years of age when she fled to a small community of seven beguines to escape her relatives who were arranging a marriage for her after her father died. She was sixteen when she entered Kerkom/Rameya (*Quinque*, 201 and 205). Grundmann, *Die Religiöse Bewegungen* (191-2), cites the cases of girls twelve and thirteen years old who acted as Ida did when faced with a matchmaking situation. According to roman law the legal age for marriage for boys was fourteen, twelve for girls (John T. Noonan, *Contraception* [Harvard, 1966] 352). This was the situation in Beatrice's lifetime. Alexander III (d. 1181) upheld those ages. See Charles Duggan, 'Equity and Compassion in Papal Marriage Decretals in England', in *Love and Marriage in the Twelfth Century*, Mediaevalia Lovaniensia, Series I, 8 (Leuven 1981) 82.

12. Oblate status was a broad category. Some oblates were adults who joined a community without the intention or the desire of becoming full-fledged members. In modern terminology, they were looking for social security, though this expression should be understood in a flexible way. See Jean Marchal, *Le 'droit d'oblat'. Essai sur une variété de pensionnés monastiques*, Archives de la France monastique 49 (Ligué-Paris, 1955). Other oblates, young boys and particularly girls, too young to be accepted as novices, were admitted because they showed some willingness to become novices at the appropriate time, when they would be better able to make a responsible choice. Such was Beatrice's case.

13. Reypens, *Vita*, 26, n. 2 estimates that during the next six years Beatrice

birthday (45,11), she decided after some hesitation (46,27) to ask to become a novice. Among the objections raised by the community was her still tender age (47,63), which meant that she was below the age officially fixed for entry and therefore lacked the required maturity (47,67: *maturitas*). Beatrice had anticipated this objection (45,18); but her determination and constancy eventually prevailed (46,38; 47,73; 49,6). This was apparently a case when an individual's petition could not simply be overruled in favour of a universal principle spelled out in juridical decrees.[14] A full year later, on some day after 16 April 1216, Beatrice made her profession.

Beatrice was not only bright but artistically gifted as well. A short

---

completed the *trivium* and the *quadrivium*. She eagerly (35,22) followed classes (25,40: *instructionis pabulum*), even when she was scarcely able to walk because of physical weakness or sickness (35,24). Alice of Schaarbeek's *Vita* mentions explicitly that at the age of seven she entered Ter Kameren to receive there an educational training (*AA SS* June 2: 477): *ibique tradita literalibus studiis*). This does not dispense with the question: can such an education be equated with the classical *trivium* and *quadrivium*? Gerard Huyghe pointed out that in accordance with a decision of the General Chapter (*Statuta* 1206,5) nuns were not allowed to educate children (*des enfants*). See his *La clôture des moniales des origines à la fin du XIIIe siècle* (Roubaix 1944) 80. This General Chapter was referring to situations of co-education where 'serious scandals' sometimes occurred when both boys and girls were accepted as students. To my knowledge, acceptance of young girls as oblates in communities of nuns was not questioned or threatened at that time.

14. Maturation being a lifelong process, the biographer has given different nuances to the expression 'constancy'. When at school in Zoutleeuw, Beatrice's earnestness (*gravitas*) is stressed as opposed to the superficiality of her fellow students (18,31); when she was determined to become a novice her 'firm proposal' (*constantia*) made the community change its mind about her degree of maturity. When she went to Rameya she looked up to the one-year older Ida of Nivelles as a mother, a leader, and a teacher (50,54). When she had her first mystical experience and was back in her own community, however, she showed a greater maturity, even 'a new and unusual fortitude and spiritual constancy, which she would have to follow in the future willy-nilly, wherever it led' (68,34). When Alexander III considered petitions related to marriage cases (see n.11), his concern was to safeguard freedom of choice, including therefore the requirement of having arrived at the age of consent. The same principle applied even more strictly to making religious profession, and the General Chapter shifted the minimum age for entrance into the novitiate back and forth from fifteen to eighteen. The principle was maintained, but its application remained subject to practical circumstances, because in this matter, no universal law was applicable always and everywhere. For a more extensive treatment of the admission of novices, see J. H. Lynch, 'The Cistercians and Underage Novices', *Cîteaux* 24 (1973) 283-97.

time after her profession her abbess sent her to the Cistercian community of Rameya (La Ramée) to learn to write manuscripts, particularly liturgical choir books (50,33). It was there that she developed an intimate friendship with Ida of Nivelles who was slightly older and more advanced in spiritual and mystical matters, at least in that year, 1216-1217.[15] This proficiency could be due partly to the period of six years or so that Ida had spent with the beguines in Nivelles. When Beatrice met her, she was already well known and respected for her unusual spiritual advancement. With Ida's guidance and friendship Beatrice made amazingly rapid progress in her own spiritual growth. When her abbess called her back to Bloemendaal (60,4), soon after her first mystical experience in early January 1217 (54,4), her community observed that a visible 'excellence of conduct and maturity of life began to shine in her whole behavior' (60,10). The signs of esteem she began to receive annoyed her so much that she decided to restrain her devotion, at least outwardly. After some months she realized that such restraint was a mistake and she returned to her former conduct. About this she wrote to Ida, sometime after 14 September 1217.

Meanwhile Bartholomew, Beatrice's father, had become a laybrother at Bloemendaal. His son Wickbert joined him there also as a laybrother, and his other daughters, Christine and Sybille, joined the same community in 1215. When Bloemendaal made a foundation at Maagdendaal near Beatrice's hometown of Tienen, Bartholomew and his four children were sent to this daughter-house.

Beatrice's diary makes no mention of this move. Following information he probably received after 1268 from Beatrice's only surviving sister, Christine, her biographer wrote of it in connection with Bartholomew. From 1221 till 1236 Beatrice remained in Bloemendaal. As she wrote her diary with no intention that it ever be made public, we should not wonder, therefore, that the *Vita* has only two indirect references to this community. One occurs in September 1232, when Beatrice was again greatly disturbed by signs of esteem and asked the advice of a wise and experienced man of Tienen (211,61). The second reference mentions the consent of Maagdendaal's abbess to the foundation of a new community, Nazareth near Lier, in 1235 (229,29).

It was in Maagdendaal that Beatrice received her consecration as a

---

15. For the problems arising from connecting the dates of Beatrice and Ida's novitiate and the level of their maturity at that time, see above n. 14, and my article, cited n. 1.

virgin by a bishop. The description given by her biographer corresponds to what we know about the *consecratio virginum* in the thirteenth century.[16] It mentions the paranymphs (76,18), some liturgical actions (76,26) and an allusion to an octave (77,50). Beatrice had to have been at least twenty-five years old for this event, though there is no compelling reason to believe that this consecration took place on her twenty-fifth birthday or even in 1225. A group of virgins was consecrated with her (76,16). In a 'television' (of which more will be said in the next volume), Ida followed from Rameya the ceremony taking place in Maagdendaal and her report is confirmed by a laybrother of Maagdendaal, probably Bartholomew visiting another daughter who had become a Cistercian nun in Rameya.[17] This text raises a question about these novices mentioned twice in Ida's confidences.[18]

In 1235, Maagdendaal decided to make the foundation at Nazareth. During the construction of the buildings, Beatrice was busy copying the choir books needed by the new community. She, her two bloodsisters, and some other nuns transferred to Nazareth in May 1236 (230,45). In

16. Philipp Oppenheimer, *Die consecratio virginum als Geistesgeschichtliches Problem. Eine Studie zu ihrem Aufbau, ihrem Wert und ihrer Geschichte* (Rome, 1943); René Metz, *La consécration des vièrges dans l'église romaine. Étude d'histoire et de liturgie* (Paris, 1954). Colomba Hart published a paper 'Consecratio Virginum: Thirteenth Century Witnesses', in *The American Benedictine Review* 23 (1972) 258-74, where (262-3) Beatrice's consecration is described according to her *Vita*.

17. Reypens, *Vita*, 49*.

18. A bishop has little to do with novices. Their profession was referred not to the bishop but to the abbot, gradually including the abbess. See Joseph Canivez, *Statuta Capitulorum Generalium Ordinis Cisterciensis 1116-1786*, 8 vols (Leuven 1933-41) [henceforth cited *Statuta*] 1242,16; 1243,6; 1244,8. Confusion came from the ambiguity created by using the term *benedictio* for profession and the consecration of virgins. The General Chapter had to clarify the issue by stating that if a *benedictio* is solemn it meant a *consecratio* and was reserved to bishops (*Statuta* 1231,53; 1241,5). Beatrice's *Vita* mentions explicitly her and her companions' *consecratio* by a bishop. If Roisin (*L' Hagiographie*, 55-59) is correct in pointing to Goswin of Bossut as the possible biographer of Ida of Nivelles, why did he speak twice of novices when relating what Ida had told him or what somebody else could have told him about her 'television'? The point is more serious than it appears at first sight. The abbess of Marquette (near Lille, then in Flanders), in trouble with authorities in the Order, had asked a diocesan archdeacon to preside at a profession in her community; this called forth a punitive intervention from the General Chapter (*Statuta* 1243,65). The explanation of the text as written by Ida's biographer seems to be that he repeated the mistake the General Chapter had recently warned against or would warn against.

the beginning, at least, she took care of the novices (230,52), and might even have been interim superior. In 1237, when an abbess was elected, she was appointed prioress at the insistence of the whole community (231,62). Beatrice held this office for more than thirty years until her death.

Nazareth, at first located in a swampy area, moved to a higher and better location on the other end of Lier in 1245. Neither Beatrice nor her biographer mention this move.

Toward the end of her life Beatrice wrote her small but dense treatise, *Seven Manieren van Minne*. Looking back over the evolution of her spiritual and mystical experiences, she gathered everything under one dynamic concept: *Minne*.[19]

Around Christmas 1267, Beatrice became critically ill and on 29 August 1268 she died,[20] or better, 'crossed over' to the Father (see Jn 13:1). She had known many crossings in her life, and had aspired with deep longing and burning desire—both bitter and sweet—to be allowed to cross over definitively to see God face to face and to be united with him forever.

On the surface, the life of this thirteenth-century Cistercian nun seems uneventful, but considering what her biography reveals about her, one is overwhelmed by the keenness of her mind, the depth and warmth of her heart, the impetuosity of her desire not only to be with God, but to become what God wanted her to be. The dynamism of her whole life revolved not around me-and-God, but around God-and-me. God was and remained her source and goal, and when she crossed over, she had come full circle.

19. Vekemans, 'Vita Beatricis en Seuen Manieren van Minne. Een vergelijkende studie', *OGE* 46 (1972) 3-59; 51.

20. Reypens (*Vita*, 55*) has pointed to the biographer's mistake in writing first that she died at the end of August 1268 (272,15) and then, a few lines below, dating it to 'Kalendas Augusti' or 29 July (274,31). Reypens convincingly justifies the view that 29 August is the right date.

CHAPTER TWO

THE BIOGRAPHY AND THE BIOGRAPHER

THE SOURCES

T O WRITE THE *VITA*, Beatrice's biographer used Beatrice's diary or autobiography, some later notes, her treatise on the *Seven Manieren*, and information gained from the nuns who lived with her.

Today four copies of Beatrice's *Vita* are known.[1] The oldest, manuscript B, is preserved in the Royal Library in Brussels, MS 4459-70, which contains several spiritual writings, collected at the request of John of St Trond, a monk in Villers when he was chaplain to the Cistercian nuns of Vrouwenpark in Wezemaal, ten miles north of Leuven. The manuscript was finished in 1320, but some parts, including Beatrice's biography (f.66-138), could have been written at the end of the thirteenth century. A second manuscript in the same library, MS 1638-49, was written in 1493-94 as the fourth part of a *Legendarium* formerly belonging to the priory of Corsendonck. The third copy, known as G is MS 165 of the University Library in Ghent. Written in 1650-1660 by the Bollandists with a view to a never realized publication in the *AA SS*, it contains only Beatrice's biography, collated with the manuscript of Corsendonck, which made the latter of negligible importance for the critical edition. The fourth, known as V, is part of the *Hagiologium*, written in 1476-84 by John Gielemans of Rooklooster near Brussels, and is now in the Nationalbibliothek in Vienna, series nova, 12707, f. 296-335. MS V, the best of the four, has been used for the critical edition and collated with B and G.

Of the treatise *Seven Manieren*, three copies survive; manuscript H (written about 1400) now in the Royal Library of The Hague; manuscript V (dated between 1400 and 1450) in the National-

---

1. Dr Reypens describes them more extensively in his critical edition of the *Vita*, 17*-23*. My purpose here has not been to present a new critical edition, but to make the work widely available.

bibliothek in Vienna, and manuscript B (written about 1400), now in the Royal Library in Brussels.[2]

THE BIOGRAPHER

In the margin of manuscript B there is an annotation in a later hand to the effect that the *Vita* was written by William, a Benedictine monk of Affligem, who later became abbot of St Trond. This attribution seems to be founded on a misinterpretation of a reference William once made to a Cistercian nun.[3] Until recently this nun was thought to be Beatrice of Nazareth; in fact it concerns another contemporary Beatrice, also a Cistercian nun and mystic, who lived in the abbey of Zwijveke near Dendermonde in Flanders.[4] Until more proof can be produced, the identification of William of Affligem as Beatrice of Nazareth's biographer can be set aside.[5]

Beatrice's *Vita* was written not long after her death in 1268. the author seems not to have known her personally, but addresses his conclusion to the nuns who had lived with her and those who had not. This allows us to fix the years when the biography was written at about 1275. In the prologue[6] and in the conclusion the writer gives some hints about himself. He calls himself the nuns' brother and fellow-servant

2. For a detailed description, see R-VM, *Seven Manieren*, 111* 123*. Vekeman and Tersteeg published diplomatically *Beatrijs van Nazareth. Van Seuen Manieren van Heiliger Minnen* (Zutphen, 1970) according to MS B. It is the result of the collaboration, for over a year, of university professors and students of the University of Nijmegen on the 'project: Beatrijs van Nazareth'. In this edition the treatise is 582 lines long.

3. N.M. Häring, 'Der Literaturkatalog von Affligem', *RBén* 80 (1949) 64-96; 95. See G. Hendrix, 'Cistercian Sympathies in the 14th Century *Catalogus virorum illustriorum*', *Citeaux* 27 (1976) 267-278, demonstrating that the *Catalogus* is the work of an anonymous Cistercian, who wrote it about 1320.

4. Reypens, 'Nog een dertiendeeuwse mystieke Cisterciërnon' *OGE* 23 (1949) 225-46; Id., 'Een derde Beatrijs in onze dertiendeeuwse Letteren? Beatrijs van Dendermonde', *OGE* 37 (1963) 419-22.

5. G. Hendrix calls 'fortuitous' the presence in the *Catalogus* of chapters 51-56 dealing with Cistercians— and the reference to some material from William of Affligem related to a certain Cistercian nun. For references see above n. 3, 274.

6. Henriquez omitted it from Beatrice's biography in his *Quinque prudentes Virgines*. P.V. Bets published it in *AHEB* 7 (1870) 77-82, using MS B. It is reproduced in Dr Reypens' critical edition.

(1,5; 273,5) who set to work at their request (273,1). Dr Reypens, correctly, looked toward St Bernard's abbey in Hemiksem near Antwerp, some thirty kilometers from Nazareth, to see whether a monk of St Bernard's could have had the qualifications.[7] And indeed the *Obituarium* of St Bernard's abbey lists some twenty-five monks who through the centuries functioned as chaplains in Nazareth.[8] At first sight the most likely candidate seems to be a certain Fulgerius (d. 1307) who is listed as the chaplain on and off for some thirty years, beginning in 1275. Unfortunately this information is tainted by the falsifications of Alexander Butkens, which will be treated in another paper.

In his introduction to the *Vita*,[9] Dr Reypens says that the author was chaplain in the modern sense of the word and not one of the *capellani* who appeared in medieval communities of Cistercian nuns. This detail is not as obvious as it looks. Many but not all communities of Cistercian nuns had two priests, one called the *confessarius* (confessor) and the other *capellanus*, a kind of assistant to help out on feastdays when two Masses were celebrated. But in the thirteenth and fourteenth centuries the *capellanus* was not necessarily a monk. The *Statuta* of the General Chapter,[10] and the *Nomasticon Cisterciense*, the codified legislation of 1240 and 1256,[11] in a section concerning the nuns have several paragraphs on *fratres capellani clerici*, clerics who promised obedience to a local abbess and performed certain duties, but were distinct from the confessor or 'chaplain' of today.[12]

The fact that in his opening sentence the biographer addresses him-

---

7. Nazareth was under the immediate jurisdiction of the abbot of Cîteaux, and the abbot of St Bernard's was supervisor by delegation. In 1448, abbot Philip of Clairvaux appointed a monk of Aulne as chaplain in Nazareth and stated explicitly that the abbot of Cîteaux was the immediate superior. See R. De Ganck, 'Over de benoeming van een nieuwe rector te Nazareth in 1448', *Cîteaux* 5 (1954) 45-54.

8. B. Van Doninck, *Obituarium monasterii Loci Sancti Bernardi* (Lérins, 1901).

9. *Vita*, 32*-33*.

10. *Statuta*, 1254,5, for instance.

11. Edited by Juliano Paris (Paris 1664) 363, and by H. Séjalon (Solesmes 1892) 581.

12. A *capellanus*, distinct from the 'chaplain-confessor', is mentioned in the biographies of Ida of Nivelles (*Quinque*, 208), Ida Lewis (*AA SS* Oct. 13: 117,35), and Ida of Leuven (*AA SS* April 2: 283, 5 and 7). There are cases, as in Flines near Lille, then part of Flanders, where several *capellani* were present for devotional purposes that would no longer be accepted today. See E. Hautcoeur, *Histoire de l'abbaye de Flines*, 2nd ed. (Lille 1909) 47-48; 438-40.

self to 'his respected lady abbess' (1,3) does not necessarily identify him as a chaplain-confessor, but might more appropriately point to a *capellanus*, a cleric who had made of vow of obedience to 'his' abbess of Nazareth. He mentions the customs of 'that' monastery (28, 106; 48,93) though they were uniform throughout all Cistercian communities. He speaks about 'that' Order (37,25) and about 'blessed Bernard' (234,6), whereas a Cistercian monk would rather have spoken of 'our Order' or 'our holy Bernard' or 'our holy father Bernard'. These details indicate that the author was likely to have been one of those *fratres capellani clerici*, a member of the community of Nazareth, rather than a professed monk of the Cistercian Order. It does not matter much. The Bollandists noted in MS G that the author of Beatrice's *Vita* (a monk-chaplain or a cleric-*capellanus*) is anonymous. He can therefore still be called the 'chaplain'.

The chaplain-biographer states that he used Beatrice's diary-notes, *cedulae* (4,34), which in his conclusion he calls 'the book of her life' (274,19), 'her book' (276,39), which she had kept so secret that not even her bloodsisters in the same community knew of its existence (4,43). Shortly before she died, so he writes, 'no longer in danger of self-complacency for the many graces she had received' and 'for the sake of her neighbors' needs she brought it forth openly in due time' (6,61).

Besides Beatrice's diary he collected verbal communications from reliable (*fideles*) people, the nuns of Nazareth and particularly from her bloodsister Christine, who survived her and succeeded her as prioress (269,117). Beatrice's autobiography covers only some twenty years of her life. After she became prioress in 1237, she seems to have jotted down some notes, not part of 'the book of her life'. These notes were collected and presented in chapters eleven, twelve and thirteen of the *Vita's* third book.[13] Her biography ends with a lengthy chapter on her love for God and a shorter one on her love for neighbor. The lengthy chapter is nothing but an unsuccessful incorporation of her treatise, the *Seven Manieren van Minne*. The biographer does not mention it as a

---

13. While the chaplain could follow Beatrice chronologically in her autobiography, the loose notes she wrote down in Nazareth were collected in the three chapters mentioned and were apparently not dated. At this point the biographer says that 'though we in no way doubt that many more than the former things happened by heavenly grace during this long time [the three decades in which she was prioress] which followed' (233,114), he chose to stand by his lack of information and did not make anything up on his own.

separate treatise (276,39).

He affirms that although he had read several biographies,[14] Beatrice's *Vita* is his first attempt at this kind of writing, in which he is an inexperienced newcomer (3,20). One meets such disclaimers in most biographies as part of that genre. Instead of writing with 'the exquisite ornaments of contriving rhetoric', he claims he will use simple words (3,27). He may have thought he did, but in fact, his style is heavy and the construction of his sentences often complicated, cascading into excessive verbosity. But 'he has done what he could' (274,43), 'according to his small capacity' (182,207).

THE BIOGRAPHER'S CREDIBILITY

The chaplain sought to bolster his credibility (3,28) by stating that he should not be considered the author of the biography (5,50; 275,34). The authorship belonged to Beatrice herself (4,36). She wrote her experiences down with her own hand, and her credibility was beyond any doubt (5,54). All he had done was to translate her vernacular into Latin (4,34; 273,4). He did so 'not impelled by the levity of arrogance or by the temerity of vainglory, but animated only by charity, the mother of virtues' (3,24). On his own he has added[15] and changed little (4,33).[16] He is sometimes careful to state that Beatrice's notebooks confirmed what he was saying;[17] or that he had had to rely on verbal communica-

14. He certainly knew the biography of Ida of Nivelles (50,36) and probably that of Lutgard (d. 1246). He too needed 'to take some rest and breathe a little' (182,208) in writing the *Vita*, as did Lutgard's biographer. See G. Hendrix, 'Primitive Versions of Thomas of Cantimpré's *Vita Lutgardis*', *Citeaux* 29 (1978) 153-206; 159. As we have already mentioned, he was familiar with the biography of Arnulph of Villers.

15. The additions are mostly his moralizing comments and appear in smaller type at the end of most chapters in the critical edition. The first chapter which is a short biography of Bartholomew, Beatrice's father, the chapter about Nazareth's foundation, the charisms mentioned in the last chapter about 'love of neighbor' are all his works as well. These are not spoken of in the 'book of her life', and refer probably to the last three decades of her life in Nazareth. However, this chapter about her charisms is not without the generalizations so often found in this kind of biography.

16. The chaplain did not realize how much his own heavy style contrasts with the simple, dense, and to the point articulations of Beatrice's treatise in the vernacular; her style, in its turn, does not translate easily into correct Latin.

17. *Vita* 20,29; 48,94; 69,70. He says it also in 252,212, where he

tions (269,117); or that he had no sources from which to draw information and kept silent for that reason (233,112). When he did not know something for certain but tendered his own opinion, he admitted it explicitly (242,49); or would let events speak for themselves, doing his best to describe them (49,27). Occasionally he shows a credulity common to his time, but not acceptable in ours.[18]

His contact with Beatrice's writings elicited a great admiration for her, and although he seems to have regretted that he had no miracles to report, he did not invent any but pointed to 'the spiritual miracle' of her heroic holiness (245,75). Beatrice herself wrote little in her autobiography or in her treatise about events in her community or in society. These things fell outside the scope of her work. The biographer respected her discretion and did not supply information. Dates and times reported in the autobiography appear in the *Vita*, without further elaboration. He neglected to mention the passage in Ida of Nivelles' biography telling of Our Lady's request that Beatrice love her with as much affection as she had for Ida.[19] The biographer's sincerity and integrity are not in doubt, but by our standards he could have been more investigative. He lived under the feudal system and knew better than we do how it worked. But nowhere does he show evidence of having consulted official documents to verify the three alleged foundations of Bartholomew. *Capellanus clericus* or not, he had a tendency to moralize, but cannot be said to have been excessively moralistic in the context of his own society. He could have been more cautious in double-checking before believing what some witnesses, especially Christine, told him. To his credit, it should be noted, he dared to challenge his readers when he defended his opinion that in 1231 Beatrice had a face-to-face vision of God (175,89).

There is little doubt that the chaplain was Flemish; in several instances he has twisted Flemish colloquialisms into Latin. In many places his sentences have a Teutonic cadence of many inserted subsentences or phrases. He never quotes from or refers to the Latin classical writers whom he probably considered pagans. Occasionally he uses words of Greek origin, as when he speaks of *cedulae* instead of *paginae*, but this trait was not unusual in his day. Thirteenth-century

---

integrates her treatise.

18. He could have known the biography of Mary of Oignies by (the later cardinal) James of Vitry, but he is less given to credulity than was James (*AA SS* June 4: 637-38), reproduced in Reypens, *Vita*, 224-26.

19. *Quinque*, 262.

biographers could not compete with their contemporary theologians, who all too often were eager to display their erudition. At times Beatrice's biographer was sloppy in his use of the reflexive pronoun *se*, but he knew contemporary medieval Latin very well. Often he shows himself to be a stylistic acrobat, delighting in long sentences intersected with triadic eurythmics such as *tam-tam-tam; quot-quot-quot; haec-haec-haec; neque-neque-neque*, or with diadic correlatives such as *tam-quam; tanto-quanto; totiens-quotiens; hic-illic; hinc-illinc*. He liked to play on words using in the same sentence or paragraph nouns, adjectives, verbs and adverbs with the same root. Examples abound, as for instance: *copiosa, copiose, copiosiora; delectabilis, delectabiliter, delectatio; consolatio, consolatoria, consolaria, consolari*. For all his Teutonism he was fond of a flowery style and of euphonics, as *verbum desolatorium, aliud consolatorium*, or *beata felicitas et felicissima iocunditas*, a style not always easy to render in English. He seems to have been at home with the tricks of the hagiographical genre, using apostrophes, exclamations with a repeated 'O', or interrogations such as *Quid miri?; Quid mirum?* or playing with assonances and alliterations. He had a knack for finding the right adjective to stress the following substantive, whatever topic he was speaking of. The nuns of Nazareth had in their chaplain a man who handled his literary skills well. One of the more important elements of his translation is what he called in one place a 'coloration' (4,34). A few times, but not often, his coloration is like a veneer which permits the underlying vernacular to be glanced or guessed at, though this by no means replaces the original itself. It would be unfair to say that he mistreated Beatrice's vernacular. Nor would it be correct to maintain that he intentionally corrupted the original text, for we have to allow any translator some leeway.

HIS METHODOLOGY

The biographer himself explained the methodology he followed. He had at his disposal Beatrice's autobiography, some later notes, her treatise, and oral communications of the Nazareth nuns. All of these together constituted 'very extensive and interminable material' (276,43) of 'excessive depth' (275,35). Not wishing to 'generate weariness' (275,33), he preferred to keep the average reader in mind. He declared that he had 'chosen a certain middle way, doing what I could, lest I seem to have altogether omitted the many things that the holy Beatrice discussed in her

book (and so I might be said to have thus truncated a large part of her volume), or lest, on the other hand, I should describe everything I received and so should have sweated oversuperfluous, rather than necessary, matter' (276,39). He decided therefore 'to weave his writing in a simple way [another commonplace in biographies] for the sake of simple people' (3,26) who were better served by an edifying account (16,6; 233,114; 275,29 and 32) than by a tedious story which would 'cause more harm than good to those with minds less practiced in these matters' (275,37). 'Even if it [the biography] is not as complete as I should have made it, still I think it tolerably sufficient' (269,113). 'In a few words I have given to the wise—to whom it suffices to have touched a few points—the occasion of investigating the greater mysteries of charity, and have satisfied the fastidious with a kindly short compendium' (276,45). In other words, he has made a selective choice, avoiding tediousness for the average reader and giving 'the wise' enough information to ponder Beatrice's spiritual journey.

This indicates that the biographer felt he had given a fair, objective, substantial account of all the material at hand. The *Vita*, and even more the treatise, show Beatrice's depth. The way the chaplain wove the treatise into the *Vita* shows that he considered the *Seven Manieren* a further evolution of Beatrice's reflections upon experiences she described in her autobiography. It shifts from the christological and trinitarian mysticism of the *cedulae* to one of *Minne*,[20] a shift the chaplain did not sufficiently recognize. And this is what leaves the 'short compendium' as he called it (276,47) too short for us, if not for the chaplain's average and 'wise' readers.

THE MISSING AUTOBIOGRAPHY

Why did the treatise in the vernacular but not the vernacular autobiography survive? Dr Reypens is of the opinion that the chaplain was responsible for the disappearance of the original autobiography because he saw no need to preserve it once he had finished the Latin translation.[21] This could very well be the case but may not offer the complete explanation as far as the biography is concerned. It does not, however, explain the treatise, which he (mis)used while the vernacular text did sur-

---

20. H. Vekeman, '*Vita Beatricis* en *Seven Manieren van Minne*. Een vergelijkende studie', *OGE* 40 (1972) 3-54; 6-8.
    21. *Vita*, 44*.

vive. The chaplain could not alone have been responsible for the disappearance of the *Vita*, for he could not have disposed of it without the
consent of the abbess and her council, of which Christine was the sen-
ior member. If the original was never seen or heard of after the translation was made, this may reflect the advice of the abbess to whom, as
her rightful superior, Beatrice had given it. This does not mean that the
chaplain did not play a role in its disappearance. The disappearance
may have happened at his suggestion, or at least by his acquiescence to
the abbess and her council, if the idea originated there. A look at some
circumstantial evidence before and around the year 1275, when the *Vita*
was presumably written, may help clarify the matter.

Besides episcopal synods and inquisitions,[22] there was also at the
time a papal inquisition. One of the first inquisitors, famous in
Beatrice's lifetime, was the overzealous Robert le Petit, better known as
Robert le Bougre, since he had been an heretic before becoming a
Dominican and, from 1233 till 1244/45, a papal inquisitor.[23] Hadewijch
wrote in her 'List of the Perfect' that Robert had a beguine executed
'because of the righteous *minne*'.[24] It so happened that Robert le
Bougre established his headquarters in Cambrai, the diocese in which at
that time Nazareth was located.

According to Thomas of Cantimpré, the bishop of Cambrai died in
1247 in the Benedictine abbey of Affligem, some thirty kilometers west
of Brussels, on his way to Antwerp to investigate heretics.[25] His succes-
sor was no less zealous in searching out heresy, as we see from his actions at Antwerp around 1252.[26] Because anybody, orthodox or heter-
odox, might become suspect, not least the beguines,[27] Urban IV in 1262

22. See, for instance, D. Lambrecht, *De Synode in het oude bisdom
Doornik gesitueerd in de Europese ontwikkeling* (Dissertation, Ghent 1976)
263-427, where the author describes the procedure used in the thirteenth
century in the diocese of Tournai, the neighbor of Cambrai. The methods used
in Tournai's synodical investigations are quite unacceptable to our modern
sense of democracy.

23. C.H. Haskins, *Studies in Medieval Culture*, 2nd ed. (New York, 1965)
Chapter X: 193-244: 'Robert le Bougre and the Beginning of the Inquisition in
Northern France; and Georges Despy, 'Les débuts de l'Inquisition dans les
anciens Pays-Bas au XIIIe siècle', *Problèmes d'Histoire du Christianisme* 9
(Hommage à Jean Hadot), C. Cambler ed. (Brussels, 1980) 71-104.

24. VM, Hadewijch, *Brieven*, I:189, l.193.

25. Paul Fredericq, *Corpus documentorum Inquisitionis haereticae
pravitatis Neerlandicae* (Ghent-The Hague, 1889) vol. I:110-19.

26. *Ibid.*, 120-21.

27. McDonnell, *The Beguines*, 506: 'For the Belgian sisters [Here

sent two papal bulls to neighboring Liège to take the especially vul-
nerable beguines under his protection.[28] The duke of Brabant, backing
the inquisitors in 1280, found it necessary to take the beguines of
Antwerp and several other places under his protection in 1285.[29] In 1272
Albert the Great, lecturing in neighboring Cologne, wrote—not an inquisitorial protocol—but a scholastic exercise, later confirmed by a
document in Nördlingen, in the heart of Swabian Ries, about heretical
mulieres religiosae who went off the track by embracing pantheistic
theories couching their 'mystical experiences' of Christ in grossly
erotic overtones.[30] In 1273, in preparation for the II Council of Lyons
the next year, Gregory X received three reports about what should be
done in regard to religious:[31] Humbert of Romans, a former master general of the Dominicans, covered the situation in southern France;[32] the
bishop of Olmutz described East Germany; and Gilbert of Tournai, a
Franciscan who had become bishop of Tournai, submitted a report entitled *Collectio de scandalis ecclesiae.*[33] In it he complained

> that there were among us women called beguines, some of
> whom blossom forth in subtilties and rejoice in novelties.
> They have interpreted in vernacular French idiom the mys-
> teries of Scripture which are scarcely accessible to experts in

---

beguines] who in the main constituted a front against heterodoxy, danger
lurked not in the particular condition of their existence but in the clerics and
laymen who took advantage of the unprotected status of semireligious'.

28. P. Fredericq, *Corpus documentorum*, 132. Curiously enough, two quite
long poems in French, both written about 1300, speak very favorably of the
beguines. Alfons Hilka, using a manuscript from Lille and another from Metz,
published these under the title 'Altfranzösische Mystik und Beguinentum', in
Zeitschrift für romanische Philologie 47 (1927) 121-70.

29. Fredericq, *Corpus ducumentorum*, 144 and 146.

30. Grundmann, *Religiöse Bewegungen*, 406-38; R.E. Lerner, *The Heresy
of the Free Spirit in the Later Middle Ages* (Berkeley-Los Angeles-London,
1972) 13-19; 61-84.

31. For a short and adequate overview of these three tracts, see
Grundmann, *Religiöse Bewegungen*, 334-40.

32. Edward Tr. Brett, *Humbert of Romans. His Life and Views of
Thirteenth-Century Society* (Toronto, 1984) *Opusculum Tripartitum*, 176-94.

33. Published by Autpert Stroick, '*Ausgabe der Collectio*', Archivum
Franciscanum Historicum 24 (1931) 33-62.

divine writings. They read aloud in common irreverently and boldly, in conventicles, convents and public squares.[34]

Gilbert of Tournai, a neighbor of the bishop of Cambrai, complained also about a *mulier religiosa* who had gained renown because she bore the stigmata (*Christi stigmatibus insignita*) and he had asked for an inquiry to still rumors.[35] Gossip seems to have been one of the side effects of inquisitorial procedures. James of Maerlant wrote in 1271 about gossip by 'that paepscap', meaning clergyman. Van Maerlant was a learned layman from Damme near Bruges who that year published his *Rijmbijbel* (Bible in Rhyme) in the vernacular, and around that time a long poem *Vander Drievoudeghede* (On the Trinity). Though his writings were orthodox, he was called up three times by ecclesiastical authorities and criticized by some clergy because he had dared to expose such delicate matters in the vernacular 'to simple people'.[36] And this was not the last word or the last reaction against such writings in the vernacular.

Nazareth, located in the diocese of Cambrai and in the vicinity of Antwerp, could not have been oblivious to everything that was happening around 1275, the supposed year of the biography's Latin translation. Beatrice's treatise survived in its original, vernacular text, but it contains only a single reference to the Trinity.[37] Her autobiography had several trinitarian passages and other theological matter, all written in the vernacular. It seems quite possible that the abbess and the chaplain of Nazareth inferred from the circumstances that it was wiser to destroy

34. The translation is taken from McDonnell, *The Beguines,* 366.

35. A. Stroick, who identified the author, ('Der Verfasser und Quellen der Collectio de scandalis ecclesiae, *Archivum Franciscanum Historicum* 23 [1930], 3-41; 273-99; 433-66) says that the bishop probably had Elisabeth of Spaalbeek in mind. A. Bussels is of the opinion that Elisabeth was a Cistercian nun in Herkendrode. See *Cîteaux* 2 (1951) 43-54. Grundman (*Reliöse Bewegung* 339, n. 38) points to Ida of Leuven, Christine of Stommeln, and some unnamed Dominican nuns. We have to discount Ida of Leuven because her stigmatization occurred before she became a nun in Roosendaal around 1230 (Jo Van Schoors, *Ida van Leuven* [Diss. Leuven, 1982] 102), while bishop Gilbert of Tournai wrote his *Collectio* in 1273.

36. C.C. De Bruin, 'De prologen van de eerste Historiebijbels geplaatst in het raam van hun tijd', *The Bible and Medieval Culture,* W. Lourdaux and D. Verhelst, eds. (Leuven, 1979) 190-219; 194-99.

37. R-VM, *Seven Manieren,* 31, 1.48.

the original, preserving it in the Latin translation, adapted—as the biographer put it—to 'the simple', about whom the authorities claimed to be so concerned.

THE METHOD
OF EDITING THE
LATIN TEXT

MODUS EDENDI

Quoad textum ipsum.

Textum codicis V damus ut jacet, cum modo scribendi eius, resolutis tantum signis abbreviationis. Haec signa ordinaria sunt nec ullam difficultatem praebent. Ubi dubitari possit de resolutione, monemus in apparatu.

Lectiones ex aliis codicibus in textu assumptae vel a nobis suppositae, inter uncos acutos imprimuntur, lectionibus codicis V in apparatu retentis. In quo apparatu hae solae lectiones variantes ponuntur quae vel aliquo modo ad sensum pertinent.

Rarissime obvenientes inutiles repetitiones verborum, et alia suppremenda, inter uncos rectos ponuntur.

In V disiuncta sed in nostro usu unita verba, parva linea iunguntur, v. g. *post ea quam* hic imprimitur *post-ea-quam*.

Unci rotundi partes quarundam phrasium includentes, non inveniuntur in manuscripto, sed a nobis sunt additi, ad faciliorem intelligentiam intricati modi dicendi, multiplicatis incisis propositionibus gravati. Quidam loci in corpore textus minore caractere distinguuntur, ut a translatore additi aedificationis causa, vel aperte in ipsa autobiographia non inventi. Quod valet tantum de longioribus locis, cum impossibile sit particulatim omnia dignoscere quae soli translatori attribuenda sint in suo modo dicendi, contrahendi vel amplificandi. Reconstructio textus ipsius Beatricis impossibilis est.

Ad faciliorem indicationem locorum *Vitae* ad quos remittitur in introductione et in decursu editionis, distribuimus textum in numeros, crassiore caractere impressos. Initia novorum foliorum vel paginarum in codicibus italico caractere indicantur.

The Method of Editing the Latin Text

Léonce Reypens, SJ

From the *Compendium introductionis neerlandicae of Beatrijs van Tienen, 1200-1268.* Antwerp: Uitgave van het Ruusbroecgenootschap, 1964. Used with permission.

The Text

We reproduce the text of Codex V as it stands, with its orthography, but with the abbreviations spelled out in full. These abbreviations are ordinary ones and present no difficulty. Where there is some doubt about the meaning, we mention the fact in the apparatus.

Readings from the other codices that have been adopted into the text and phrases we have supplied are printed within angular brackets , < >, with the readings of Codex V retained in the apparatus. In the apparatus have been given only those variant readings which in some way affect the sense.

The very rare useless repetitions of words and other omissions have been placed within square brackets [ ].

Words which are separate in V but which are written as one word in our usage, are hyphenated, v.g. *post eq quam* is here printed as *post-ea-quam.*

The round brackets ( ) enclosing some phrases are not found in the manuscript, but have been added by us to help unravel intricate sentences, burdened with many incidentals. In the body of the text the use of small type distinguishes certain passages which have been added by the translator for the sake of edification, or which have obviously been added to the autobiography. This is done only for the longer passages, since it is impossible to separate in each and every instance what should be attributed only to the translator and his way of phrasing, summarizing or amplifying Beatrice's text.

To facilitate finding places in the *Vita* to which reference is made in the introduction and notes, we have divided the text into numbered sections, with the numbers printed in bolder type. The beginnings of new folios and pages as given in the codices are shown in italic type.

Quoad notas.

Duplex datur series notarum. Prima lectiones variantes codicum G et B praebet, in quibus enumerandis codex G semper prius ponitur, ut ab antiquo exemplari ipsius abbatiae Nazarethanae transscriptus. Quae ex G vel B in textum ipsum assumpta sunt et ibi inter uncos acutos ponuntur, ut plurimum ex ipsa juxtapositione lectionum variantium in apparatu comprobantur. Ubi opus est, pressius justificantur. Altera series notarum spectat ad argumentum ipsum textus.

Quoad interpunctionem.

Gielemans, scriba codicis V, interpunctionem suam curat. Adhibet punctum simplex, punctum duplex et punctum uncum, *haakpunt* Neerlandice dictum. Comma nostrum ignorat.

Quae signa pro nobis non semper eundem valorem habent. Nam in corpore phrasis punctum commati nostro respondet, non nostro puncto. Duplex autem punctum scribae, interdum nostro duplici puncto, aliquam explicationem introducenti, saepius tamen nostro puncto-cum-commate, vel nudo nostro commati respondet.

Punctum uncum vero, raro adhibitum, majori intervallo, ordinarie nostro puncto-cum-commate, sed interdum etiam nudo commati nostro respondet.

Haec relative accurata punctuatio codicis V, antiquae praelectioni potius accommodata, nostrae consuetudini in legendo insufficiens remanet, praesertim respectu stili tam intricati translatoris *Vitae*. Quapropter nostram interpunctionem adiunximus, ita tamen ut italicis caracteribus notetur, rectis vero ipsius scribae servetur. Nam nostram punctuationem, ut quidam faciunt, inter uncos ponendo, typographicum aspectum paginarum hirsutum fecissemus.

The Notes

Two series of notes are provided. The first gives the variant readings of codices G and B. G transcribed from the ancient copy belonging to the abbey of Nazareth always appears first. The readings adopted into the text from G and B and placed within angular brackets are confirmed for the most part by comparison with the variant readings in the apparatus. When necessary they are justified in more detail. The other series of notes treats the meaning of the text.

The Punctuation

Gielemans, the writer of codex V, provided his own punctuation. He used the period, the colon and the hooked dot, or 'haakpunt' as Netherlanders say. He did not know our comma.

For us these signs do not always have the same value. In mid-sentence his period corresponds to our comma. His colon sometimes corresponds to ours, introducing some explanation, but more often it corresponds to our semi-colon or simple comma.

The hooked dot, rarely used and only at intervals, ordinarily corresponds to our semi-colon, and sometimes to our colon.

This relatively careful punctuation of codex V accommodates the text more to the ancient way of reading, but is insufficient for modern reading habits, especially in regard to the very intricate style of the translator of the *Vita*. We have therefore added our own punctuation printed in italics, with the scribe's punctuation kept in ordinary type. If we had put our punctuation within parentheses, as some do, the typographical face of the page would have been too rough and uneven.

L.R.

TRANSLATORS NOTE

Biblical References

Biblical references are given at the bottom of the pages of the English translation. Literal quotations are set in italics; paraphrases or combined citations and allusions to biblical texts are in roman. Because the biographer used the Vulgate text of the Bible, the references retain that enumeration. Abbreviations of the books of the Bible, however, follow those used by the Jerusalem Bible.

R.D.G.

CORRIGENDA TO THE LATIN TEXT

These corrections repeat and augment a preliminary list published by Anselme Hoste in *Librije*, 1966.

Instead of paragraph, line		*read*
14,115	: quadenti	gaudenti
22,49	: au	aut
30,10	: flagenllando	flagellando
31,25	: hec	hoc
31,26	: adhorrebat	abhorrebat
32,49	: cinqulum	cingulum
35,21	: aggreuata	aggrauata
36,13	: cergo	ergo
51,65	: vererabilem	venerabilem
51	: lines 66-67	transp. 67-66
60,8	: incorparata	incorporata
62,68	: ed	ad
67,29	: promixo	proximo
6977	: promissorum	correct, see 66,59
70,103	: neuum	nexum
71,18,1	: signalicum	signaculum
83,14	: asperauit	aspirauit
92,43	: corde.	, corpore. in V
98,136	: comma after discrimine	not after necessario
105,4	: ab	ad
119,26	: surculo	sarculo
123,76	: al	ad
127,50	: ara, leuatum	ara leuatum
158,55	: apperitus...ingeritus	appetitus...ingeritur
159,72	: languorum	languorem
159,76	: illius,	illius
170,17	: al	ad
180,172	: quad	quod
181,181	: exilia	ex ilis
184,25	: 187	184

187,79	: exigentium	exigentiam
189,115	: flagellandum	flagellandam, sic G
198,55	: posset	possent
199,66	: diuinis	diuinus
202,47	: aquiescens	acquiescens
202,47	: affectu	effectu
203,55	: amens jacens	amens, jacens
211,55	: sapientis	sapienti
211,65	: victa	vincta
214,26	: comparauit	comparuit
216,84	: inexeperti . . . teneris	inexperti . . . terresis
230,53	: ipsaque	ipsasque
231,61	: exigentium	exigentiam
232,92	: vilitatiis	vilitatis
232,104	: eo	ea
242,60	: adiocari	advocari (?)
243,60	: christi	christe
253,241	: absorta	absorpta
253,365	: 356	365
259,502	: quam	quem
260,555	: carcecis	carceris
261,563	: imporunitate	importunitate
262,300	: 300	600
265,51-52	: implotantibus	implorantibus
265,52	: tantibus	rantibus

THE LIFE
OF
BEATRICE OF NAZARETH

(f° 296 a)   <PROLOGUS>

1 Incipit prologus in venerabilis beatricis vitam, priorisse quondam in nazareth [1].

Uenerabili domine sue, dei prouidentia monasterij de nazareth ordinis cisterciensis., Cameracensis dyocesis, abbatisse [2]., eiusdemque loci venerando co-
5   nuentui :, frater earum et conseruus. : In domino salutem., et cum electis
virginibus ornatis lampadibus in sponsi thalamum introire.

2 Scripturus vitam venerabilis beatricis, vestri quondam [3] monasterij perfectissime monialis., in primis vestre deuotionis opem efflagito, : quatenus, ad
perficiendum opus quod iniungitis, vires mihi vestris orationibus impetretis ;
10   ne, post-ea-quam posuero fundamentum et non habuero sumptus ad perficiendum., in illud euangelicum incidam improperium, vt et michi non immerito dici
valeat : ' hic homo cepit edificare et non potuit consummare.' [4] Nam et-si
varios sanctorum triumphos, hystorica narratione depictos[.] ab alijs, ipse
perlegerim [5]., necdum tamen huiuscemodi locutionis vsum attigi : quippe cui,
15   nichil penitus de proprijs viribus confidenti, nunc vsque potius aliene decorem
eloquentie mirari libuit. quam vigorem experientie, titubantibus et infirmis
adhuc gressibus, imitari.
3 Non ergo mireris, o lector, sicubi forsitan, in narrationis progressu, minus
congruenter <insertum> [6] quid occurrerit ;, cum videris ad scribendi studium
20   ex solo caritatis precepto me pertrahi : qui necdum, assuefacto narrationis vsu,
vel primam balbutientis lingue rubiginem elimaui. Sed quid magis conueniens,
aut quid magis consonum rationi ; , quam vt in primo progressionis exercitio
nouus tyro facilem a lectore veniam consequatur; quem, ad arripiendum dictandi
studium, non arrogantie levitas, non vane glorie temeritas // *fol. 296 b*
25   impulit., sed sola mater virtutum caritas animauit ? Hac ergo duce, viam utique
non expertam nouus viator ingrediar :, et simplicibus simplex texens eloquium,
beate memorie beatricis vitam, vtcumque potero, non exquisitis rethoricorum
scematum ornamentis., sed verbis humilibus et rei geste veritatem continentibus
explicabo [7].
30   **4** Si quis vero de facienda fide super hijs que dicturus sum me conueniat., et
veritatis a me testimonium, curiosius rerum indagator, exposcat : huic sane

PROLOGUE

1. **B**eginning of the prologue of the life of the Venerable Beatrice, formerly prioress in Nazareth.

To his respected Lady who is, through God's providence, abbess of the monastery of Nazareth of the Cistercian Order in the diocese of Cambrai, and to the respected convent of the same place, their brother and fellow-servant: greetings in the Lord, and may they enter the chamber of the bridegroom with the chosen virgins, with their lamps lighted.[1]

2 Intending to write the life of the Venerable Beatrice, a former very perfect nun of your monastery, I entreat first of all the help of your devotion. Obtain for me by your prayers the strength to achieve the work you requested. Otherwise, after having laid the foundation and lacking the means to finish, I might fall into that evangelical disgrace, and deserve—not unmeritedly—to have it said of me: this man began to build, but could not finish.[2] Even if I have read the various triumphs of the saints in historical narratives written by others, I have not yet attained the level of such speech. Consequently, not trusting in my own strength, up to now I have rather taken delight in marveling at the beauty of others' eloquence than in imitating the vigor of the experiment with my still weak and stumbling steps.

3 Do not therefore wonder, dear reader, if in the progress of my story something incongruous should appear to be included, for you will perceive that I am drawn to write only by the precept of charity, even though I am not yet familiar with composition and have not filed the rustiness away from my stammering tongue. But what is more appropriate or more in tune with reason than that as a newcomer in my first attempt at writing I should easily find pardon? In undertaking this writing I am not impelled by the levity of arrogance or by the temerity of vainglory, but am animated only by charity, the mother of virtues. Under her guidance, indeed, I walk along a path as an inexperienced traveller. Weaving my writing in a simple way for the sake of simple people, I shall try to explain the life of Beatrice of blessed memory as well as I can, omitting the exquisite ornaments of elaborate rhetoric, but using instead simple words to express the truth of what happened.

4 But if someone challenges me to prove the things I am going to say, and as a curious investigator demands from me a witness to the truth, I answer him

---

1. Mt 25:7   2. Lk 14:30

breui satisfactione respondeo, me solum huius operis translatorem existere non
auctorem ; quippe qui de meo parum addidi vel mutaui [8] :, sed, prout in
cedulis [9] suscepi, oblata verba vvlgaria latino < tantum > eloquio coloraui.

35 Ceterum hec ipsa cui sermo noster in hoc translationis opere famulatur., hec
inquam huius auctoritatem operis sibi non immerito vendicat :, que sola,
proprij viuacitate spiritus, interiora mentis sue penetrare potuit ;, et ex ea
misteriorum suorum archana producere :, super quibus, in toto vite sue progressu, preterquam internum arbitrum cui nullum latet secretum, testem et

40 conscium non admisit. ' Quis enim nouit hominum que sunt in homine ;, nisi
spiritus hominis qui in ipso est ? ' [10] Quod et-si de quolibet homine veraciter
dici valeat ;, venerabili tamen beatrici tanto profecto specialius conuenit :,
quanto studiosius intra profundissimum mentis sue receptaculum ineffabilis
< dona > gratie, non sine multo labore pariter et timore, fauente superna

45 clementia., cunctis vite sue temporibus occultauit. Quis denique vel extraneus
aut ignotus in illud secretissimum triclinium mentis sue potuisset irrumpere.,
vel absconditum in agro cordis sui thesaurum diuine gratie, propalando //
fol. 296 c detegere. , cum et proprias spiritu carneque germanas, quas in eodem
monasterio consortes habuit, referatur ab eo velut extraneas exclusisse [11].

50 **5** Hec nimirum ideo prelibaui. , ne quis huius operis auctorem me crederet. ,
ac proinde que dicuntur velut a me conficta respueret :, sed potius, auctricis
nomine patefacto, deuotus lector attenderet, non ex mendaciorum tenebroso
latibulo., sed ex luculente veritatis fonte perspicuo, totam narrationis nostre
seriem emanasse. Quis enim vel insani capitis estimet venerabilem beatricem

55 aut falsum aliquid aut confictum de semetipsa proferre vel scribere potuisse ;,
que totum in experientie libro legit et didicit [.] quod, eo veratiori quo fideliori
stilo, suis postea manibus exarauit ?

6 Perpendat itaque lector prouidus ad quantum discretionis culmen mens huius
sancte mulieris excreuerit ;, que superne thezaurum gratie sic intra pectoris

60 sui claustra contra spirituales insidias occultare studuit :, et rursus in oportuno
tempore, tunc videlicet cum easdem insidias, elapso pene cursus sui tempore,
minime formidabat. , hunc [12] ipsum nobis, conseruis suis, vtiliter erogauit [13].
Cum autem dicat in euangelio dominus "Attendite ne iusticiam vestram

in all simplicity that I am only the translator of this work, not the author. Of my own I have added or changed little; rather I have only given a latin coloring to the vernacular words as they were given to me in diary-notes. She who is served by our work of translation rightly claims its authorship. Moreover she alone, by the brightness of her own vigorous spirit, was able to penetrate the innermost depths of her mind and bring forth its own secrets and mysteries. During her whole lifetime she admitted no one as a witness or confidant in these things, except the interior judge to whom nothing is hidden. 'For what man knows the things of a man, but the spirit of a man that is in him'?[3] And although this can truthfully be said of anyone, it pertains more especially to our venerable Beatrice, as she more carefully hid within her capacious mind the gifts of ineffable grace all the days of her life.[4] And this she did with great labor and fear, by the help of divine mercy. What outsider or unknown person could have broken into that most secret chamber of her mind, or could have uncovered and divulged the treasure of divine grace hidden in the field of her heart,[5] when it is said that she excluded outsiders from it, even her own bloodsisters, sisters in spirit too, who lived in the same monastery with her?

5 I have set forth these things at the outset lest anyone take me to be the author of this work and therefore reject what is said, believing it to be made up by me. Instead, now that the name of the authoress has been made public, the devout reader may expect that our whole story has flowed, not from some dark mendacious hiding place, but from the bright shining font of truth. Who could be so insane as to think that the venerable Beatrice would proffer or write something false or fabricated by herself, for she read and learned in the book of experience everything which she later wrote with her own hand in a manner as truthful as it was faithful?

6 Let the prudent reader carefully weigh the heights of discretion to which the mind of this holy woman was raised, for she thus zealously hid from spiritual dangers the treasure of heavenly grace within the cloister of her heart. Later, when the opportune time came at the end of her life, no longer fearing these same dangers, she usefully bequeathed this treasure to us, her fellow journeyers. The Lord says in the Gospel: 'Take heed that you

---

3. *1 Co 2:11*   4. Si 1:21   5. Mt 13:44

faciatis coram hominibus vt videamini ab eis " [14]. , <e>t rursus alibi „ Sic
luceat lux vestra coram hominibus vt videant opera vestra bona[.] et glo-
rificent patrem vestrum qui in celis est " [15] : huius vtriusque dominici pre-
cepti superficialem discordantiam sic in vnam obeditionis sententiam [16] con-
cordauit, vt et hostis antiqui versutias, secretum suum intra se vigilanter
occultando, deluderet., et rursus illud in palam opportuno tempore proferendo,
proximorum necessitatibus erogaret. Sicque, diuina disponente clementia, factum
est vt lucerna, diu latens sub modio, tanto postea, revelata luce, clarius eniteret
in publico :, quanto studiosius ad lucendum iam diu preparata fuerat in occulto.
<S>ed iam ad narrationis ordinem // fol. 296 d accedamus.

do not do your justice before men, to be seen by them',[6] and again elsewhere: 'So let your light shine before men, that they may see your good works, and glorify your Father who is in heaven'.[7] Beatrice so combined in one obedience the seeming discrepancies of these two precepts of the Lord that she foiled the strategies of the ancient enemy[8] by first hiding her secret carefully within herself, and then bequeathing it for her neighbors' needs by bringing it forth openly in due time. And so, through God's benevolent arrangement, it happened that the lamp long hidden under a bushel[9] finally did shine out clearly in public after it had been long and carefully prepared in secret for such shining. But now to our narrative.

6. Mt 6:1   7. Mt 5:16   8. Eph 6:11   9. Mt 5:15

7 SEQUUNTUR CAPITULA PRIMI LIBRI*

De ortu eius et de moribus ac vita venerabilis bartholomei patris eius. (8-15) i.

De infantia eius. (16-19) ij.

5   De eo quod beghinis sociata fuit et scolas frequentauit (20-22) iij.

De eo quod regularem habitum assumpsit. (23-29) iiij.

De penitentia et mortificatione carnis eius. (30-33) v.

De infirmitatis incommodo quo puericie sue tempore grauabatur. (34-35) vj.

10   De penuria quam in victu sustinuit et <de vestitu>. (36-41) vij.

De ordinatione et exercitio meditationum cordis eius. (42-44) viij.

Qualiter ad nouiciatus habitum aspirauit. (45-48) ix.

De professione eius et de eo quod ad rameyam monasterium ad discendam artem scriptoriam missa fuit. (49-53) x.

15   De raptu eius et celica visione sibi in spiritu demonstrata. (54-59) xi.

De eo quod seductor dyabolus eam a sancto proposito suo reuocare conatus est. (60-64) xij.

De consolatione diuina quam sensit in perceptione eucharistie. (65-66) xiij.

20

De subtilitate et fortitudine spiritus quam in perceptione sacra-. menti a domino consecuta sit. (67-70) xiiij.

Item de ordinatione et exercitio meditationum eius. (71-72) xv.

De celestibus consolationibus : , et ductu diuine gratie qua se ad spirituales profectus sensit cotidie promoueri. (73-75) xvj.

25

De eo quod ab episcopo consecrata fuit. (76-78) xvij.

De frequentatione sacramenti corporis et sanguinis christi. (79-82) xviij.

Expliciunt capitula.

Sequitur vita venerabilis ac deo dilecte beatricis quondam monialis ac priorisse in nazareth tribus distinctis libris comprehensa. Incipit liber primus.

7   THE CHAPTERS OF BOOK ONE

The end of the Chapters.

Here follows the life of the venerable Beatrice, dear to God, formerly nun and
prioress in Nazareth, condensed in three distinct books. Here begins the first book.

¶ DE ORTU EIUS ET DE MORIBUS
ET VITA VENERABILIS BARTHOLOMEI PATRIS EIUS
Primum capitulum

(f° 297 a) **8** Igitur in oppido [.]cui thenis vetustas nomen imposuit., temporali quidem <ducum> brabantie vel lotharingie di-
tioni subiecto;, leodiensis vero presulis in dyocesi constituto,
parentibus mediocribus alumpna christi beatrix exordium huius
vite sortita est.[1] Pater eius, bartholomeus vocatus, huius seculi
labili honestate mediocriter quidem inter suos enituit;, at uero
pijs operibus et proborum actuum assidua iugitate multo clarior in
oculis diuine maiestatis apparuit :, vt sequens plenius lectio de-
monstrabit. Trium quippe monasteriorum ordinis cisterciensis is
fundator extitit[2]:, in quibus perpetue sanctitatis et beneficentie
monimenta non tam laudanda quam imitanda, posterorum memorie delegauit. Mater vero virginis, gertrudis dicta., miro pietatis affectu, studio deuotionis et castitatis amore prepolluit :; et
domui sue bene preposita., viro subdita, deo placita., continuis
bonorum operum incrementis opinionis sue memoriam, etiam inter
matronas sui temporis, efficaciter ampliauit.

9 Ab hijs ergo, diuina preordinante clementia, liberorum gene-
rosa propago descendit : quam pater bartholomeus ipsi patri misericordiarum, a quo <datam> acceperat, integro postea numero
consignauit. Primogenitum quippe filiorum suorum in monasterio
premonstratensis ordinis, auerbodium nominato :, regulari canoni-
corum observantie subdidit.[3] Unam autem ex filiabus in monasterio cisterciensis ordinis, quod rameya nuncupatur :, diuini cultus
obsequio mancipauit.[4]

BEATRICE'S ORIGIN
AND THE CHARACTER AND THE LIFE
OF THE VENERABLE BARTHOLOMEW, HER FATHER
Chapter One

8 In the town from of old called Tienen, subject to the temporal authority of the dukes of Brabant or Lotharingia and constituted within the limits of the diocese of the bishop of Liège, the child of Christ, Beatrice, was born of modest parents. Her father, named Bartholomew, stood out respectably among his fellow citizens of the middle class in this transient world, but in the eyes of the divine Majesty he shone still more brightly because of his pious deeds and upright works, as the following story will make more fully manifest. He became, indeed, the founder of three Cistercian monasteries, through which he left to the memory of posterity monuments of enduring holiness and beneficence, to be not so much praised as imitated. The mother of our virgin, Gertrude by name, was remarkable in the wonderful warmth of her piety as well as in her zealous devotion and love of chastity. She governed her house well, was subject to her husband, and was pleasing to God.[1] Her many good works increased her honorable memory among the women of her time.

9 By divine mercy and providence, a generous progeny came forth from these parents. Father Bartholomew gave all his children to the Father of mercies from whom he had received them.[2] He subjected the firstborn of his sons, Averbode by name, to a monastery of the regular canons of the Praemonstratensian Order. He devoted one of his daughters to the service of divine worship in a Cistercian monastery, called Rameya (La Ramée).

---

1. 1 Tm 3:4   2. 2 Co 1:3

10 Ipse vero, post dilecte coniugis obitum, in monasterio prefati
cisterciensis // f. 297 b ordinis a se fundato[5], et vallis florida nun-
cupato, cum tribus filiabus[6] et vno superstite filio[7], suscepto religionis habitu, se conuertit[8] :; in quo, fortis athleta contra spiritualia nequitie in celestibus, annis sex omnipotenti domino strenue
militauit[9]. Deinde in mentem beati viri, reuelante domino, subijt,
vt, diuini cultus ampliandi gratia, monasterium aliud de nouo
construeret ; et in eo, creatori suo die noctuque seruientium, eiusdem ordinis examen sanctimonialium aggregaret : quod et factum
est. In dicti quippe thenensis oppidi territorio monasterium ordinis
cisterciensis vir strenuus, auxiliante dei gratia, fundauit[10] et statuit, vallis<que> virginum ei nomen imposuit :; in quod postmodum omni cum sobole sua priori monasterio deputata, se transtulit., et annis .xiiij.[11] inibi per ordinis obseruantiam creatoris sui
se beneplacito conformauit. Quibus itidem expletis, etiam tertium
eiusdem ordinis monasterium, sancte trinitatis venerator eximius,
exorsus est in lyrensis oppidi confinio[12] dedicare :; quo rursus,
adiuuante superna clementia, laudabiliter et egregie consummato.,

10 Bartholomew himself, after his beloved wife died, went to a monastery of the above-mentioned Cistercian Order which he had founded, called Florival (Bloemendaal), where he received the habit with his three daughters and one remaining son. There, as a strong athlete against the powers of spiritual evil in high places,[3] he strenuously served his Omnipotent Lord for six years. Then, at the Lord's revelation, it came into the blessed man's mind that for the sake of spreading the divine worship he should again construct another monastery, and to it should attach a group of nuns under the supervision of the same Order, serving their Creator day and night. And this came to pass. In the territory of the said town of Tienen the vigorous man decided to construct, with the help of God's grace, another monastery of the Cistercian Order and gave it the name Maagdendaal (*Vallis Virginum*). Later on he transferred to it himself with all his progeny, sent there by the first monastery, and for fourteen years he conformed himself to the pleasure of his Creator by the observances of the Order. After this lapse of time the great venerator of the Holy Trinity founded a third monastery of the Order within the boundary of the town of Lier. Here again, with divine help, he established that third one in a praiseworthy and respectable way.

3. Eph 6:12

vir deuotus, ab illo sempiterni floris orto florigero., nazareno videlicet oppido, mutuato vocabulo, nazareth ei nomen imposuit, et
cum prefata prole sua, christi miles emeritus, in eo deceto famu-
laturus creatori suo domino, se transuexit.

50 **11** Fuit autem hic vir beatissimus omni vite sue tempore circa
diuini cultus ampliandum decus, vigilans et sollicitus., proximorum
indigentie subleuator assiduus :, et nichilominus, in sui domatione
corporis, asper et rigidus., in sustentatione sobrius et modestus.
Tam intime quoque zelus animarum wlnerauerat cor illius :, vt
55 omnibus ad se venientibus edificationis eloquia propinaret., multos, opitulante christi gratia, de tenebrosis extractos peccatorum
latibu- // *f. 297 c* lis, ad statum emendatioris vite conuerteret :,
multos etiam, ab huius seculi nexibus absolutos, ad regularis
obseruantie normam dirigens., per religionis habitum et votum
60 professionis, christo domino consignaret. Erga pauperum etiam
indigentiam, pro facultate virium supportandam, deuotus christi
pauper tam largus pariter et beneficus apparebat :, vt quotiens
ad monasteriorum negotia procuranda foras necessitas exire com-
pelleret., aut vtilitas admoneret, stipem semper in sinu gereret,
65 quam occurrenti pauperi vir misericordissimus misericorditer
erogaret.
Tantam etiam fidelium defunctorum animabus, ad penas purgatorij dei iudicio destinatis, compassionis affluentiam habuisse
dinoscitur :, vt cotidie psalterium integrum, ex psalmi peniten-
70 tialis, id est quinquagesimi, repetitione creberrima compensatum,
omnipotenti domino pro illorum liberatione persolueret; et nichilominus orationibus disciplinisve corporalibus, aut ceteris carnis
afflictionibus., illarum quas patiebantur erumpnas vir pijssimus
assidue releuaret.
75 **12** Quis autem umquam otiosum hunc vidit ; quis deprehendit
tepidum vel remissum ? Diebus, operi manuum insistens, marthe
vicem agebat extrinsecus :; at vero noctibus, ad pedes domini cum
maria residens., orationum simul et meditationum officio, partem
optimam, que non auferetur ab eo [13], continuatis vigilijs acquire-
80 bat. Numquam autem, vt ipse fatebatur, in tantum exteriori solli-

And the devout man imposed on it the name Nazareth, a name borrowed from the town of Nazareth, the flower-bearing, from the birth of the sempiternal Flower. Together with his aforementioned progeny the veteran knight went there henceforth to serve the Lord, his Creator.

11 During his whole life this devout man was vigilant and solicitous about the divine worship, constantly concerned to relieve the needs of his neighbors. He was nevertheless very harsh and rigid in taming his body, sober and modest in sustaining it. Zeal for the salvation of souls had so intimately wounded his heart that he gave all those who came to him edifying words to drink. Through the help of God's grace he was able to convert to a better life many whom he drew from the darkness of their sins. He brought also to the Lord many loosed from bondage to this world, guiding them to the pattern of regular observance through the religious habit and the vows of profession. This devout poor man of Christ, concerned with the needs of the poor to the extent of his abilities, showed himself so generous and kind that, whenever necessity compelled or utility admonished him to go out for some monastery business, he always carried some money with him which he would mercifully give to any poor fellow he met.

He was known to have an abundance of compassion for the souls of the faithful departed, who through God's mercy had to suffer the pains of purgatory. He daily recited the whole psalter or its equivalent in the frequent repetition of the penitential psalm, the fiftieth, praying the Omnipotent Lord for their liberation. At the same time, through his prayers and bodily discipline or through other bodily afflictions, this devout man continually sought to alleviate them from the sufferings they endured.

12 Who ever saw him idle? Who caught him tepid or inactive? By day working with his hands he outwardly acted the part of Martha, but at night, sitting with Mary at the Lord's feet, through his prayers and continuous vigils he acquired the best part that would not be taken from him.[4] By his own admission, he could never be so pressed

---

4. Lk 10:42

citudine grauari potuit. , quod deuotionis feruor in eius corde
decresceret : , aut intentionem orantis occupatio superueniens impediret. Memoriam quoque dominice passionis in pectore frequenter habuit et in ore : ; presertim in horis quibus a sancta ecclesia
85   per orbem terre recitatur dominum ihesum, nostre redemptionis
intuitu, voluntarie passionis obprobria pertulisse. [14] Numquam a
dei laude vacare. , numquam edificationis verbo saturari potuit : ;
sed susceptum [15] in terra cordis sui, absconditum studiose recon-
didit <et> // f. 297 d vsquequo fructum faceret, habundantissimo
90   lacrimarum ymbre, cotidie dulciter irrigauit.
13 Quis vero puritatem spiritus. , verborum subtilitatem. , intellec-
tusve profunditatem huius sancti viri digne valeat explicare ? Frequenter illius spiritus iudiciorum dei profunda magnalia penetrare
promeruit : ; frequenter illi pius dominus, orationibus aut medi-
95   tationibus occupato, secretorum suorum mirabilia reuelauit. Est et
illud in beato sene laudabile. , quod, annis ferme decem antequam
ex hoc carnis ergastulo solueretur, omni pene die dominico, cum
magno deuotionis affectu multaque lacrimarum habundantia, procurabat se refici dominici corporis sacramento : mirabilem in hijs
100   omnibus prebens intuentibus exempli materiam; quippe mirantibus
hominem annorum plus minus . xcv . tam alacriter in via mandatorum dei incedere. , robustosque iuuenes et corpore validos, alacri
voluntatis incessu mentisque virtuosis passibus, infatigabiliter
anteire.
105   14 Cum vero bonorum omnium remuneratori complaceret illius
laboribus finem imponere. , fidelisque milicie prolixos agones perpetue remunerationis felici commercio compensare : , decidit vir
beatus in lectum egritudinis. , et, lentis febribus estuando, paulatim
vite termino cepit miles christi, carnis exesa corpulentia, propin-
110   quare. Cui cum ex filiabus eius due deuotissime femine, christina
videlicet et hec <nostra> beatrix, cuius in hoc opere describende
vite deseruire proponimus. , merentes et flentes pariter asside-
rent : , ipse, vvltu iocundissimo conuersus ad eas. , tali sermonum

by exterior cares that the devotional fervor in his heart diminished, nor would an oncoming occupation impede his attention to prayer. He had the memory of our Lord's passion in his heart and on his lips, especially at the times when Holy Church throughout the world told how the Lord Jesus bore the shame of his voluntary passion for our redemption. He never ceased praising God; he never had enough of the edifying word, but having received it in the soil of his heart, he buried it zealously and watered it sweetly and daily with the abundant rainfall of his tears until it should bear fruit.[5]

13 Who could expound the purity of spirit, subtlety of speech, and profound intellect of this holy man? Frequently his spirit deserved to penetrate into the deep mysteries of God's judgments; while in prayer or meditation the Lord would often reveal to him the marvels of his secrets. It is praiseworthy in the blessed old man that for nearly ten years before he was delivered from the prison of his body, he took care to be nourished by the Sacrament of the Lord's Body nearly every Sunday with deeply felt devotion and abundance of tears. In all this he gave an admirable example for others to see. They marvelled that a man of more or less ninety-five years advanced with alacrity in the way of God's commandments and untiringly surpassed robust young men, strong in body, thanks to the eager movement of his will and the strivings of his virtuous mind.

14 When it pleased the rewarder of all good works to put an end to his labors and to compensate the long struggles of his faithful service with an eternal reward—a happy exchange—the blessed man took to his sickbed. Sweating with a low fever and losing weight, the soldier of Christ, little by little began to approach the end of life. His two devoted daughters, namely Christine and our Beatrice (whose life we propose to describe), both sat with him mourning and weeping. Turning his face joyfully toward them, he tried to

5. Mt 13:44

ordine cepit dolorem flentium mitigare. : ,, Cessate inquit a fleti-
115   bus et lamentis, filie mee dilectissime : , quin potius mihi qaudenti
pariter congaudete ; certus enim <existo> quod, cum hoc carnis
onus ipse deposuero, bene mecum aget omnipotens : qui me, licet
peccatorem, dignatus est in electorum suorum numero computare.
Et hoc etiam // f. 298 a [etiam] vobis annuncio, quod non solum
120   super salute propria me pius dominus consolari dignatus est : ,
verum etiam super omnium liberorum meorum vtriusque sexus sem-
piterna predestinatione, diuina reuelatio certum me reddidit. , et
eorum, in eterna iocunditate, me fruiturum consortio, certe demonstrationis indicio declarauit''. Hec cum ore mellifluo vir beatus, dul-
125   cique verborum serie perorasset. , haut multo post tempore, letali
morbo corpus decrepitum acrius infestante. , bartholomeus, ihesu
christi famulus, senex et plenus dierum, ad extrema peruenit : ;
et, viuifici sacramenti viatico premunitus. , in confessione vere
fidei, carnis eductus ergastulo, fidelis seruus et prudens in gau-
130   dium domini sui, regnaturus in secula, feliciter introiuit [16].

15 O vere beatum virum cuius anima tanto sine fine gloriosior
apparebit in celi palacio : , quanto per multa virtutum exercitia. ,
claris etiam clarior enituit in hoc mundo.

Sepultus est autem in nazareth monasterio [17]. , quod olim, vt pre-
135   diximus, ipse fundauerat in lyrensis oppidi territorio : , prestante
domino nostro ihesu christo. , qui cum patre et spiritu sancto viuit
et regnat deus in secula seculorum. Amen.

soothe the grief of his weeping daughters and spoke to them thus: 'Stop weeping, my dearest daughters. You should be as joyful as I am. For I am certain that when I lay down this burden of my flesh, the Almighty will treat me well, for he has accepted me, sinner though I am, among the number of his elect. And this also I can tell you, that our loving Lord has not only been willing to console me about my own salvation, but divine revelation has given me the certainty that all my children of both sexes are eternally predestined. He has shown me by indubitable signs that I will enjoy their company in eternal bliss'. Shortly after the blessed man had said all these words sweet as honey, the deadly disease attacked his languishing body more sharply, and Bartholomew, the servant of Jesus Christ, old and full of days, came to his last moment.[6] Fortified with the life-giving Sacrament as viaticum, confessing the true faith, the faithful and prudent servant left the prison of the flesh and entered into the joy of his Lord,[7] to reign for ever.

15 What a truly happy man, whose soul in heaven's palace will appear endlessly more glorious as he outshone all in this world through many exercises of virtue.

He was buried in the monastery of Nazareth, which he had founded, as we said, in the territory of the town of Lier, by the concession of our Lord Jesus Christ, who with the Father and the Holy Spirit lives and reigns, God forever and ever. Amen.

6. 1 Ch 23:1   7. Mt 25:21

⁌ DE INFANTIA EIUS
Secundum capitulum

16 Hijs ergo de vita venerabilis bartholomei, patris secundum carnem nostre sanctissime beatricis, per excessum, breuitatis causa
5 compendiose digestis : , ad ipsius vite materiam, de qua modice. , diuine laudis et legentium edificationis causa digressi fuimus. , narrationis nostre stilum decetero conuertamus.

Que licet a magnis coram deo parentibus originem duxerit, et religionis tytulo decoratis : , sublimioribus tamen ipsa sublimior et
10 perfectis perfectior, illorum gloriam quoque suis virtutibus ex-tulit. , et copiosiori perfectionis lumine copiosius illustrauit.

17 Siquidem infantie sue primo <limine> sic bonis moribus iam cepit illa pol- // f. 298 b lescere : , vt ab ipso materno semine, diuine gratie secum videretur indicia produxisse. Prius enim quam,
15 solidatis labijs, ad plenum valuisset humana verba vel edere uel proferre. , mirum dictu, sic omne scurrile vel turpe verbum indi-gnanti corde detestari cepit et spernere : , vt nullus ex fratribus, nullus ex familiaribus domus sue tale quid effutire, beatrice pre-sumeret audiente. Nam si quem horum tale <quid>, ipsa presente
20 vel audiente, protulisse contingeret ; , miro rectitudinis armata zelo christi iuuencula. , mox apud patrem huius reum transgressio-nis instantius accusauit [1] : , et quem per semetipsam emendare non poterat, implorata seueritate paterna, simul cum eo delin-quentem vt potuit emendauit.

25 Quid enim? Vt video, iam completum in nostra cernimus beatrice [:] quod olim ysaias sanctus precinuit de filio prophetisse : prius enim quam, formatis ad plenum vocabulis, hec patris nomen aut matris exprimere potuisset, iamiam humani generis aduersario festinauit iniquitatis sue detrahere spolia : , cum ab ore carnalium, quod idem aduersarius impellebat ad verba maledica, pro
30 iuste correptionis sarculo, hec viciorum explantare iam studuit incentiua.

18 Quid vero de morum eius grauitate dicturus sum : , cum raris-sime vel risu solutam ; , vel puellaribus iocis, quibus illa delectari solet etas, hanc quisquam deprehenderit occupatam ? Siquidem

HER INFANCY
Chapter Two

16 We have composed in shortened form these things about the life of blessed Bartholomew, the father of our saintly Beatrice according to the flesh. Now let us turn our pen to the matter of her life, from which we digressed slightly for divine praise and the edification of the reader.

Though she was born of parents who were great in God's eyes, adorned with the reputation of being very religious, she was more sublime than the sublime and more perfect than the perfect. She exalted their glory by her own virtues, and made them illustrious by the more copious light of her perfection.

17 Indeed from the beginning of her infancy she was so vigorous in good morals that from her mother's womb she seemed to have brought forth with her signs of divine grace. Before her lips were trained enough to utter fully human words, she—wonderful to say—began to detest and disdain with an indignant heart every indecent or bad word. None of her brothers or of the familiars at home would have dared to chatter such words in Beatrice's presence. If one of them happened to say something of that kind in her presence or within her hearing, the girl with the weapons of a wonderful upright zeal for Christ, would immediately tell her father about this transgression. While she could not correct it by herself, she implored her father's severity and together with him corrected the culprit as she could.

What about all this? As I see it, we perceive fulfilled in our Beatrice what the holy Isaiah formerly foretold of the prophetess's son.[1] Before she was able to speak plainly and pronounce her father's or her mother's name, she hastened to drag away from the enemy of the human race the spoils of his wickedness. By using the hoe of deserved correction, she strove to uproot the spark of vices, the evil words forced from the mouths of the worldly by the same adversary.

18 What shall I say about her seriousness? Who ever caught her engaged in the girlish jokes in which that age delights, as she was

1. Is 8:4

extra limites domus sue raro quidem ab aliquo videri potuit : ,
35 sed multo rarius, ad vacandum ociosis aut ludicris coevarum se
puellarum contubernio sociauit. Et, mirum in modum, cum iam
<necdum> agnosceret nec quid amandum quidve <respuen-
dum> foret. , adhuc infantili mens obcecata caligine, preuideret : ,
ita tamen nescio quid diuinum eius inhesit affectui, vt, in appe-
40 tendo vel in eligendo. , seu etiam reprobando, soli se videretur
submittere rationi. Nichil enim horum // f. 298 c que corporali
cernuntur intuitu. , non aurum vel argentum. , non preciosarum
cultum vestium : , non denique vel ipsos parentes habuit in affectu.
Et licet illam dominicam <improbationem> qua dicit. : ' si quis
45 amat patrem suum aut matrem plus quam me non est me
dignus ' ². , necdum vel legerit vel audierit, illis tamen nimis re-
solutum affectum impendere, hoc solo rationis impulsu super-
uacuum iudicauit. Mirabilem quoque pietatis gratiam eius pectori
pius dominus iam impresserat ; , vt si quando tenera membra,
50 prout moris est, ad ignem calefactionis gratia contulisset. , super-
uenienti pauperi mox locum cederet : , et ad angulum domatis, vbi
nullius alterius frequentabatur sessio. , turtur domini simplicissima
conuolaret. Ibi, vel<ut> quelibet extranea, quietis causa, sedebat
solitaria et tacebat : , et nulli <quauis> importunitate molesta. ;
55 sed omni familie pro viribus obediens et subiecta. , gratum vix
silentium resoluebat, etiam cum necessarijs indigebat.
19 Hijs igitur et alijs virtutum flosculis, quibus infantilem etatulam
virgo christi beatrix in dies attentius exornabat, ab eius matre,
sagaci discretionis odore, non sine multa congratulatione cordisque
60 leticia, deprehensis : , ingeniosam filiam, iam futurorum prouida,
scolari studio mox <censuit> applicandam ³; in quo <tantum>
cepit, auxiliante superna gratia, repente proficere : , quod, iam

rarely given over to laughter? She rarely could be seen by anyone outside the walls of her house, and more rarely still would she join the girls of her own age in their idleness and games. It is wonderful that when she was still not yet capable of recognizing what was to be cherished or rejected, her childish mind, still in darkness, had foresight. I do not know what divine [gift] it was which affected her so that in desiring, choosing and rejecting she seemed to submit only to what was rational. Nothing seen with bodily sight, whether gold or silver, or taste for exquisite dresses seemed to affect her. Not even for her own parents did she have affection. Though she had not yet read or heard of the Lord's condemnation where he says: 'If anyone loves father or mother more than me, he is not worthy of me',[2] she judged it superfluous, on the impulse of reason alone, to give them a too unrestrained affection. The good Lord had also marked her heart with a great compassion: when it happened that she approached the fire to warm her tender members in the usual way, she would quickly yield her place if a poor man approached. The Lord's simple turtledove would fly off to a corner of the house which no one else often frequented. There, like an outsider, she sat alone and was silent[3] for the sake of quiet. She was never troublesome to anyone by any sort of rudeness, but was obedient and subject to all her family, according to her capacity. She scarcely broke her pleasing silence even when she needed something.

19 Her mother perceived with sagacious discretion and much rejoicing of heart these and other flowerings of virtue with which the virgin of Christ, Beatrice, was daily more adorned in her infant years. Foreseeing the future, she thought that her clever daughter should soon be set to study. Beatrice, with the help of heavenly

2. *Mt 10:37*   3. Lm 3:28

quinquennis effecta, daui<d>icum illud psalterium absque quolibet offendiculo valuisset ex ordine recitare. Sed quid mirum si
65   purum ingenium, in tali etate, verba foris sonantia discere potuit ; ,
quod [4] paulo post etiam ipsorum sensuum alta misteria, non magistrali peritia. , sed sola sancti spiritus duce gratia, penetrauit.

❡ DE EO QUOD BEGHINIS SOCIATA FUIT
ET SCOLAS FREQUENTAUIT
Tercium capitulum

20 Evolutis igitur annis sex, cum iam puericie terminos. , id est
5   annum etatis septimum, attigisset : , mater eius venerabilis, ad
immorta- // f. 298 d litatis perpetue libertatem, per mortis compendium emigrauit. Porro venerandus pater virginis, dilecta con-
iuge viduatus. , hanc, de qua loquimur, filiam tenere diligens. ,
et future perfectionis, ex modo conuersationis, aliquantula iam
10 indicia deprehendens : vt liberius ad virtutis prouectum conscenderet, in oppido cui lewis vocabulum est illam deuoto beghinarum
collegio sociauit [1]. , et tam magistre, mulieri religiose scilicet et
deuote, quam ceteris consororibus sub eius regimine domino famulantibus, bonis informandam moribus. , erudiendam exemplis
15 et virtutibus adornandam, hanc pius pater attentius commendauit.
Quibus virgo domini ex paterna iussione voluntarie sociata, miro
dilectionis affectu singulas illius deuoti collegij socias et consortes. , et precipue venerabilem illam, cuius magisterio delegata
fuerat, instructicem, mox cordi suo cepit imprimere : , et vt ipsa
20 testante didicimus [2]. , numquam vel ipsis progenitoribus suis tam

grace, began to progress so rapidly that at the age of five she could recite David's psalter without flaw and in the right order. But it is wonderful that her clear intellect at such an early age could learn the outward words. For soon afterwards that intelligence would penetrate the high mysteries of their meaning, not with a skill gained from a teacher, but led only under the direction of the Holy Spirit's grace.

HOW SHE WAS ASSOCIATED WITH THE BEGUINES
AND WENT TO SCHOOL
Chapter Three

20 When she had completed her sixth year and had reached the end of early childhood, the seventh year, her venerable mother, through the shortcut of death, migrated to the freedom of perpetual immortality. Whereupon the virgin's venerable father, bereaved of his beloved wife, tenderly loving this daughter and perceiving from her conduct some signs of her future perfection, entrusted her to a devout group of Beguines in a town called Lewis (Zoutleeuw), so that she might more freely make progress in virtue. The pious father recommended her with careful attention to the mistress, a religious and devout woman, and to the other sisters who were serving the Lord under her leadership, to form his daughter in good manners, teaching her with examples and adorning her with virtues. Thereupon, the Lord's virgin, willingly united to them by her father's command, soon began with a wonderful love to impress on her heart the individual members of that devout group, especially the venerable instructress to whose teaching she was assigned. As we learned from her own testimony, she never gave even her own parents

largum dilectionis affectum impresserat. , quam suis ex tunc consodalibus infundebat. Sed et ipsa non minus ab hijs quoque
redamari potuit : , quippe quam diuina clementia singulari gratio-
sitatis dulcedine perlustrauit. Erat enim conuersatione simplex et
timida. , locutione verax et prouida : , sed et obsequio cunctis
obediens et subiecta.

21 Per idem quoque tempus a patre magistris liberalium < artium >
est commissa, disciplinis scolaribus, quibus iam a matre, sicut
prediximus, iniciata fuerat, expeditius informanda ³. Ubi cum inter
multitudinem scolarium cogeretur toto die deuotissima christi
discipula residere : , horum tamen que ab hijs gerebantur vel
dicebantur nichil penitus aduertebat. Sed et quantum potuit ab
illis corpore pariter et animo sequestrata, facie quoque auersa, soli
lectionis studio quam a magistro memorie commendandam acceperat intendebat. In tantum enim illorum confabulationes //
f. 299 a et consortia vitare studuit ; , vt nec in faciem quidem
alicuius eorum aspectum vmquam libens impresserit. ; nec in necessitatis quidem articulo [.], cuiquam horum adiungere se presump-
serit. , sed sic inter multos ac si sola fuerit, etiam mente solitaria,
perdurauit. Multotiens quidem, ob tantam sui custodiam, ab alijs
argui, ab alijs subsannari. , grauitatem morum eius inuidentibus,
eam contigit : ; sed quantum ob hoc a conscolaribus plus molestie
seu verecundie pertulit. , tanto firmius in hoc laudabili proposito
perdurauit.

22 Libet parumper hoc in loco subsistere : , et illis, quas nostro tempore iam
videmus puellis, exemplum recolende probitatis ante mentis oculos reuocare.
Perpendant igitur huiusmodi, que iuuenum suspecta colloquia, non solum euitare
non satagunt. , sed etiam incautorum aut non auertentium [.] aspectibus importune plerumque se ingerunt; nolentes au renitentes ad voluptuosas affectiones imprudenter emolliunt : gestibus et nutibus, impudicis quoque respec-
tibus, latentis interius indicia blandientis lasciuie foras euomunt. Attendant
inquam electam hanc dei virginem, per totum et eo amplius anni circulum,
inter scolares quam plurimos ita solitariam accubasse : , vt nullus eam depre-
hendere potuerit, non dico suspecta miscuisse colloquia. , sed nec in necessitatis quidem tempore cuiusquam subsidium implorasse.

as much love as she gave her companions at that time. She herself
could be loved no less in return by them, since the divine mercy
adorned her with singular sweetness and charm. In her relation-
ships she was simple and timid, in her speech truthful and prudent,
and in her compliance obedient and subject to all.

21 At the same time she was entrusted by her father to teachers of
the liberal arts, to be more readily instructed in the scholarly studies whose beginnings her mother had taught her, as we have already said. Although the devout disciple of Christ was obliged to
spend the whole day with the crowd of students, she paid no attention whatever to what they did or talked about. Keeping herself
apart from them in body and mind as far as she could, with face
turned away she gave full attention to reading what she had received from the teacher for memorization. She so strove to avoid
her fellow students' talk and company that she never impressed
her appearance on any of them, neither did she presume to join any
of them even when she needed something, but amid so many, she
remained as if alone, solitary even in mind. Because of such self-
control she was frequently criticized by some and laughed at by
others who envied her serious manners, but the more harassment
and shame she endured from her fellow students, the more
resolutely she continued in her laudable intention.

22 Let us dwell for a while on this topic, and recall this example of
memorable virtue to the girls of our time. Let this example be pondered
by those who not only do not avoid suspicious conversations with boys,
but who often thrust themselves boldly upon the gaze of the incautious or
those who do not turn away. Those who refuse their pleasure-seeking
affections, they imprudently soften up; by gestures and nods and im-
modest glances they vomit out signs of the beguiling lechery lurking
within them. Let them look at this chosen virgin of God who for a whole
year and more lived so solitary among so many students that no one
could catch her. I do not say that she took part in suspicious conversations, but she did not even ask anyone's help in time of need.

⁌ DE EO QUOD REGULAREM HABITUM ASSUMPSIT
Quartum capitulum

23 Anno igitur, a tempore quo beghinarum cetui adiuncta fuerat, reuoluto[1]:, pater filiam ad se reuocatam super omnimoda sui conuersione, blando cepit alloquio conuenire. Cuius liberrimam voluntatem, et fixum in domino virginale propositum deuotus pater intelligens, omnipotenti domino copiosas gratiarum actiones retulit:; et dilectum pignus vallis floride monasterio, quod, vt prediximus, ipse fundauerat, inuehens beatricem. sanctimonialium cetui per assumptionem initialis habitus adunauit[2]. Quantis // *f. 299 b* vero lacrimis et suspirijs, non ex fellis amaritudine., sed ex feruentissima cordis deuotione passim prorumpentibus, virgo christi primum hunc habitum conuersionis induerit., non est mee paruitatis exprimere:, quia nec sue possibilitatis fuit illas eodem in tempore cohibere.

24 Induta vero nuptiali veste solempniter et festiue., confestim aurem cordis attentissime cepit ad omnem regularis obseruantie disciplinam., et ad omne verbum edificatorium inclinare., singulas ordinis obseruantias inuestigando perquirere:, sed et pro captu intelligentie singula queque tenaci memorie commendare. Si quando vero de diuinis sermo, precipue de salutari redemptionis nostre misterio et passionis dominice sacramento, audiente christi discipula, subintrauit:, ita <feruenti> queque studio collegit in memorie cofino;, quod vel fragmentum ex eis que recitabantur in terram non caderet:, sed nunc consodalibus omnia replicando., nunc meditationis studio singula retractando., non prius

HER TAKING THE REGULAR HABIT
Chapter Four

23 After a year had passed from the time she had been sent to the Beguines, the father recalled his daughter home and began gently to test her about her total conversion. When her devout father understood the strength of her free choice and her virginal resolve fixed on the Lord, he gave abundant thanks to the Lord Almighty. He brought his beloved treasure, Beatrice, to the monastery of Florival, which he himself had founded, as we said, and joined her to the community of nuns by the taking of a beginner's habit. It is beyond my poor powers to express with what tears and sighs, springing not from bitterness but from fervent devotion, Christ's virgin received this first habit of conversion, just as it was not possible for her to restrain her tears at that time.

24 Once she had been clothed in the wedding garment with solemnity and festivity, she immediately began to incline the ear of her heart attentively to the whole discipline of regular observance and to every edifying word, investigating each of the Order's observances and commending them to her tenacious memory according to her understanding. If a sermon on divine things came within earshot of this disciple of Christ, especially if it concerned the mystery of our redemption or the Lord's passion, she fervently collected everything in the basket of her memory so that no fragment of what was said should fall to the ground.[1] At one time repeating everything to her companions, at another going over everything in meditation, she would not give

---

1. Mt 15:27; Jn 6:12

sompnum oculis et dormitationem palpebris indulgeret., quam, omnibus ordinate compositis, collectum ex hijs mirre fasciculum inter gemina, congratulationis scilicet et compassionis ubera collocaret.

25 Ex tunc siquidem, austro superni respectus et gratie, mentem venerabilis beatricis, velut ortum irriguum, superni roris et pluuie stillicidio visitante, continuo liquefacta ceperunt illius aromata super mel et fauum dulciora diffluere et suauissimum vt ita dixerim odorem in naribus domini sabaoth inspirare. Erat quippe videre deuotam christi iuuenculam, nunc protractis in longum orationibus cum suspirijs et lacrimis insistentem; nunc acris flagellationibus corpus omne mactantem : ; nunc continuatis ieiunijs artus teneros macerantem ; nunc a perfectioribus edificationis instructionisve pabulum expetentem : ; nunc quoque sodalibus et coeuis, illud idem quo iam // f. 299 c interius ipsa refecta fuerat, ad vsum similem erogantem. ; <s>ic denique, tam in actis quam in dictis, mores suauissimos omni tempore componentem : , vt nichil de perfectionis statu sibi deesse crederet. , qui tam perfectos inchoationis actus in ea diligenter exploraret. Nichil enim ex hijs que ad macerationem carnis vel spiritus humiliationem pertinere noscuntur, eius experientiam effugere potuit : ; sed multa quoque, non tam teneris puellis quam fortissimis etiam viris pene importabilia, feruenti zelo sibimet intrinsecus <simul et extrinsecus> adaptauit.

26 Per idem tempus psalterium beate virginis, quod ex angelice salutationis tam crebra repetitione compensari solet quam daui-<d>ici psalterij psalmorum numerus se extendit, cotidie cum genuflexionibus exsoluere consueuit[3] : , donec a deputata sibi custode deprehensa, grauiterque redarguta. , iam ab hoc oneroso labore quiesceret ; nec tamen opus tante pietatis omnino preter-

sleep to her eyes or slumber to her eyelids[2] until she had arranged everything in an orderly way and had collected from there a bundle of myrrh[3] to be placed between her two breasts of thanksgiving and compassion.

25 From this time on, the south wind of divine grace and benevolence[4] visited the mind of the venerable Beatrice which was like a garden watered[5] with the drops of heavenly dew and rain. Her aromas, continuously liquified sweeter than honey and the honeycomb,[6] spread themselves abroad, filling the nostrils of the Lord of hosts with the sweetest fragrance, so to speak. The devout youngster of Christ was to be seen, now intent on long prayers with sighs and tears, now immolating her whole body with sharp flagellations, now weakening her tender limbs with prolonged fasts, now seeking the food of edification and instruction from the more perfect, now distributing to her companions and contemporaries for their use the same fare by which she had been interiorly nourished. Her manners both in action and in speech were always so sweetly composed that anyone who carefully examined such perfect beginning actions would believe that nothing of the state of perfection was lacking in her. Nothing known to pertain to the chastising of the flesh or the humiliation of the spirit could escape her experience. Many things, moreover, which were almost unbearable not only to tender girls but also to the strongest men, she zealously applied to herself, both interiorly and exteriorly.

26 At the same time she used to recite daily, with genuflections, the psalter of the Blessed Virgin which consists of as many repetitions of the angelic salutation as there are psalms in David's psalter. When she was caught by the sister in charge of her and severely reprimanded, she stopped this burdensome practice. However, she did not at that time forego totally such a work of

2. Ps 131:4   3. Sg 1:12   4. Ps 77:26
5. Is 58:11   6. Ps 18:11

misit eodem in tempore : , sed quod verbis et genuflexionibus
decetero non audebat efficere. , saltem, quiescentibus labijs, intra
se, meditationis exercitio, studuit adimplere. **27** Verum cum ex
⁶⁰ dimensione virium corporalium proprie fragilitatis defectum attendere iam cepisset. , et obliuionis simul et ignorantie, que bonis
moribus insidiari non desinunt, improbitatem vehementer perti-
mesceret ; , timens ne forte, multorum exemplo, spiritu quidem inchoantium sed carne consummantium, ipsa quoque a bono propo-
⁶⁵ sito, lassato spiritu, ignauie torpore deficeret : saluberrimum
contra pestem huiusmodi. , et dignum memoria consilium adinuenit. , quo non solum ea que pertimescebat incommoda declinauit. ,
verum etiam intentionem cordis, ad omne bonum iam patulam et
erectam, in bono conseruauit proposito. , et perseuerantie industria
⁷⁰ consummauit. Vnam si-quidem ex coeuis, quam ceteris deuotiorem
et ad virtutis studium promptiorem aspexit, ex aliarum numero //
f. 299 d preelectam, firmissime dilectionis glutino cordi suo deuota
iuuencula sic impressit. , vt in duobus corporibus anima una et
cor unum, prout de antiquis christi discipulis legitur et in actibus
⁷⁵ apostolorum <habetur> ⁴. Hac ergo sodalitate per communem
consensum inita. , et per fidem mutuam confirmata. , talis inter
vtrasque firmatur pactio, talis conuentio stabilitur : vt sese vicaria
commonitione, verbo pariter et exemplo, cum vtilitas id exposcit,
invicem excitare debeant. , ad profectus studium incitare non
⁸⁰ differant ; et si quando temptationis laqueum cuiuscumque antiquus hostis illarum alteri presumat inicere : , insimul in eum pari
constantia consurgentes, ipsius dolos ad nichilum redigant. , eum-
que de finibus suis procul eiciant et expellant. Hac demum inter
deuotas christi tyrunculas pactione firmata. , videres opere perfi-
⁸⁵ cere quod fortissima fide conceperant : et nunc de regularibus
obseruantijs sese mutuo commonentes. , nunc ad agendam penitentiam de commissis se inuicem animantes. , nunc de virtute
obedientie, de sui custodia. , de frequentandis orationibus. , ordinandis meditationibus et ceteris virtutum operibus exequendis. ,
⁹⁰ audires frequenter mutuo colloquentes.

piety, for what she dared not do any more by words and genuflections, she tried to fulfill at least in an unspoken way, interiorly as an exercise of meditation. **27** When she began to pay attention to her own frailty, because of her limited bodily strength, she was much afraid of the wicked forgetfulness and ignorance which lie in wait for good morals. Fearing lest her good resolutions collapse into torpor and sloth, her spirit being worn out, after the manner of many who begin in the spirit but end in the flesh, she found a healthy counsel against this plague, and one worth remembering. By it she not only avoided the drawbacks she feared, but preserved the intention of her heart, now open and alert to every good in its good resolve and completed what she had set out to do with industrious perseverence. The devout girl Beatrice pressed firmly to her heart with the lime of love one of her companions her own age, whom she saw to be more devout and ready of virtue than the others. She did so in such a way that one soul and one heart existed in the two bodies,[7] as we read of Christ's first disciples and as is said in the Acts of the Apostles. By this companionship, begun by common consent and confirmed by mutual trust, such an agreement and covenant was established between them that they were bound to stir each other up by admonition in word and example when this was useful, and to rouse each other's effort toward progress. And if the ancient enemy should presume to cast the snare of some temptation around one of them, they would both forthwith be firm in standing up to him with the same firmness and bring his tricks to nothing, casting him out of their bounds. With this agreement concluded between the devout beginners in Christ, you would see them accomplishing in deed what they had conceived with vigorous faith. You would hear them admonishing each other about regular observances, animating each other to penance for misdeeds, and frequently talking together about the virtue of obedience, self-custody, prayers to be repeated, meditations to be arranged and other works of virtue to be accomplished.

7. Ac 4:32

28 Erat nichilominus eis pro consuetudine, clam ad nocturnas vigilias, quietis hora, consurgere : ; easque, non ex ordine quidem, vt in choro psallebantur, librorum dumtaxat impediente carentia, decantare :, sed, quod solum poterant, dominicarum orationum numerosa replicatione satagebant eas deuotissime compensare [5]. Cetera vero, que sine libris expedire valebant, id est de beata virgine matutinas, defunctorum quoque vigilias, ante fores ora- torij, furtiuis decantationibus exsoluebant : ; et quod residuum erat temporis, vsque dum pene matutina synaxis expleretur in choro psallentium. , iste, salutaribus insistendo meditationibus, vtiliter expendebant. Quibus rite peractis, ad strata sua clanculo redeuntes. , et, ne deprehenderentur ab // f. 300 a alijs, pre con- uentu reditum modice maturantes. , saluberrimo quodam dolo. , non tam illas quas sibi deputatas habuere magistras, quam ipsum quoque doli <primum> artificem et auctorem, frequentissime seduxerunt. Monastica quippe consuetudo uigens in ipso monas- terio. , tale quid, personis dumtaxat huiusmodi, pro debilitate vel impotentia corporis, attemptandum minime concedebat.

29 O mira potestas :, o ineffabilis nostri dignatio redemptoris. Ecce qui dudum super altitudinem nubium in lateribus aquilonis sedem ponere dispo- suerat [6]. , ecce qui flumina absorbebat, habens fiduciam vt et iordanis influeret in os eius [7]. , ecce qui tot gentes et regna, necdum carne velata dei sapientia [8], sibi subegerat : nunc a duabus christi virgunculis velut inermis atteritur. , velut insensatus illuditur. , et tamquam excors et timidus ab antique ditionis, non quidem proprie sed inuase, finibus effugatur. O vere felicissimam beatricem ; , que dum, talibus intenta studijs, spiritui corpus obediendo seruire docuit. , de totis tenebrarum harum rectoribus, adiuuante christi clementia, mirabili victoria triumphauit.

28 They had the custom of rising secretly for night vigils when all was quiet. They could not sing them as they were sung in choir, for lack of books, but doing what they could, they labored to compensate devoutly by the frequent repetition of the Lord's Prayer. What they could do without books, that is, matins of the Blessed virgin and vigils of the dead, they sang softly in front of the closed doors of the oratory. They spent the time left over usefully in godly meditations till vigils were almost finished in the nuns' choir. When they had finished their devotions properly, they stole away to their beds, hastening their return a little before that of the community so as not to be caught by the others. Thus they misled with very excellent trickery not so much the mistresses set over them, as the first maker and author of trickery. The monastic custom in force at that monastery did not permit vigils to persons of weak or feeble body.

29 O wonderful power, O the ineffable goodness of our Redeemer! See the one who formerly thought to establish his throne above the height of the clouds in the sides of the north;[8] the one who drank up rivers and was confident that the Jordan would run into his mouth;[9] the one who subdued under him so many nations and kingdoms when the wisdom of God was not yet veiled in flesh. Now he is trodden down as if unarmed by Christ's two little virgins, is laughed at as stupid, and is chased as if senseless and timid out of his ancient domain, not properly his but invaded by him. O truly happy Beatrice, who intent on such efforts, taught her body to obey the spirit, and who triumphed in a wonderful victory over all the rulers of this darkness,[10] thanks to Christ's mercy.

8. Is 14:13   9. Jb 40:18   10. Eph 6:12

☞ DE PENITENTIA ET MORTIFICATIONE CARNIS EIUS
Quintum capitulum

30 Sed vt iam planiora fiant et aptiora que dicimus : , de genera-
libus ad specialia descendamus. Et primum, de ipsius domatione
5   corpusculi locuturi. , quibus operibus penitentie teneros artus in
ipsis diebus adolescentie macerauit. , non tam verbis intelligere
quam aliquantula saltem experientia conicere studeamus. Moris
quippe fuit huic deuotissime, plerumque virgis acerrimis : , interdum etiam aculeatis taxi ramusculis corpus tenerum a planta
10   pedis ad pectus vsque flagenllando dirumpere. ; sed et stratum
suum, a summo vsque ad deorsum, acutis taxi folijs operiendo
construere ; , quibus tenerrima iacentis membra sic diris punctionibus arcebantur : vt vix aliqua <corporis> eius particula valuisset illesa, sub tanto punctionum discrimine, // f. 300 b perma-
15   nere. Sed ne solum noctibus huiusmodi se cruentaret supplicio
et dies absque penali tormento vacua pertransiret : , ipsa quoque
taxorum folia per diem in sinu suo gestauit acerrima ; quibus
eo nimirum atrocius pungebatur. , quo vigilantis sensus, eorum
importuna lesione, cogebatur incessabiliter affici : , et, quocumque
20   se verteret, nouis semper punctionibus infestari.
31 Nec hoc tamen, licet admodum diro contenta supplicio fuit
aut cruciatu valido christi virgo : , sed renes suos et latera funibus, aut contortis restibus insuper accingebat. Lineum quoque
vestimentum, quod humane carnis teneritudini familiari quadam
25   mollitie deseruire videtur : , hec velut superfluum, ymo quasi
venenum aliquod adhorrebat. Lignum etiam aut lapidem, pului-
naris loco, capiti suo ad soporandum in lectulo reclinato, frequentissime substernebat : ; lectulum quoque sibi <substratum>,
quotiens absque reprehensionis nota valebat, de sub lateribus suis,
30   nocturnis temporibus, extrahens : , in stramenti duricia se volue-
bat. Sed et brumali tempore, nudis genibus et poplitibus. , vel
in glacie, vel in niue, genuflexiones quam plurimas sub nocturno
silentio faciebat. Et vt paucis multa concludam. , nichil de talibus
aut similibus, ad corporis domationem carnisve macerationem
35   accommodis. , quod vel vires sui corporis omnimodo non ex-

HER PENITENCE AND MORTIFICATION OF THE FLESH
Chapter Five

30 But to make our words clearer and more appropriate, let us come down from generalities to specifics. First of all, since we are going to speak about the mastering of her frail body by works of penitence during the days of her youth, let us strive less to understand by words than to conjecture by at least a little experience. She was accustomed to beat her tender body, from the soles of her feet[1] up to her chest, using sharp twigs and even the prickly branches of the yew tree. She also strewed her bed, from top to bottom, with sharp yew leaves; by them her tender limbs were so hedged in that scarcely any part of her body remained unscratched by the punctures. But lest she wound herself only at night with this torment and pass her days without it, she carried the prickly yew leaves in her bosom during the day, and was more harshly pierced by them as her waking senses were forced to be continuously aware of the nagging hurts, and to be constantly harassed with fresh pricks wherever she turned.

31 Nor was Christ's virgin content with this harsh and excruciating torment; she also girded her loins and sides with ropes and twisted cords. The linen undergarment which affords the tenderness of human flesh a certain familiar softness she abhorred as superfluous and indeed as something baneful. Also, she very often put a piece of wood or a stone under her head in place of a pillow to sleep on. As often as she could do so without reproach, she would pull her bed out from under her body at night and would stretch out on the hard floor. In winter time in the quiet of the night she would multiply her genuflections on bare knees in the ice or snow. To cut the matter short, Christ's devout beginner never omitted any of these or similar things suitable to subduing the body or tormenting the flesh, no matter how hard and unbearable they seemed, unless they altogether exceeded the strength

---

1. Jb 2:7

cederet., vel regularis ordo permitteret:, hec deuota christi
tyruncula, quantumcumque durum aut importabile visum fuerit,
omittebat. Et hoc quidem in diebus puericie sue., cum necdum
primum adolescentie, id est etatis annum quintum decimum.,
40 attigisset [1].

32 Ceterum in fortiori etate, viribus corporis simul cum deuotionis
feruore crescentibus:, hijs, que iam recitata sunt, operibus penitentie non contenta., de spinosis restibus contorto funiculo, frequenter ad carnem vtebatur pro cingulo., qui sua longitudine
45 renes eius et latera circumflexione gemina circuibat [.] // f. 300 c
<e>t tot cotidie tenero corpori intorquebat vvlnera., quot,
spinarum intertextus aculeis, immensa sui longitudine, duplicatis
reflexionibus in latum extensus, ipsi corpusculo fortius inherebat.
Nec isto tamen contenta supplicio., cinqulum, multa nodositate
50 contortum, eidem funiculo connectebat:, vt si qua pars corporis
spinarum acerbissimam punctionem potuisset euadere., saltem
huius nodositate durissima coartata, nullatenus absque supplicio
remaneret. Aliud quoque cingulum, quinquaginta nodorum duricia
conglomeratum, istis omnibus superaddidit:, quem [2] et tunice
55 superposuit, vt et alios [3], introrsum absconditos:, artiori ligatura
constringeret., et sua nodositate lateribus imminens, supplicium
supplicio geminaret. Hijs omnibus nichilominus et corrigiam superposuit;, qua sic cetera firmiter introrsus astringeret., vt nec
in partem alterutram aliquotiens se valeret inflectere:, nec
60 sursum caput erigere., sed nec deorsum absque dolore fortissimo
reclinare.

Tybias etiam cum cruribus huiuscemodi funiculis et restibus
constringebat.; et sic demum omne corpusculum flagris et punctionibus atterebat:, vt <non> iacendo, sed modice reclinando
65 sompnum caperet., et si quando dormitatio sompnolentas palpe-
bras occuparet., hinc vel inde spinarum punctionibus coartata,
expergefactis oculis a sompno continuo resiliret. Solebat autem
hec spinarum restium et funium tormenta bis in ebdomada semelve
deponere., non vt corpori, subtracto supplicio, commodi quippiam

of her body or were not allowed by the regular customs. And all this was done in the days of her childhood, when she had not yet attained adolescence, that is, the age of fifteen.

32 Moreover, later, when her bodily strength and devotion increased, she was no longer satisfied with the penances already mentioned, but made a rope with thorns woven into it, and this she often used on her flesh as a belt. Its length went twice around her waist, and daily caused her tender body more wounds as its great length and many thorns dug deeply into it. Not content with this torment, she made out of the same rope a belt twisted with many knots so that if some part of her body could escape the sharp pricking of the thorns, it would still not remain without torment, being at least constrained by these hard knots. To these she added another belt, composed of fifty hard knots, which she wore over her tunic more tightly to compress the other hidden inside, and to pile torment on torment. Yet to all these she added also a leather strip which pressed hard on the others inside, so that at times she could not bend one way or the other, or lift or lower her head without fierce pain.

She would even bind her shins and legs with the same kind of ropes and cords. Thus she wore her frail body down with whips and piercings. She would sleep not lying down but reclining slightly, and if sometimes sleep took hold of her drooping eyelids, she would be pricked in one place or another by the thorns and would immediately open her eyes and start from her sleep. Yet once or twice a week she used to lay aside these torments caused by the thorny ropes, not to indulge her body or to spare it, but to

70 indulgendo deferret aut parceret :, sed vt, reparatis viribus, fortiori zelo solite passionis incentiua resumeret., et necdum obductis cycatricibus noua wlnera veteribus intorqueret.

33 Talibus ergo supplicijs hec tyro [4] christi strenua, corpusculum suum iugiter affligebat extrinsecus : ; qualia, nostris temporibus, eo sunt vtique rariora,
75 quo, refrigescente caritate multorum, iam in toto terrarum orbe regnat iniquitas., et ab hominibus seipsos amantibus, id est a // f. 300 d delicatis et mollibus., estimantur huiusmodi grauiora. Fortasse tamen dicet aliquis quod durus et importabilis est hic sermo., cum audit venerabilem beatricem tot nodosis funibus., tot spinarum acerbis punctionibus omne corpus ad plantam
80 pedis vsque disrumpere., et nichil eorum inexpertum derelinquere que, commodi causa, delicati solent homines euitare ; sed si diligenter attendat, hinc tormentorum dampnationis eterne supplicia., hinc beatitudinis perpetue gaudia repromissa :, non estimabitur importabile quod toleratur in tempore., dum per temporalem tolerantiam ad perpetue libertatis gloriam felici quis posset
85 commercio peruenire.

⁋ DE INFIRMITATIS INCOMMODO QUO PUERICIE SUE TEMPORE CONTINUE GRAUABATUR
Sextum capitulum

34 Sed hijs, continuationis causa, de operibus penitentie, que in fortiori
5 etate virgo christi tolerauit in corpore, prelibatis :, ad annos puericie [1] reuertamur., et quod restat afflictionis et tolerantie paulatim ex ordine prosequamur. Vt ergo veridica illa sententia qua dicitur oportere nos per multas tribulationes regnum dei consequi, confirmaretur in hac dei famula :, pius dominus, vt eternis eam ex tormentis eriperet, virga correctionis,
10 per omne fere tempus adolescentie, flagellauit ; et nunc tercianis, nunc acutis febribus., interdum etiam pustularum et vlcerum eruptionibus a planta pedis vsque ad verticem, adeo sauciauit :, vt [2] quemdam alterum iob in ea cerneres, sedentem in sterquilinio, saniemque testa redentem., omnipotenti domino super afflictione
15 fortissima deuotas gratiarum actiones referre, et illud beati viri memorabile verbum dicentis. : ' si bona suscepimus de manu

resume her usual sufferings with more zeal and restored strength, and to add new wounds to old ones, not yet healed over.

33 By such torments Christ's vigorous recruit continuously afflicted her body from without. Such torments are all the more rare in our times as the charity of many grows cold and iniquity reigns over the whole world,[2] and these sorts of things seem excessive to lovers of self, that is, to the soft and delicate. Perhaps someone will say that this kind of talk is harsh[3] and unbearable when he hears how the venerable Beatrice harassed her body even to the soles of her feet with so many knotty ropes and sharp, piercing thorns, and left untried none of the things which delicate people usually avoid for the sake of ease. But if the pains of eternal damnation on one side and the promised joys of eternal happiness on the other are carefully examined, whatever is borne in time will not be thought unbearable as long as, by a happy exchange, a person can arrive at the glory of unending freedom through some temporal endurance.

THE TROUBLESOME INFIRMITY BY WHICH SHE WAS CONTINUALLY BURDENED DURING HER CHILDHOOD
Chapter Six

34 For the sake of continuity we have treated in advance the penitential works which Christ's virgin bore in her body when she was older, but let us now return to her childhood and tell gradually in an orderly way the rest of her affliction and endurance. That the true saying that it behooves us to enter the Kingdom of God through many tribulations[1] should be confirmed in this servant of God, the good Lord, to snatch her from eternal torments, scourged her with the rod of correction during almost her entire adolescence. He so wounded her now with tertian fever, now with high fever, sometimes with the eruption of pustules and open ulcers from the sole of her foot to the top of her head,[2] that one could see in her another Job, sitting on a dung heap, scraping away the corruption with a tile,[3] and giving devout thanks to Almighty God for her heavy affliction, repeating the memorable saying of this blessed man: 'if we have received good

2. Mt 24:12; 1 Jn 5:19   3. Jn 6:61
1. Ac 14:21   2. Jb 2:7   3. Jb 2:8

domini;, quare mala non sustineamus:?' hylari wltu et leto
corde frequentissime decantare.

35 Tante quippe, per omne tempus huius visitationis sue, fuit
hec fortitudinis et patientie., quod, licet ex omni parte dolore
corporis aggreuata, pedibus suis vix posset incedere, rarissime
tamen scolare, cui tunc deseruiebat exercitium, // f. *301 a* satagebat omittere:; quin potius, reptando, vel conductum suum
aliarum manibus committendo, ad scolas vsque procedens, ne sine
doctrine viatico tempus videretur ociosa transigere., deputate
lectioni modis omnibus studuit interesse; vnde frequenter accidit,
vt, infirmitatis nimie pondere pregrauata, manibus alienis ad stratum deportata recederet, et, vellet nollet, infirmitati cederet:que, si
martirij tempus adesset., persequentium gladio cedere non nouisset. Et in
hoc nichilominus venerabilis christi discipula studiosis scolaribus exemplum
perseuerantie non incongruum prebuit:, quam nec infirmitatis pondus importabile, ab exercendi studij proposito reuocauit.

⁋ DE PENURIA QUAM IN VICTU SUSTINUIT
ET < DE VESTITU >
Septimum capitulum

36 Quid autem de venerabilis beatricis, quam in diebus istis, vna cum infirmitatis onere, supportauit defectu necessariorum et iugi penuria referemus?
Dederat ei quippe dominus cor timidum et verecundie gratia
decoratum:, vt, quantumcumque neglecta super vite necessarijs
a ceteris ipsa fuisset, numquam ad petendum horum quippiam,
quibus tamen valde necessario indigebat, oris sui labia resoluisset;
quin potius semetipsam a quibusdam gaudebat negligi:, sciens
per talem patientie semitam eum, qui pauperibus spiritu celorum
regnum in euangelio repromittit[1]., christianum debere quem-
libet imitari. Sic cergo, christum, caput suum, per tribulationes
varias insequendo., gaudebat oppido christi virgo deuotissima
pro eo quod, hinc infirmitate continua, illinc necessariorum indigentia grauabatur:; nichili pendens quod extrinsecus tolerabat
in corpore., dum per asperitatem tolerantie potuisset ad creatoris
sui gratiam peruenire.

things from the Lord's hand why should we not receive the bad too?'[4] Frequently she sang this with a happy face and a joyful heart.

35 All throughout this visitation she possessed such fortitude and patience that, even though burdened with pain in every part of her body and scarcely able to walk on her feet, she was careful almost never to miss the classes to which she was then going. Rather, either creeping along or supported by the hands of others, she went to class, lest she seem to pass her time idly if she went without the food of learning. Therefore it often happened that she was overwhelmed by excessive sickness, and was carried back to bed by others, and had to yield to sickness whether she wanted it or not. If it had been a time of martyrdom, she would never have yielded to the sword of persecution. And yet in this matter Christ's venerable disciple gave a not unworthy example of perseverance to zealous students, for not even the unbearable weight of sickness kept her from her resolution to study.

HER EXTREME POVERTY IN FOOD AND CLOTHING
Chapter Seven

36 What shall we say about the lack of food and clothing which the venerable Beatrice endured then, along with the burden of sickness? The Lord had given her a timid heart adorned with bashfulness so however much she was neglected by others in regard to the necessities of life, she never opened her mouth to ask for any of them, although she needed them very much. Rather she rejoiced that she was neglected by some, knowing that every Christian by such patience should imitate him who promised the Kingdom of Heaven to the poor in spirit.[1] Thus, therefore, Christ's devout virgin rejoiced greatly to follow Christ, her Head, through many tribulations, being weighed down both by continuous sickness and lack of necessities. She counted as nothing what she bore in her body outwardly, as long as she could arrive at the grace of her Creator by the harshness of what she endured.

4. *Jb 2:10*   1. Mt 5:3

37 Nonnumquam quippe contigit vt, a custodibus obliuioni tra-
20   dita., et velut adolescentula non equa lance compassionis cum
ceteris prouectioribus ipsius monasterij ponderata, ab egritudinis
cui incumbebat lectulo, // f. 301 b non sine graui molestia, refectionis tempore se leuaret, et ad refectorium, victum quesitura,
recederet; vbi non lautas epulas, quarum vel nullus, vel rarus
25   vsus in illius ordinis refectorijs inuenitur ²., non denique vel
infirmitati sue congruentes inuenit :, sed vel panem siccum., vel
<unum> ex hijs que sanis preparabantur ad refectionem pul-
mentum, ex satis incondito confectum legumine, reportauit ; quo,
licet inuito et renitente stomacho, famis eam importunitati satis-
30   facere oportuit : ; vel si nullatenus admitteretur ab eo., seu cum
non valuisset ad efferendum consurgere., per totum diei spacium,
a ceteris neglecta, christi paupercula ieiunauit.

38 Tantam quoque vestimentorum indigentiam quasi continue
patiebatur in diebus adolescentie sue vel etiam puericie :, quod,
35   discissis aut denigratis incedens adoperta tunicis., ab intuentibus
non de ipsius collegij gremio aliqua., sed pro mercedis stipendio
seruiens ancillula putaretur. Superueniente vero venerabili patre
suo ³., uel ceteris propinquis., quorum nunnumquam ad eam
inuisendam copia confluebat :, mutuata a coeuarum suarum aliqua
40   se veste contexit :, et sic propinquis suis occurrens., illorum
diligentie, quam ad ipsam videbantur gerere., sueque verecundie
satisfecit. Et licet venerabilis pater virginis, vtpote generalis
temporalium bonorum eiusdem monasterij dispensator, hunc dilecte filie sue defectum perfacile corrigere potuisset :, maluit
45   tamen hec agna christi patientissima fame coartari et frigore.,
quam indigentie sue tolerantiam, vel ipsi patri suo, vel alteri
cuilibet indicare ⁴. **39** Nam hyemis tempore frequenter adeo superueniente frigore stringebatur., vt, congelatis poplitibus, nec pedi-

37 Sometimes when it happened that she was forgotten by those in charge, and, as a young girl, not treated with compassion equal to that given the older sisters of the monastery, she would rise from her sickbed at mealtimes only with great difficulty and go to the refectory looking for food. There she did not find rich fare, which is hardly ever used in the refectories of that Order, nor even anything suited to her illness, but she would bring back dry bread or some dish of rough vegetable prepared for the healthy. With this she had to satisfy her gnawing hunger, in spite of her unwilling or rebellious stomach. If she could not eat the food at all, or if she could not rise to get it, Christ's poor little one, neglected by the others, would fast all day long.

38 She suffered from such a lack of clothing nearly all the time in her adolescence and even her childhood that, wearing torn or soiled tunics, she seemed to onlookers not to belong to the congregation, but to be a little servant girl working for wages. When her venerable father came, or other relatives of whom a number sometimes came to see her, she dressed herself in clothing borrowed from her companions and so went to meet her relatives, satisfying in this way the loving concern they seemed to have for her and her own bashfulness. Although the girl's venerable father was the general manager of the monastery's temporal goods and could easily have corrected this neglect of his beloved daughter, Christ's patient lamb preferred to be pressed by hunger and cold rather than tell her needs to her father or anyone else.

39 In winter time she was often so stricken with cold that her knees were frozen and she could not walk on her feet, or apply her

bus suis potuisset incedere : , nec manus ad quodlibet necessarium
⁵⁰ et vrgens obsequium applicare⁵. Verum hanc eius tolerantiam,
multum quidem per omne modum in sui natura commendabilem. ,
accedens etiam patientie virtus adeo decorauit : , vt numquam
hanc patientie // f. 301c sectatricem, sub tanto vel infirmitatis
pondere desudantem, murmurare quis audierit. , aut signum
⁵⁵ saltem aliquod impatientie deprehenderit. ; sed in omnibus, omnipotenti domino gratiarum referens actionem. , semet in anteriora
semper extendit : , et que retro fuerant obliuiscens, sese ad sec-
tandam patientiam animauit.

40 Erat quippe desiderium deuote iuuencule penas peccatis suis
⁶⁰ debitas in hoc seculo luere ; , quatenus, superueniente vocationis
sue tempore⁶, ad creatoris sui presentiam sine quouis valuisset
offendiculo peruenire⁷. Hoc autem desiderium cordis sui, deuotis
orationibus, in diuine maiestatis presentia, recitauit assidue ; ,
hoc crebris suspirijs et gemitibus adimplendum cotidie domino
⁶⁵ commendauit : ; et propterea, quidquid extrinsecus ei molestie
superuenire potuit, eo nimirum alacrius pertulit. , quo, de pij
domini bonitate confisa, molestias corporales in recompensationem illius futuri purgatorij quod timebat, indultas sibi diuinitus
estimauit.

⁷⁰ **41** Quid enim futura timeret incendia vel tormenta ; , que crucis christi morti-
ficationem iugiter in suo corpore baiulauit ? Illi sane future pene supplicium
expauescant, qui toto vite sue tempore, superflua curiositate, cure carnis
inseruiunt ; , qui vel modicum quidem durum aut asperum pro christo pati
refugiunt : , qui totum delectationis sue fructum in terrena voluptate requirunt.
⁷⁵ Hij inquam tam purgatoria quam eterna supplicia pertimescant. Porro venerabili beatrici nichil horum timendum fuerat. , que, sine qualibet exorbitatione,
precedentis ad vitam redemptoris sui vestigijs, a primo natiuitatis sue die, ad
extremum vsque resolutionis sue terminum, inherebat.

hand to any necessary or urgent service. Yet the virtue of patience so adorned this endurance in itself in every way very commendable by its nature, that no one ever heard a murmur or even any sign of impatience coming from this seeker of patience, laboring under such a weight of sickness. Rather in everything giving thanks to the all-powerful Lord, she reached out to what lay before her, and forgetting what was behind she stirred herself[2] up to pursue patience.

40 It was indeed this devout girl's desire to expiate in this world the punishments due her sins, so that when the time of her call came she could come into her Creator's presence with no obstacle of any sort. This heart's desire she repeated assiduously with devout prayers in the presence of the divine Majesty. She also commended it daily to the Lord with frequent sighs and groans. Moreover, any annoyance coming to her from without she endured more eagerly as, trusting in the goodness of her Lord, she thought that bodily annoyances were divinely given in place of the future purgatory she dreaded.

41 Why should she who always bore in her body the mortification[3] of Christ's cross fear future fires and torments? Let them indeed fear future punishment and torment, who all their lives long serve and care for their flesh in superfluous ways, who avoid suffering and difficult hardship for Christ's sake, and who seek all their delight in earthly pleasure. Let these, I say, fear punishment both in purgatory and forever. But nothing of this kind was to be feared by the venerable Beatrice, who without any deviation followed the footsteps of her Redeemer leading the way to life, and this she clung to from the first day of her birth until the very end of her life.

2. Ph 3:13   3. 2 Co 4:10

ℂ DE ORDINATIONE ET
EXERCITIO MEDITATIONUM CORDIS EIUS
Octauum capitulum

42 Hijs ergo de statu exterioris hominis eius, admodum compendiose premissis., superest vt precedentem ipsam ad interiora
sequamur., et de cordis ordinatissima puritate narrationis nostre
iam seriem ordiamur.
// f. *301 d* Erat maximum studium huic deuote iuuencule, iuxta
sapientis consilium omni custodia seruare cor suum [1]:, ne quando,
suadente maligno, vel aperta malicia per [h]ostium consensus
influeret:, vel occulta suggestio., seu cuiuslibet negligentie vel
modica porcio subintraret. Vt autem ad hanc cordis omnimodam
puritatem facilius potuisset ascendere:, obseratis exteriorum sensuum <officinis>, in interioribus cordis sui semetipsam inclu-
serat. Vbi, non solum illicitarum aut noxiarum motu cogitationum
expulso., verum etiam honestarum in suo genere, sed cordis eius
puritati minime congruentium tumultu sedato, quasi columba
simplex in foramine petre residens., in cauerna wlnerum ihesu
christi nidum habitationis sue locauerat :; ex quo diebus singulis
omnia que pro nostra redemptione mediator dei et hominum.,
homo christus ihesus, in tempore quo inter homines homo conuer-
satus est, aut patrauit aut passus est, a prima die sancte natiuitatis vsque in horam ascensionis sue., quecumque videlicet ex
hijs, audiendo legendoue, memorie commendauerat., humili meditationis scrutinio perquirebat, et singulis immorando singulariter,
cum gemitibus et suspirijs, gratiarum actiones pio domino, super
tot miserationis sue beneficijs, affectu plenissimo per singula
refundebat. Vt autem, omnibus ex ordine recitatis que vel in natiuitatis tempore christus infans pertulit, vel in iuuenili etate
miracula demonstrauit, aut in virili robore passionis obprobria,
sputa, flagella, crucem mortemque sustinuit., aut post mortem,
inferni portas confringendo suosque de tenebris eripiendo, potenter expleuit. , ad ascensionis dominice gloriam vsque meditando
peruentum est : ibi progressus sui metam sistere [.] consuescebat,

THE ORDERING AND EXERCISE
OF THE MEDITATIONS OF HER HEART
Chapter Eight

42 Now that we have set forth very succinctly the foregoing matter of her outer life, it remains for us to follow her into her inner life. Let us begin our narrative with her well-organized purity of heart.

This devout girl had the greatest zeal in keeping her heart with all watchfulness,[1] according to the counsel of the wise man, lest at any time, by persuasion of the evil one, open malice should enter through consent to her enemies, or some hidden suggestion, or lest some little negligence should sneak in. To rise more easily to this all-embracing purity of heart, she locked up the outer shop of her senses, so to speak, and enclosed herself in the recesses of her heart. There she not only expelled the movements of illicit and harmful thoughts, but also calmed the tumult of those that were honest enough in their own way but quite unsuitable to the purity of her heart. Dwelling like a simple dove in the clefts of the rock,[2] she made her nest in the hollows of the wounds of Jesus Christ. Everything she heard or read concerning what the man Christ Jesus, mediator between God and men,[3] did or suffered for our redemption while he lived as a man among men, from the first day of his holy birth to the hour of his ascension—all this she daily remembered and pondered in humble meditation. Dwelling on each aspect individually, with groans and sighs, she gave thanks to the loving Lord for all the benefits of his mercy, and this she did with full affection. In her meditations she used to recount in an orderly way what the infant Christ bore at the time of his birth, the miracles he manifested in his youth, the disgrace, the spittle, the scourges, the cross and death he endured in the manly strength of his passion, and what he powerfully accomplished after his death, smashing the gates of hell and snatching his own people from the darkness. Thus she also arrived in her meditation at the glory of the Lord's ascension. There she used to halt, thinking herself

1. Pr 4:23   2. Sg 2:14   3.1 Tm 2:5

35 indignam se reputans ad sublimiora post christum ascendere. .
que se necdum estimabat huius prerogatiuam gratie, condigno
virtutum exercitio, meruisse.

43 At licet, vt p. ʾdictum est, ad sublimiora conscendere non
presumeret, // f. *302 a* apud se tamen in humilitate cordis sui
40 residens, omnipotentis dei clementie semetipsam orationum instantia commendabat., et patris quidem omnipotentie necessarium
infirmitatis humane defectum :, nequando, semetipso grauatus, in
yma viciorum excideret., erigendum confirmandumque deuotione
qua poterat offerebat. Filii vero sapientie cecitatis et ignorantie
45 sue tenebras illustrandas attentius committebat. At vero clementie
sancti spiritus affectiones intimas cordis sui moderandas ordi-
nandasque., ne umquam ad illicitorum appetentiam inordinate
defluerent, deuotis precibus ingerebat. Sicque toti deifice trinitati
sese totam interius exteriusque commendans, eleuato corde, miti-
55 gatis affectibus, sensibusque sedatis :, eo securius quo sublimius
in sinu diuine protectionis et gratie quiescebat. Singulis quoque,
tam nocturnis quam diurnis synaxibus, illud dominice passionis
quod in eadem hora perpessus est., hec, deuoto meditationis
studio, percurrebat : ; et nullo penitus impedimento reuocari pote-
60 rat ab hoc salutari proposito., quin potius idipsum diebus ac
noctibus., deputatis ad hoc, vt predixi, temporibus incessabiliter
exercebat.

44 Tribus etiam ex causis specialiter hec deuota diebus singulis
compunctionis lacrimas, id est pro hijs que dominus ihesus christus
65 in carne mortalitatis nostre dura tolerauit et aspera ; , pro peccatis suis et presentis vite miseria :, sed <et> pro eo quod celesti
adhuc exulabat a patria, cum orationibus et suspirijs flens largiter
effundebat. Sicque, contrarijs contraria medicando, secularium
curarum tumultus noxios., omnes inimici blandientis adulationes
70 deceptorias, aut quelibet cetera quibus ad peccati consensum
impelli poterat, hec fortis virago procul e cordis sui finibus ex-
pellebat., <i>n omnibus tamen premissis nichil aut parum egisse
se reputans., quippe que, juxta latitudinem cordis sui, desiderio
quod gestabat intrinsecus // f. *302 b* ad plenum satisfacere non
75 valebat.

unworthy to ascend after Christ to loftier heights because she thought she had not yet deserved such a privilege of grace by a worthy exercise of virtues.

43 Though she did not presume to ascend the heights, as we said, staying within herself in the humility of her heart, she urgently commended herself in prayer to the mercy of the all-powerful God, offering to the same Father, with what devotion she could, the necessary weakness of human nature to be strengthened and lifted up, lest burdened with itself this weakness should fall into the abyss of vices. To the wisdom of the Son she more attentively committed the darkness of her blindness and ignorance to be enlightened. To the mercy of the Holy Spirit she commended in devout prayers the intimate affections of her heart to be moderated and ordered, lest they should ever slip away to illicit desires. Thus she recommended herself wholly, both inwardly and outwardly, to the whole deifying Trinity with uplifted heart, pacified affections, and calmed senses. In this way she rested the more securely and more sublimely in the bosom of divine protection and grace. At all the choir offices by night and day in devout zealous meditation she held in her mind that part of the Lord's passion which he suffered at that hour. She could not be kept back by any hindrance from this salutary purpose, but rather, as I have said, she practiced it day and night unceasingly at the appointed hours.

44 With an abundance of prayers and sighs this devout girl daily shed tears of compunction for three particular causes: for all the harsh and rough things suffered by the Lord Jesus Christ in our mortal flesh; for her own sins and the misery of the present life; and for her continued exile from the heavenly fatherland. Thus this strong heroine, healing contraries with contraries, drove far from her heart the harmful tumult of worldly cares, all the deceptive adulations of the fawning enemy and whatever else could draw her to consent to sin. Yet in all this she judged herself as having done nothing or little, because she could not to her heart's content fully satisfy the desires she bore within her.

¶ QUALITER AD NOUICIATUS HABITUM ASPIRAUIT
Nonum capitulum

45 Vt autem, puericie tempore iam decurso, succedentis adolescentie terminos incepit attingere [1]., miro quodam et insatiabili
desiderio cepit ad nouiciatus statum et habitum aspirare :, tanto
se fore presumens diuine clementie gratiorem, quanto per artiorem
ordinis obseruantiam eius amplexibus inherere se firmius., suique
iam in parte degustata dulcedine se fruituram expeditius estimabat. Ceperat autem hoc salubre desiderium ab olim, id est in primo
conuersionis sue tempore [2], cum iugi feruoris augmento in corde
suo miro modo succrescere : sed postquam etatis annum quintum
decimum attigit., ita, iam dilatatis affectibus et viribus ampliatis,
hoc ipsum intra sese consurgere sentiebat ;, et adeo tam fortiter
inualescere :, quod nullo rationis freno preualuit illius impetuo-
sum excessum, absque cordis sui lesione grauissima, de cetero
cohibere. Hucusque tamen, etsi cum graui molestia tam renitentem
illius impetum intra seipsam absconderat ; eo quod a magistratu
sibi preposito, tum propter etatis sue defectum., tum propter
virium corporalium imbecille subsidium, (si, ad id quod deside-
rauerat expetendum, semetipsam, oblatis precibus, ingessisset) :,
repulsam et correptionem sibi referendam incurrere formidabat.
Diutius tamen huius importuna susurria supportare non preualens., ad vniuersalem matrem misericordie, matrem humane salutis
et gratie, totam cum suspirijs et lamentis se contulit :; et cre-
berrimis cordis gemitibus, fletibus multiplicatis et precibus.,
ipsius fidele patrocinium implorauit.
46 Prius tamen quam ad propalandum cordis sui desiderium
semetipsam animare presumeret., ad pleniorem sui cognitionem
cepit oculos cordis attollere, mores quoque suos inuestigando
perquirere., ne forte quippiam incultum seu inordinatum lateret
// f. 302 c intrinsecus., quod, post susceptum professionis habitum, ipsam valeret a perfecte conuersationis, ad quam aspirabat,
proposito reuocare. Proinde, tam actibus exterioris hominis quam

HOW SHE ASPIRED TO RECEIVE THE NOVICE'S HABIT
Chapter Nine

45 As Beatrice was passing from girlhood and entering adolescence she began to aspire to the novice's habit and status with a wonderful insatiable desire, presuming that she would be more pleasing to the divine clemency the more firmly she clung to his embraces by a stricter observance of the Order. Moreover, having tasted some sweetness, she thought she would enjoy the same more freely. This salutary desire had begun to increase wonderfully in her heart from of old, that is from the time of her first conversion when she felt a constant increase of fervor in her heart. But after she reached the age of fifteen, with her increased affections and powers, she felt this same longing rising within her and becoming so strong that she could not rationally control or restrain its impetuous excess without causing grievous harm to her heart. Until then she had hidden that unruly impulse within herself though with great trouble, for she feared rejection and rebuke from the persons in charge of her on account of her insufficient age and weak health, if she were to thrust herself forward with many prayers to ask what she wanted. Not being able any longer to stand the importune whispers of this desire, however, she turned wholly with sighs and laments to the universal Mother of mercy, the Mother of human salvation and grace, imploring her faithful patronage with frequent groans from the heart and many tears and prayers.

46 But before she presumed to stir herself to open up her heart's desire, she began to raise the eyes of her heart to a fuller self-knowledge and to investigate her behavior, lest any neglect or disorder hiding within should hinder her from the perfection she aspired to, once she had received the habit. She examined her exterior

interioris moribus exquisitis, plurimisque correctione dignis intra
35 se repertis, vt aduertit non modici temporis et laboris esse., tot
defectuum suorum insolentias reprimere impugnando :, satis vtili
freta consilio, mox primam et precipuam illarum, quam sibi magis
officere preuidebat, totis constantie viribus cepit expugnando
lacessere., non prius intentionem reuocans ab hoc fructuoso cer-
40 tamine, quam per dei gratiam indultam sibi meruisset victoriam
optinere. Hac igitur a corde suo primitus effugata, confestim ad
alias, prout eas aut molestiores aut suo proposito contrariores
sustinuit., non quidem vno simul impetu, sed ordinatim ad singulas dimicatura se contulit. Unde factum est, vt, annuente superna
45 clementia, non prius intentionis sue propositum ab hac reluctandi
iugitate retraheret :, donec, cedente victoria, citra quam spe-
rauerat ad votum singulas illarum expugnaret.
47 Necdum tamen ipso, quod sibi statuerat, expleto tempore vel
negotio consummato., feruoris desiderij sui nimis impatiens, im-
50 plorata diuina clementia, quam ante iam longanimi assiduitate
placare studuerat., firmam spem et fiduciam habens in domino,
venerabilem tunc temporis abbatissam eiusdem [3], totumque simul
conuentum miro deuotionis affectu supplicatura aggreditur :, et
vt nouiciatus habitu debeat innouari., cum lacrimis et suspirijs ab
55 ea suppliciter exoratur. Quam dum virgo domini petitionem,
optimo sapientie sale condito, verborum ordine perorasset :,
videns, tam ipsam abbatissam quam ceteras dei famulas insolito
pre stupore pallescere., beatricis in faciem omnes simul aspectum
imprimere., magnanimitatem cordis et desiderij sui vires atten-
60 dere., modum petitionis et ordinem, ipsius negotij circumstantias
inter sese discutere :, quidve responsionis exoranti referri deberet,
// f, 302 d studiosis apud se retractationibus explorare. Sed,
habita deliberatione, pro tempore confestim etatis infirmitas.,
impotentia virium., et non preparata necessariorum impensa sibi
65 simul a cunctis obicitur :, et a proposito, quod ex iuuenilis animi

actions and interior behavior, and found in herself many things in need of correction. When she noted that it would take no little time and effort to fight the many shortcomings of her defects, she took some very useful counsel and began to assault with all the forces of her constancy the first and greatest of these, which she saw hindering her the most. She did not withdraw her attention from this fruitful struggle until by God's grace, she deserved, to obtain the victory. Having chased from her heart the first defect, she immediately turned her combat against the others, to the degree that they were more troublesome or contrary to her resolve. She did this not in a single movement but in an orderly way, one by one. Thence it came to pass that by the divine clemency she did not withdraw her resolute intention from this continuous struggle until she had victoriously overcome every one of her defects sooner than she had hoped.

47 The time she had set herself was not yet expired nor was the process ended when she grew impatient with the great fervor of her desire. Imploring the divine mercy which she had striven to please beforehand by her unremitting zeal, with firm hope and trust in the Lord, in a suppliant way and with wonderful devotion, she approached the venerable abbess then in office and the whole community. She begged her with tears and sighs to allow her to be renewed by the novice's habit. When the Lord's virgin had set forth her petition in a methodical way, salted with wisdom, she saw the abbess and the other handmaids of the Lord turn pale with unusual amazement. They all fixed their gaze on Beatrice's face, noticed her magnanimity of heart and strength of desire, and discussed among themselves the manner and order of her petition and the implications involved. They considered carefully among themselves what response should be given to the petitioner. But after their deliberation they objected without delay to her still tender age, her lack of strength, and her inability to finance the necessary expenses. They all exhorted her not to delay from withdrawing quickly from a proposal which seemed to come more

leuitate potius quam ex deliberato consilio procedere videbatur,
vt maturius resilire non differat ab omnibus exhortatur. Sed
deuotissima christi virgo, non solum hijs omnibus a firmato iam
dudum in mente proposito reuocari non potuit :, quin etiam,
accepta responsione voluntati sue contraria., nulla se deinceps
a suo proposito <retardari> posse molestia., vel edita vel
illata⁴., palam coram omnibus affirmauit. Quid multa? Vicit
beatricis constantia; nec petitionis effectus diu differri potuit.,
cuius desiderium in corde dilecte sue diuina clementia celitus
inspirauit⁵.

48 Annuit igitur abbatissa petitioni deuote iuuencule :; cunctisque
simul assentientibus, induitur veste candida., veste leticie., noui-
ciali videlicet habitu :, quo, ceteris conformata, decetero iugum
domini suaue, quod eatenus apud se tulerat in occulto., liberiori
iam studio simul et animo, non vetaretur etiam in publico baiulare. Quanta vero leticia mentem eius inebriauerit illo die⁶.,
et-si mee non est facultatis exprimere, potest tamen ex eo conici
vel in parte, quod nec reuerentia dominice passionis, quam eodem
in tempore sancta per orbem terre celebrare solet ecclesia; (erat
quippe dies illa preclara qua dominica cena cum discipulis habita
memoratur) : sub debite maturitatis operculo foris ᴄᵤmpentem
in gestu cordis sui leticiam non potuit cohibere. O quam gra-
tanter, o quam delectabiliter in stramento sequenti nocte corpusculum absque reprehensionis nota locauit :, quod et-si pridem
crebrius actitauerat., increpantis tamen magistre sententiam exinde
sepissime reportarat. Nunc vero tanto iocundius ea nocte quieuit
in palea :, quanto securius id facere // f. 303a licuit,, ipsius
monasterij regularia⁷ non excedendo, sicut olim consueuerat,
instituta. Numquam enim in omni vita sua, ipsa teste, delectabilius
cubauerat :, presertim quia cunctis cresi diuitijs, ymo totius mundi
delicijs ipsam, cui incubuit, duriciam palee preferebat.

from youthful instability than from well-considered counsel. But Christ's devout virgin not only could not be deterred by all these objections from the proposal already long settled in her mind, but also could not accept a reply contrary to her wishes. She declared clearly in front of everyone that she could not be hindered in her proposal by any vexation in word or deed. Why say more? Beatrice's constancy won, nor could the outcome of her petition be long delayed once the divine mercy had inspired the desire in the heart of the beloved.

48 The abbess therefore agreed to the devout girl's petition, and with the consent of all she was clothed in white garments, the garments of joy, that is, the novice's habit. Now, like the others, she was not forbidden to wear, even in public with a freer zeal and spirit, the Lord's sweet yoke[1] which till then she had borne in secret. Since it is beyond me to express the joy which inebriated her mind that day, it can be guessed at least in part: not even reverence for the Lord's passion, which Holy Church throughout the world was celebrating then (it was the noble day when the Lord's supper with the disciples was being commemorated) could restrain the joy of her heart. She could not, despite her maturity, contain herself from breaking out in happy gestures. O how joyfully and delightfully she laid her frail body to rest on the straw ticking the following night without any note of blame. Even though she had often done this before, yet very frequently she had gone to bed bearing the rebukes of her mistress. Now she rested on the straw that night more joyfully because she could do so more unconcernedly, not having transgressed the rules of the monastery as she had formerly done. As she herself testified, she had never lain down with more pleasure in all her life, because she preferred the hard straw on which she lay to all the riches of Croesus, indeed to the pleasures of the whole world.

1. Mt 11:30

Verum hijs sub breuitatis compendio prelibatis. , ad cetera trans-
eamus : et qualiter ad professionis gratiam hec sancta peruenerit,
exigente narrationis ordine, prosequamur.

❡ DE PROFESSIONE EIUS
ET DE EO QUOD AD RAMEYAM MONASTERIUM AD
DISCENDAM ARTEM SCRIPTORIAM EMISSA SIT
Decimum capitulum

⁵ **49** Expleto itaque probationis anno, quo, sub nouiciatus habitu,
se studuerat, omni qua valebat instantia, regulari obseruantie
conformare :, iuxta monastici tenorem decreti, ad professionis
votum christi virgo suscipitur. , et omnimodo, iam corpore simul
et animo, sponsarum christi collegio sociatur. Tunc vero primum
¹⁰ <videres> expletum illud feruentissimum et longissimum desiderium cordis sui :, quod ne quando perficeretur ipsa manente
in corpore, pre nimio iam dudum consueuerat desiderio formidare.
Vt vero professionis tempus appropinquare iam cepit, et in
proximo sociandam ancillarum christi collegio se preuidit, quociens
¹⁵ id ad memoriam reuocauit., tam ingens lacrimarum affluentia,
pre maxima gratitudine, solebat ex eius ocellis erumpere., quod
nulla potuisset eas instantia cohibere. Sed et ipso professionis
die, quasi fluentes ex fonte riuulos, ita, resolutis capitis catha-
ractis, ex oculis lacrimas effundebat :; quas irrefrenabilis <que-
²⁰ dam> animi gratitudo, cordisque propensa leticia, remotis verecundie simul et rationis obstaculis, incessanter effluere faciebat.
Sic denique deuota christi famula, deuoto incorporata collegio. ,
qualem conuersationem inter socias moniales ex eo tempore ducere
ceperit., quam integre totam ordinis obseruan- // ƒ.303 b tiam
²⁵ exercuerit., quam feruenter aliarum onus in suis humeris ipsa
portauerit ;, et precipue qualem se sponso suo christo domino
presentauerit :, quantum dictantis possibilitas ad hoc assurgere
poterit., sequens lectionis series explanabit.
50 Igitur cum, exacto probationis anno, sanctimonialium esset
³⁰ adunata collegio., consilio venerabilis abbatisse, post modicum

Now that we have briefly set forth these matters, let us proceed to others, and explain as order demands, how this holy person arrived at the grace of profession.

HER PROFESSION
SHE IS SENT TO THE MONASTERY OF Rameya
TO LEARN THE ART OF WRITING MANUSCRIPTS
Chapter Ten

49 When the year of probation was over, during which time she strove in the novice's habit to conform to the regular observance with all possible constancy, Christ's virgin was accepted for the vows of profession according to monastic rule, and was joined to the community of Christ's spouses both in body and in soul. Then you would see fulfilled for the first time that most fervent and deep-seated desire of her heart, which by reason of her excessive desire she had long feared would never come to pass while she lived in the flesh. When the time of her profession began to draw near and she foresaw that she would soon be joined to the community of Christ's handmaids, such a huge flood of grateful tears flowed from her eyes each time she recalled this that no effort could restrain them. On the very day of her profession tears came rolling down from her eyes as rivulets from a spring, as though cataracts inside her head had been released. With the removal of the obstacles caused by shyness and reason, an unrestrainable gratitude and great joy of heart made her tears flow ceaselessly. What follows will explain, as far as the writer can express it, how Christ's devout servant, incorporated into the devout community, began to behave among her fellow-nuns from then on, with what integrity she cultivated the entire observance of the Order, with what fervor she took the burdens of others on her shoulders, and especially how she presented herself to the Lord Christ, her bridegroom.

50 United with the community of nuns after the year of probation, Beatrice was sent after a short time by the counsel of the venerable

temporis interuallum, ad quoddam eiusdem ordinis monasterium,
rameya nuncupatum. , (vbi scribendi facultatem addisceret. , quam
postmodum in scribendis libris sue necessarijs ecclesie frequen-
taret), comitante se christi gratia, destinatur. Vbi venerabilem
[35] ydam niuellensem, magni meriti dominam, eiusdem loci monialem,
inuenit ; que qualis quantive meriti fuerit apud deum. , ex libro vite
sue discere poterit quisquis gesta miraculorum eius vel legere vel
audire[1] voluerit : , que mirabiliter in suo tempore, fauente superna
gratia, perpetrauit[2]. Huic igitur beate femine, deuota iuuencula
[40] quodam nexu caritatis inseparabiliter semetipsam adiunxit. , verbum edificationis ex ore suo cotidie diligenter expetijt. , exceptum
in terra cordis sui fructifera, seminauit : ; sicque factum est, vt,
ex mutue <societatis> frequentia, contraherentur ex tunc spiritualis quidam inter vtrasque dilectionis federa, que, post etiam,
[45] indissoluta manserunt ipsis persistentibus in hac vita[3]. Illa
quippe, quam prefatus sum, niuellensis yda, reuelante sancto
spiritu, beatricem nostram, in specialem sponsam, a domino fore
proculdubio didicit assumendam : , eiusque plenitudinem gratie
superabundanter in anime sue receptaculo perfundendam ; et
[50] propterea sese totam illius obsequijs diligenter exposuit. , eam
sibi totam applicuit et salutaribus monitis omni qua potuit sollicitudine informauit. Nec tantis ingrata beneficijs, virgo deuotissima, quamcumque potuit, reddidit vicem in obsequio. , ipsam
vt matrem diligens. , vt ductricem sequens. , vt nutricem amplec-
[55] // f. 303 c tens. , quippe cuius dulci cotidie mulcebatur alloquio : ,
cuius instruebatur assidue verbo pariter et exemplo[4].
51 Mirabatur autem humilis christi iuuencula super beate femine,
quam erga se considerabat, obsequiosa cotidie diligentia : , prorsus
indignam se reputans ad tantum familiaritatis archanum admitti ; ,
[60] presertim illius quam immensi meriti apud deum et apud ho-

abbess to a monastery of the same Order called Rameya, and the grace of the Lord accompanied her. There she was to learn the art of writing manuscripts, which she would later use in writing the books necessary for her own church. At Rameya, she met the venerable Ida of Nivelles, a woman of great merit and a nun of that place. Whoever wishes to read or hear the account of her miracles, marvelously performed during her life by divine grace, can learn from her biography what sort of person and of what merit she was in God's sight. It was to this blessed woman that the devout girl attached herself inseparably by a bond of love. Every day she carefully sought a word of edification from her mouth, and when she received it, she sowed it in the fertile soil of her heart.[1] So it was that from their close companionship together a certain alliance of spiritual love was contracted between them which, even afterward, remained intact as long as they lived. Ida of Nivelles learned by revelation of the Holy Spirit that our Beatrice would surely be taken by the Lord as his special spouse, and that the fullness of his grace would be poured superabundantly into her soul. Therefore Ida gave herself wholly to Beatrice's service, and took Beatrice wholly to herself, forming her with all possible solicitude by good advice. Nor was the devout girl ungrateful for such benefits, but returned the service as best she could, loving Ida as a mother, following her as a leader, and cherishing her as a teacher, for she was daily charmed by her sweet speech and carefully instructed by her word and example.

51 Christ's humble maid, Beatrice, was amazed at the daily attentive care which this blessed woman Ida gave her, thinking herself quite unworthy to be admitted to the secrets of such familiarity, especially since she had no doubt about Ida's great merits with God

1. Mt 13:24

mines., magne nichilominus auctoritatis et opinionis, existere minime dubitabat :; cum, ex aduerso, nec alicuius momenti se reputaret aut meriti., nec aliquatenus digne se posse tam sublimi familiaritatis obsequio deliniri.

65 Proinde vererabilem ydam vna dierum, super hijs rei veritatem familiaritatis obligatio., sedulitas in obsequio., gratiositas in exploratura, constanter aggreditur., et quid sibi velit hec tante colloquio :, presertim apud se, tam humilem et paruam., tam ab ipsa meritorum et vite dissimilitudine differentem., tam humili

70 quam familiari colloquio sciscitatur.

Ad hec venerabilis yda.: „ Non tantum, inquit, pro meritis aut virtutibus quibus in presenti te decorari conspicio., tam indisso- lubili caritatis affectu te diligo :, quantum pro hijs quibus te certissime scio futuris temporibus a domino sublimandam. Etenim

75 pius misericordiarum dominus super te sue miserationis oculos indubitanter aperiet., teque in sponsam sibi fidelissimam eliget :, sueque plenitudine gratie te perfundet [5]. Tu vero, tantis eius beneficijs omnino satage te non ingratam in oculis sue maiestatis

80 ostendere :, e vasculo cordis tui si quid in eo superfluum delites- cit, curato diligenter effundere :, et quantum in te est locum acceptabilem in corde tuo diuine gratie preparare. Non enim qui cepit in te iam aliqua sue liberalitatis indicia demonstrare., manum solite pietatis a te reuocabit vllo modo :; cuius gratie

85 dona melliflua siquidem bene dispensare curaueris in hoc seculo., multiplicabit et gloriam in futuro ".

52 Qua responsione beatrix // f. 303 d accepta, mirabiliter exul- tabat in domino :, firmam spem habens et plenam fiduciam de promisso. Siquidem tanti meriti feminam, tanta gratiarum affluen-

90 tia redimitam., nullatenus hec tam sedulo perorasse certissime confidebat :, nisi de superne claritatis lumine protulisset idipsum quod, absque dubitationis obstaculo, voce tam libera promittebat. Quapropter non modici desiderij cepit intra se facibus estuare., quatenus hec beata, de qua tante perfectionis future testimonium

95 acceperat, speciales apud altissimum orationum hostias pro se dignaretur offerre :, seque, deuotis precibus, omnipotentis dei clementie commendare. Super hec itaque rursus beate femine,

and men, or her great authority and reputation. On the other hand, Beatrice thought herself of no importance or merit, and wholly unworthy to receive such sublime and affectionate services.

One day she resolutely approached the venerable Ida about the truth in these matters, namely, the bond of familiarity, the careful service, the kindhearted inquiries, and she asked in a humble familiar way what Ida had in mind in such converse, especially with her, so lowly and small, so unlike herself in merit and life.

To this the venerable Ida replied: 'Not so much for the merits and virtues with which I see you adorned at present do I love you with such an indissoluble charity, but rather for those by which I see for certain you will be raised up in the future by the Lord. For the loving merciful Lord will certainly open his eyes of mercy on you, and will choose you for his own most faithful spouse, and will pour out on you the fullness of his grace. Stir yourself then not to be ungrateful for such benefits in the eyes of his Majesty. Carefully empty your heart of anything superfluous lurking there and, as far as you can, prepare in your heart an acceptable place for divine grace. For He who has now begun to show some signs of his liberality toward you will in no way withdraw his habitually kind hand from you. If only you will take care to use well his sweet gifts of grace in this world, he will multiply the glory in the world to come'.

52 When Beatrice heard this answer, she exulted wonderfully in the Lord,[2] having firm hope and confidence in the promise. She was utterly confident that a woman of such merit, crowned with such an abundance of graces, would never have stated these things so carefully unless she had deduced by a clear heavenly light what she so freely promised without any trace of doubt.

As a result, Beatrice began to be stirred up with no small desire that this blessed woman from whom she had received testimony of such future perfection, should offer special prayers to the Most High for her and should recommend her with devout supplications to the mercy of the Almighty God. Again she approaches this blessed

2. Lk 1:46

supplicationes oblatura, se sociat :, et vt desiderium suum,
annuendo precibus suis, adimpleat., deprecatur iterum humiliter
et exorat. Cui rursus yda beatissima sic respondit. : ,, Quid
inquit, a domino, filia, consequi., vel per me tibi impetrari
desideras in instanti ? Scito me paratam ad parendum in omnibus
tuo beneplacito :, nec michi cuncteris desiderium tui cordis edi-
cere quod tibi superna gratia dignabitur inspirare ". Ad hec
iterum humilis christi famula. : ,, Rogo, mi domina, inquit., vt
apud misericordem dominum tuis michi precibus obtinere stu-
deas., vt illius gratie singularis gustu me recreet et participio
confortet, cuius dulcedinem solis dat electis et specialibus suis
in hoc seculo sibi famulantibus, experiri ". [6] Tunc yda. : ,,Esto,
inquit, parata in diem sancte natiuitatis dominice., quo desiderium
cordis tui, gratiam infundendo quam postulas, pius dignabitur
dominus irrefragabiliter adimplere [7] ".

53 Qua responsione beate femine rursus accepta., leta supra
modum efficitur :, et in diem sibi prefixum gratiam visitationis
dominice cum preparata sollicitudine prestolatur. Quid plura ?
Adest dies sancte natiuitatis dominice [8], beatrice optante per
horas singulas infusionem gratie : ; // f. 304 a sed eo die quod
acceperat in promisso., diuina clementia rem et rei processum
aliter ordinante., prout iam dudum optauerat non contigit eue-
nire. Nullum enim gustum vel experimentum gratie quam sperabat
illo die percipere potuit. Super quo, licet admodum merore con-
fecta fuerit :, patienter tamen et humiliter huius grauaminis apud
se molestiam tolerauit., nimirum : peccatis suis exigentibus hec
reputans accidisse quod celestis gratie fruitionem illo sanctissimo
die non meruerit impetrare. Super quo venerabilem ydam conque-
rendo rursus aggreditur :, et quid cause fuerit., hoc sibi cur
acciderit., humili precum instantia percunctatur. Cui denuo beata
femina sic respondit. : ,, Non, inquit, peccatis tuis exigentibus,
vt suspicaris, id accidit :, sed scito certissime, quod infra diem
octauum, ab illo primo die natiuitatis dominice computandum
hoc quod speras eueniet ; nec me perperam tibi respondisse putare

woman Ida with her request, and again humbly begs and prays her
to fulfill her desire by agreeing to her requests. To which the most
blessed Ida responded: 'My daughter, what do you desire to obtain
from the Lord, or to beg for yourself through me right now? Know
that I am willing to yield in every way to your wish. Do not
hesitate to tell me your heart's desire, which heavenly grace will
deign to inspire in you.' To this Christ's humble handmaid
replied: 'My lady, I ask that through your prayers to the compassionate Lord you strive to obtain for me that he will reinvigorate
me by the taste of, and strengthen me by sharing in, that particular
grace whose sweetness he grants to be experienced only by his
elect and special servants in this world.' Then Ida said: 'Be prepared on the day of the Lord's holy birth when the good Lord will
irresistibly fulfill the desire of your heart, granting you the grace
you ask for'.

53 She rejoiced exceedingly over the blessed woman's reply, and
on the assigned day she awaited the grace of the Lord's visit by
careful preparation. Why say more? The day of the Lord's holy
birth arrives, and every hour of it Beatrice longs for the infusion of
grace; but on that day the promise she had received did not take
place as she had long desired, for divine clemency had arranged
the thing and its process differently. She could perceive no taste or
experience of the hoped-for grace on that day. She bore within
herself the annoyance of this disappointment patiently and
humbly, though much grieved by it, thinking that her sins required
that she not obtain the enjoyment of the heavenly grace on that
most holy day. She again approached the venerable Ida to bemoan
this, and humbly asked why this had happened to her. The blessed
woman answered: 'This did not happen because your sins demanded it, as you suspect; but know for certain that what you hope
for will happen before the octave day, counting from the first day of
the Lord's birth. Moreover, you should not think that I answered

te conuenit :, et-si quod promisi die natiuitatis dominice non
euenit., quia sanctum circumcisionis diem [9] cum octauis interia-
centibus [10], quisquis operationis diuine misterium, hijs diebus ex-
135   pletum, efficaciter honorare voluerit., sub vnius dominice natiuitatis die rationis iudicio compilabit.

Quod iterum consolationis a beata femina responsum accipiens, in
spem mirabiliter erecta refloruit :, et denuo promissam gratiam, tam
diebus quam noctibus, et precibus instanter expetijt., et magnis
140   desiderij affectibus tempus sue visitationis humiliter expectauit.

⁋ DE RAPTU EIUS
ET CELICA VISIONE SIBI IN SPIRITU DEMONSTRATA
Undecimum capitulum

54 Prefatis ergo diebus, id est octauis dominice natiuitatis diem
5   ex ordine subsequentibus necdum expletis [1]., cum pio misericordiarum domino sue pietatis opus in beatrice, deuota sua
famula, perficere complaceret :, accidit vna dierum., vt secundum
exigentiam temporis completorio, quod aduesperascente // f. 304 b
iam die psallebatur in choro, cum ceteris ipsius loci monialibus
10   interesset. Cumque, residens inter psallendum, ab omni forensi
strepitu modice quieuisset., magnoque conamine cor suum ad
dominum eleuasset :, venit in mentem eius illius tenor antyphone
quam hijs diebus, in nimiam commendationem caritatis diuine,
sancta consueuit ecclesia recitare. Est autem hec antyphona. :
15   ' Propter nimiam caritatem suam qua dilexit nos deus, filium suum
misit in similitudinem carnis peccati vt omnes saluaret ' [2]. Cuius
antyphone verba diligenter examinans., magnamque in hijs laudis
diuine materiam inuestigans, ipsum filium, hac verborum recordatione concepta, deuoto meditationis incessu, sursum, vsque dum
20   ad patris presentiam meditando conscenderet, cum laudibus et
gratiarum actionibus humiliter est secuta [3]. Quo cum meditando

you wrongly even if what I promised for the day of the Lord's birth did not happen, for whoever wishes effectually to honor the mystery of the divine operation fulfilled during these days will combine in his mind the holy day of the Circumcision, and the intervening octaves, as one with the day of the divine nativity.'

Having received this consoling answer from the blessed woman, Beatrice revived, being wonderfully lifted up by hope. Again she constantly sought for the promised grace day and night in her prayers, and she awaited with humility and great desire the time of her visitation.

HER RAPTURE
AND THE HEAVENLY VISION SHOWN TO HER IN SPIRIT
Chapter Eleven

54 The aforesaid days, that is, the octaves which follow Christmas day, were not yet finished when it pleased the merciful Lord to perfect the work of his love in Beatrice, his devout handmaid. It happened one day that she was present with the other nuns in choir at the singing of compline toward dusk, as the season demanded. Seated during the psalmody, she had quieted herself a little from all outside noise, and with a great effort had raised her heart to the Lord. Into her mind came the text of that antiphon which Holy Church is accustomed to sing on these days in high commendation of God's love. This is the antiphon: 'Because of the surpassing charity with which he has loved us, God sent his Son in the likeness of sinful flesh to save all'. Carefully thinking over the words of this antiphon, and investigating the abundant matter of divine praise contained in them, Beatrice with devout meditation, praise, thanksgiving and all humility followed the Son as he ascended right up to the Father's presence. When she had arrived there in

peruenisset, et vlterius ascendere non valeret :, iterum venit in
mentem eius illud quod diebus paschalibus in responsorio psal-
litur⁴. : ' et dauid cum cantoribus cytharam percutiebat in domo
25   domini '. ⁴

55 Quibus verbis cum meditando rursus intenderet., et ea sedulo
ruminaret :, in excessu<m> mentis sue continuo rapta prosilijt.
Viditque, non corporalibus sed intellectualibus., non carnis sed
mentis oculis, sublimem et deificam trinitatem, supra mirabiliter,
30   in claritatis sue decore sempiterneque virtutis sue omnipotentia,
relucentem ; et dauid, cum cantoribus illius superne iherusalem,
in psalterio simul et cythara, maiestatem diuine potentie magnifice collaudantem : ; sanctorum spirituum agmina, supercelestium-
que virtutum ordinata collegia, summe deitatis presentiam in-
35   cessabiliter intuentes., intuendo feruenter amantes., amando
laudum iubilos, in tranquillo pacis silentio, summe trinitatis essentie mirifice decantantes ⁵. Cum quibus ipsa quoque, cui hec videre
concessa sunt, cum ad magnificandam creatoris sui pre- // f. 304 c
sentiam intentionem affectumque sedulo conaretur erigere :, con-
40   tigit vt, finito˙completorio, conuentus sanctimonialium, pausandi
gratia dormitorium ascendens, ad strata sua recederet., ipsa
nichil horum aduertente que gerebantur extra se :, sed adhuc
immobiliter in contemplationis sue dulcedine permanente. Cumque, alijs recedentibus, ipsa sola, quasi dormiens, inclinata deorsum
45   in subsellio resideret :, vna consodalium suarum, illam sompno
depressam existimans, propiusque accedens, oram vestimenti, quo
desuper induta fuerat, attraxit modice., sic credens a sompno
dormitantem sociam excitare. Sed illa, nec sic quid extra se fieret
aduertente, <perstitit> altera., vestimentum, vt a sompno dormi-
50   tantem excuteret, instantius attrahendo., et ad excitandum, quam

meditation and could not ascend higher, again there came to her mind the responsory sung at Easter time: 'And David with the singers played the harp in the house of the Lord'.

55 Meditating on these words with great attention and ruminating them carefully, she immediately leapt up there, seized in an ecstasy of mind. Not with bodily but with intellectual eyes, with eyes not of the flesh but of the mind, she saw the divine and sublime Trinity shining marvelously in the beauty of its splendor and the omnipotence of its eternal excellence. And she saw David with the singers of that heavenly Jerusalem magnificently praising the majesty of divine power on the lute and harp.[1] She saw the throngs of holy spirits, the orderly array of supercelestial powers who gazed ceaselessly on the supreme Godhead, loving it fervently in gazing on it, and in loving it singing out wonderfully in the tranquil silence of peace their jubilees of praise to the essence of the supreme Trinity. While Beatrice was also trying carefully to raise her attention and love to magnify the presence of her Creator in union with these spirits, it happened that compline was over and the community of nuns went up to the dormitory to their beds to sleep. Beatrice, paying no attention to what was going on around her, remained immobile in the sweetness of her contemplation. While she sat alone, bent over on the bench as though dozing, one of her companions, thinking her asleep, came close and gently pulled the end of her dress to rouse her from sleep. When Beatrice even then did not notice her surroundings, the other nun kept on pulling her clothing more insistently to waken her whom she thought

1. Ps 150:3

certissime corporali sompno dormire putauerat, insistendo :, donec
eius importunitate, resumptis sensibus exterioris hominis, in se
reuerteretur., sibique redderetur noua celestium mirabilium con-
templatrix.

55 **56** Ad se ergo reuersa, cum a celestibus delicijs ad humane
conditionis miserias reuocatam se conspiceret., et se in terris
positam, que paulo ante celestium spirituum gaudijs interfuerat,
inueniret : cepit vehementer suspirando lacrimas effundere., fa-
ciemque tam effusis fletibus irrigare., quod illam excitatricem
60 suam oppido conturbatam ex eo reddiderit., putantem sibi corporalis alicuius molestie repentinum incommodum imminere. Residens ergo iuxta flentem et merentem sociam, monialis caput eiu-
lantis in sinu suo reclinauit :, et, quantum sub silentio [6] licuit,
lacrimas tergendo flentemque fouendo, merenti compassiuo deuo-
65 tionis obsequio ministrauit.

Post paululum igitur, ad stratum reducta, cum apud se quid sibi
paulo ante contigerat meditando reuolueret., et vbi fuerit et quid
viderit ad memoriam reuocaret :, tam ineffabili gratitudine mentisque insolita iocunditate cepit interius affici., quod illius im-
70 mensa prodigalitas nullo sensu <a non> ante // *f. 304 d* experiente intelligi potuisset., nullo vel ab experto valeret verborum
ordine demonstrari.

Accidit autem eadem in hora quiddam mirabile. : beatricem videlicet ex multa lacrimarum habundantia tam perfectam corporis
75 sanitatem consequi :, quod eodem in tempore nullo se sentit
infirmitatis pondere molestari., quamuis omni illo die tam grauem
obsessionem in membris suis experta fuerit., vt se putauerat
immenso febrium estu, vel alterius cuiuslibet infirmitatis insolentia
fatigari. Quod quidem preter naturalem rerum ordinem accidisse
80 nemo qui dubitet :, cum ex lacrimarum effusione, si nimia fuerit,
magis debilitari necesse quis habeat quam a debilitatis pondere
releuari.

57 Cum autem in hac iocunditatis immoderata leticia pauco tempore permansisset, accidit venerabilem ydam. cum alijs quibusdam
85 ex eodem collegio monialibus, ad ipsam gratia visitationis acce-

most certainly asleep. Finally through the other's importunity,
Beatrice returned to her outer senses, and thus the new con-
templator of heavenly marvels was restored to herself.

56 When Beatrice returned to herself and saw that she had been
recalled from heavenly delights to the miseries of the human condition, and found herself on earth whereas shortly before she had
shared the joys of the heavenly spirits, she began to sigh and sob
violently, bathing her face with such tears that the nun who had
aroused her was much shaken, thinking she had suddenly taken
sick. Sitting down next to her weeping and grieving companion,
she lay the head of the wailing nun on her lap, and as far as she
could during the great silence, she showed her compassionate devotion and care by wiping her tears and comforting the crying
woman.

After a little while Beatrice was taken to bed. When she turned
over in her mind what had just happened to her, and remembered
where she had been and what she had seen, she began inwardly to
be filled with unspeakable gratitude and unusual delight because
God's immense prodigality could in no way be understood by
someone who had not previously experienced it, nor could it be
demonstrated in words even by an experienced person.

Something wonderful happened then. Beatrice came to such a
perfect bodily health from that abundance of tears that she no
longer felt the troublesome burden of sickness, though all day long
she had been so oppressed in her members that she had thought
she had a great fever or some other infirmity. No one would doubt
that this happened outside the natural order of things, since a person must necessarily be weakened by such a great flood of tears
rather than be relieved of weakness.

57 When she had remained a short time in this unrestrained
delight, it happened that the venerable Ida came to visit her with
some other nuns of the same convent, and they perceived that
something new and unusual had happened to Beatrice in body or in

dere, quibus iam innotuerat aliquid noui, vel in corpore vel in
mente, sibi, ex eo quod plus solito se gerebat, insolentius accidisse :, cuius tamen secreti misterium hanc solam latere non
potuit., que hoc, paulo ante, suis apud deum precibus impetrauit.

90 Vt igitur cateruatim ad se propius illas vidit accedere., tantum,
pre maxima gratitudine, mox cepit in risum erumpere :, quod
illarum presentiam nulla potuisset cordis tolerantia sustinere.
Siquidem videbatur ei quod in partes cor suum, nimia gratitudinis
affluentia, scinderetur : si venerabilem ydam ad se propius ali-

95 quatenus accedere contigisset.

58 Ne ergo deprehenderetur amplius ab hijs immensa cordis sui
quam patiebatur insania :, cepit intra se, sine verborum strepitu,
optando protinus affectare vt lucernam, que totum illud dormitorium illustrabat, extingui contingeret., quatenus immoderata

100 risus sui intemperantia per visum saltem alijs non pateret. Quod
ita factum est :; nam continuo lucerna deorsum extincta cecidit.,
et sic tenebrosum totum // f. 305 a illud dormitorium reddidit :,
et, diuino parens imperio, beatricis, dei famule, desiderio satisfecit.
Tunc vero rursus, et-si non videretur, audiri tam…ι se timens ab

105 alijs., iterum ad dominum, effusis precibus, se conuertit, ei
supplicans vt venientes ad se moniales, a se recedere faceret :.
et ab earum presentia, quam ferre non potuit, ipsam denuo libe-
raret. Sed et hoc ita factum est. Nam ille, priusquam ad eam
propius accessissent., diuinitus admonite, recessere continuo :,

110 et dei electam, soli deo vacare volentem in nouitate gratie quam
acceperat, abeuntes sine molestia relinquere. Ab hijs ergo christi
famula diuinitus expedita, tanto sincerius accepte gratie nouis
fruitionibus incumbebat :, quanto sub nocturnis tenebris et silentio, dormientibus alijs., aut quid sibi tunc acciderit ignorantibus,

115 liberius id licebat. Siquidem in longum protracto spacio, delectabiliter in noue gratie dulcedine se exercens, tam immoderatis,
vellet nollet, risibus insistebat :, vt ne ridentis sonus deprehenderetur ab alijs, eadem nocte frequentissime domino supplicaret.
Infuse quippe noue gratie dulcedo, sic, eatenus huiusmodi iocun-

120 ditatis inexpertam, effecerat, vt crebro sub eadem nocte, se sibi
videretur in aere volitare.

59 Quid miri ? In cellam quippe vinariam introducta., nichil aliud quam
ebrietatem eructare potuit, ebrietatem inquam non sensuum exteriorum aliena-

mind, because she behaved in an unusual way. But it was only from
Ida that the mystery of the secret could not be hidden, for Ida had
sought this from God shortly before by her prayers. When Beatrice
saw them approaching her in a group, she immediately began in immense gratitude to break out in loud laughter, because she could in no
way stand their presence by any patience of her heart. Indeed it
seemed to her that her heart would be torn to pieces by excessive
gratitude if the venerable Ida should come any closer to her.

58 That the great madness she experienced in her heart might not be
even more apparent to these nuns, Beatrice began to wish within herself, without any sounds of words, that the lamp which lit the whole
dormitory would go out, so that at least the immoderacy of her laughter
would not be seen by them. And so it happened. The lamp immediately
fell down and went out, leaving the whole dormitory in darkness.
Obeying the divine command, it satisfied the desire of the servant of
God, Beatrice. Then afraid of being heard by them, even if not seen, she
again turned to the Lord in prayer, begging him to make the approaching nuns withdraw from her, freeing her again from their presence
which she could not bear. This also happened, for before coming any
closer to her, they were divinely warned and immediately withdrew,
leaving God's chosen one free from trouble when she wanted to attend
freely to God alone in the newness of the grace just received. Christ's
handmaid, thus divinely freed of them, applied herself to the new enjoyments of the grace received more sincerely as she was at greater
liberty to do so in the darkness and silence of night, while the others
were asleep or did not know what was happening to her. Then for a
long time she busied herself delightfully in the sweetness of this new
grace, and persisted in this immoderate laughter, whether she wanted to
or not, so that she often asked the Lord that night that the sound of her
laughter not be heard by the others. The sweetness of this new infused
grace so affected her, who had known no such delight before, that often
during that same night she seemed to herself to be floating in the air.

59 Why wonder at this? Brought into the wine cellar,[2] she could only get
drunk, with the drunkenness not of the outer senses causing an alienation

---

2. Sg 2:4

tionem extrinsecus operantem. , sed mentem interius ineffabilis gratitudinis et
125   leticie plena dulcedine iocundantem. Perpende, lector, quanta beatitudine
sanctorum spiritus, ipsi summo bono perpetualiter inherentes, perfruuntur in
patria: , si beatricis spiritus, tam effluentem delectationis habundantiam, hinc
sub momento retulerit, adhuc subsistens et permanens in hac vita.

Nec enim tante beatitudinis copia repente disparuit ; , sed per
130   mensem integrum et eo amplius in eius spiritu celestis dulcedo
gratie continue perdurauit [7]. Ex hoc tempore, mirabiliter in spiritu
recreata, plenioris amplexibus caritatis // f. 305b ipsi summo bono
decetero se impressit : , et ad omnipotentis dei seruitium et omnem
tolerantiam. , illuminatis mentis oculis, informatis affectibus, omni
135   reiecto torporis obstaculo sese cotidie renouauit.

⸿ DE EO QUOD SEDUCTOR DYABOLUS EAM A SANCTO PROPOSITO SUO REUOCARE CONATUS EST
Duodecimum capitulum

60 Paucis ergo post hec diebus expletis, cum iam satis in arte
5   scriptoria profecisset [1], beatrix, dei famula, rameye monasterio
valedicens, ad'suum, id est vallis floride monasterium, a venerabili
abbatissa reuocata regreditur [2]: , et ei, cui per professionis votum
ab olim incorparata fuerat, amico collegio denuo sociatur. Reuersa
vero, mox in omni conuersationis sue modo tanta cepit excellentia
10   morum et vite maturitas enitescere : , quod palam erat omnibus
eam intuentibus, in scola sancti spiritus hanc eam conuersationis

of the outer mind, but delighting the inner mind with the full sweetness
of unspeakable gratitude and joy. Consider well, dear reader, what
beatitude the spirits of the saints enjoy in heaven, always clinging to the
supreme Good. Beatrice's spirit, still in this life, received such an overflowing abundance of delight in just a short moment.

Neither did this abundance of happiness quickly disappear, but
for a whole month and more the sweetness of heavenly grace continued in her spirit. From this time on, marvelously renewed in
spirit, Beatrice clung to the supreme Good with the embraces of a
fuller love, and daily renewed herself in total patience in the service of almighty God, with her mind's eyes enlightened, her affections well formed, and all torpor cast away.

THE DEVIL TRIED TO SEDUCE AND RECALL HER
FROM HER HOLY INTENTION
Chapter Twelve

60 A few days after this, since Beatrice had already made good
progress in the art of writing, the servant of God bade farewell to
the monastery of Rameya, and returned to her own monastery of
Florival, recalled there by her venerable abbess. There she was
again united with her loving community into which she had been
incorporated previously by her vows of profession. Once she was
back, such an excellence of conduct and maturity of life began to
shine in her whole behavior that it was clear to all who saw her
that it was in the school of the Holy Spirit that she had received

normam et proficiendi studium excepisse. Ex omni siquidem
populari tumultu, cunctoque forensis impedimenti strepitu, corpore
simul et animo reuocata, cepit orationibus incessanter insistere,
meditationis officium omni conatu virium, exquisitis ad hoc horarum spacijs, exercere : preter ea que foris erant instantia coti-
diana, iugisque custodia regularis obseruantie ;, cuius etiam nexibus adeo se deuinxerat :, vt ab ipsis quoque sodalibus, et-si
veneratione precipua coleretur., ob hoc tamen arguebatur e regione frequentius, quod, amica solitudinis et silentij, raro nimis
et numquam voluntarie, sibi, quas edificatorijs ad-prime sermonibus informare potuerat, ipsam sui presentiam exhibebat.

61 Verum, cum hijs et alijs proficiendi studijs in semita mandatorum dei sui per singulos dies conaretur incedere :, videns et
inuidens humani generis inimicus, quod eam apertis incursibus
et preuisis infestationibus a proficiendi firmo proposito nequaquam posset excutere., nullaque valeret instantia reuocare ;,
sese in angelum lucis continuo transfigurans, aggressus //
f. 305 c est illud beatricis inuincibile pectus exquisita deceptionis
stropha concutere :; et, sub virtutis specie, virtutum cultrici
strenue, pro nectare venenum in poculo propinare. Cum enim
humilis ancilla christi conspiceret, ab omnibus in communi, singulari venerationis prerogatiua se coli, specialique reuerentia pro
virtutum suarum et morum exigentia commendari ;, mox immi-
nentis periculi cepit intra se casum vehementer expauescere : et ne
in vane glorie foueam, huiuscemodi venerationis aliquando delectata, corrueret., immodici timoris angustia formidare. Proinde,
ne de cetero tam effusa de se laudis fama conualesceret, et
humilitatis sue thezaurus extractus in publico, pro vane glorie
vili commercio deperiret :, cepit apud se mox deliberando propo-
nere, quod in conspectu dumtaxat hominum ab orationum instantia., lectionum aut meditationum, genuflexionum aut com-
punctionum[3] salutari frequentia se vellet, sine maioris proficiendi
desiderij preiudicio, cohibere : sanctius nimirum existimans ad
tempus exigue negligentie detrimentum incurrere :, quam per
inanis glorie fastum a bono quandoque proposito, suadente dyabolo, resilire.

this manner of life and zeal for improvement. She withdrew herself in body and soul from all popular excitement and every noisy
outer hindrance. She also began to pursue incessant prayer, and
applied herself to meditation with all her energy, seeking long
hours to devote to this task. Besides those things which were outward, there was also her daily insistence upon, and continual care
for, the regular observance, the obligations of which she took so
seriously that, although she was greatly venerated by her companions, they rather frequently chided her that, as a lover of
solitude and silence, she very rarely, and never willingly, gave her
presence to them, whom she could very well have edified by her
conversation.

61 But while Beatrice was trying to progress daily in the ways of
God's commands by these and other methods, the envious enemy
of the human race, seeing that he could not shake her with open
attacks or anticipatory plots from her firm purpose of progress,
and could not restrain her by any pressure, transformed himself
into an angel of light and approached to attack Beatrice's invin-
cible breast with a carefully thought-out trick. Under the appearance of virtue he meant to slip poison instead of nectar into the
cup of this zealous cultivator of virtue. When Christ's humble
handmaid saw she was reverenced by everyone in general, and was
specially commended for her virtues and character, she immediately began to be immoderately afraid of a fall and terrified lest
she become delighted with this veneration and fall into the pit of
vainglory. Consequently, lest her widespread reputation increase
and the treasure of her humility be dragged out in public and
perish in a cheap exchange for vainglory, she began by deliberat-
ing with herself, to resolve, only in the sight of men, to restrain
her constant prayer and the salutary frequency of her reading,
meditation, genuflections, and breast-beating, but without
prejudice to her desire for greater perfection. She thought it more
holy to incur the loss caused by a little negligence for a time, than
some day to have to reject her good resolve through the haughti-
ness of vainglory, under the devil's persuasion.

62 Sicque factum est, vt columbina simplicitas, absque serpentis astucia volens incedere, caribdis [4] discrimini nimis improuide se ingereret :, priusquam exosum scille [5] periculum ad plenum effugere potuisset. Nam cum in conspectu intuentium simplex dei famula, que superius enumerata sunt virtutum operibus insistere formidaret., et propterea sese nimis incautius ab hijs frequenter abstinendo retraheret :, accidit vt a solito feruore proficiendi, zelus in eam mox, torpescendo, deficeret ; et cum ex vno latere sanctitatis nomen effugeret., ex altero desidie squalore, male cauta, sauciata succumberet [6] :, et nisi pius misericordiarum dominus in necessitatis tempore subueniret, iamiam, decedente sibi victoria, beatrici triumphator malignus spiritus insultaret. Sed benignissimus dominus, qui suis in euangelio dicit. : ' Ecce ego vobiscum sum omnibus diebus vsque ad consummationem seculi ' [7] :, etiam hanc dilectam // f. 305 d suam in huius status periculoso discrimine non deseruit., sed ad solitum proficiendi studium, cum voluit et quando voluit, expulsis ignorantie tenebris et inimici rugientis insidijs effugatis., ineffabili miserationis sue clementia reuocauit.

Nam cum a paschali tempore, per sex mensium ferme spacium, id est vsque ed sancte crucis exaltationem que mense septembri in ecclesia celebratur [8], in hoc torpore desidie continue permansisset, et iam non tam abstinentia bonorum actuum., sed et verbis et gestibus, equo plus, admodum insolentior appareret :, misertus ancille sue misericors pater totius misericordie., lumine gratie sue denuo care sue pectusculum illustrauit., et priorum actuum exercitium., et antiqui profectus solitum incrementum ad memoriam sibi reuocans, eam ad repetendum quod omiserat intrinsecus mirabili desiderio mirabiliter animauit.

63 Vt enim detrimentum prioris profectus sui cepit aduertere., seseque respexit in ymo relapsam que prius in sublimi perfectionis gradu constiterat., antiqui seductoris deceptam astutia, recidisse : <prius quidem vehementer admirans, quod, sub tam simplicis intentionis specie, potuerit in tam profundam deceptionis foueam

62 So it came to pass that, with dove-like simplicity wanting to proceed without the cunning of the serpent,[1] she imprudently ran into the danger of Charybdis before she could fully escape the hateful peril of Scyllae. When the simple servant of God feared being too involved in the aforesaid virtuous works in the eyes of men, and therefore rather imprudently often withdrew from them, it happened that her zeal became sluggish and quickly flagged in its usual fervor. While on the one hand she was fleeing a reputation for holiness, on the other she was succumbing to the wound of squalid sloth through lack of caution. Had the loving merciful Lord not come to her help in the time of need, the evil spirit would have triumphed over Beatrice, the victory going to him. But the kind Lord who says to his own in the Gospel 'Behold, I am with you all days, even to the consummation of the world',[2] did not desert this beloved one of his in her peril, but with his ineffable mercy recalled her, when he willed and because he willed, to her usual zeal for progress, expelling the darkness of ignorance and putting to flight the ambushes of the raging enemy.

After she had continued in this torpor and sloth for about six months, that is, from Eastertide till the Exaltation of the Holy Cross celebrated by the Church in September, and it seemed highly insolent, and unusual, to abstain not only from good acts but also words and gestures, the Father of all mercies[3] took pity on his handmaid and again illumined her dear heart with the light of his grace. He recalled to her memory her former acts and her usual progress in times past, and he animated her from within with a wonderful desire to seek again what she had neglected.

63 When Beatrice began to notice the loss of her former progress, and saw that she, who had been in a high state of perfection, had fallen low by the cleverness of the ancient seducer, she first marveled that she could have fallen into such a deep pit of deception

---

1. Mt 10:16   2. *Mt 28:20*   3. 1 Co 1:3

incidisse.>, <m>ox mirum in modum erexit semetipsam contra
se, totis cordis et corporis sui conatibus, a se torporis inuisum
pondus excutiens, et prioris vsum deuotionis instantissime repe-
85   tens ;, id quod, per maligni dolosam astutiam, in se torpendo
perdiderat., recuperare pro posse modis omnibus satagebat. At
quoniam intentionis sue vires, quibus semetipsam in statum deuotionis pristine conabatur erigere., debilitatas oppido sentiebat :,
ad sinum ineffabilis misericordie dei sui, lacrimando simul [.]
90   et eiulando se contulit :, reamque se clamitans, reatus sui veniam
humillime petijt : ; et ne decetero, tam inutilis occasionis pretextu,
tale quid attemptare presumeret, pactum cum domino subijt,
quod et fide media confirmauit.

64 Sed quid benignissimus misericordiarum pater et totius conso-
95   lationis dominus, electissime famule sue de- // f. *306 a* negare
potuit., quam toto cordis affectu reuertentem ad se penitendo
conspexit., et prioris fidelitatis velle federa resarcire, tam studioso
conamine deprehendit. Proinde serenitatis sue faciem ad dilectam
suam iterum, absque mora, conuertere non despexit :, sed reuer-
100 tentis manum dexteram misericorditer apprehendere studuit., qui
quando voluit, hoc ipsum, fideli sue, reuersionis propositum inspirauit. Nec mora, beatrix, <adiuvante> superna clementia, studium quod omiserat iterum arripiendo, solito cautius exercere non
distulit :, et vt quisquis sibi de fallacis insidijs inimici, suo doctus
105 experimento, precaueat., omnibus ista legentibus in exemplum
que sibi contigerant, perpetue commendanda memorie, dereliquit [9].

¶ DE CONSOLATIONE DIUINA QUAM SENSIT
IN PERCEPTIONE EUCHARISTIE
xiij. capitulum

65 Qualiter autem hanc pius dominus, in hoc procelloso necessi-
5   tatis turbine, misericorditer ad se reuocare dignatus sit, et in
potiori proficiendi studio, gratie sue munimine, confirmauerit :,
opere precium est vt continuata narrationis serie subnectamus.
Cum enim, a perceptione <viuifici> sacramenti dominici corporis

under the appearance of so simple an intention. Then she quickly straightened herself up, shaking off the hateful burden of torpor with every effort of heart and body, eagerly seeking again her former devotion and trying in every way possible to recover what she had lost in torpor through the cleverness of the devil. But because she found her strength of mind, by which she tried to rise to the level of her former devotion, much weakened, she betook herself to the ineffably merciful bosom of her God, weeping and wailing. She proclaimed her guilt and humbly sought pardon. And she made a covenant with the Lord, confirming it by means of a faithful promise that she would never again try anything like that under such a useless pretext.

64 But what could the ever-kind Father of mercies and Lord of all consolation[4] deny his chosen handmaid whom he saw returning to him penitently with all her heart's affection and willing to repair with full effort the alliance of her former fidelity? Without delay he did not refuse to show the face of his serenity again to his beloved; he who, when he willed, had inspired this intention of returning in his faithful one, quickly and mercifully took her right hand when she did return. Without delay, Beatrice, by divine mercy, took up again the endeavor she had dropped, and practiced it with more caution than usual. She left the account of these things which had happened to her as a perpetual memorial to all who would read them, so that everyone, taught by her experience, would beware of the cunning ambushes of the enemy.

THE DIVINE CONSOLATION SHE SENSED
IN THE RECEPTION OF THE HOLY EUCHARIST
Chapter Thirteen

65 It is worthwhile to add, as a sequel to this narrative, how the good Lord mercifully recalled Beatrice to himself in this stormy vortex of need, and how by the protection of his grace, he confirmed her, with a stronger zeal for progress. When Beatrice in her sloth and torpor

4. 2 Co 1:3

et sanguinis aliquantis iam diebus abstinens., in torporis sui
10 desidia se gessisset :, accidit vt quedam ex sanctimonialibus,
admodum sibi familiaris et intima., [1] diuino nutu celitus inspirata,
quodam dierum illam, improuise quidem sed satis instanter aggressa, commonere cepit et cogere quatenus ipsi <viuifico>
sacramento communicare satageret :, et eius se participem efficere
15 non pigeret. Quod cum, ob reuerentiam tanti misterij primitus
quidem, quod <ad hoc> se per medelam confessionis minime
preparauerat, ad effectum ducere formidaret :, per ebdomade
quippe curriculum confessionem non fecerat delictorum :, institit
nichilominus altera, nec a coactione prorsus desistere voluit.,
20 donec illius consensum, ad percipiendum eadem in hora salutare
misterium dominici corporis, excitauit.

66 Nec mora, cum iam, appropinquante termino, virgo domini vel
// f. 306 b preparare se per confessionis suffragium, vel retroce-
dendo diutius subterfugere non valeret :, totam se conuertens
25 ad dominum, in timore cordis et conscientie, delictorum suorum
indulgentiam instantissime cepit ab ipso fonte misericordie domino
postulare :; sicque, timorato corde versus altare pedetentim incedens, antequam ad sacrosancte perceptionem eucharistie peruenisset, aperte sunt catharacte capitis eius :, et ceperunt ab oculis
30 eius, in habundantia plene consolationis et dulcedinis effuse lacrime distillare :, quibus intra semetipsam oppido confortata, cum
maiori fiducia iam ad viuificum sacramentum appropians, eius
saluberrimo meruit eodem in tempore participio recreari. Siquidem,
huius particeps iam effecta, continuo virtutem illius experiendo
35 cepit agnoscere, pristinique torporis et <ignorantie> tenebris,
infuso noue gratie lumine, penitus effugatis :, in maiorem sui
cognitionem erecta., simulque in eminentioris spei et fiducie culmine collocata, propensiori cognitionis intuitu, dilectoris et dilecti
sui cepit et tunc et deinceps in se beneficia recognoscere :; de-
40 gustatisque caritatis sue primitijs., eo decetero firmius quo
suauius, illius deliciosis amplexibus inherere.

had abstained for some days from receiving the life-giving Sacrament
of the Lord's Body and Blood, it happened that one of the nuns, very
familiar with and close to her, came up to her unexpectedly one day
and, divinely inspired, began quite insistently to warn her and to press
her to communicate in this life-giving Sacrament, telling her not to be
loathe to share in it. Although Beatrice at first feared to follow her advice out of reverence for so great a mystery, because she had not prepared herself for it through the remedy of confession—she had not
been to confession of faults for a week—the other nun insisted and
would not leave off pressing her until she had aroused her consent
to receive the saving mystery of the Lord's Body that very hour.

66 There was no time for delay for, with the hour now upon her,
the Lord's virgin could neither prepare herself with the help of
confession, nor any longer take refuge in withdrawal. She turned
wholly to the Lord in fear of heart and conscience, and urgently
began to beg pardon for her faults from the Lord, the very wellspring of mercy. And so, advancing slowly toward the altar with
fearful heart, before she arrived to receive the holy Eucharist, her
facial cataracts were opened and copious tears began to flow from
her eyes, tears full of consolation and sweetness. Much
strengthened interiorly by them, she approached the life-giving
Sacrament with greater confidence and deserved at the same time
to be remade by this salubrious participation. Indeed, by sharing in
it, she immediately began to recognize by experience its power to
expel the darkness of her former torpor and ignorance through the
infusion of the light of new grace. Straightened up in greater self-
knowledge and placed at the same time on a higher level of loftier
hope and confidence, she began to recognize more clearly in herself then and thereafter the benefits of her lover and beloved. Having tasted the first fruits of his love she clung thereafter to his
delicious embraces all the more firmly as they were sweeter.

⁋ DE SUBTILITATE ET FORTITUDINE SPIRITUS QUEM IN PERCEPTIONE SACRAMENTI A DOMINO CONSECUTA EST

xiiij. capitulum

67 Sub eodem quoque tempore, misso nuncio [1] venerabili, cuius supra mentionem fecimus [2], yde nyuellensi, de cuius patrocinio magna cordis fiducia presumebat :, illius preterite perturbationis sue modum et causam euidenter exposuit., emendaturam se priorem negligentiam, annuente domino, fideli sponsione promisit., et vt orationum suarum suffragio diuinam sibi propitiaret clementiam, supplex christi famula suppliciter exorauit. Cui beata femina continuo remandauit, vt salutifero redemptionis nostre misterio, dominici videlicet corporis viuifico sacramento, communicare satageret :, et pius dominus, indulta [3] negligentia quam timebat, et noue // f. 306 c dulcore gratie mentem eius, solita pietate, perfunderet, ipsaque, recepta consolatione diuina, per noue gratie nouam experientiam, statum vite veteris emendaret. Qua responsione beate femine magnifice recreata, cepit continuo, preparando cordis vasculo, totis viribus intentionis insistere.; confessionis sarculo quidquid in se viciosum, arguente conscientia, putabat euellere.; studiosis orationibus incessanter incumbere.; regularis tenorem obseruantie plus solito custodiendo se stringere :, ceterisque virtutum operibus, ad receptionem diuine gratie, mentem infatigabili studio preparare. Et hec quidem nimia simplicitate actitabat decepta :, putans <exterioris laboris exercitio> gratiam que gratis datur acquirere., donumque incomparabile, compensatiuo corporalium actionum commercio, comparare. Sic denique, pro modo possibilitatis sue., domo conscientie renouata., promixo sequenti die dominico viuificum salutaris eucharistie sacramentum humili corde suscepit :, et, vt sibi mandatum fuerat, eterne vite pabulo se refici procurabat.

68 Nec fefellit eam illa veridica promissio quam acceperat ; sed, post perceptionem diuini pignoris mox in spiritu mirabiliter ani-

THE SUBTLETY AND STRENGTH
OF SPIRIT WHICH BEATRICE OBTAINED
FROM THE LORD IN THE RECEPTION OF THE
BLESSED SACRAMENT
Chapter Fourteen

67 At the same time, through the venerable messenger whom we mentioned above, Beatrice gave a clear account of her recent disturbance and its cause to Ida of Nivelles, in whose patronage she greatly trusted, and faithfully promised to amend her previous negligence, with God's help. As a suppliant handmaid of Christ she begged Ida to obtain divine mercy for her through her prayers. The blessed woman immediately sent back word that Beatrice should be careful to communicate in the salvation-giving mystery of our redemption, that is, the life-giving Sacrament of the Lord's Body, and that the merciful Lord would pardon the negligence she feared and would with his accustomed kindness, pour into her mind, the sweetness of new grace. She herself would amend her former life through the reception of divine consolation, that is, a new experience of new grace. Greatly renewed by this blessed woman's reply, Beatrice straightaway began with all her strength to prepare the vessel of her heart. She thought to tear out with the hoe of confession whatever was faulty in herself, according to her conscience; to give herself incessantly to zealous prayers; to bind herself to the regular observance more than usual; and to prepare her mind untiringly by the other works of virtue for the reception of divine grace. She acted this way deceived by excessive simplicity, thinking to acquire by exterior labor the grace which is freely given, and to buy the priceless gift with the price of bodily activities. Thus renewing the house of her conscience as best as she could, on the next Sunday Beatrice received the life-giving Sacrament of the saving Eucharist with a humble heart, and took care to refresh herself with the food of eternal life, as she had been told to do.

68 Nor was Beatrice deceived by the truthful promise she had received, but wonderfully animated in spirit soon after the reception

mata, noua quadam fortitudinis et constantie spiritualis insolen-
35 tia⁴ roboratam se sentiebat intrinsecus : quam, vellet nollet,
ipsam sequi decetero., quocumque procederet, oportebat. Tam
illuminatum quoque spiritus intellectum eo in tempore, domino
largiente, suscepit ; vt, roboratis discretionis obtutibus <subli-
matisque> rationis viribus., in qua sibi foret ambulandum de
40 cetero viam⁵ veritatis, infallibili iudicio rationis agnosceret :, et
inter bonum et malum., inter prophanum et vtile, subtili discretionis examine iudicaret. Tunc etiam, in subtilitate spiritus, euidenter aduertit inconsulte se per recompensationis commercium,
ad impetrandam superne liberalitatis gratiam, aspirasse, sciens et
45 intelligens illius dona, iuxta sui nominis ethimologicam inter-
pretationem, a domino cui vvlt, et quomodo vel quando wlt,
absque recompensationis mercede distribui., et ab eo qui dat
affluenter et non improperat, absque venali- // f. 306 d tatis
pactione gratuito dispensari. Proinde super tanto presumptionis
50 excessu ream se iudicans., omnipotentis dei iudicio satisfacere
studuit :, et vt numquam decetero proprijs viribus ad donum
diuine gratie promerendum assurrecturam se fore presumeret,
sese domino per sponsionem voluntariam obligauit. Ab illo quoque
tempore fortiori desiderio., virtutum studijs inseruire proposuit ;
55 vagos cogitationum recursus, operum locutionumque pruritus ad
vsum emendatioris vite conuertere studuit : ; et ne in vacuum
gratiam dei receperit, in puritate cordis et conscientie sue se
victuram., et, diuino beneplacito sese <conformaturam> decetero, fixo proposito repromisit.
60 **69** Nec defuit forti volentis desiderio, fortior superueniens operis
executio : sed spiritus fortitudinis quem acceperat, omne quod
mentis affectus interius concipere poterat, hoc per executionem
operis in dei beneplacito dirigebat. Tantam quoque, sub eodem
tempore, mentis intelligentiam, acumen discretionis, et subtilitatem
65 spiritus est adepta :, quod ex omni re quam, ipsa presente, vel
corporaliter actitari, vel recitari quouis verborum ordine, contigis-

of the divine pledge, she felt herself interiorly strengthened by a
new and unusual fortitude and spiritual constancy which, whether
she liked it or not, she would have to follow in the future, wherever
it led. By the Lord's gift she then received such an illuminated spiritual insight that with strengthened discretion and increased powers
of reason, she would thenceforth know with infallible judgment the
way of truth in which she would have to proceed, and would judge
subtly between the good and the evil, the profane and the useful.
Then indeed by her subtlety of spirit she saw clearly how foolishly
she had aspired to obtain the supremely free gifts by exchange and
repayment. Now she knew and understood that the Lord's gifts, according to the etymology of the word, are distributed by him to
whom and how and when he willed, without the reward of
recompense.[1] They are dispensed freely without the venality of a
pact by him who gives abundantly and without restraint. Then judging herself guilty of great presumption, she sought to satisfy God's
judgment, and obliged herself by a voluntary promise never in the
future to presume that she could attain the gift of divine grace by
her own efforts. From that time on she intended to serve the works
of virtue with a stronger desire, and she strove to convert to the improvement of life her wandering thoughts and the itch to act and to
speak.[2] And lest she receive the grace of God in vain, she promised
again with a firm purpose that she would live in purity of heart and
conscience, and that she would conform herself to the divine good
pleasure.

69 A stronger determination to carry out what she intended was not
lacking to Beatrice's strong desire and will. With the spirit of fortitude she had received, she directed toward God, in a way very pleasing to him, everything she could inwardly conceive of. At the same
time she was given such intelligence of mind, such keenness of discretion and subtlety of spirit that, from anything done in her presence
or spoken in any way whatever, she knew, with her vivacious reason

1. Jm 1:5   2. 2 Co 6:1

set., aliud edificationi sue proficuum, viuaci iudicio rationis, eli-
ceret. , et in vsum profectus sui, subtilitate sensus, etiam si minus
congruum aut fructuosum id fuerit : , virtuosa quadam violentia
70   retorqueret. Nam vt, ipsa confitente [6], didicimus, numquam dies
aliqua. , numquam vel raro, per continue sequens septennium [7],
hora preterijt : , in qua docilis christi discipula doctrine studio
non profecit. Omne quippe quod a retroactis temporibus, aut ob
ingenij tarditatem, aut obliuionis vel ignorantie cecitatem, memorie
75   commendare neglexerat ; , hoc, instar rapidi torrentis, in vnam
simul congeriem adunatum, ante mentis sue cotidie refluebat
aspectum : ; et ex omni vel singulo promissorum [8], quantum edificationi sue pro tempore suppetebat, tantum discretionis et intelligentie receptaculo, per dies singulos, instar filiorum israel olim
80   in deserto gomor [9] manna colligentium, hauriebat.

70 Super hec omnia, totis intentionis sue conatibus, // *f. 307 a*
ad plenam sui cognitionem attingere satagebat : , timens ne quid
intra se delitesceret, aut, occulta callidi hostis immissione, subre-
peret, quod, in via mandatorum dei incedentis gressum offen-
85   deret. , aut a cepto quandoque proposito reuocaret. Et quoniam
obliuionis sue defectum, in hoc studioso proprie cognitionis exercitio, precipue suspectum habuit. , artem <qua> tam nociuum
obliuionis obstaculum opportune retunderet, et a memorie sue
finibus indesinenter expelleret. , inspirante dei gratia, satis pro-
90   ficuam, et intentionis sue proposito satis accommodam, adinuenit.
Crucem quippe ligneam, vnius palmi longitudinis, nodoso funiculo
sibi stricte colligatam. , die noctuque gestabat in pectore ; cui
tytulum dominice passionis. , horrorem extremi iudicij. , iudicisque
seueritatem inscripserat : , et cetera que iugiter proponebat in
95   memoria retinere. Aliud nichilominus dominice crucis signaculum,
in pargameni cedula depictum, etiam gestabat in brachio colli-
gatum : ; tercium quoque coram se, cum scribendi vacabat officio,
depictum habebat in assere ; , quatenus ad quecumque loca se
diuerteret. , aut quidquid operis extrinsecus actitaret : , omnis obli-
100   uionis effugata caligine, per dominice crucis signaculum, id, de

how to draw something useful for her own edification. With a kind of virtuous violence and subtlety of sense she would turn it to her own profit, even if it was somewhat incongruous or unfruitful. For, as we learned from her, never did a day pass, and never—or but rarely—did an hour pass during the next seven years in which Christ's docile disciple did not progress in eager learning. Everything she had neglected to remember from times past, either through slowness of wit or the blindness of forgetfulness and ignorance, all daily flowed together as a whole before her mind's eye, like a fast torrent. From all this she daily drew with the vessel of discretion and understanding as much as she needed for her edification at the time, like the children of Israel in older times gathering a gomer of manna in the desert.[3]

70 In addition to all this, Beatrice strove with all her might to attain full self-knowledge. She feared lest anything should lurk within her, or might creep into her through the clandestine plotting of the clever enemy, which would trip her up as she was journeying in the way of God's commandments, or might sometime recall her from her settled purpose. In this earnest practice of self-knowledge she chiefly distrusted the defect of her forgetfulness, and by God's grace, she found a quite profitable and, for her purpose, appropriate method of beating down this obstacle of forgetfulness and expelling it continuously from the limitations of her memory. Day and night she wore on her breast a wooden cross, about a palm in length, tightly tied with a knotted string. On it was written the Lord's passion, the horror of the last judgment, the severity of the judge and other things she wanted always to keep in mind. Besides this she also carried tied to her arm another image of the Lord's cross painted on a piece of parchment. She had a third, painted on a piece of wood, set before her when she was writing, so that wherever she went, or whatever exterior work she did, all forgetfulness would be banished, and by means of the image of the cross

---

3. Ex 16:16

cuius amissione timebat., impressum cordi suo in memoria
firmiter retineret. Sicque factum est, vt per iugem memoriam
dominice passionis omnem neuum obliuionis abstergeret: et ad
profectum virtutis omni tempore vigilantior appareret.

❡ ITEM DE ORDINATIONE ET
EXERCITIO MEDITATIONUM EIUS
xv. capitulum

71 E t quoniam, vt prediximus, aliquantulum a perfectionis itinere,
5   maligni spiritus astutia retardante, digressa fuerat:, opere precium erat vt iterum ordinando cordis hospicio sollerter intenderet., et sese totaliter in omnipotentis dei beneplacito renouaret.
Studebat igitur per aliquantulam vite conformitatem, cordis videlicet humilitatem et spiritus paupertatem, omnimoda qua valebat
10   intentionis instantia, creatoris sui ves- // f. 307 b tigijs inherere.
Sed et illa que dudum, carne velata, dei patrauerat sapientia, pro
captu memorie, deuote meditationis officio, recitabat assidue:;
miroque pietatis affectu vniuersa simul amplectebatur in genere.,
sed speciali memoria, delectando super omnia, quiescebat in domi-
15   nica passione. Ibi refectionem spiritus insistebat queritando cotidie:; ibi se gaudebat omne quodcumque saluti sue proficuum
esse poterat., aut affectui delectabile, disponente superna clementia, sine typo[1] vel mora celeriter inuenire. Quotiens autem
alicuius perturbationis incommodo, cuiusque noxe piaculo se lesam
20   interius sentiebat:, confestim ad pedes domini crucifixi, coram
ipsius ymagine, se prosternere consuescebat; et super delicto
venia, vel super tribulationis incommodo medela consolationis ab
ipso fonte misericordie pertinaciter expetita:, mox effectum
petitionis sue, per exauditionis experientiam, sentiebat. Non solum
25   enim pius dominus id quod ab <ipso> petebatur indulsit continuo:, sed semetipsum quoque fore mercedem et premium, ecclesie sue[2] fideli stipulatione promisit[3] et censuit in futuro.

she would keep impressed on her heart and memory whatever she feared to lose. Thus it came to pass that she removed the flaw of forgetfulness through the constant remembrance of the Lord's passion, and she seemed always more vigilant in progressing in virtue.

AGAIN, THE ORDERING AND EXERCISE OF BEATRICE'S MEDITATIONS
Chapter Fifteen

71 In that Beatrice had departed a little from the way of perfection through the deception of the evil spirit, as we said, it was worthwhile for her carefully to set in order again the house of her heart, and to renew herself wholly in God's good pleasure. Therefore she tried with all possible energy to follow in her Creator's footsteps through a little conformity of life, namely humility of heart and poverty of spirit. But she also carefully summoned from her memory in devout meditation whatever the Wisdom of God veiled in flesh had done, and she embraced everything in general with a wonderful devotion, but with a special remembrance she rested with delight in the Lord's passion. There with daily insistence she sought food for her spirit; there, by divine mercy, she delighted in finding quickly, without visual images and without delay, whatever was useful to her salvation or delectable to her affection. As often as she felt inwardly harmed by some troublesome disturbance or some injurious misfortune, she used to prostrate herself immediately at the feet of the crucified Lord, before his image. There she would persistently seek pardon for her fault or ask for some consoling remedy for the troublesome disturbance from the very wellspring of mercy. Soon she felt the effect of her petition and an experience of being favorably heard. Not only did the loving God immediately grant her what she sought from him, but he promised himself faithfully as the reward and recompense for his church, and he obliged himself to do so in the future.

72 Exinde vero, per continuum ferme quinquennium[4], tam firmiter impressum habebat mentis intuitum in memoria dominice
passionis., vt vix vmquam ab <illius> suaui meditatione recederet:; sed singulis que pro humana salute pati dignatus est,
miro deuotionis affectu, iugique meditatione medullitus inhereret.
Hoc scuto, contra spiritualia nequitie in celestibus[5], incedebat
armata continue., nec erat vbi, per consensus introitum, inique
suggestionis aut praue delectationis iaculum, aduersarius humani
generis immitteret ad mentem eius:, cum hoc scuto memorie
dominice passionis admissum, absque nocendi qualibet efficacia,
continuo resiliret. Sic igitur omnis cordis eius intentio, diuino
confirmata beneplacito, subsistebat interius:; sic omnis locutionis
aut operis executio foris, diuine complacentie lumine renitebat.
Sic, inquam, virgo domini, iugi meditationis intuitu, retractandis
diuine gratie beneficijs // f. 307 c insistebat:; sic totis affectionis
et intentionis sue viribus, eidem a quo data susceperat., laudum
hostias incessanter cum gratiarum actionibus exsoluebat.

⁋ DE CELESTIBUS CONSOLATIONIBUS ET
DUCTU DIUINE GRATIE QUA SE AD SPIRITUALES
PROFECTUS SENSIT COTIDIE PROMOUERI
Sextum decimum capitulum

73 Sed quia rationis equitas hoc exigere videbatur, vt amanti
sponse sue vicem sponsus amando rependeret. (quam, vt verius
eloquamur, amando <preuenerat> et excitauerat ad amandum):,
vt pius dominus, hanc quam prediximus vicem euidentibus signis
ostenderet., ad beatricem suam wltum misericordie sue sensibiliter
omni tempore conuertebat. Quotiens enim aut per orationis officium., vel meditationis exercitium, ad ipsam dilecti sui presentiam,
eius fruitura solacio, se transferret:, totiens ab ipso se preuentam, in benedictionum suarum dulcedine, sentiebat. Tam suaui
ergo diuine pietatis experientia, celestique dulcedine confortata.,

72 Thereafter for about five unbroken years she had the mental image of the Lord's passion so firmly impressed in her memory that she scarcely ever quit this sweet meditation, but clung from the bottom of her heart with wonderful devotion to everything he deigned to suffer for the salvation of the human race. Always armed with this shield she advanced against the spirits of wickedness in high places, and nowhere through any opening of consent could the enemy of the human race cast a dart of evil suggestion or wicked pleasure into her mind, since whatever entered, immediately bounced back from this shield of the Lord's passion without any harmful effect.[1] Thus the whole intention of her heart, confirmed by divine approval, held firm within; thus every outward execution of word or deed shone with the light of God's good pleasure. In this way the Lord's virgin by continuous meditation kept on re-thinking the benefits of divine grace and with all the strength of her affection and intention she offered the sacrifice of praise and thanksgiving to him from whom she had received these gifts.

THE HEAVENLY CONSOLATIONS AND THE LEADING OF DIVINE GRACE BY WHICH SHE FELT DAILY MOVED FORWARD IN SPIRITUAL PROGRESS
Chapter Sixteen

73 Since it seemed fair and reasonable to demand that the bridegroom lovingly reciprocate the love of his bride (although, to speak more truly, he anticipated her in love and roused her to love), as a loving Lord he used at all times to turn the face of his mercy toward his Beatrice in a perceptible way, so as to show, as we said, this reciprocation by evident signs. Each time she turned to the presence of her beloved in prayer or meditation in order to enjoy his consolation, she felt herself anticipated by the sweetness of his blessing. Strengthened by so delicate an experience of divine tenderness and so heavenly a sweetness,

---

1. Eph 6:12

¹⁵ mira gratitudine sic cotidie liquescebat intrinsecus, vt vix pedibus
suis incedere., vix corpus suum, exteriorum sensuum valuisset
officio supportare. Quid mirum si carnis fragilitas ibi succumbat
exterius;, vbi spiritus, ad altiora leuatus, in suo naturali situ
interius, celesti confortatus robore, subsistebat? At quoniam pium
²⁰ dominum electe sue vicem amando rependisse prediximus:, iam
quibus aut qualibus modis hoc intra semet experiebatur actitari
virgo domini, subnectamus.

74 Aliquotiens enim vt magister <discipulam>., ita dilectam
suam, qualiter vixerat., aut qualiter viuendum foret de cetero,
²⁵ certis eam indicijs, non sono vocis, sed inspirationis leniter in-
fluente susurrio, intrinsecus instruebat.; aliquotiens vt ductorem
et rectorem itineris, ambulantem secum in hac labilis vite semita,
perpendebat:, et quocumque se verteret, aut quorsum incederet,
precedentem dominum inoffensis passibus subsequi alacriter as-
³⁰ suescebat.

Aliquotiens etiam ipsum // *fol. 307 d* vt pastorem ouium., sese
vero velut eius dilectam et electam ouiculam attendebat:, quam,
in vberrimis gratie sue pascuis incedentem, ipse dirigebat attentius.

³⁵ Interdum etiam ipsum vt patrem, multiplicis gratie plenitudine se,
velut electam filiam, locupletare volentem., et omnium virtutum
insignijs adornare:, non sine gratitudinis admirabili dulcedine
sentiebat.

Nonnumquam autem velut sponsum dominum, sese vero velut
⁴⁰ sponsam eius electam., et perpetue gratie et decoris anulo
subarratam ¹, et remunerationis future dotalicio iam dotatam, in
spiritu preuidebat.

In quolibet vero modo considerationis, istorum scilicet quos superius explanauimus., tanta letitie spiritualis et iocunditatis grati-
⁴⁵ tudine replebatur interius;, vt super omnem humanarum virium
possibilitatem esset tantum exultationis pondus in domicilio cordis
abscondere:, et indomitum et effrenem spiritum, ne foras violenter erumperet., in fragili carnis ergastulo retinere. Unde frequenter accidit:, vt, vellet nollet, is quem tolerabat interius mentis

Beatrice daily melted inwardly with a wonderful gratitude until
she could scarcely walk on her feet or support her body with the
help of the exterior senses. What wonder that the frail flesh succumbed outwardly, while her spirit, raised to higher things and
strengthened by heavenly vigor subsisted interiorly in its own
natural site? Because the Lord returned the love of his chosen one,
as we have said, let us add an account of how the Lord's virgin
experienced this within herself.

74 Sometimes he would inwardly by certain signs instruct his
beloved, as a master does a pupil, on how she had lived or should
live in the future, not with the sound of his voice but with the gentle whisper of his inspiration. Sometimes Beatrice would consider
him as her guide and leader, walking beside her on the slippery
path of this life. Wherever she turned or went she used to follow
the Lord who went before her, eagerly and without stumbling.
Sometimes she saw him as a shepherd, and herself as a beloved
and chosen ewe lamb which he carefully directed to the richest
pastures of his grace. Sometimes she used to perceive him—not
without wonderfully sweet gratitude—as a father wanting to enrich
his favorite daughter with the fullness of many graces and to adorn
her with the marks of every virtue.

Sometimes she foresaw him in spirit as her bridegroom and lord,
and herself as his chosen bride, having in her ring the pledge of
perpetual grace and comeliness and already endowed with her future dowry.

Beatrice used to become inwardly so filled with spiritual joy
and gratitude at all the considerations we have explained above
that it was beyond human possibility to hide such a weight of
exultation within the dwelling place of her heart and to keep this
wild and unrestrained spirit from breaking violently out of the
fragile prison of the flesh. Therefore it frequently happened that,
whether she willed it or not, her interior jubilation of mind

50 iubilus, per aliqua demonstrationis indicia foris erumperet, et vel
    risu vel tripudio, gestu vel alio quovis indicio se prodendo, quid
    iubilantis mens pateretur interius, extrinsecus indicaret. Nec
    dubium quin, in gratiarum donıs vberrimis quibus assidue dita-
    batur interius, quotiens et meditando reuolueret :, ampliorem
55 gratiarum actionis et laudis materiam inueniret. Sic denique spiri-
    tus illius in hijs mirabilibus absor<p>tus fuerat et a terrenis
    abstractus, solisque gratiarum actionibus occupatus :, vt, ebetatis
    obtusisque sensibus, quod videbat non agnosceret., quod audie-
    bat non intelligeret., aut quod gustare solebat, per saporis indi-
60 cium discernere non valeret.
    75 Fuit autem in huius admirabili status obseruantia per unius
    aut circiter anni spacium :, quo denique transcurso, sinuque sa-
    pientie et scientie // f. 308 a longo virtutum exercitio dilatato.,
    mutatus est hic status in alterum :, et-si minus forte laboriosum,
65 non minus tamen, vt estimo, fructuosum. Nam ex omnibus que,
    presente venerabili beatrice, recitari pro tempore contingebat.,
    de quibuscumque sermo fieret, etiam si de vanis et ociosis is in
    medio prosiliret., ordito prius themate, sermocinantium more,
    collectis omnibus et per partes ordinate distinctis., intra se
70 verbum edificationis elicuit :, et ad laudem creatoris sui singula,
    mirabili subtilitatis scemate reducendo., etiam in talibus profectus
    sui materiam exquisiuit. Fuit etiam in hoc statu secundo proposito,
    similiter vnius anni spacio : quibus duorum annorum curriculis
    per labentia tempora defluentibus, admodum delectabiliter inter
75 sponsi sui brachia collocata., dulcem amoris sompnum, absque
    quolibet infestationis offendiculo, diuina se protegente gratia,
    capiebat.

    ❡ DE EO QUOD AB EPISCOPO CONSECRATA FUIT
                    xvij. capitulum

    76 Per idem quoque tempus [1] accidit vt, cum alijs ad hoc depu-
    tatis virginibus, episcopali officio virgo domini beatrix in virginali
5   proposito confirmari deberet :, et per integram castitatis et fidei

would break out in some manifestation, and the mind's inner jubilation would betray itself outwardly either in laughing or dancing a gesture or some other sign. No doubt she would find more ample matter for thanksgiving and praise as often as she turned over in her mind the abundant graces with which she was steadily enriched interiorly. Thus her spirit was so absorbed in these wonders, so withdrawn from earthly things and so occupied with thanksgiving alone that, with senses weakened and dulled, she would not recognize what she saw or understand what she heard, nor could she tell by taste what she usually relished.

75 Beatrice was in this admirable state for about a year. Once this stage was over, her capacity for wisdom and knowledge was so expanded by long practice of the virtues that this stage was exchanged for another. If this later stage was perhaps less laborious, I think it was no less fruitful. Whatever happened to be told in Beatrice's presence, no matter what the subject was, even vain and idle things, she would first set the theme in order. Collecting all the parts and distinguishing them in an orderly way, as preachers do, she would draw something edifying out for herself. By reducing everything, by a wonderfully subtle formula, to her Creator's praise, she sought matter for her progress even in that kind of thing. She was in this second stage also for a year's time, and during these two years of ever-passing time she lay with great pleasure in the arms of her bridegroom and slept the sweet sleep of love, without any hostile obstacle, divine grace protecting her.

SHE WAS CONSECRATED BY THE BISHOP
Chapter Seventeen

76 It also happened at this time that, together with other virgins so designated, the Lord's virgin Beatrice should be confirmed in her virginal resolve by the episcopal office, and sealed for Christ the

sponsionem ipsi virginum sponso christo domino consignari[2].
Quod intelligens, immenso gaudio replebatur., et mox, omni
deuotionis instantia, tanto se dignam misterio pro viribus suis
conabatur efficere:, multoque deuotionis apparatu, quo celesti
10   sponso procederet obuia, pendente modico tempore dilationis,
interim se studuit adornare.
Sed quid plura? Adest dies ad hoc misterium explendum ap-
tissimus., dies videlicet ascensionis dominice[3]., dies quo trium-
phantem in celo ecclesiam dignatus est redemptor noster dominus,
15   per glorificatam humanitatis sue presentiam eterno sibi connubio
desponsare. Nec mora., congregatus virginum cetus ante presu-
lem[4], more consueto consecrandus adducitur:, // f. 308 b inter
quas, apto loco, christi sponsa venerabilis astantium obsequio
collocatur. Adest et pontifex, officiumque ex more per ordinem
20   super vnamquamque singillatim exequitur:, ac per manus im-
positionem omnis illa multitudo virginum, anulo desponsationis
eterne sponso, ihesu domino, typice subarratur[5].
Vt autem ad electam domini ordinatim quod faciendum fuerat
<exequendo peruentum est> :, mox, mirum in modum intra se
25   <rapta>., celestique iubare perlustrata., vidit intellectualibus
oculis omnia que venerandus pontifex[6], legendo, benedicendo.,
coronam capiti, digito misticum anulum imprimendo, ceteraque
ad officium huiusmodi pertinentia per ordinem exequendo., sub
eodem tempore foris visibiliter actitabat in corpore;, dominum
30   nostrum ihesum christum, eternum et verum pontificem, intus in

Lord, the spouse of virgins, through the integral promise of chastity and fidelity. Learning of this, Beatrice was filled with immense joy. Quickly she tried with all her might and devotion to make herself worthy of so great a mystery, and during the short delay she tried carefully to adorn herself with great devotion to go out to meet the bridegroom.[1]

Why say more? The most fitting day to carry out this mystery arrives namely the day of the Lord's ascension when our redeemer, by the presence of his glorified humanity, wedded the church triumphant in heaven to himself in an eternal marriage. Without delay the group of virgins is brought before the prelate to be consecrated in the usual way, and Christ's bride is placed among them in a suitable place, with attendants standing around. The bishop is ready and discharges his duty over each of them in the usual way and order, and by the imposition of his hands all that multitude of virgins is symbolically betrothed to the Lord Jesus, the eternal bridegroom, by the ring of betrothal.

When the bishop came in the usual course to do what was to be done to the Lord's chosen, she was wonderfully seized from within and enlightened with heavenly brightness. She saw with the eyes of her mind that everything the venerable pontiff was doing in a visible bodily way—reading, blessing, placing a crown on her head and a mystical ring on her finger and the other actions pertaining to this office—our Lord Jesus Christ, the true and eternal

---

1. Mt 25:6

anima sua sensibiliter exercere. Nam ab ipso sponsationis
anulo subarrata, non transitorie sed perpetue fidei sponsionem
eodem accepit in tempore; non solum propitiationis gratiam
in hoc seculo :, sed et perpetue beatitudinis gloriam in futuro,
35 domino sibi finaliter promittente.

77 Quam sponsionis prerogatiuam cum accepisset electa domini.,
tanta mox interius.iocunditatis et exultationis repleta est dulcedine :, quod, exteriorum sensuum officio quiescente, quid secum
extrinsecus ageretur nequaquam potuisset aduertere :, sed quo-
40 tiens ad pontificem, aliquid illorum que huic ministerio congrue-
bant debuisset acceptura accedere., nonnisi manibus obsequentium
sustentata, suam valuisset illi presentiam exhibere. Sed et expleto sacramentali officio, per totum illum diem et-si frequentia
populi fuerit vndique constipata :, nichil tamen <eorum> que
45 videre vel audire de rebus exterioribus eam contigit, vel discernere vel aduertere potuit ; sed cuncto rerum forensium strepitu quiescente :, delectabiliter inter sponsi sui brachia requieuit.
Tanta vero fuit illa spiritualis dulcedinis habundantia quam ex
hac interna desponsatione // f. 308 c sua virgo domini est
50 adepta :, quod per totam continue sequentem ebdomadam, ac si
iugiter a celesti sponso, secum inter flores et lilia quiescente, per
idem <tempus> amplexata fuerit., ita feruens et recens, incessanter illius in anima perdurauit. Et vt olim beato patriarche
iacob dies quibus pro rachel eum seruisse scriptura commemo-
55 rat [7]., pauci videbantur pre amoris magnitudine :, sic etiam
abbreuiati dies illi beatrici, sponsi sui copia perfruenti., sub
celerrimo videbantur breuitatis compendio pertransire.

78 Sed numquid illius anima liquefacta est vt dilectus eius
locutus est [8]? Huius rei testes fuerunt ille, plene dulcedinis et
60 deuotionis, ex oculis eius distillantes in habundantia lacrime.,
quarum impetum ante sponsi faciem, quotiens ad mentem illi
redijt :, et-si voluisset, nulla tamen valuisset cohibere instantia.
O vere felicem huius animam., quam eternus cum patre dei filius, in huius se-
65 culi procelloso turbine fluctuantem adhuc, in sponsam sibi, cum tantis gratiarum arris, aptare dignatus est:; cui christus dominus, ante carnis depositionem,
inter electas virgines mansionem [.] non distulit in celesti thalamo preparare.

pontiff was doing sensibly in her soul. For betrothed by the engagement ring, she then received at the same time the pledge not of a transitory but of an everlasting fidelity, for the Lord promised her forever not only the grace of forgiveness in this life, but also the glory of perpetual happiness in the next.

77 When the Lord's chosen one, Beatrice, had received this privilege of betrothal, she was immediately so filled with sweet joy and exultation that she took no notice of what was going on around her, since her outer senses were asleep. As often as she had to approach the bishop to receive some of the things pertaining to this rite, she could not present herself to him unless supported by the hands of those around her. When the sacramental rite was over, even though she was closely surrounded by people all day long, she could not notice or attend to anything she happened to see or hear around her. All the noise of outer things was hushed, and she rested sweetly in the arms of her spouse. Such was the abundance of spiritual sweetness which the Lord's virgin received from this inner betrothal that, for the entire week following, the abundance remained continuously in her soul as glowing and as new as if she were constantly embraced the whole time by the heavenly bridegroom resting with her among the flowers and lilies. And just as Scripture says that the days the blessed patriarch Jacob served for Rachel's sake once seemed few to him because of the greatness of his love,[2] so also the days seemed short and to pass very quickly to Beatrice who was enjoying the abundant riches of her spouse.

78 Did her soul melt when her beloved spoke?[3] The witnesses were tears full of sweetness and devotion flowing abundantly from her eyes. Even if she had wished to stem their flow before his face, no insistence could stem them, whenever the thought of the bridegroom came to her mind. O truly happy soul which the Son of God, co-eternal with the Father, deigned to prepare as his bride with such pledges of grace while she was still tossed to and fro on the stormy waves of this life. For her, Christ the Lord did not delay preparing a dwelling place in the heavenly bridal chamber with the chosen virgins, even before she had laid aside the flesh.

2. Gn 29:18   3. Sg 5:6

¶ DE FREQUENTATIONE
SACRAMENTI CORPORIS ET SANGUINIS CHRISTI
xviij. capitulum

79 Quis digne referre valeat, cum quanta deuotionis affectione
sacramentum dominici corporis hec beata frequentare consueuerit ;
quantum spiritualis delectationis in eius perceptione gustauerit. ,
quis dignis sermonibus explicabit? Tanto quippe desiderio solebat
ad communionem illius viuifici corporis aspirare continue : , quod,
appropinquante termino quo salutari sacramento communicare
proposuit, non solum mens illius interius spirituali <repleretur>
dulcedine. , verum etiam ad omnia membra corporis foras erum-
pens delectatio, velut nectar inebrians, eam, spirituali quodam
tripudio, fecerit exultare. Vt autem percipiendi tempus aduenit,
et hoc sacriste, secundum morem, innuere debuit, cuius obsequio
desiderium suum adimplere necessarium habuit. , continuo, liquefacto // f. *308 d* corde, lacrimarum potius habundantia, vel
quadam immoderati risus insolentia, desiderium cordis sui, quam
signo prodidit : , et quantumcumque renitendo resistere voluisset,
quod interius sentiebat per talia foris indicia demonstrauit.

80 Recepto vero salutis nostre viuifico pabulo, tota mens illius
diuine consolationis et gratie plenitudine replebatur continuo : ,
sicque confestim exteriorum sensuum destituebatur officio, quod
nec pedibus incedere nec manibus valuisset aliquid operis exercere.
Frequenter etiam accidit, vt per totum diem vix vnius verbi
sonitum vel edere vel proferre potuerit : , sed, pre nimia spiritualis
dulcedinis habundantia, viribus corporis destituta, languescens in
lectulo decumbebat. Sed quid miri? Sicut enim cera liquescit a facie
ignis. , deus quippe noster ignis consumens est[1] : , sic spiritus
illius a facie deifici sacramenti. , corpusque a facie spiritualis
iocunditatis, ab interioribus ad exteriora manantis. , et sese per
corporis membra mirabili quadam dulcedine diffundentis ; , quotiens ad id,[2] communicando, propinquare se contigit : , totiens,
pre maxima gratitudinis affluentia, liquescere consueuit.

HER FREQUENT RECEPTION OF THE SACRAMENT OF
CHRIST'S BODY AND BLOOD
Chapter Eighteen

79 Who can worthily tell with what devout affection this blessed one was accustomed frequently to receive the Sacrament of the Lord's Body? Who shall fittingly explain in words what spiritual delight she tasted in its reception? With such desire did she aspire continually for Communion with that life-giving Body that, when time for Communion came, not only was her mind filled with inner spiritual sweetness, but the delight breaking out in all the members of her body, like an inebriating nectar, made her move excitedly in a kind of spiritual dance. When the time to receive came and, according to custom, she had to give the sacristan notice (it was through the sacristan's compliance that she had to fulfill her desire) she showed her heart's desire more by the melting of her heart, the abundance of her tears or her unusual unrestrained laughter than by a sign. By such outer disclosures she showed her inner feelings, however hard she willed to resist.

80 Beatrice's whole mind was immediately filled with the fullness of divine consolation and grace when she had received this life-giving food of our salvation. Forthwith she lost the use of her outward senses so she could neither walk nor do any work with her hands. It often happened that for the whole day she could speak scarcely a single word, but lay languid and helpless in bed because of the excessive spiritual sweetness. But why wonder at this? Just as wax melts before the fire[1]—and our God is a consuming fire[2]—so her spirit melted before the deifying Sacrament, and her body before the spiritual joy flowing out from her interior and diffusing itself throughout her members with a wonderful sweetness. Thus she used to melt with enormous gratitude as often as she approached the Sacrament to communicate.

1. Ps 67:3   2. Dt 4:24, Heb 12:29

81 Fuit autem in hoc statu per annorum multa curricula [3] : ;
sed postea, copiosius superna se perlustrante clementia, mutatus
est hic status <admirabilis> in alium, magis vtique mirabilem. ,
magisque proficuum. Nam vt prius ad perceptionem salutaris
eucharistie, liquefactis viribus, languescere consueuit in corpore : ,
sic e contrario, sub illo secundi status tempore, quotiens ad
viuificum hoc sacramentum hanc contigisset accedere. , vim in
se diuine virtutis experiens. , ab omni, si qua grauabatur, egritu-
dine, repente conualuit in perceptione spiritualis alimonie, . diuina
se gratia visitante.

Sed non mirereis, o lector, si, secundum diuersos status
anime beatricis, hoc sacramentum, cum vnum idemque subsistat in se, tam
diuersos effectus habuerit : ; cum idem sit, et dulcedo lactentium, et refectio
robustorum.

82 Hec ergo de profectu fidelis anime paucis ideo prelibauimus,
quod, demonstratis ascensionis gradibus. , qualiter ad perfectionis
statum, continue proficiendo, beatrix nostra peruenerit. , sequenti
relatione sub ∥ *f. 309 a* compendio demonstremus. Verum, vt
narrationis progressibus lectoris tedium non incurrat. , superest vt,
vbi a primo statu, videlicet inchoantium, ad secundum, id est
proficientium, hec dei famula transmigrauit. , finem hic primus
liber accipiat : ; vt, reparatis viribus, ad ea que sequuntur liberius
exprimenda, sermo noster in antea conualescat.

Explicit liber primus.

81 Beatrice was in this state for many years, but later by a more abundant divine mercy this admirable state was exchanged for another, more wonderful and more profitable. Whereas earlier she used to languish in body and lose her strength when she received the Eucharist, on the contrary in the second stage, whenever she approached this life-giving Sacrament, she experienced the divine strength in herself and quickly recovered from all sickness, if she had any, by receiving the spiritual food and the visitation of divine grace.

You should not be astonished, dear reader, if this Sacrament, which remains one and the same in itself, had such different effects according to the different states of Beatrice's soul, since the same thing gives sweetness to the suckling and nourishment to the robust.

82 We have set forth in a few words the progress of a faithful soul so that, having shown the steps of her ascent, we may show briefly in the following narrative how our Beatrice, by continuous progress, arrived at the state of perfection. But in order that the reader not grow weary at the steps of the narration, it seems fitting that the first book should end here when the servant of God had passed from the first stage, that of beginners, to the second, that of the proficient. In this way our discourse may rather gain strength to express more freely the matter which follows.

HERE ENDS THE FIRST BOOK

83 INCIPIUNT CAPITULA LIBRI SECUNDI.

Expliciunt capitula.

Siquitur liber secundus. Et primo :

83   THE CHAPTERS OF BOOK TWO

The end of the Chapters.

Book Two follows, beginning with:

¶ DE FREQUENTATIONE SACRE SCRIPTURE IN QUA VENERABILIS BEATRIX STUDIOSE SE EXERCUIT
Primum capitulum

// fol. 309 b **84** In superiori libro pauca de multiplici gratiarum infu-
sione, qua dilectam suam dominus, in benedictionum suarum dulcedine,
preuenire dignatus est, sub compendio demonstrauimus : ; nunc autem qualiter
accepta dona gratie, studiosa negotiatione fideliter ampliauerit. , et pecuniam
domini sui sollerti vigilantia dispensauerit in hoc seculo. , prout ipse dominus
annuerit, et quantum id breuius explicare potuerimus ostendemus. At quoniam,
inter omnia que proficientibus in huius vite via magis vtilia comprobantur. ,
sacra scriptura potissimum locum obtinet ; , vtpote que, tendentium ad patriam
preuia, suo conductu fidelium gressus dirigit. , prima suo lumine tenebras
erroris expellit : , et, quasi pro muro a dextris gradientium et sinistris, iter
preuia preparat et ostendit ; , idcirco de hac primam narrationis nostre seriem
inchoabimus : , et quam studiose beatrix nostra suis eam temporibus exercuerit ostendemus.

85 Aperuerat quippe diuina gratia sensum dilecte sue vt intelli-
geret scripturas ; et propterea omnes, tam actionum suarum quam
affectionum motus, intrinsecos videlicet et extrinsecos, iuxta
consilium scripturarum informare studuit. ; et quodcumque sibi
proficuum in huius vite transcursu vel fuit, vel fore potuit. , hoc,
ex omni scripturarum campo latissimo, cotidie, totis ingenij sui
viribus, exquisiuit. Sicque factum est vt, iuxta scripture consilium,
aduersario carnis sue, donec cum <illo> graderetur in huius vite
via, cito <contendens>, et illicitos motus noxiarum voluptatum
ad nichilum assidue redigendo supprimeret : , et totam vite sue
continentiam. , nouis cotidie <virtutum> floribus adornaret.

Nam ex omnibus que vel legere vel audire consueuit, illuminato
nimirum intellectu. , granum e palea, videlicet e littere cortice
nunc moralem nunc misticum sensum elicere studuit : , et secundum ea que vel *// f. 309 c* subtiliora vel profundiora, diuino
dictata spiritu <pro salutis humane subsidio>, repperit. , ad
sublimitatem perfectionis tendere didicit : , nichil horum quasi
neglectum preteriens, in quibus aliquam instructionis aut edificationis materiam deprehendit.

THE FREQUENT USE OF SACRED SCRIPTURE AND THE VENERABLE BEATRICE'S EARNEST STUDY OF IT
Chapter One

84 In the previous book we showed briefly a few of the many graces with which the Lord, in the sweetness of his blessings, deigned to anticipate his beloved, but now we shall show, with the Lord's help and with what brevity we can, how Beatrice in a faithful, zealous, businesslike way increased the gifts of grace received, and managed her Lord's money in this world with alert watchfulness.[1] But Sacred Scripture holds first place among everything which proves most useful to those progressing in this life, because it goes before the faithful, directing their steps on their way to the homeland.[2] It first expels the darkness of error by its light, and like a wall to the right and left of those on the march, it goes before, preparing and showing the way. Therefore we shall begin our narrative with Scripture, and show how zealously our Beatrice devoted herself to it.

85 Divine grace had opened the beloved's faculties to understand the Scriptures, and therefore she was zealous to form all her actions and affections, within and without, according to the counsel of the Scriptures. Daily with all her might she sought in the vast field of the Scriptures what was or could be profitable to her passage through life. Thus, as Scripture advises, quickly coming to grips with her enemy the flesh, while she was still on the way with him in this life,[3] she carefully suppressed and brought to nothing the illicit movements of evil pleasures, and daily adorned her general self-restraint with fresh flowers of the virtues. From everything she used to read or hear, she carefully sought with her enlightened mind to draw the wheat from the chaff,[4] that is, now the moral and now the mystical meaning from the hull of the letter. She learned to tend toward the heights of perfection by means of the subtler or deeper things she discovered dictated by the divine spirit for human salvation. She neglected and passed over nothing in which she found some matter of instruction or edification.

---

1. Lk 19:23   2. Ex 14:29   3. Mt 5:25   4. Mt 3:12

86 Vnde frequenter accidit, vt de profundis misteriorum diuine pagine, siquando lectio suis se conspectibus ingessisset quam, proprij viribus ingenioli, nullatenus intelligere valuisset :, ne diutius incassum fatigaretur illius spiritus, repente gratia spiritus
40 sancti, illuminans intellectum illius, <affuerit>., et quasi fulgur de celo veniens in huiuscemodi studentis ingenium, in momento temporis illustrauit., et quesitum diutius intelligentie fructum, non quidem ad fruendum iugiter quod humanis sensibus impossibile fuit., sed ad vtendum eo pro tempore demonstrauit.
45 Nam quotiens illum oculis demonstratum intelligentie, viuacitate sensus apprehendere memorieque commendare disposuit :, totiens, suo frustrata desiderio., quod querebat humani vires ingenij prorsus excedere, docente experientia, protinus intellexit.
Miro quoque caritatis affectu desiderare consueuerat, vt omnes
50 quos in sorte sanctorum eterna predestinatione dominus euocare dignatus est, archana sacre scripture misteria, quibus ad bene viuendum informari poterant, intelligere valuissent. At quoniam effectum huius desiderij nequaquam assequi potuit :, super hoc saltem, alios pro facultate virium oportunis temporibus instru-
55 endo., suo vel in parte desiderio satisfecit.

℩ DE FREQUENTATIONE
ET EXERCITIO TEMPORIS
Secundum capitulum

87 Erat enim huic dei famule sollicitudo permaxima., ne quan-
5 tulamcumque temporis particulam incassum amitteret :, et, sine profectus sui lucro, vel modica concessi temporis portio deperiret. Tanta quippe fuit, in spiritualibus exercendis negotijs, et tam vigilans illius occupatio :, vt in omni tempore, circa concepta negotia procuranda, tempus sibi defuerit., aut quod negligentibus
10 aut remissis interdum superesse consueuit. (hijs inquam quorum intentio // f. 309 d magis otijs quam negotijs omni vacare delectabatur in tempore)., huius [1] presertim, ad explendum sue inten-

86 Thus it often happened that, if ever her reading concerned some mysterious matter in the divine pages of Scripture which she could not at all understand with her limited powers—lest her spirit weary itself in vain for a long time—, the grace of the Holy Spirit was suddenly present enlightening her intellect. Coming like a flash of lightning from heaven[5] into the mind of this student, it immediately illumined it, and showed that the long sought for fruit of understanding was not for continual enjoyment—a thing impossible for human senses—but to be used at that time. Whenever she sought to apprehend with her keen sense and to commend to her memory what had been shown to the eyes of her intelligence, she was frustrated in her desire and immediately understood by experience that what she sought exceeded human capacity.

With a wonderful charity she used to desire that all those whom the Lord had called by eternal predestination[6] to the heritage of the saints should be able to understand the mysteries of Sacred Scripture by which they could be formed to right living. But since she could in no way attain this desire, by teaching others at opportune times she satisfied her desire, at least in part.

HER USE OF TIME
Chapter Two

87 Beatrice was extremely solicitous not to lose the smallest particle of time or to let any part of the time granted slip away without profit and progress. Such was her vigilant attention to spiritual exercises that time was always lacking for what she had undertaken, and while negligent and slack religious (I mean those who delight in ease rather than in effort) sometimes used to have time to spare, God's virgin complained of not having time enough to

5. Lk 17:24   6. Col 1:12

tionis votum, virgo dei continua se querebatur indigentia laborare.
Proinde, non sine graui cordis sui molestia sufferre potuit, quod
plerosque robustos et corpore validos interdum vacantes otio
deprehendit :, cum e contrario tanta illius in rebus spiritualibus
excercitatio fuerit, quod nulla temporis protractione, singulis
singulariter immorando, quod exequebatur explere potuerit., sed,
sola impediente temporis angustia, frequenter infecta, nonnumquam etiam intacta, superexcrescentia sibi negotia necessario
dereliquit.

88 Nam instar torrentis rapidi, superuenientium incessanter occupationum cumuli[2], cum illorum[3] quibus in mente beate femine
vacationis tempus expeteret. (non habentis interdum vnde quod
petebatur exsolueret.) ita fortissimum huius virginis animum
quasi procellosis fluctibus obruebant :, vt plerumque, caligante
iudicio rationis quid prius, quidve posterius admittendum fuerit.,
aut quantum horum cuilibet immorandum, aduertere vel discernere
non valeret. Quod enim discernendi tempus esse potuit ;, ubi
singule virtutes,· suis agminibus constipate, pari simul impetu,
per continue recordationis impulsum illius in animo confluentes,
nunc componendis moribus., nunc affectibus ordinandis, nunc
agendis gratiarum actionibus., nunc contemplationis oculo dei
beneficijs intuendis., ceterisque spiritualibus exercitijs, quorum
non erat numerus, exequendis, hunc[4] indesinenter inuigilare
<compellerent>., et, velut infatigabili quadam improbitate mutuo
decertantes, ad priorem queque promotionis gradum, impetuosis
moribus adspirarent.

89 <At> quoniam, vt prediximus, ad vacandum singulis[5], impediente temporis dumtaxat indigentia, prout oportunum fuerat
intendere non valebat, ex <illarum qualibet> vnum, quem magis
sibi proficuum existimabat, articulum eligens, vt a memoria non
excideret, in scriptis hunc redigere consuescebat:; et post <hoc>

fulfill what she had vowed. It cost her great grief of heart to see so many of the robust and able bodied meanwhile lolling in idleness, while she, on the contrary, was so busy in spiritual exercises that by no extension of time could she dwell on them one by one, but from sheer lack of time she often had to leave her ever-increasing affairs unfinished, and sometimes could not even begin them.

88 Like a rushing torrent the heaps of unceasing, endless occupations, with their deadlines to be met, so overwhelmed, as if by stormy waves, the energetic mind of this virgin, who sometimes had no means of meeting them, that often her judgment as to what to do first and what second was darkened, and she could not decide how much time was to be spent on each. For what time for discernment could there be when each of the virtues, crowding together in their ranks, flowing steadily into her mind and memory, compelled her constantly to be alert now to compose her conduct, now to order her affections, now to give thanks, now to watch for God's benefits with a contemplative eye, and to engage in all the numberless exercises of the spiritual life? Each of these virtues vied with one another in a kind of tireless competition to gain first place.

89 But since for sheer lack of time, she could not conveniently attend to each of the virtues as she should have, as we said, she used to take one point—whatever she thought more useful—and set it down in writing so it could not slip away from her memory. After this, asking the help of divine mercy, she would divide her

// *f. 310 a,* in adiutorium inuocata diuina clementia, per singulos
45 temporis portionem partita [6], nunc hos nunc illos [7] oportunis
meditationibus exercebat [8]. Sicque factum est vt spiritualibus
<occupationibus> iugiter impedita, nec a bonorum operum exe-
cutione, pro temporis nimia parcitate, deficeret :, nec, illius aliquando prolixitate grauata., vel modicam eius particulam otijs
50 indulgeret. In dominicis vero festiuitatibus, et sanctorum natalicijs
occurrentibus pro consuetudine retinebat, vt ipsi materie de qua
solempnitas agebatur pro tempore, ad hoc deportata portiuncula
temporis, officio meditationis intenderet. Et sic per succedentia
tempora, gratiarum actioni iugiter immorans, et in templo cordis
55 sui domino solempnizans, <apud> se cotidie spiritualia gaudia
renouaret.

90 Intellexerat etiam, ex iugi experientia, multa se diuine gratie
munera percepisse :, et plurima percepturam fore. Quapropter,
in omni tempore, magna premebatur sollicitudine, quatenus iam
60 adepta dei beneficia sic in opera pietatis exercitando conuerteret,
vt, in diuine presentia maiestatis, et iam indultis aliquatenus se
dignam ostenderet., et in posterum indulgenda, per nullam sue
presumptionis incuriam, impediret. Quantum etiam superne dulcedine gratie, copiosius infundebatur interius :, tantum nimirum,
65 eius beneficijs indigniorem se reputans, sub diuini timoris iugo
districtius se premebat. Nec defuit electe sue, diuini respectus
miseratio :; sed quo, sub potenti manu dei, semetipsam humiliauit
attentius., eo se nimirum sentiebat, in die visitationis, per infusionem gratie plenioris, a domino sublimius exaltari. Ob hoc
70 ergo, singulari quodam affectu temporis beneficium in veneratione semper habuit ; et sic in omni tempore suis profectibus
intendere studuit :, ac si, finito tempore quod presens fuit, aliud
postea non succederet ad exequendum quod preteritis ante temporibus inchoauit.

time among the individual points and meditate now on some, now on others. Even though she was always hindered in her spiritual occupations, she did not fail in doing good works for lack of time, nor did she allow herself the least bit of ease despite being burdened with the great number of them. On Sundays and the feast-days of the saints she had the custom of setting aside a certain portion of time to meditate on the theme of the solemnity. Thus as time passed she continued constant in thanksgivings, offering the Lord worship in the temple of her heart and daily renewing spiritual joys within herself.

90 From constant experience she understood that she had received many gifts of divine grace, and that she would receive many more. Therefore she was always very anxious to turn to the practice of works of piety the divine benefits she had already received, so that in the presence of the divine Majesty she might show herself to some degree worthy of what she had received and not impede future gifts by some presumptuous carelessness. The more plentifully infused she was inwardly with the blessings of heavenly grace, the more unworthy of such benefits she thought herself, and the more strictly she bent under the yoke of divine fear. But there was no lack of the mercy of divine grace in his chosen one, and the more carefully she humbled herself under the mighty hand of God,[1] the more sublimely exalted she felt herself on the day of visitation[2] by the infusion of more plentiful grace. Therefore she always venerated the gift of time in a special way, and she was always zealous for her progress, as if, when the present moment passed, there would be no more time in which to carry out what she had previously begun.

1. 1 P 5:6   2. 1 P 2:12

⦉ DE TRIPLICI
EXERCITIO SPIRITUALIUM AFFECTIONUM
Tercium capitulum

91 Et quoniam de tempore iam pauca prelibauimus, // f. *310 b*
superest, vt ad ea que gessit in tempore reuertamur. Cum ergo
virgo Christi totis intentionis viribus ad <perfectionis> vite
fastigium aspiraret, triplici sollicitudine cepit affici quodam in
tempore :, quarum exercitio nitebatur omnipotenti domino seruitium beneplacitum et gratum obsequium exhibere. Harum sollici-
tudinum prima fuit de peccatis suis condigne satisfactionis voluntas et affectio. Secunda de receptis a deo beneficijs deuota
gratiarum actio. Tercia vero, per caritatis obsequia, diuine voluntatis honorisque promotio.

In primo statu recogitabat assidue, qualiter, per ordinatam emen-
dationem vite et condignum fructum penitentie, valuisset attingere
quid sibi defuit ; aut quid sibi necessarium extitit ad <assequen-
dum> ipsum fructum penitentie quem quesiuit, iugi meditatione
conabatur inquirere :, et inuenit : meram de commissis penitentiam,
in via perfectionis necessario debere virtutes ceteras anteire.

92 Verum, cum eam quam in diebus suis egerat penitentiam, ad
omnimodam delictorum suorum expiationem, ad plenum sufficere
posse non crederet., et de multis quas in sua conuersatione
deprehendit negligentijs., ad multa se teneri penitentie opera,
proprie discussionis examinata[2] iudicio, minime dubitaret : ne,
propter inopiam penitentie, omnipotenti deo grauioribus delictorum debitis obligata maneret ;, omne quodcumque, diuina clementia fauente, bonum opere perpetrauerat., aut quidquid aduer-
sitatis in corpore vel in corde pertulerat., hoc, omisse loco
penitentie, creatori suo christo domino consecrabat.

Nec hoc tamen satisfactionis contenta genere, per idem tempus
erexit se contra se mirabili zelo penitentie, cotidianis gemitibus, lacrimis et singultibus, ac etiam corporalis discipline castigationi-

THE TRIPLE EXERCISES OF HER SPIRITUAL AFFECTIONS
Chapter Three

91 Since we have just set forth a few things about time, it remains for us to consider what Beatrice did with her time. Since Christ's virgin aspired to the heights of the perfect life with all the force of her intention, she began at a certain time to be affected by a threefold solicitude by which she strove to offer Almighty God a pleasing service and an agreeable obedience. The first of these solicitudes was the will and the affection of making worthy satisfaction for her sins. The second was giving devout thanks for the benefits received from God. The third was the advancement of the divine will and honor by the duties of love.

In the first state she carefully considered how she could attain what she lacked through an orderly amendment of life and worthy fruits of penitence, or else she tried by continual meditation to inquire what remained necessary for her to attain the fruits of the penitence she sought. She found that a pure unmixed penitence for faults committed must necessarily precede the other virtues on the way of perfection.

92 However, she could not believe that the penance she had so far done in her life could fully suffice for the total expiation of her faults, and when she examined herself, she little doubted she was obliged to many works of penitence for the many negligences she found in her life. Therefore, in place of her penitence she consecrated to Christ the Lord, her creator, any good work she accomplished by the help of divine mercy, or any adversity she suffered in body or heart, lest she remain in debt to Almighty God for her graver faults through lack of penitence.

But not content with this type of satisfaction, Beatrice at the same time straightened herself up with a marvelous penitential zeal, purifying herself with daily sighs, tears, and sobs as well as with physical discipline. Proclaiming herself guilty for each lapse,

bus se purificans. , ream se per singula clamitans, ream se iudicans, et quasi nichil dignum venia, preteritis temporibus, in
35   conspectu diuine maiestatis ob- // f. *310 c* -tulerit, ita se, continuis
operibus penitentie, per illud tempus ad placandam diuine pietatis
clementiam animauit. Non solum autem ad satisfaciendum domino
de commissis hunc penitentie laborem exercuit : , sed vt, elimata
peccatorum scoria, purum et mundum in se diuine gratie, cuius
40   infusionem prestolabatur omni tempore, domicilium prepararet,
hijs operibus omnibus penitentie sese, cotidiane renouationis
exercitio, reparauit. ; Sanctum quippe sciens <S>piritum discipline fictum effugere. , nec in <corde> peccatis subdito, delica-
tam illius gratiam habitare.
45   **93** Cum autem in hoc penitentie laborioso studio per vnius mensis
spacium, aut circiter, omnipotentis dei famula se gessisset, deprehendit in via virtutis minus quam putauerat <in hoc statu se
proficere>, minusque quam decebat honoris et reuerentie, diuine
maiestatis aspectui se prebere. Quapropter, omisso, de quo pre-
50   diximus, interim hoc minus fructuoso statu penitentie : , mox ad
secundum illum, id est gratiarum actionis statum se contulit. , et
peccata sua vel dimittenda, vel etiam vlciscenda diuine iusticie,
pro sue voluntatis arbitrio, reseruauit.
Sicut ergo sub illius prioris status tempore totas intentionis sue
55   vires ad agendos dignos fructus penitentie puniendasque tam
cogitationum quam operum minutias excitauerat : , ita, sub hoc
secundo statu, totas eque vires affectionis sue, recogitandis et
recognoscendis, largitatis diuine collatis sibi beneficijs, tam naturalibus quam gratuitis, indesinenter applicuit ; et copiosam per
60   singula materiam gratiarum actionis inueniens. , diuine largitatis
magnificentiam copiose per singula benedixit.
94 De naturalibus quidem, quod ad ymaginem suam illam creauerat, et memoriam, rationem intellectumque contulerat. , ei deuotas
gratiarum actiones exhibuit : ; de gratuitis vero, tanto nimirum
65   <deuotiores>] obtulit. , quanto copiosiora dona gratie sibi collata
// f. *310 d* diuinitus, ex ipsorum donorum singulari magnitudine,
deprehendit. Siquidem preter ea que cum omnibus simul christia-

and judging herself guilty, and as though she had offered nothing worthy of pardon in the sight of divine Majesty in times past, she stirred
herself at that time to appease divine mercy by continuous works of
penitence. Yet not only did she exert this penitential labor to satisfy the
Lord for past offences, but she also re-fashioned herself by all these
penitential works in an effort at daily renewal in order to prepare in
herself, once the dross of sin had been eliminated, a pure and clean
dwelling place for divine grace, whose infusion she at all times
awaited. She knew that the Holy Spirit of discipline flees from the
deceitful[1] and that his delicate grace does not dwell in a body subjugated to sins.

93 When this servant of Almighty God had exerted herself in this
laborious penitential zeal for about a month, she noticed that she had by
these means progressed in the way of virtue less than she had thought
and that she was showing less honor and reverence in the sight of the
divine Majesty than was fitting. Wherefore for the time being she
dropped this less fruitful state of penitence of which we have been
speaking and quickly betook herself to the second stage, that of
thanksgiving, leaving her sins to be either forgiven or avenged by divine justice, as he thought best.

Just as in the former state she had aroused all the energy of her intention to bringing forth worthy fruits of penitence[2] and to punishing small
failures of thought and deed, so in this second state she unceasingly
applied the energy of her affection to re-thinking and recognizing the
benefits of divine generosity lavished on her, both those given naturally
and those given gratuitously. Finding abundant matter for thanksgiving
in each of them, in each she abundantly praised the magnificence of
divine generosity.

94 For the natural qualities Beatrice gave God devout thanks that he
had created her to his own image and had given her memory, reason,
and understanding. For the gratuitous, however, she gave yet more
devout thanks, for she grasped, through their singular magnitude, the
greater abundance of the graces divinely given her. In addition to

1. Ws 1:4   2. Mt 3:8

nis, tytulum videlicet christianitatis et lauacrum regenerationis,
acceperat., hoc specialiter ei de gratuitis dei donis accreuerat :,
70   quod innocentem et immaculatam, corde simul et corpore, de
mundanis fluctibus ad portum monastice tranquillitatis aduexe-
rat.; quod bone voluntatis propositum perseueranter in eius
corde firmauerat.; quod ab vniuersis mortalium peccatorum sordibus impollutam illius affectionem, omni vite sue tempore, custo-
75   dierat.; quod denique mentem eius celesti benedictione cotidie,
respectuque superne dignationis et gratie visitabat. Super hijs
omnibus et singulis, assueta repetitione, bonorum omnium largi-
tori singulares gratiarum actiones exhibuit, et non tam de commissis, de quorum indulgentia presumebat, quam de ceteris a
80   quibus illam innoxiam et immunem superna miseratio custodierat.,
assiduas, omnipotentis dei clementie, gratiarum hostias offerebat.
Pluris equidem estimabat quod a perpetratione criminum hanc
diuina clementia, sub vmbra sue protectionis, absconderat :, quam
si omnium peccatorum genera commisisset, et ea, gratuite mise-
85   rationis indulgentia, dominus a recordationis sue memoria de-
leuisset.
95 De spiritualibus quoque nostre redemptionis operibus, quibus
dominus jesus christus, nascendo de virgine, cum hominibus
conuersando, predicando, baptizando., miracula faciendo., tan-
90   demque crucis obprobria perferendo., moriendo, resurgendo.,
nostreque nature substantiam in diuine maiestatis dextera collo-
cando, salutis nostre negotium explere dignatus est.: hec deuotissima, deputatis ad <hoc> horarum spacijs[3], speciales illi gratiarum actiones eo nimirum deuotius obtulit :, quo, per hec nostre
95   redemptionis opera, confractum antiquum dampnationis cyro-
graphum., et reparatum totius humane salutis beneficium intellexit. Post hec etiam de cunctis operibus misericordie, que per
celestium et terrestrium creaturas copiose distribuitur, // f. 311 a
et precipue de salutifero sui corporis et sanguinis sacramento,
100   quod humano generi, tam in sui commemorationem, quam in
sustentationem et viaticum in huius peregrinationis exilio, dere-

what she had received with all Christians, namely the title of Chris-
tianity and the laver of regeneration,[3] these special benefits had come
to her by God's free gift: that he had brought her, innocent and un-
stained in heart and body, from the eddies of the world to the harbor
of monastic tranquillity; that he had steadily strengthened in her heart
the intention of her good will; that he had kept her affections from all
sorts of pollution and the filth of mortal sin all during her life; and
finally that he daily visited her mind with heavenly blessing, and with
the gaze of his favor and grace. To the giver of every good gift she
repeatedly gave individual acts of thanks for each and every one of
these things, and constantly offered sacrifices of praise to the mercy
of Almighty God not so much for what she had committed (she
presumed their forgiveness) as for the other things from which divine
mercy had kept her innocent and free. She valued more the fact that
divine mercy had hidden her in the shadow of its protection from
committing crimes than if she had committed all kinds of sin and the
Lord had blotted them out from his memory by a free gift of his
mercy.

95 At the hours of the office assigned to them, Beatrice very devoutly
gave thanks for the works of our redemption by which our Lord Jesus
Christ deigned to carry out the work of our salvation: by being born
of a virgin, living with men, preaching, baptizing, working miracles,
and finally, bearing the disgrace of the cross, dying, rising again, and
placing the substance of our nature at the right hand of the divine
Majesty.[4] This she did more devoutly as she understood that the old
writ of damnation was destroyed,[5] and the salvation of all mankind
repaired through this work of our redemption. In addition, she
copiously thanked divine liberality and bountiful generosity for all the
merciful works which God abundantly distributes through heavenly
and earthly creatures, and especially for the health-giving sacrament
of his body and blood, which he left to the human race both as a

---

3. Tt 3:5   4. Heb 12:2   5. Col 2:14

liquit :, hec, diuine liberalitatis et munificentie largitatem, copioso
gratiarum actionis obsequio, magnifice collaudauit.

96 Cum autem in hoc statu gratiarum actionis paulo morosius
quam in illo priori., de quo prefati fuimus, incessabili studio se
gessisset, ad illum quem tercio loco posuimus statum, indilate se
contulit :; in quo diutius quoque quam in duobus prioribus, in-
stinctu diuine complacentie. perdurauit. Fuit autem ipsi in hoc
statu, summum et insatiabile desiderium omnipotenti deo gratum
atque beneplacitum seruitutis offerre <ministerium>., nichilque
penitus horum inexpertum derelinquere, quibus, suffragante corporalium virium adminiculo, creatori suo gratum valuisset obsequium exhibere.

Tantam vero desiderij latitudinem in hoc statu conceperat :, et
voluntatis insatiabilem appetitum., vt, expletis omnibus quecumque iuxta virium facultatem agenda susceperat., nichil dignum
diuino conspectui patrasse se crederet :, et inutilem semper ancillam se reputans, ex amplitudine desiderij, cui nullo laboris
obsequio satisfacere potuit, incommoditatis afflictionisque dis-
pendia non minima sustineret.

97 Omnis quippe voluntas et desiderium beate femine semper
erecta manebant ad dei beneplacitum exequendum :; et idcirco
nullo discretionis consilio, desiderio suo modum imponere potuit,
<quia>, super omnem corporalium <virium> sufferentiam,
ad exequendum voluntatis diuine beneplacitum, dilatatis affectionis viribus, sic excreuit., vt omnes mortis species gra-
tanter pertulisset in corpore., sed <et> infernalium penarum
libenter sustinuisset tormenta pro tempore :, dum per <hoc>
ad expletionem insatiabilis desiderij sui, quod de diuine maiestati
gratum obsequium exhibendo conceperat., aliquatenus potuisset,
corporalium virium opitulante suffragio, perueni- // f. 311 b -re.

98 Verum, quoniam hoc assequi prorsus impossibile iudicauit.,
cum hinc mira diuine caritatis dulcedine traheretur intrinsecus.,
illinc ex insatiabilitate concepti desiderij grauaretur., affecta
medullitus, sic diuersis et pene contrarijs affectionibus onerata :

reminder of himself and as its support and travelling provision in this wandering exile.

96 When Beatrice had conducted herself with constant vigor in this state of thanksgiving a little longer than in the prior state of which we spoke, she forthwith betook herself to that state we put in third place, and in this, at the instigation of divine good-pleasure, she remained longer than in the former two. Here she had a huge and insatiable desire to offer Almighty God a sweet and pleasing ministry of her service and to leave untried nothing by which she could offer pleasing obedience to her creator, as far as bodily strength allowed.

In this state she conceived such a vast desire and insatiable appetite of will that she thought she was doing nothing worthy of divine notice, no matter what she undertook and fulfilled according to her strength. Always considering herself a useless servant,[6] she suffered no small discomfort and grief from the amplitude of her desire which she could not satisfy by any service or labor at all.

97 The entire will and desire of this blessed woman always remained erect and alert to follow God's good-pleasure. She could impose no discreet measure on her desire, because in the expanding force of her affection she so grew to follow the divine good-pleasure that, regardless of any bodily suffering, she would willingly have borne in her body any sort of death. She would even have gladly suffered the torments of hell for a time, provided she could in this way to some extent fulfill by her physical energies her insatiable desire to please the divine Majesty.

98 But Beatrice judged this to be wholly impossible, and being interiorly drawn one way by a wonderful sweetness of divine love and another way being burdened with insatiable desire, she felt affected to the marrow of her being by diverse and almost contrary

6. Lk 17:10

virium etiam corporalium, in tanto discrimine necessario, detrimenta sustinuit. Vnde et hijs diebus in egritudinis languorem incidit., quam non sine graui quoque molestia pertulit., donec pius misericordiarum dominus et hunc statum, de quo prediximus, in 140 alium, electe sue condescendens inedie, pietate solita, commutauit.

⸿ DE EO QUOD IN CONUERSATIONE CETERARUM MONIALIUM PROFECTUS SUI LUCRUM <EXQUISIUIT>
Quartum capitulum

99 Erat quoque beate femine consuetudo laudabilis, vt omnes
5 quos dei seruitio mancipatos per habitum religionis aspexerit:, velut sanctos et electos dei <famulos> honoraret., et in vnoquoque virtutem quam imitaretur exquireret, presertim in sanctimonialibus monasterij sui; quarum mores et vitam omni sollicitudine considerationis oculo satagebat inspicere:, quatenus, ex
10 aliene comparatione perfectionis, in oculis suis ipsa sibi vilesceret., et quod imitaretur virtutis exemplum, in ceteris inueniret. Cum autem in hoc statu considerationis, oculos intentionis sue cepisset attollere., et, instar apis argumentose, de diuersis floribus mellis sue dulcedinem haurientis: huius obedientiam., illius
15 patientiam., alterius deuotionem., alterius misericordiam., sicque per singulas deducto consideratjonis intuitu, ceterarum virtutes fulgore lucido cerneret enitescere., <c>epit, hinc quidem, <ex> eo quod tot virtutes bonorum operum in hominibus inuenisset., exultando diuiine bonitati gratiarum actiones exsoluere:, illinc
20 vero, quod aliarum comparatione nichil virtutis eatenus acquisisse se crederet., magnis dolorum stimulis estuare. Satagebat itaque virgo domini, totis intentionis sue conatibus, ad virtutum illarum executionem semetipsam accingere.; et // f. 311 c quidquid in aliarum conuersatione vel honestum <deprehendit
25 aut utile>, totum proprijs conabatur viribus adimplere. **100** Verum, cum in hoc quoque laborioso negotio multo iam tempore desudasset, et nimis arduum ad explendum, pro desiderij sui latitudine, deprehenderet:, omissis interim alijs, ad quarum

affections. In this crisis she unavoidably suffered the loss of her physical energies. Therefore at that time she fell into languor and sickness which she bore with great difficulty till the Lord of mercies came with his usual kindness to the aid of his famished chosen one and changed this state we have been speaking of to another.

HOW SHE SOUGHT PROFIT AND PROGRESS IN HER COMPANIONSHIP WITH THE OTHER NUNS
Chapter Four

99 The blessed woman Beatrice had the laudable custom of honoring as holy and chosen servants of the Lord all those whom she saw consecrated to divine service by the religious habit, and of seeking in each of them virtue to imitate, and this especially in the nuns of her own monastery. With utter watchfulness of a perceptive eye she pondered their conduct and life so that by comparison with others' perfection she might abase herself in her own eyes and find in others a model of virtue to imitate. When in this state of reflection she began to raise her eyes and, like a busy bee gathering its sweet honey from different flowers—this one's obedience, that one's patience, another's devotion, another one's mercy and so on—looking at them one by one, she saw the virtues of the rest shining brightly. Then she began, on the one hand to give exultant thanks to divine goodness because she found so much virtue and so many good works among human beings and, on the other hand, to be much disturbed and pained because she believed she had so far acquired no virtue in comparison with them.

The Lord's virgin then girded herself with all efforts of her intention to imitate their virtues, and she tried to accomplish with her own energies whatever she found respectable or useful in their behavior.

100 When she had exerted herself for a long time in this laborious occupation and found it too hard to accomplish because of the breadth of her desires, she proposed looking at and imitating one

similitudinem mores et actus suos iam diutius expleuerat, vnam
30 ex aliarum numero, quam in perfectionis itinere ceteris instantius
ambulare conspexit., oculis considerationis <sue> deinceps,
imitandi causa, proposuit; et qualiter in ordinis obseruantia,
modo conuersationis, orationum meditationum<que> frequentia., ceteris quoque virtutum operibus exercendis, illam gerere se
35 conspexit:, ita, conformatis moribus ad illius similitudinem, per
viam virtutis incedere studuit., donec, per assiduum imitandi
laborem, illius moribus etiam et suos aptissime conformauit. Siquidem ex illius imitatione, multarum negligentiarum ineptias
euitare didicit., eiusque laudabili studio prouocata, in via manda-
40 torum dei sui, decetero sollicitius ambulauit.

❡ DE DUABUS CELLIS QUAS IN CORDE SUO CONSTITUIT
Quintum capitulum

101 Cum ergo venerabilis jesu christi famula, mirabili feruore
deuotionis ad assequendum dilecti sui fauorem et gratiam aspi-
5 raret:, cepit quodam tempore[1] seuere, circumspectionis oculis,
angulos intentionis et affectionis <sue> discutere., ne quid
forsan in illis ipsis, vel igorantie vel negligentie latesceret quod
oculos diuine maiestatis offenderet, et eius contra se indignationem
aliquatenus prouocaret.
10 Cum ergo predictum inquisitionis <officium> exercere cepisset,
et scrutari iherusalem in lucernis[2]:, duas quasdam, id est cordis
pigritiam eiusque comitem indiuidu<a>m., illius[3] videlicet in-
constantiam, latentes in secreto quodam illius angulo deprehendit.
Mox ergo, contra premissa tarditatis et inconstantie morbosa
15 contagia, totis inuectionis et indignationis studijs excitata, //
f. 311d duas in corde suo cellulas e regione constituit:, in
quibus, ad expugnanda prefata contagia pariterque a cordis sui
finibus expellenda., contraria medicamina collocauit.

nun out of them all, whom she saw walking in the way of perfection more earnestly, for a while leaving aside the others whose lives and deeds she had long been imitating. In whatever way she saw this one nun behave in regard to the observances of the Order, her mode of life, the frequency of her prayers and meditations, and the other exercises of virtuous works, Beatrice would try to walk in the same way of virtue, conforming her behavior to that of the other, until by the assiduous labor of imitation she had aptly conformed her own behavior to the other's. Thus by imitating the other nun, she learned to avoid many silly negligences, and she was stimulated by the other's praiseworthy zeal to walk more solicitously in the way of the commandments of her God.

THE TWO CELLS SHE ESTABLISHED IN HER HEART
Chapter Five

101 Because the venerable handmaid of Jesus Christ aspired with a marvelous fervor and devotion to win the favor and grace of her beloved, she began at a certain time to examine severely the intricacies of her intentions and affections with circumspection, lest any ignorance or negligence be concealed in them to offend the eyes of divine Majesty and to provoke his indignation against her in the slightest.

When she had begun this inquiry and this search of Jerusalem by torchlight,[1] she found lurking in a certain secret corner of her heart two things, laziness and its inseparable companion, inconstancy of heart. Quickly therefore she aroused herself against these deadly diseases of indolence and inconstancy, using all her skill in invective and indignation, and against them she established in her heart two cells in which she stored medicine to fight them and drive them from her heart.

1. Zph 1:12

102 In inferiori igitur cella peccata sua vel negligentias, aut cetera
quibus ad humilitatis studium excitari potuit, contra morbum
inconstantie, per contrariam affectionem dimicatura, constituit : ;
quibus et generales humane conditionis miserias, in augmentum
roboris et solamen auxilij, superaddidit. ; quas etiam, senario
numero computatas, in suo <quaslibet> ordine, deuote recordationis officio, collocauit [4].

Harum prima est illa miserabilis humani generis et dura peccandi
<conditio>:, quam nec infans valet effugere cuius est unius
diei vita super terram.

Secunda est illa non minus miserabilis humane conditionis afflictio., qua varijs passionibus indesinenter afficitur., et fame, siti
et frigore, nuditate ceterisque corporalibus miserijs et infirmitatum
passionibus oneratur.

Tercia vero, numquam in eodem statu permanens et mutans
humane conditionis instabilitas:, que, dum varijs, per singula
momenta, desideriorum passionibus et temptationum incitamentis
affligitur., numquam in tranquille pausationis portu, confirmata
plene fruitionis copia, desiderio stabilitur.

At vero quarfum esse dixerim. : huius mundi continuum et plenum
doloribus et erumpnis exilium :, cuius dispendiosa protractio,
cum humanam affectionem mundanis fluctuationibus obruit., ad
perpetue libertatis desiderium ascendere non permittit.

Quinta vero mundani huius exilij tenebrosa prolixitas et obscu-
ratio veritatis : ; que dum cordis oculos excecat interius., etiam
<exterioris> actus hominis frequenter in peccatorum labem
precipitat, et illius gressus a via rectitudinis alienat.

Porro sexta mortalitatis est ineuitabilis et inuisa condicio : ;
que, dum repente non preuidetur adesse, se denunciat, volentes
// f. 312 a nolentes<que>, de commissis rationem reddituros,
ad extremum vsque [ad] quadrantem, diuino nos cotidie iudicio
representat.

Has ergo quas prediximus necessarias conditionis humane mise-

102 In the lower cell she placed her sins and negligences, or other things which could stir her zeal for humility, thus fighting against the disease of inconstancy by a contrary affection. To these she added the general miseries of the human condition, to build up her strength and prescribe assistance. She stored them in her devout memory in their own order by sixes.

The first of these is that miserable and enduring wont of the human race to commit sin, something not even an infant alive one day on earth can avoid.

The second is that no less miserable affliction of the human condition by which it is endlessly affected by various sufferings and burdened with hunger, thirst, cold, nakedness, and other bodily miseries and the sufferings of infirmity.

The third is the instability of the human condition, always changing and never remaining in the same state. While it is knocked about at every moment by passionate desires and temptations, it never attains stability of desire in the haven of a quiet resting place, confirmed in the copious abundance of enjoyment.

The fourth, I would say, is the long-drawn-out exile of this world, full of sorrows and troubles. While its harmful protraction overwhelms human affection with worldly fluctuations, it does not permit it to rise to the desire for everlasting freedom.

The fifth is the long darkness of this earthly exile and the obscuring of the truth, which blinds the inner eyes of the heart and also frequently hurls the actions of the outer man into the ruin of sin, and draws his steps away from the path of righteousness.

The sixth is the inevitable and hateful condition of mortality. When not foreseen to be close, it abruptly announces itself and daily presents us, willing or unwilling, to divine judgment, where we shall have to give an account of what we have done and pay to the last penny.

Beatrice stored in the lower cell of her heart these necessary

rias., aliasque, ad expellendum inconstantie morbum, vt iam
prelibauimus, efficaces, in inferiori cordis sui cella constituit :,
et quotiens ab illius [5] importunitate vexari se doluit., totiens ad
55   hanc [6] fugiendo se contulit, et, predictis humiliationis humane
collectis in vnum antidotis, donec a finibus cordis sui debellata
recederet [7], illius infatigabiliter <insolentiam> expugnauit.

103 In <superiori> vero cellula, quecumque bona vel naturalia
vel gratuita, diuina pietate largiente, receperat :, contra torporis
60   infestationem dimicatura. composuit. Insuper et illa spiritualia
dona fidelitatis et gratie, quibus se cotidie preueniri, in bene-
dictionibus dulcedinis diuine, perpendit :, necnon et omnia gene-
ralia que pro reparatione salutis humane pius dominus, nascendo.
patiendo, moriendo, seu etiam resurgendo vel ad celos ascen-
65   dendo, patrauit., cum hijs que, in medio terre, pro commoditatibus
nature humane, momentis singulis operari non desinit., <h>ec,
inquam, et hijs similia, de scripturarum ortis in recordationis
cophinum vndecumque collecta, simul cum propriarum beneficijs
gratiarum, in superiori, sicut prediximus, cellula collocauit.

70   **104** Sicque factum est, vt, quotiens aut inconstantie morbo
aut ignauie torpore vexata, nimia se grauari importunitate
conspiceret :, ad harum alterutram confugiens, importunas illarum molestias, contrarijs collectarum virtutum agminibus, a
cordis sui finibus effugaret. Cum enim inconstantie leuitas
75   illius animum titillare presumpsit :, tunc, vt prediximus, ad
inferiorem cellam indilate confugiens, cum innumerabiles humane conditionis miserias ibidem in vnum recordationis cumu-
lum <adunatas> perspexit :, non erat vnde iam amplius in-
solescere libuit. Sicque, fugata procul inconstantie leui- // f. 312 b
80   -tate, vite maturitas et morum grauitas in <domicilio> cordis
sui locum sibi potissimum, <securo> potita <dominio>, ven-
dicauit. Similiter et cum torporis grauitas ingruebat., ad supe-
riorem mox cellam se transferens, innumeris dei beneficijs et

miseries of the human condition and the others mentioned above which are effective in expelling the disease of inconstancy. As often as she grieved to find herself vexed importunately by inconstancy, she fled to this cell, and collecting together these antidotes to human humiliation, she would untiringly assault the insolence of this vice until, overcome, it withdrew from the territory of her heart.

103 In the upper cell she gathered whatever goods, natural or gratuitous, divine kindness had bestowed on her, and she arranged them for her fight against attacks of torpor. Moreover she pondered those spiritual gifts of fidelity and grace by which she was daily outstripped by blessings of divine sweetness and all those general deeds which the loving Lord did for the reparation of human salvation by being born, suffering, dying and also rising again and ascending into heaven, together with his ceaseless activity at every moment in the midst of the earth for the advantage of human nature. These and others like them, gathered in the basket of memory from all over the gardens of Scripture, together with the benefits of her own graces, she placed as we have said in the upper cell.

104 Thus it happened that as often as Beatrice was vexed by the disease of inconstancy or by cowardly sloth and saw herself excessively burdened with them, she would flee to one of these cells and drive their rude attacks from her heart with the opposing troops of the stored-up virtues. When the fickleness of inconstancy tickled her soul, then she would, as we said, promptly fly to the lower cell where she would gaze into the innumerable combined miseries of the human condition, gathered up by her memory; then there was no more room for inconstancy to wax stronger. So with light inconstancy put to flight, maturity of life and serious demeanor claimed first place in her heart and enjoyed secure dominion. Similarly when torpor lay heavy on her, she quickly moved to the upper cell and was soon cheered by the innumerable benefits of God and

gratiarum donis in ea repertis, exhilarata continuo, non erat iam
85 amplius vnde, alicuius molestie pondere grauata, torpesceret.,
aut, desidie molibus onerata, succumberet :; sed statim in illius
animo iocundata serenitas, aut renouata securitas, effugatis
contrarijs passionibus, enitebat.

❡ DE QUINQUE SPECULIS CORDIS SUI
Sextum capitulum

105 Talibus ergo considerationis studijs, virgo domini diebus ac
noctibus occupata., cum ab pleniorem sui cognitionem festinaret
5   attingere:, nec, iuxta desiderium cordis sui, premissis meditationum occupationibus ad plenum id valeret efficere:, nouas
quasdam, et suo proposito commodiores, excogitabat assidue;
per quas ad sui cognitionem [et], abiectionem., <humiliationem,
se> sperabat efficacius peruenire.
10 Erectis ergo rursus quinque speculis coram oculis cordis sui:,
faciem interioris hominis in hijs, iugi meditatione, satagebat inspicere. Quorum primum fuit celum supra se.; secundum terra
subter se.; tercium proximus iuxta se; quartum vero dominus
jesus christus, expansis in cruce brachijs, ante se.; quintum
15 autem mortis assidua recordatio penes se.
106 In primo, diuini timoris, oblatam <adspectibus> considerationis sue materiam satis accommodam et copiosam inuenit. Nam
quotiens ad celorum fastigium oculos eleuauit:, totiens illi distric-
tus iudex et iustus dominus, aspectu sue diuinitatis omnia
20 conscientiarum abscondita penetrans, ad mentem redijt.; et ne
quid delitesceret in abscondito cordis sui, quod oculos seueritatis
illius offenderet, acerrimi stimulata timoris aculeo, formidauit.
Quapropter, vt omni tempore suis grata aspectibus appareret.,
omni custodia cor suum communire non distu- // f. 312 c lit:,
25 et, tamquam sponsa suis decorata monilibus, in virtutum se
ornamentis <adspectui> diuine presentie, deuota sollicitudine,
continue preparauit.
107 In secundo speculo, materiam humilitatis, oblatam oculis sue

the gifts of grace found there. Then there was no room for her to become torpid, weighed down by some trouble, or to succumb to some heavy burden of sloth. Instead, a joyful serenity or renewed security quickly shone forth in her soul, while the contrary passions were put to flight.

THE FIVE MIRRORS OF HER HEART
Chapter Six

105 When the Lord's virgin, Beatrice, taken up with these considerations day and night, hastened to come to greater self-knowledge and could not do so fully according to her heart's desire by the aforesaid meditations, she eagerly devised new ones, more suited to her purpose, by which she hoped to attain more effectively to self-knowledge, abjection, and humiliation.

She erected five mirrors before the eyes of her heart, and strove by constant meditation to perceive the face of her inner man in them. The first of these was heaven above her; the second, the earth beneath her; the third, her neighbor next to her; the fourth, the Lord Jesus Christ with arms outstretched on the cross before her; and the fifth, the assiduous remembrance of death alongside her.

106 In the first mirror she found presented to her gaze and consideration abundant matter well-suited to the fear of God. For as often as she raised her eyes to the heights of heaven, the strict Judge and just Lord who with his divine glance penetrates everything hidden in the conscience, returned to her mind, and she feared with sharp, cutting fear lest anything lurk in the secret of her heart which might offend those severe eyes. Therefore she did not delay fortifying her heart with great care, that she might please his gaze at all times and, like a bride adorned with her jewels, she continuously prepared herself carefully with the ornaments of virtue for the divine presence and sight.

107 In the second mirror Beatrice constantly saw matter for

considerationis, indesinenter aspexit : ; nam [1] quid fuerit aut quid

³⁰ fore debuerit ostensa cordis aspectui <conculcare> sub pedibus
suis, illi, per singula momenta temporum, ipsa terre vilitas in-
dicauit.

108 In tercio vero speculo materiam caritatis erga proximorum
exercendam dilectionem inuenit. Nam cum ad ymaginem dei fac-

³⁵ tum hominem et ad eius similitudinem ymaginatum aspexit :,
ad illius dilectionem ex precepto caritatis se teneri, docente
rationis iudicio, certissime recognouit.

109 In quarto compassionis et deuotionis materiam copiosam
repperit. . quotiens ad pendentem dominum in cruce, considera-

⁴⁰ tionis oculum eleuauit. Cum enim speciosum forma pre filijs
hominum, confossum et cruentum in cruce pendentem inspexit.,
et illius plagis atque vvlneribus oculum meditationis adhibuit :,
quasi cera liquescens a facie ignis., ita, compassionis igne liquefacta, illius anima tota simul in calice christi vvlnerum emanauit ; .

⁴⁵ <Hec> illius requies <hec> delectatio :, <hec>, contra mundi
miserias et erumpnas huius seculi., illius refugium et protectio
semper fuit. Quamobrem in hoc <dulcissimo> recordationis
speculo, cordis aspectum imprimere semper habuit dulce :, et
illius suauissima dulcedine delectata, ceteris prelibatis, illud deuo-

⁵⁰ tius omni tempore coluit., et quasi iugiter presentem christum
in cruce pendentem aspexit ; ita deuote, meditationis intuitu,
illius memoriam in mente retinens :, per obliuionis obstaculum
hanc a corde suo recedere non permisit.

110 Ad quintum vero speculum quotiens aspectum recordationis

⁵⁵ attollere contingebat., totiens, per timoris spiritum, ad recogita-
tionem mortis extremique iudicij pauefacta, continuo ad omnem
se patientiam, humilitatem., obedientiam morumque constantiam
// *312 d* accingebat., sciens se tanto gratiorem diuino tunc appa-
rituram conspectui :, quantum, virtutum lumine clariorem, tem-

⁶⁰, pore sue vocationis eam <contingeret> inueniri.

humility offered to her consideration, because the vileness of the earth shown to her indicated that at every moment she was trampling underfoot what she was and would have to become in the future.

108 In the third mirror she found matter for the charity to be exercised in the love of her neighbors, for, since she saw man made to the image of God and framed according to his likeness, she recognized with certitude and by reasonable judgment that she was bound by the precept of charity to love him.

109 In the fourth mirror Beatrice found copious matter for compassion and devotion as often as she raised her eyes to consider the Lord hanging on the cross. When she saw him who was beautiful above the sons of men,[1] pierced through, bloody and hanging on the cross, and when she meditated on his stripes and wounds, then her whole soul, melting with the fire of compassion like wax melting before the fire, flowed totally into the chalice of Christ's wounds. This was her rest, this her delight; this was always her refuge and protection against the miseries and troubles of this world. Therefore she always found it sweet to apply her heart's gaze to this sweetest mirror of remembrance. Delighted with it, she always cultivated it more carefully than the others, and almost always saw Christ hanging on the cross in front of her. Thus devoutly keeping his memory in mind by meditation, she did not let it depart from her heart through forgetfulness.

110 As often as she happened to raise the glance of her remembrance to the fifth mirror, she was frightened by the recollection of death and the final judgment, and immediately girded herself to practice all patience, humility, obedience, and constancy of behavior, knowing that she would then appear more pleasing to the divine gaze as she would be found more outstanding in the radiance of virtues at the time of her call.

1. Ps 44:3

ℂ DE SPIRITUALI MONASTERIO
QUOD IN CORDE SUO CONSTITUIT
vij. capitulum

111 Aliam quoque considerationis materiam, sub eodem tempore [1],
satis mirabilem, satisque proficuam adinuenit; in qua multo
feruore deuotionis exercitare se studuit, sperans per diuersa
meditationum exercitia, fugato <torpore> desidie, profectus sui
fructum facilius acquirere quem quesiuit.

Ad similitudinem ergo visibilis claustri, quod per materiales officinas disponitur, et prelatorum officio gubernatur:, virgo domini
spirituale claustrum in corde suo constituit:; et, de diuersis
collectam virtutibus, tam prelatorum quam ministrantium nume-
rosam in eo multitudinem aggregauit.

112 Huic autem monasterio deus omnipotens abbatis officio
prefuit, qui et ipsum edificando constituit., et interius exteriusque, virtutis sue potentia, conseruauit. Virtus autem dilectionis
et spiritualis affectionis intentio, prelati sui comites indiuidue,
disponenti de profectibus huius claustri [2], studiosum satagebant
obsequium exhibere.

Sub hoc autem abbate, ratio secundum, id est abbatisse locum
et nomen obtinuit; cui similiter, in vita sua ne per temerarium
iudicium insolenter quid ageret., virtutum custos discretio ministrauit. Priorisse vero loco pariter et officio, sapientie virtus huic
monasterio prefuit:; que, post abbatissam, ceterarum virtutum
officia, conseruando quaslibet in suo robore, gubernauit.

Sub hac quoque, prudentia subpriorisse gessit officium:; que
<sub actus> extrinsecos, vt ad ordinis obseruantiam prompti
semper existerent., eos iugiter instruendo bonisque moribus in-
formando, potissimum tenuit principatum.

Caritas autem huius claustri fuit celleraria:; que, dum in dei
proximique dilectione semetipsam exercitare non desinit., //
ƒ. 313 a omne quod in gratiarum donis a deo collatum accepit.,
ad proximorum subleuandam indigentiam subministrat liberaliter
et effundit.

THE SPIRITUAL MONASTERY
SHE ESTABLISHED IN HER HEART
Chapter Seven

111 About the same time Beatrice found another kind of consideration, quite wonderful and quite profitable. In it she exercised herself with much devout fervor, hoping by different meditative exercises to put torpor to flight and to acquire more easily the fruit of the progress she sought.

The Lord's virgin established in her heart a spiritual cloister resembling the visible cloister which is arrayed with material workshops and governed by prelates, aggregating from the different virtues in it a great multitude of prelates and subordinates.

112 Almighty God held the office of abbot of this monastery; he built it and preserved it, within and without, by the strength of his power and virtue. But love and spiritual affection, the close companions of their prelate, zealously busied themselves obeying the one who provided for the welfare of this cloister.

Under this abbot, reason held the second place and name, that of abbess. Discretion, the guardian of virtues, ministered to her, lest, through rash judgment, she do anything insolent and out of place in her life. The virtue of wisdom held the place and the office of prioress in this monastery. Subordinate to the abbess, she regulated the duties of the other virtues, keeping them all in their own firmness.

Under her, prudence discharged the job of subprioress; she had the important task of teaching, supervising exterior exercises, so that they would always be at hand according to the Order's observances.

But charity was the cellarer of this cloister. Continuously exercising herself in the love of God and neighbor, she liberally ministered and poured out whatever gifts and graces she received from God to relieve the needs of her neighbors.

35 Compassio vero vicem et officium infirmarie non inconuenienter
exercuit :; que cunctis infirmitate corporum sive morum op-
pressis., deuoto condescensionis obsequio ministrauit.

113 Cantrices vero, iuncta simul cum constantia [3] gratitudo, diuinis vacando laudibus inter se tali concentus suaui modulo con-
40 cordabant :, vt et gratitudo diuine pietatis clementiam deuotis
laudibus indesinenter attolleret., et ne per leuitatis excessum
aliquotiens inordinate difflueret., illius impetum, iuncta sibi constantia, refrenaret. Fides autem et spes sacristarum officio funge-
bantur in hoc spirituali monasterio :; que, dum ex se virtutes cete-
45 ras illustrabant., quasi tot lucernis atque lampadibus quot diuersarum virtutum generibus, huius claustri templum eximie deco-
rabant. Oratio vero deputata fuit vt altari semper assisteret :, et,
numquam ab iniuncto vacans officio, presertim in diuini sacramenti presentia, pro suis aliorumque necessitatibus vtilitatibusve
50 continue domino supplicaret.

114 Sobrietas et patientia prefuerunt simul refectorio :, quatenus,
in ciborum habundantia, sobrietas excessum in appetendo comprimeret ;, et, ea deficiente, mentis impetum a murmure patientia
cohiberet.

55 Negotiorum vero curam sollicitudo susceperat; que singulos cordis
affectus et membra corporis, ne vel ad momentum temporis
resoluerentur otio, pertinaciter ad deputata sibi ministeria dirigebat.
Castitas seu pudicitia fuit in hoc monasterio fenestraria :; que
dum fenestris quinque sensuum, caste circumspectionis officio,
60 prefuit., immaculatam interius, virginalis puritatem innocentie
custodiuit.

Hospitalitas autem hospitumque receptio deputata fuit considerationis obsequio :; que, iuxta meritorum exigentiam, superuenientes
quasque cogitationes admittere studuit., et, receptis in hospicio
65 cordis vtilibus et // f. *313 b* honestis., importunas quasque vel
inutiles ab hospicij sui terminis effugauit.

Ad portam vero monasterij prouidentia se collocauerat :; que,
quid intromittendum excludendumve rationis foret iudicio., dis-
creto circumspectionis oculo diligentius obseruabat [3].

Compassion quite rightly exercised the role and duty of infirmarian, and ministered graciously with devout service to all who were weighed down by weakness of body or of character.

113 The chantresses, gratitude and constancy, agreed together in applying themselves to the divine praises with gentle harmony that gratitude might ceaselessly praise the divine loving-mercy, and together with constancy, her companion, curb her impulse lest she sometime be inordinately carried away by an excess of levity. in faith and hope discharged the duty of sacristans in this spiritual monastery. While by themselves they made the other virtues illustrious, they adorned this monastic church remarkably with as many lamps and torches as there are different kinds of virtues. Prayer was assigned to be forever present at the altar, never taking time off from her duty, ceaselessly interceding to the Lord for her own and others' needs and advantages.

114 Sobriety and patience together were in charge of the refectory, so that when there was an abundance of food, sobriety would restrain excessive appetite, and when food was short, patience would restrain the urge to murmur. Solicitude received charge of business affairs. She resolutely directed the affections of the heart and the bodily members, lest they be idle at the tasks assigned them even for one moment of time. Chastity or modesty was in charge of the parlors of the monastery. Being in charge of the five windows of the senses, she kept the purity of virginal innocence unsullied under her chaste circumspection.

Hospitality and the reception of guests were the assigned task of consideration. She endeavored to admit each incoming thought according to its merits. Receiving those useful and upright into the guesthouse of the heart, she drove the bothersome and useless away from that hospice.

At the gate of the monastery vigilance stationed herself, and with the discreet eye of circumspection carefully observed what should be admitted or excluded according to the judgment of reason.

⁷⁰ Huius autem monasterij custodes fuerunt humilitas et obedientia : ; que prescriptum virtutum conuentum ita circumcinxe-
runt, ex omni parte, sua custodia. , quod illarum nulli, presump-
tione propria, regularia claustri sui transcendere licuerit instituta.
115 Has omnes virtutes virgo domini, diebus singulis ad hoc
⁷⁵ speciali deputato tempore, post completorium scilicet, ad discussionis sue capitulum conuocabat ; et a supremis ad infimas
vsque cogitationes mittens accusatricem conscientiam. , quantum
eo die profecerint quantumve defecerint. , qualiter administra-
tiones suas gesserint. , vbi vel quantum excesserint, instantius
⁸⁰ <explorabat>. Si quas autem negligentes repperit aut remissas : ,
harum loco semetipsam, ad abbatisse, rationis scilicet iudicium
euocatam, de commissis suis acris se increpationibus accusabat.
Abbatissa vero, patris abbatis, id est dei omnipotentis, eam iudicio
presentabat : ; a quo suscepta, iusto iudicio, iuxta quod magis
⁸⁵ minusve deliquerat. , impositum sibi, de psalmorum lectionibus ⁴
aut genuflexionibus disciplinisve corporalibus, onus penitentie
cotidie reportabat.

⁋ DE DUABUS MONASTERIJ SUI CUSTODIBUS
HUMILITATE SCILICET & OBEDIENTIA
Octavum capitulum

116 Cum autem circa gubernationem, correctionem, reformatio-
⁵ nem huius claustri multo tempore desudasset ; , factum est, vt,
nimia considerationum harum inquietudine fatigata, pondus solli-
citudinis huius sustinere diutius, pre multo penarum atque curarum tedio, non valeret. Quapropter, hac omissa sollicitudine. ,
ex dictarum virtutum numero duas tantum eligere studuit, idest
¹⁰ predicti claustri custodes. : humilitatem // f. *313 c* scilicet et
obedientiam : ; ad quarum exercitium, eo quod illarum efficatia
sub eo tempore plus indiguit, tanto liberius quanto iam expeditius,
de cetero se conuertit.

Humility and obedience were the wardens of this monastery. They so surrounded and guarded this convent of virtues on every side that none of them might transgress the regular boundaries of this cloister by their own presumption.

115 Every day at a set time, that is, after compline, the Lord's virgin Beatrice summoned all these virtues to an examination in chapter and, using conscience as an accuser, she insistently explored all her thoughts from the greatest to the least, how they had progressed or failed that day, how they had handled their administration, how or how far they had erred. If she found any of them negligent or slack, then she called herself in their place to the judgment of the abbess, that is, reason, and accused herself sharply for what she had done. But the abbess referred her to the judgment of the father abbot, Almighty God. Received by him, she daily brought back the burden of penance justly imposed on her— psalms, genuflections and bodily disciplines—according to how much or how little she had failed.

HUMILITY AND OBEDIENCE: THE TWO GUARDIANS OF HER MONASTERY
Chapter Eight

116 When she had toiled a long time in the governance, correction, and reformation of this cloister, it happened that she, worn out by the great disquiet of these considerations, could no longer bear the weight of this solicitude because of the vexation of many pains and cares. Therefore dropping this solicitude, Beatrice chose only two of the virtues, the guardians of the aforesaid cloister, humility and obedience. She turned to the practice of these more readily and more easily because she felt a great need for them at that time.

Studuit ergo, modis omnibus, ad sui cognitionem aciem mentis
attollere. , quatenus, ex ipsa sui cognitione, sibiipsi vilesceret : ,
et, iuxta verbum propheticum, in medio suiipsius. , humiliationis
sue materiam inueniret. Semetipsam igitur paruam et vilem reputans. , ceteris quibusque, tam maioribus quam minoribus, in omni
loco reuerentiam et honorem exhibuit : ; et quasi quelibet illarum
ex prelationis officio sibi preposita fuerit, ita, toto deuotionis
affectu singulis se subiciens, etiam illarum quamlibet honorauit.
Siquando semetipsam honorari seu commendari contingebat a
ceteris. , pro hoc ipso tantum magis ipsa, suo iudicio, despectiorem
se credidit : , quanto superuacuis honoribus se grauatam ab alijs
potius quam honoratam estimauit.

117 Quotiens autem a ceteris aut castigari, contempni vel vitu-
perari se contigit, aut illatam contumeliam imminere perspexit : ,
totiens, ad tutissimum patientie sinum confugiens, omne quod
aduersum occurrit, mire gratitudinis brachijs amplexari non distulit ; et quasi, pro sua correctione vel emendatione, specialiter a
diuina pietate sibi concessum idipsum in munere suscepisset : ,
ita corde letissimo, totius ignara rancoris aut murmuris, impositum
in humeris suis onus contumelie baiulauit.

In tantum igitur in hijs virtutibus, illas iugiter insectando, profecerat : , quod, tam minoribus quam maioribus, tam subditis quam
prelatis, ad parendum in preceptis, indifferenti zelo, debitricem
se crederet ; et quidquid ab aliqua pro mandato reciperet, non
ex necessitate uel ex tristitia, sed hylari spiritu, velut ex debito
protinus obediret. Sic ergo cum <omnibus> indifferenter obediendo se subdidit : , harum virtutum fructum suauissimum, annuente domino, meruit apprehendere quem quesiuit.

She applied herself, therefore, in every way to focusing her mind on self-knowledge so that by it she might despise herself and find within herself the matter of her humiliation, according to the prophetic word.[1] She reckoned herself small and of little value, and showed reverence and honor in every place to all the others, great and small. She honored each of them, subjecting herself to them with devotion and affection, as if each of them had been set over her as some kind of superior. If ever she happened to be honored or praised by them, she believed herself more despicable for this very reason, that she considered herself more burdened with empty honors than honored by others.

117 As often as she happened to be chided, scorned, or blamed by others, or perceived insult hanging over her, she fled to the ever-safe bosom of patience and quickly embraced every adversity with the arms of a wonderful gratitude. She bore the burden of insult laid on her shoulders with a joyful heart, wholly without rancor or murmuring, as if she had received from God's loving kindness, a special gift meant for her correction and amendment.

By her constant pursuit Beatrice made such progress in these virtues that she thought herself obliged to obey with equal zeal the orders of small and great alike, subjects as well as superiors. Whatever she received as a command from anyone, she obeyed immediately out of duty, not by necessity or with sadness, but with a cheerful spirit. Therefore, because she subjected herself to everyone impartially, she deserved to obtain, with God's help, the sweetest fruit of these virtues which she sought.

1. Jr 23:9

// f. 313 d

C DE ORTO FRUCTIFERO CORDIS SUI

ix. capitulum

118 Sub alio quoque tempore hec dei famula, per aliam considerationis speciem, ortum fructiferum in territorio cordis sui plantare
studuit : , in quo diuersarum virtutum olera seminauit.

Hunc autem ortum diuina gratia circumquaque muniuit : , et
contra spirituales nequitias[1] hunc, quasi murus, ex omni parte,
firmissima sui custodia, circumclusit. Prouidentiam autem ad
portam illius. , custodis atque portarie loco, constituit. ; per cuius
industriam, ne in vanum gratiam dei reciperet, ab orti sui finibus
omnem dissolutionis et insolentie proteruiam effugauit.

Numquam autem huic orto suo diligentius excolendo, sua presentia defuit ; sed per inquisitionem morum et actuum. , per
explorationem cogitationum, locutionum et operum, hunc cotidie
circumfodit : , fimo confessionis peccatorum suorum impinguauit. ,
et, cotidiano lacrimarum ymbre diligentius irrigatum, ad faciendum fructum acceptabilem domino, vigilanti circumspectionis
industria, preparauit.

119 Fuit autem, per omne tempus huius considerationis, in orto
suo iugiter excolendo continua sollicitudine virgo domini mirabiliter occupata, ipsum cotidie sagaci perlustratione circuiens : ,
et, ne qua labruscarum aut tribulorum in eo frutecta succrescerent,
quibus virtutum olera grauata succumberent. , intenta sollicitudine
diligentius inuestigans.

Hic igitur viciorum vrticas et tribulos cotidiane surculo confessionis euulsit : ; illic virgulta rosarum atque liliorum inseruit. Hic
fomenta[2] viciorum explantare non distulit : ; illic diuersa virtutum
semina seminauit. Nec dubium quin, talibus occupationum studijs
impedita, tanto plus laboris habuerit : , quanto sincerius ad perfectionis culmen aspirans, semper noxiarum, quas euelleret, her-
barum culmos repperit; in quibus euellendis eo studiosius illam nimirum exer- // f. 314 a citari oportuit. , que superflua hec et sponte

THE FRUITFUL GARDEN OF HER HEART
Chapter Nine

118 At another time this servant of God, by another kind of consideration, endeavored to plant a fruitful garden in her heart and in it she sowed the plants of the different virtues.

Divine grace walled this garden round on every side, and against the spirits of wickedness[1] firm self-control enclosed it entirely like a wall. It established solicitude at its gate as guard and portress, and by her care drove from her garden all impudence, dissoluteness, and insolence, lest she receive the grace of God in vain.[2]

Beatrice was never remiss in the careful cultivation of this garden, but through inquiry into her habits and acts, by exploration of her thoughts, words and deeds, she daily dug around it. With the dung of her confession of sins she enriched it, and by the hard work of careful circumspection she prepared it, carefully watered by the daily shower of her tears, to bear fruit acceptable to the Lord.

119 All during the time of this meditation the Lord's virgin was wonderfully occupied in cultivating her garden with continual solicitude, going around it daily, keenly examining it; she investigated it carefully with intense solicitude lest thickets of wild vines or thorny plants grow up to smother the plants of virtue.

By the hoe of daily confession Beatrice uprooted the nettles and thorns of vices, and planted rose bushes and lilies instead. Here she quickly tore out the stubs of vices, there she sowed the various seeds of virtue. No doubt impeded by such undertakings she had to work harder as she aspired more sincerely to the height of perfection and so always found stalks of harmful weeds to root out. In this work she had to be more energetic as she understood that

1. Eph 6:12   2. 2 Co 6:1

nascentia [3], nisi resecarentur assidue, profectum impedire ferti-
35 lium [4]., et eas facilius opprimere deprehendit. Sciebat quippe
sensus hominis pronos semper in malum existere [5] :; quapropter
in hijs excolendis eo viuatius instandum censebat esse continue,
quo, per cotidianum experimentum, in multis nociuis illorum
cernebat germina viciosa., (nimirum ob neglectum circumspectio-
40 nis debite) sponte quidem sed perniciose nascentia, pullulare.

        ❡ DE EO QUOD AD COGNITIONEM
    SUI IPSIUS OMNIMODAM ASPIRAUIT
          Decimum capitulum

120 Cum vero multo iam tempore, talibus occupata negotijs, in
5 orti sui negotio laborasset :, post hec, ad omnimodam et plenam
sui cognitionem, sub eodem tempore, magno cepit desiderio
aspirare. Satagebat ergo, diebus et noctibus, omnes exterioris
hominis actus et mores inquirere :; sed et affectiones singulas
cordis sui non cessabat, districte circumspectionis et inquisitionis
10 obtutibus explorare.
Cum autem per vnius fere mensis spacium in hoc inuestigationis
scrutinio continue laborasset, et nec virium suarum industria, nec
sensus acumine, quem querebat sue cognitionis statum ad plenum
apprehendere valuisset :, accidit vt, quodam tempore matutino, se
15 suis viribus diffisa, decetero, supplicandi gratia, totam intentionem
suam ad dominum deuota mente conuerteret; et, vt cognitionis
sue <quem> querebat statum, oculis sue considerationis ostenderet., preces, cum gemitibus et lacrimis, in diuine maiestatis
presentia, cumularet. Nec distulit pius dominus electe sue quod
20 postulabat impendere :; sed mox, illuminato spiritu cordisque
reseratis oculis, quam querebat sue cognitionis ostensionem, ab
ipso fonte misericordie meruit obtinere. Patefactis ergo proprie
cognitionis oculis, in-primis exteriores actus moresque perquirere
studuit :, ac deinde // f. 314 b profunditatem cordis sui, subtilis-
25 sima considerationis acie, perlustrauit.

these excessive and spontaneous growths would crowd out the fertile plants and easily smother them unless they were carefully cut back. She knew that man's senses are always prone to evil.[3] Therefore she thought that efforts to cultivate good plants were always more to be insisted upon because she knew from daily experience that, no doubt for lack of due care, the bad seeds would sprout spontaneously and dangerously in many harmful ways.

HOW SHE ASPIRED
IN EVERY WAY TO SELF-KNOWLEDGE
Chapter Ten

120 When Beatrice had worked for quite some time in her garden, she began at the same time to aspire, with great longing, to total and complete self-knowledge. She occupied herself day and night, therefore, inquiring into all the acts and habits of the outer man, but did not cease to explore strictly and cautiously each affection of her heart.

When she had been laboring steadily for about a month at this investigation, and neither by her efforts nor by her acumen had managed to grasp fully the degree of self-knowledge she sought, it happened one morning that, distrusting herself, she devoutly turned her whole intention to the Lord in supplication and increased her prayers, with sighs and tears, in the divine presence, asking that he show to the eyes of her consideration the knowledge of herself that she sought. Nor did the loving Lord delay granting his elect what she asked. Her spirit was quickly enlightened and the eyes of her heart were opened, and she deserved to obtain from the very fountain of mercy the indication of self-knowledge she had sought. With the eyes of self-knowledge now opened, she applied herself first to inquire into her exterior acts and habits, and then she scrutinized the depths of her heart with keen and subtle consideration.

3. Gn 8:21

121 Cum ergo, tam de naturalibus quam gratuitis bonis, vsibusque singulorum, qualiter ea videlicet in lucrum detrimentumve proprium exercitando conuerterit, attente cepisset inquirere :, continuo multarum negligentiarum frutices, quos antea, caligantibus oculis cordis sui, videre non poterat :, ex neglectu diuine gratie pullulantes, apertis cernebat obtutibus eminere. Naturalem quoque decorem anime, quem ex eterne similitudine diuinitatis impressum acceperat cum ad ymaginem et similitudinem suam illam deus creauerat., non modice <diffiguratum> ex eo cepit attendere[1], quod nobilissimam illius puritatem prout a deo collatam acceperat, per naturalium bonorum exercitium ex ipsius nature fertilitate nascentium, abstracta et illecta per affectiones contrarias, eatenus neglexerat custodire.

122 Sunt autem hec bona naturalia : naturalis videlicet et nobilis illa superbia, qua potiora vel sublimiora semetipsa querit amat et affectat anima :, qua iuxta consilium rationis caduca transcendit lubrica :, quaque detestatur et spernit, ex contrarie radice superbie pullulantia viciorum omnium incentiua.

Sunt et alia bona naturalia. : subtilitas et acumen ingenij :, que mentem eleuant ad indaganda queque subtilia. Naturalis quoque simplicitas, que inter diuersa mundi offendicula tanto liberior incedit et absque calumpnia :, quanto magis curiose diuersarum rerum indaginis expers fuerit et ignara. Per primam, id est ingenij subtilitatem, solet animus in celestium contemplatione proficere :; per secundam vero, summo bono simplici desiderio, tanto firmius quanto magis expeditius, inherere.

Est et aliud naturale bonum. : innata seueritas, cuius naturaliter interest omnia viciorum genera detestari semper et persequi :; quam, ne motu suo fines equitatis excedat., // f. 314 c aut, caligante iudicio rationis, in preceps corruat., iustitie normam in omnibus conuenit imitari.

Hanc e regione respicit illud naturale bonum :, pacis amans, cordis quieta tranquillitas :; que, dum, pacis consilio, nulli pro-

121 When Beatrice began to inquire attentively into the natural and gratuitous gifts, and how in her use of them she had turned them to her profit or loss, she perceived right away many brambles of negligence thriving on her neglect of divine graces, which she could not see earlier because her heart was blinded. She began to notice that the natural beauty of soul which she had received from the impressed likeness of the eternal Godhead when God had created her to his own image and likeness, was not a little disfigured. She realized that diverted and enticed by contrary affections, she had neglected to preserve, through the exercise of natural goods arising from the fertility of nature itself, the noble purity of soul she had received from God.

122 These are the natural goods: a natural and noble pride by which the soul seeks, loves, and pursues things better and more sublime than itself; by which through use of reasonable judgment it transcends what is frail and slippery and by which it detests and spurns all the incentives of vice springing up from the root of the opposite sort of pride.

Other natural goods also exist: subtleness and keenness of wit which raises the mind to investigate various subtleties. Also natural simplicity which walks more freely and without falsehoods amid the various stumbling blocks of the world as it is more inexperienced in and ignorant of curious investigation of various matters. Through the first, that is, subtlety of wit, the soul usually advances in the contemplation of heavenly things; through the second, it clings more firmly and more promptly in simple desire to the supreme Good.

There is another natural good: innate severity, which by its own nature always detests and attacks every kind of vice. It should act in accordance with the norms of justice in everything, lest it exceed the bounds of equity in its motives, or plunge over a precipice if reasonable judgment is clouded. This natural good respects the norms of justice. It is peace-loving, quiet tranquillity of heart. Out of desire for

prias acquiescit irrogare molestias, etiam equanimiter iniurias
60 sustinet alienas.

123 Sunt etiam alia nature bona quamplurima., qualia sunt:
<generositas>., largitas., habilitas., affabilitas., et cetera multa
similia., diuersis quidem diuersimode:, sed, ad acquirendum
vnum remunerationis denarium eterne., a domino distributa;
65 que, dum secundum mensuram donationis christi, illius dispen-
sante gratia, quisquis acceperit, eo grauius de suscepto talento
se puniendum esse meminerit:, quo minus ad laudem illius a quo
datum accepit, in suos aut proximorum vsus necessarios, idipsum,
iuxta concessam <sibi> cooperantem gratiam, erogarit.

70 Quod cum, illo cognitionis sue radio perlustrata beatrix, ihesu
christi famula, diligentius inspexisset., et nichilominus, ex hijs
naturalibus bonis ea, que sibi spiritualiter ex omnibus appropriata
fuerant, inuenisset, perpenderetque quid aut quantum ex eorum
neglectu, prout superius diximus, amisisset:, visum est ei summo-
75 pere necessarium hoc existere, quod puritati nature tota virtute
conformare se disceret, et, al illius assequendam rectitudinem, affectus sui conamine se conuerteret., seque in hac <ipsa> limpi-
dissima puritate <de cetero>, iuxta datam sibi gratiam, exerceret.

124 Mox igitur, accingens fortitudine lumbos suos, et manum
80 suam mittens ad fortia:, hoc opus arduum aggressa est continuo., non prius ab hoc laborioso quieuit exercitio., donec,
reformatis in se nature viribus atque virtutibus, ipsam nature sue
puritatem in eo statu, diuina fauente gratia, reparare meruit.,
in quo collatam illam sibi diuinitus ab initio recognouit.

85 Sic igitur, in huius puritate decoris iugiter procedendo, non prius
gressum ab hoc virtuoso sui profectus itinere reuocauit:, quam
ad illam perfectionem spiritus, id est assecutionem veritatis, //
f. 314d omnia tam spiritualia quam corporalia suo iustissimo
moderamine dirigentis, incedendo peruenire promeruit:, in qua
90 decetero, tanto nimirum expeditius quanto purius, ab huius luce
veritatis illuminata mentis intelligentia, de virtute in virtutem
proficiens, ambulauit.

Ad quem statum, cum, opitulante superna gratia, profectu celeri

peace it inflicts its own troubles on no one and even bears others' injuries with calmness.

123 Very many other natural goods exist, such as generosity, liberality, ability, affability and many more suchlike things, distributed by the Lord in different ways to different people, in order to acquire the one denarius of eternal reward. Whatever anyone receives from the grace of Christ, according to the measure of his giving,[1] let him remember that he will be the more severely punished for the talent received[2] unless he turns it to the praise of him from whom he received it and uses it for his own and his neighbors' needs, according to grace given him and working in him.

When Beatrice, the servant of Jesus Christ, had carefully considered this under the ray of self-knowledge, and discovered which of these natural goods from among so many had been given to her spiritually, and weighed what and how much she had lost by their neglect, as stated above, it seemed to her supremely necessary that she learn to conform herself with all her strength to the purity of her nature, and turn herself wholly to the pursuit of that rectitude, and exert herself moreover in that limpid purity according to the grace given her.

124 Quickly girding her loins with strength[3] and putting out her hand energetically to strong things,[4] Beatrice undertook this arduous work without delay, and did not rest until, by God's grace, she had restored the purity of her nature, by the reformation of her capacities and virtues, to that state in which she knew it had been given her by God from the beginning.

Thus, in proceeding always along this line of purity and beauty, she did not draw back from the path of virtuous progress until she reached that perfection of mind, the attainment of truth, which with right guidance directs all spiritual and bodily things. In this perfection she walked, going from virtue to virtue[5] with equal promptness and purity, her mind enlightened by truth.

After Beatrice had arrived at this state quickly with the help of

1. Eph 4:7   2. Mt 25:28   3. Pr 31:17   4. Pr 31:19   5. Ps 83:8

peruenisset :, mox illius dona gratiε qui dat affluenter et non
95 improperat, in hoc proprie <cognitionis> beneficio recognoscens ;, ipsum datorem omnis gratie magnifice benedixit :, et
ymnum 'te deum laudamus' <ipsi> deifice trinitati, pro speciali
laudis obsequio, decantauit. <Ex> tunc igitur et deinceps,
christi famula in pleniore sui cognitione permansit :, et in pro-
100 pensiori bonorum copia, tam <gratuitorum> quam naturalium.,
in puritate conscientie cordisque dulcedine, creatori suo domino
decetero ministrauit.

⁌ DE QUADAM ORDINATIONE VITE SPIRITUALIS QUAM ALIQUANTO TEMPORE EXERCUIT

Capitulum xi

125 Per idem quoque tempus, virgo domini, super huius mundi
5 dispendioso cepit exilio mirabiliter affici :, et, ad requiem patrie
celestis aspirans., in terrenis et transitorijs, cum propheta, renuit
consolari illius aniɱa. Sed pius misericordiarum dominus, hanc
ad perfectioris vite fastigium eleuare disponens, non ad requiem
sed ad laborem eam iterum inuitauit. ; et nouam conuersationis
10 normam, qua se regeret atque, virtutum commercio, censum
diuine gratie potiorem acquireret., illi sub eodem tempore, sancti
spiritus gratia, demonstrauit.
Huius vero norme tenorem, hoc modo diebus ac noctibus indesinenter exercuit :: vt, cum, nocturno tempore, primum, ad officium
15 matutinale, signum pulsari consuetum [1], illius auribus, sonitus sui
clangorem infudit., confestim erecta, viuifice crucis signaculo se
muniret :, et, vt omnes cogitationum, locutionum et operum, que
sequenti die fuerat patratura processus, ad laudem et honorem
sancte et indiuidue trinitatis dirigerentur., humili prece domino
20 supplicabat. // ƒ. 315 a Post hec autem orationem dominicam,
trina repetitione, perlegebat ex ordine :, sicque, spiritu feruenti,

God's grace, she recognized in this boon of self-knowledge the gracious gifts of him who gives abundantly and does not upbraid,[6] and magnificently praised the giver of every grace, singing the hymn *Te Deum laudamus* to the divine Trinity as a special act of praise. From then on Christ's servant remained in a fuller knowledge, and served the Lord her creator with a more abundant supply of goods, both gratuitous and natural, in purity of conscience and sweetness of heart.

A CERTAIN ORDERING OF HER SPIRITUAL LIFE THAT SHE PRACTICED FOR A TIME
Chapter Eleven

125 At the same time the Lord's virgin began to be wonderfully affected by the harmful exile of this world, and she aspired to the rest of the heavenly homeland, her soul refusing, with the prophet, to be consoled with earthly and transitory things.[1] But the loving merciful God, planning to raise her to the heights of a more perfect life, again invited her not to rest but to labor, and, by the grace of the Holy Spirit, showed her at the same time a new norm of living by which to govern herself and how to acquire a richer income of divine grace by trading with the virtues.

Day and night she constantly exercised this norm in the following way. When at night the usual first signal for rising for the matins office sounded in her ears, she would immediately sit up and fortify herself with the sign of the life-giving cross. With humble prayer would she beg the Lord that all her thoughts, words, and deeds the coming day would be directed to the praise and honor of the holy and undivided Trinity. After this she recited the Lord's prayer three times in a row. Thus she would promptly

6. Jm 1:5   1. Ps 76:3

alacriter a stratu suo dissiliens., ad diuinum se satagebat officium, cum maturitate debita, preparare.

126 Inchoato <vero> matutinali officio, diuini respectus auster
²⁵ afflabat illi continuo, totumque liquefaciens cor illius, per ocu-
lorum rimas non cessabat educere lacrimas ex deuotionis fluuio : ;
quas nimirum, eo tempore, tanto liberius effundebat, quanto
secretius, absque teste uel conscio., solius diuine maiestatis obtutibus ex intimis educebat [2].

³⁰ Expleto vero matutinali officio, ad exercitium meditationis ex
more se contulit : ; in qua, donec ad missale vocaretur officium.,
omnes defectus suos omniaque delicta, delectatione, consensu,
cogitatione vel opere perpetrata, si<n>gillatim ante mentis oculos
sagaci memoria reuocauit ; et ex eorum vilitate seipsam diiudi-
³⁵ cans : , pro hijs cor contritum et humile, cum debito satisfactionis
obsequio, cotidie domino presentauit. Vnde frequenter accidit.,
vt pro defectibus et peccatis suis domino supplicans, non prius
caput ab oratione leuauerit :, quam diuine consolationis presentem experiretur gratiam quam optauit.

⁴⁰ In missa vero totam considerationem ad saluberrimum illud et
viuificum dominici corporis sacramentum conuertere consueuit :.
et quanto miserationis affectu pius dominus, in pignus dilectionis
et augmentum virtutis <hoc> ecclesie sue, per omnia seculorum
tempora frequentandum exercendumue reliquerit., hoc, cum hu-
⁴⁵ mili gratiarum actione spiritualique dulcedine <delectationis>,
assidue ruminabat.

127 Quodam etiam tempore, domino reuelante, mandatum accepit, vt in hora sacrificij, tempore videlicet eleuationis, pro cunctis
fidelibus christianis humiliter intercederet, et eorum aduocatam
⁵⁰ ad supplicandum, pro quibus, in crucis ara, leuatum sacri-
ficium propiciabile sui corporis deo patri christus obtulit, in diuine

jump from her bed with a fervent spirit, and carefully prepare herself for the divine office with appropriate composure.

126 Once the office of matins started, the south breeze of divine
gaze[2] immediately blew over her and liquified her whole heart, and
constantly drew tears from her eyes in a rivulet of devotion. These
tears she shed then more freely, because secretly, without witness or
observer, [and] intimately, in the sight of the divine Majesty alone.

When matins were over, she usually gave herself to meditation.
Doing this until she was summoned to mass, she recalled to mind,
with keen memory one by one all her defects and faults committed
by delight, consent, thought, and deed. Judging herself by their
baseness, she daily presented a humble and contrite heart[3] to the
Lord, with due satisfaction for them. Therefore it often happened
that in her supplication to the Lord for her faults and sins, she did
not raise her head from prayer until she had experienced the grace
of the divine consolation she desired.

At Mass she used to turn her whole attention to the salutary and
life-giving Sacrament of the Lord's body; and everything that the
loving Lord left to his Church—and with what affection—to be
used throughout all ages as a pledge of his love and for an increase
in virtue. This she used to ruminate on assiduously with humble
thanksgiving and spiritual sweetness of delight.

127 At one time, by divine revelation, Beatrice received the command humbly to intercede for all the faithful Christians at the moment of the sacrifice, that is, at the elevation, and to hold herself,
particularly at that time, in the presence of divine Majesty, as an
advocate for those for whom Christ offered his body on the altar of

2. Lk 12:55   3. Ps 50:19

maiestatis presentia, sub illo presertim tempore, se preberet. //
ʃ. *315 b* <Quod> mandatum et deuote suscepit et deuotius
adimpleuit:; ac pro suis aliorumque necessitatibus exorando, quod
residuum erat temporis, ad horam vsque terciam, <in precibus>
consummauit.

128 Ab hora vero tercia vsque ad sextam, <omnem> dominice
passionis seriem ante mentis oculos presentem habuit:, et illius
obprobria, sputa, colaphos et flagella, ceteraque que pro nostra
redemptione pius dominus in cruce pertulit, humili memoria
retractando., ad vicem compassionis illo tempore semetipsam
instantius excitauit.

A sexta vsque ad horam nonam, ad similitudinem conuersationis
jhesu domini, quam, inter homines homo, doctrina pariter et
exemplo suis sequacibus demonstrauit., hec deuotissima, vesti-
giorum suorum emula, conuersationem suam, qualiter videlicet
ipsum (dicentem in euangelio 'discite a me quia mitis sum et
humilis corde') per viam humilitatis et patientie sequeretur., vt
potuit ordinauit.

Ab hora nona vsque ad vesperam, de collatis sibi a deo beneficijs,
generaliter cum omnibus creaturis et specialiter cum electis.,
deuotas omnipotenti deo gratiarum actiones exhibuit. At vero
suam, in hoc statu, gratiarum actionis insufficientiam non ignorans., omne quodcumque patrauit aut pertulit., in vsum gratiarum actionis mente deuotissima commutauit.

129 Post vespertinam vero synaxim., qualiter hec omnia, statutis
temporibus, eo die frequentauerat:, acutissimo retractationis
oculo vigilanter indagare consueuit:; et si fortassis in aliquo,
vel excedendo vel omittendo, deliquisse se repperit., super hoc
semetipsam acriter accusando, de commisso, pro culpe modo, per
emendationis fidelissimam sponsionem, omnipotentis dei clementie
continuo satisfecit. Post completorium autem cor suum ad cor
dilecti sui constanter applicuit; cuius admirabili dulcedine recreata., cum puritate spiritus et pace consciencie, deinceps ad
pausandum se contulit:; et, sic sopitis sensibus affectibusque
pacatis., per // ʃ. *315 c* noctis residuum inter dilecti sui brachia
requieuit. Hanc autem vite spiritualis ordinationem infatigabili

the cross as an appeasing sacrifice to God the Father. This command
she received with devotion and fulfilled with yet more devotion. The
time remaining until terce she spent in prayer for her own and others'
necessities.

128 From the hour of terce until sext she kept her mind's eye upon the
whole sequence of the Lord's passion; and recalling with humble memory his disgrace, the spittle, the blows and scourges and the other things
the good Lord suffered on the cross for our redemption, she aroused
herself earnestly to reciprocal compassion.

From sext until the hour of none, according to the model which Jesus,
as a man among men, showed by teaching and example to his followers, Beatrice, the Lord's devout and eager follower, ordered her life
as best she could, to follow in the way of humility and patience the
Lord Jesus who said in the Gospel: 'Learn of me for I am meek and
humble of heart'.[4]

From the hour of none until vespers Beatrice gave devout thanks to
Almighty God for the divine benefits given her, general thanks with all
creatures and special thanks with the elect. But not being ignorant of
the insufficiency of her thanksgiving in this state, she devoutly transferred to it everything she accomplished or endured and used it as
thanksgiving.

129 After vespers Beatrice used to reconsider with an acute and vigilant
eye how she had observed all this at the proper times during the day,
and if by chance she found she had failed in something by excess or
omission, she would sharply accuse herself of what she had done, and
immediately make satisfaction to the mercy of Almighty God for it, as
for a fault, by faithfully promising amendment. After compline she
constantly applied her heart to the heart of her beloved. Recreated by
his admirable sweetness she took off to rest in purity of spirit and peace
of conscience, and thus with quiet senses and with peaceful affections
she rested in the arms of her beloved during the remainder of the night.
She practiced this ordering of her spiritual life with tireless care,

4. *Mt 11:29*

spiritu diligenter exercuit., et, donec ad aliam conuersationis
normam vocaretur a domino [3], diebus multis hanc in se, replica-
90   tione diutina, renouauit.

¶ DE GRAUIBUS TEMPTATIONUM INCOMMODIS
QUIBUS PER TRIENNIUM VEXATA FUIT
xij. capitulum

130 Post hec autem, cum in multa suauitate spiritus et conscientie
5   puritate, per iam descriptas conuersationum normas, ferme triennio diuino se beneplacito mancipasset ;, et sancti spiritus in
omnibus sequendo consilium, qui mansionem requietionis in eius
mente locauerat., nec ad dexteram nec ad sinistram a sue demonstrationis, id est veritatis semita deuiasset :, placuit illius cle-
10   mentie manum consolationis, qua dilectam suam in bonis dulcedinis sue copiose refecerat., ad tempus illi dispensatiue sub-
trahere ; et, non vt vas electionis abiciendo desereret., sed vt
dilectam suam, in temptationum certamine, cautam instructamque
redderet, multis temptationum molestijs illam voluit erudire.
15   Cum autem electa domini, spiritualis gratie se sentit dulcedine
destitutam :, repente timore grauissimo cepit affecta tabescere.,
verens <ne>, multiform<ibus> inimici laqueis irretita vel de-
ceptionibus emollita, tandem aliquando cogeretur a sancto proposito deuiare. Mox ergo, districtissimo circumspectionis intuitu,
20   cepit interiora cordis., sed et exterioris conuersationis actus moresque discutere :, et si <qua> sua culpa diuine seueritatis
offensam meruisset, ob quam illius amisisset indultam sibi prius
gratiam., non cessabat attentius explorare. Cum vero nullius [in]
se grauioris delicti consciam inuenisset :, nichilominus et de
25   leuioribus, ea confitendo diligenter, purgare se studuit ; et ne
quid contrarium voluntati diuine committeret, eo sibi sollicitius
precauere curauit :, quo se, spoliatam illa priori gratia, ruituram
sese facilius estimauit.

renewing and repeating it for many days until the Lord called her
to another way of life.

THE TEMPTATIONS WITH WHICH SHE WAS
GRAVELY HARASSED FOR THREE YEARS
Chapter Twelve

130 After this, however, when Beatrice had served the divine
good-pleasure for about three years in much sweetness of spirit
and purity of conscience according to the aforesaid norms of behavior, and had in everything followed the counsel of the Holy
Spirit who had set up his dwelling place in her mind, swerving
neither to right nor to left from the path of truth which he showed
her, it pleased his clemency for his own reasons to withdraw temporarily the consoling hand by which he had abundantly refreshed
his beloved with his goodness and sweetness. Not that he would
abandon and cast away the vessel of election,[1] but he would teach
his beloved through the battle of many troublesome temptations to
be cautious and well-instructed. When the Lord's elect felt herself
stripped of the sweetness of spiritual grace, she became suddenly
consumed with great fear that, snared by the many traps of the
enemy and softened by his delusions, she might finally be forced
out of her holy way of life. Quickly therefore she began to examine her inner heart and her exterior acts and behavior with the
strictest circumspection, and she continued the careful exploration
to see if some fault of hers had earned divine severity and the loss
of the grace formerly given to her. When she did not find herself
guilty of anything grave, she nevertheless cleansed herself even
from lighter matters by confessing them carefully, and she took
the greatest care not to do anything contrary to the divine will for
she thought she would more easily come to ruin now that she was
stripped of that former grace.

1. Ac 9:15

131 Ex eodem ergo tempore, miro modo // f. *315 d* peccatorum
omnia genera detestari cepit et odio prosequi.; sicque in cordis
et corporis puritate via cupiebat regia proficisci;, vt non minus
grauaretur cotidianis et leuibus delictorum suorum excessibus:,
quam si <pro> huiusmodi, quasi pro mortalibus et enormibus.
diuino debuisset iudicio condempnari. Creuit autem hic timor per
dies singulos., et in mente beate mulieris adeo potenter inualuit;,
vt omne quod viderat aut quod audierat alijs euenisse, sibi posse
timeret accidere:; nec solum hoc., sed et omnia genera peccatorum, que vel legendo vel audiendo perceperat., adeo suspecta
tunc temporis habere cepit., et singulari grauitate timoris horum
singula pertimescere., quod, illorum quolibet ingruente, per sub-
tractionem diuine gratie debilitatis viribus, se posse diffideret
in agresso certamine preualere.
132 Quanto vero timor hic eius in corde plus <preualuit>, tanto
magis diuersorum criminum horrendas ymagines, quas numquam
antea vel experientia vel etiam cogitatu perceperat aut accidere
posse putauerat., antiquus humani generis aduersarius, illius
cotidie meditationis aspectibus, replicatis vicibus, ingerebat.
Hinc igitur irruerunt noxiorum criminum importuna susurria.;
illinc carnalium voluptatum venenosa contagia; necnon et diffidentie seu desperationis impetuosa conamina:; quorum singula,
proprijs viciorum agminibus constipata, mentem illius, ex omni
parte vallatam, tam acriter, nunc singillatim nunc pariter inua-
debant., quod iamiam casuram, nimio pauore coartata, se crederet,
vel illorum crebris assultibus, et-si pro tempore rebellando resisteret., tandem, lassatis viribus, ad deditionem se cogi posse vehe-
mentissime formidaret.
Non solum autem timore valido., sed multa quoque verecundia
pariter et horrore cor beate femine sub eodem tempore replebatur:; cum hinc malarum cogitationum turpitudinem., et diuersorum memoriam fla- // f. *316 a* -giciorum, quorum fedas abhorrebat ymagines, non valebat effugere:, inde vero grauissime
verecundaretur, quod eas in conspectu diuine presentie sustineret.
Magnos nichilominus agones et intolerabiles molestias, a cogitationibus blasphemie, vel etiam discredentie, sub eodem tempore
christi miles inuicta sustinuit:; que tanto nimirum acerbius

131 At the same time Beatrice began to detest and in a wonderful way to hate every kind of sin, and she desired so to walk on the royal road in purity of heart and body that she would be no less burdened with small daily faults and excesses than if she had had to be condemned by the divine judgment for these as if they were enormous mortal sins. This fear grew every day, and so prevailed in the blessed woman's mind that, whatever she had seen or heard happening to others, she feared might happen to her as well. And not only that, but she began then to be suspicious of every kind of sin she had heard or read about, and to be terrified of every one of them, because she did not believe it possible to conquer any of them in open combat, now that her strength had been sapped by the withdrawal of divine grace.

132 The more this fear grew in her heart, the more the ancient enemy of the human race time and time again forced on the inner vision of her daily meditation horrible images of different crimes which she had never before experienced, or even conceived, or thought possible.

From one side troublesome whispers about harmful crimes, from another poisonous infections of carnal enjoyments, and even impetuous onslaughts of mistrust and desperation rushed in on her. Each of these vices, crowded together in their bands, now singly, now all together, invaded her mind, surrounded on all sides. They did this so bitterly that she was constrained by great fear, and thought she was on the point of falling. Even if she could resist by fighting back their frequent assaults for a while, she very much feared that in the end her strength would flag and she might be forced to surrender.

The blessed woman's heart was filled at this time not only with huge fear but also with great shame and horror, since she could not escape the shamefulness of evil thoughts and the memory of various outrages whose foul images she abhorred. She was especially ashamed to put up with these images in the divine presence. This unvanquished soldier of Christ also bore at this same time great agonies and intolerable vexations from thoughts of blasphemy and even unbelief. These two things wounded her heart more bitterly

vvlnerauerant cor illius, quanto de rebus spiritualibus (que since-
ram et integram fidem exigunt) ., ad quas, consolationis gratia,
debuisset in temptationis certamine tamquam ad portum securi-
tatis confugere. , ceteris molestijs acerbiora cogebatur dubitationis
70 susurria supportare.

133 Videns ergo circumquaque magnum pondus certaminis imminere:, cepit grauiori timore deficere. Verumptamen ex quo
necessario resistendum fuerat:, elegit potius ad mortem vsque
dimicando resistere, quam vnius mortalis peccati, cuiuscumque
75 generis id extiterit., contagiosum virus in anima sustinere. Totis
itaque conatibus., totis<que> cordis et corporis viribus, cotidie
satagebat contra dyabolicos <assultus> semetipsam hinc inde
defendere. At vbi vires <aut> ingenium <sibi> sentiebat in
resistendo deficere;, ibi diuine clementie largitatem, in auxilium
80 defensionis sue, non cessabat magnis desiderij vocibus implorare.
Non enim humane fuit industrie, tot tantosque motus temptationum, et aerearum potestatum [1] insultus, euincendo comprimere:; cum, non diebus incertis aut horarum interpolatis spacijs.,
sed continuatis diebus et noctibus, incessanter cogeretur hec
85 importunissima viciorum certamina tolerare.

In omnibus autem hijs temptationum assultibus, instar beatissimi
iob, tam fixum manebat cor illius in virtutis proposito:, quod et
si condempnandam <certissime> se presciuisset a domino.,
non tamen aliquatenus, a via virtutis exorbitando, recedere
90 voluisset.

134 Sub illo quoque tempore, frequenter illud beati iob in mente
habuit.: 'et quod verebar accidit: et venit super me indignatio
tua domine'[2]. Quod nimirum verbum eo molestiori corde reco-
luit., // fol. 316 b quo, fortiori timore grauata., quotiens illud
95 ad memoriam redijt., totiens propemodum a dei misericordia
desperauit.

Videns autem et desperationis assultum ex aduerso fortiter imminere:, satis prouide confestim ex illa parte, ne demergeretur
in desperationis fouea, communire se studuit. Et contra proposi-

in that she had to put up with whispers and doubts about spiritual things (which demand sincere and integral faith) and these were worse than her other troubles. Yet it was to these [spiritual things] as to a safe harbor that she had to fly for consolation in the struggle against temptation.

133 Beatrice began to be incapacitated by greater fear when she saw the heavy burden of struggle threatening her on every side. Yet since she had to resist anyway, she chose to fight and resist even to death rather than bear on her soul the infectious virus of even one mortal sin of any kind at all. Daily she labored to defend herself with all her efforts and with all her strength of heart and body, on this side and that, against the diabolic assaults. When she felt her strength or wit slacking in the resistance, she never gave up begging with great longing cries for the bounty of the divine mercy to defend her. For it was not by human diligence that she suppressed and conquered so many and such great temptations and assaults of the demonic powers, since it was not on different days or at widely separated hours but for days and nights on end that she had to bear this unremitting struggle with the vices. In all these assaults of temptation, Beatrice, like the blessed Job, so fixed her heart on virtue that, even had she known for certain that she would be condemned by the Lord, she would not have willed to depart or deviate in any way from the path of virtue.

134 Beatrice often at that time had in mind blessed Job's saying: 'What I feared has befallen me, and your indignation, O Lord, has come down upon me'.[2] She recalled this word with a heavier heart because every time she remembered it, she became more fearful and almost despaired of God's mercy.

But seeing that despair gravely threatened her on one side, she quickly and prudently armed herself on the other, lest she sink into the pit of despair. Against the blessed man's desolate word, she

2. *Jb 3:25-26*

100 tum verbum beati viri desolatorium, aliud eiusdem consolatorium,
hoc videlicet : 'Et si in profundum inferni demersus fuero³.,
inde me liberabis' adhibere non distulit. In quo et-si non plenam., magnam tamen consolationis gratiam repperit :, quotiens
illud, vel aliud huic simile, ad memoriam reuocauit.
105 Preter hec omnia, videbatur aliquotiens dei famule., quod omnes
vie ducentes ad celestem patriam animam christianam., laqueis et
decipulis essent advsque finem a principio circumcepte ;, per
quas tam gressu sollicito posset nullatenus proficisci :, quin ipsorum laqueorum in aliquo⁴, pedem affectus sui contingeret irretiri.
110 135 Quid ergo faceret, aut quo se verteret mens sancte femine :,
tam <graui> viciorum assultu., tam importuna cogitationum
audatia tam sepissime prouocata ? Respiciens erat ad solitum
adiutorium, et absconderat faciem suam altissimus : ; non, vt heri
et nudiustertius, palam dimicantem aut adiuuans aut pro se dimi-
115 cans., sed dimicantem a longe quasi per fenestras nunc pro-
spiciens et cancellos. Attamen vt vidit [a longe] immodici certaminis cotidie pondus accrescere., collectis in vnum cordis et
corporis viribus, ad resistendum se contulit :, et quidquid de
scripturis., quidquid de sanctorum exemplis hac illacve colligere
120 potuit., hoc ad vsum repugnandi sapienter in cordis sui domicilio collocauit.
136 Aduersum obiectos ergo laqueos illud constanter in memoria
tenuit : quod humilis quisque, per semitam regni celorum laqueo-
sam incedens, pro-vt olim bono seni anthonio per visum dominus
125 demonstrauerat, illorum⁵ solus decipulas euitabat. Quapropter,
vt et ipsa, prefatos inimici laqueos // f. 316 c aliquatenus in-
offenso pede percurreret :, omni quo potuit humilitatis officio se
deiecit., et nichil eorum, quo vel ad sui cognitionem vel ad propriam humiliationem attingere potuisset, quantumcumque vel arduum
130 vel ad peragendum difficile fuerat., inexpertum eodem in tempore
dereliquit ; quin etiam et tantam in domino fiduciam ex hac

quickly used this consoling word of his: 'Even if I were plunged into the depth of hell, you will free me from it'.[3] She found great, if not total, consolation in this as often as she recalled it or similar texts to mind.

In addition to all this, it sometimes seemed to God's handmaid that all the roads leading the Christian soul to the heavenly homeland were beset by snares and traps from beginning to end. She feared that she could never make her way along them carefully enough not to have the foot of her affection caught in one or another of the snares.

135 What could she do, or where could the blessed woman's mind turn when she was so frequently challenged by the heavy attacks of the vices and the grievous audacity of thoughts? She looked to her accustomed helper, and the Most High had hidden his face, not openly helping her in her fight, nor himself fighting for her, as he did yesterday and the day before, but watching her fight now from afar as though through windows or through lattices.[4] But when Beatrice saw the burden of the great struggle increasing daily, she gathered up her strength of heart and body, and resisted. Wisely she stored in the house of her heart whatever she could collect here and there from the Scriptures and the examples of the saints, in order to fight back.

136 In regard to the set snares, she constantly remembered that only the humble would avoid them on the snare-ridden road to the kingdom of heaven, as the Lord had once upon a time shown in a vision to the good old man, Anthony. Therefore, in order that she too might with uninjured foot to some extent avoid the aforesaid snares of the enemy, she threw herself into every humble task she could, and at the same time left untried none of the things by which she might be able to arrive at self-knowledge or her own humiliation, however hard and difficult they were. Indeed from this exercise of humility and patience Beatrice gathered such

3. *Jb 17:16; 33:28*   4. Sg 2:9

humilitatis et patientie virtuositate collegit :, quod [6] et si, preter
vnum hominem, totum genus humanum dampnandum a domino
presciuisset., vt hec tamen prerogatiua gratie sibi reseruaretur
ab ipso., quatenus, alijs pereuntibus, ad salutem <ipsa> per-
tingeret, de ipsius bonitate confisa, totis virium suarum <inten-
tionisque> conatibus efficere studuisset.

137 Cogitabat etiam quod diuine pietatis clementiam assidua [7]
tantum importunitate lacesceret, vt, iuxta quod scriptum est
'regnum celorum vim patitur' [8]., a precum instantia non ces-
sando donec aspectu solite pietatis illustraretur a domino, celorum
regno violentiam irrogaret. Habebat etiam et illam euangelicam
parabolam in recordatione continua, quam de duobus amicis
dominus texuit:, quorum vnus ad alium nocte veniens, vt sibi
tres panes commodaret humiliter exorauit [9].; <q>uo de strato
nolente consurgere, non prius refert alterum a precibus quieuisse,
quam, surgente reliquo, panes, quotquot habuit necessarios, ab
eo meruit impetrare. Hoc igitur euangelicum paradigma memoriter apud se retinens., in corde suo finali statuit deliberatione,
non prius a fletibus et a precibus, a lacrimis et singultibus abstinere:, quam, auxilio ihesu christi, debellatis cum suarum
temptationum irritamentis aereis potestatibus [10]., effractaque
cordis sui duricia., sensuum quoque suorum instabilitate sopita.,
compositis tandem moribus ordinatisque meditationibus, ab vni-
uersali generis humani domino pariter et amico., cum suis pueris
in cubili celestis patrie quiescente., panes quotquot haberet necessarios ad recuperationem sue gratie // f. 316 d mereretur:,
et-si non vt amica., saltem vt improba reportare. In eodem quippe
sequitur euangelio., dicente domino <petite et accipietis., que-
rite et inuenietis>, pulsate et aperietur vobis. In quibus nimirum
verbis <et> similibus, sicut prediximus que ex scripturis colligere potuit., et-si non plenam cordi suo pacem repperit:,

confidence in the Lord, that, even if she had known beforehand that the whole human race, save only one person, was going to be condemned by the Lord, then trusting in his goodness she would have striven with all her might and main that this prerogative of grace might be reserved for her, that she might attain salvation while others perished.

137 She also resolved to provoke the divine loving mercy with such steady importunity that, as it is written: 'The kingdom of heaven suffers violence',[5] by not ceasing her persistent prayers until the Lord looked upon her with his usual kindness, she might do violence to the kingdom of heaven. She also continually remembered that Gospel parable which the Lord wove about the two friends, one of whom came to the other by night, humbly asking him to lend him three loaves of bread. When the friend was unwilling to get out of bed, the other did not muffle his petitions until he received as many loaves as he needed from the first, who did rise from bed.[6] Keeping this Gospel paradigm in mind therefore, Beatrice made this final resolve in her heart; she would not cease her weeping and prayers, her tears and sobs until, with the help of Jesus Christ, she deserved, if not as a friend then at least as a nuisance, to wrest from the universal Lord and friend of the human race—as many loaves of bread as she needed to recover grace together with the attendant conquest of the demons and their harassing temptations, the shattering of her own hardness of heart, the quieting of her restless senses, the composure of her behavior, and the ordering of her meditation. In a continuation of the same passage, the Lord says: 'Ask and you shall receive, seek and you shall find, knock and it shall be opened to you'.[7] From these and similar words which she could collect from the Scriptures, as we said, even if she did not find full peace for her heart,

5. *Mt 11:12*   6. Lk 11:5-8   7. *Lk 11:9*

magnam tamen consolationis dulcedinem, instante temptationis periculo, degustauit.

¹⁶⁹ **138** Illud quoque, quod pius dominus ad ymaginem et similitudinem suam illam creauerat., qui non vvlt mortem peccatoris sed vt conuertatur et viuat:, dyabolicis cotidie temptationibus opponebat ; quodque tempestiuius, impollutam corpore simul et animo, ex tempestuoso mundi naufragio ad monastice stabilitatis portum aduexerat:, et inter electionis sue vasa sibi iugiter famulantia collocauerat.; illud quoque, quod, omni vite sue tempore, tam pium, tam munificum tamque misericordem, in omni necessitatis sue instantia, creatorem suum experta fuerat., cum ceteris quibusque pietatis diuine suffragijs, demoniacis cotidie suggestionibus obicere satagebat. Et licet acriter ipsum incentorem malicie sibi resistere aduerteret:, non tamen a repugnandi luctamine donec sub pedibus suis inimicos suos tandem ipsa <contereret>, auxiliante christi gratia, quiescebat.

139 In hoc siquidem laborioso certamine dilectam suam dominus annis ferme tribus, antequam ad eam plene consolandam oculos miserationis sue conuerteret, agonizare permisit ; sic tamen, et-si tribulatam corde, per omne probationis huius tempus inter pietatis sue brachia confouendo protexit, vt, fugatis inimicis, obtentaque victoria de cunctis aduerse potestatis immissionibus, nec vnum quidem noxiale piaculum superesset quod, vsque ad confessionis faciende remedium, suam in aliquo conscientiam aggrauaret.

140 Vere mirabilis deus in sanctis suis., qui sic electos suos dimicantes in certamine deserit., vt tamen pugnantium manus ad prelium et digitos eorum ad bellum instruat:; // f. 317 a sic eos, quasi derelictos, inimicorum insultibus erudiendos exponit., vt non solum a morte animas., sed et oculos eorum a lacrimis et a lapsu pedes eripiat. Sic denique faciem <sue> propitiationis ab eis abscondere meminit., vt fideliter decertantibus, victorie palmam indulgeat., et perseuerantibus coronam glorie repromittat.

¹⁹⁵ Vere laudabilem beatricem dixerim., et per omnia labentium seculorum tempora merito commendandam ;, que sic, per triennij continuum spacium, contra demones, carnem et mundum iugi certamine dimicauit., vt non solum, inuicta per tot annorum curricula, non succumberet:, sed vt, victrix, nec vnius quidem cicatricem vvlneris de prelio reportaret.

she did however taste great and sweet consolation in the midst of dangerous temptation.

138 Beatrice daily opposed to the devil's temptations the fact that the loving Lord had created her to his own image and likeness,[8] and that he does not will the death of the sinner but that he be converted and live.[9] She also daily countered the devil's suggestions with the fact that God had brought her early, and undefiled in body and soul, from the stormy shipwreck of the world to the harbor of monastic stability, that he had placed her among the chosen vessels who always serve him, and that she had always experienced her creator as most loving, generous and merciful in every urgent need, together with other proofs of the divine loving kindness. Although she perceived the author of malice resisting her bitterly, by the grace of Christ she did not rest from her struggle and resistance until she finally crushed her enemies beneath her feet.

139 The Lord permitted his beloved to agonize in this laborious struggle for nearly three years before he turned the eyes of his mercy to console her fully. Even though she was troubled in heart, he so protected her with his kindly sheltering arms during all this time of trial that, when the enemies had been put to flight and victory over all the attacks of the hostile powers had been obtained, not a single hurtful sin remained—even to be remedied by confession—to burden her conscience.

140 God is truly wonderful in his saints,[10] for he deserts his elect struggling in conflict in such a way that he instructs their hands for battle and their fingers for war.[11] He exposes and seems to abandon them to be taught by the insults of their foes in such a way that he not only snatches their souls from death, but also their eyes from tears and their feet from falling.[12] He intentionally so hides the face of his favor from them that he grants the palm of victory to those who struggle faithfully, and to those who persevere he promises the crown of glory.

I would call Beatrice truly praiseworthy and forever deservedly to be commended by the lips of worldlings because for three years running she so continuously struggled against the demons, the flesh, and the world that, unconquered, not only did she not succumb in all this time, but as victor she did not carry away a single scar or wound from the battle.

8. Gn 1:27   9. Ezk 18:23   10. Ps 67:36   11. Ps 143:1   12. *Ps 114:8*

❡ DE EO QUOD AD HORAM
A DOMINO CONSOLARI MERUIT
xiij. capitulum

141 Accidit autem vt, quodam tempore, necdum finito pre-
5   dicto certamine, virgo domini, velut ex omni parte temptationum
exercitu numeroso circumdata., maximis fatigaretur assultibus.,
diuersis cogitationum impulsibus castrum munitissimum cordis
sui grauiter impugnantibus : ; quibus omnibus vt sola resisteret,
et omnium motus expugnando comprimeret eodem tempore, nimis
10   impossibile iudicabat. Quid ergo faceret in tanto discrimine, quo
se verteret ? Cum enim blasphemie cogitationibus hinc resistere
laboraret., ex altera parte discredentie temptamenta grauiora
sustinuit : ; quibus cum ocius ad resistendum occurreret., ex parte
reliqua voluptatum feda ludibria, repugnanda deprehendit. Sic
15   igitur, ex omni parte grauissimo pondere certaminis infestata :,
cum proprias vires ad resistendum minus sufficere posse conspiceret., et iamiam inimicorum tyrannidi succumbere formidaret ;,
ad illud tutissimum diuine protectionis adiutorium confugiendo se
contulit : ; et quotiens, hinc vel inde, molestari se doluit., totiens
20   ad petram que christus est // f. *317 b* ipsos cogitatus suos alli-
dens, aduersus importunissimam illorum insolentiam, illius misericordiam instantius implorauit.

142 Videns ergo nec sic eorum proteruiam ab infestando quiescere., timensque, pre simplicitate nimia cordis sui, diuine cle-
25   mentie, tam crebris ad ipsam <confugiendo> recursibus, importunitate sua molestiam seu iniuriam irrogare ;, vt hanc ipsam
importunitatis sue molestiam equanimiter toleraret, deuotissimis
eum precibus sibi placare studuit : ; nam et-si mil<l>ies omnibus
horis hijs temptationum assultibus eam infestari contingeret.,
30   totiens ad eius misericordiam auxilium quesitura confugeret.,
et, firmam spem fiduciamque habens in eo, suam in omni tempore
clementiam imploraret., <s>ic quippe totam intentionis sue
virtutem in eo fundauerat, vt, iuxta quod apostolus de se suisque

HOW SHE DESERVED
TO BE TEMPORARILY CONSOLED BY THE LORD
Chapter Thirteen

141 Once, when this struggle was not yet over, it happened that the Lord's virgin Beatrice was, as it were, surrounded on all sides by a numerous army of temptations, and she was worn out with grave assaults and with various kinds of bad thoughts heavily attacking the well-fortified citadel of her heart. She judged it impossible to resist all this alone, and to fight off and suppress all these movements at the same time. What should she do, where should she turn in such a crisis? For while she worked to resist blasphemous thoughts here, she was subject to heavier temptations of unbelief there. And when she moved quickly to resist these, she saw that foul wanton pleasures had to be expelled somewhere else. So she was harried on every side with the heaviest battles, and when she saw that her own forces could not hold out and she feared she was on the point of succumbing to the tyranny of the enemies, she hastily fled to the safest help of divine protection. As often as she was grieved and vexed about this or that, she dashed her thoughts against the rock which is Christ,[1] imploring his mercy earnestly against their persistent insolence.

142 Seeing that even so the bold attacks were not lessening, and fearing in her extreme simplicity of heart that she was vexing or offending the divine mercy by flying to it with such frequent recourse, Beatrice tried to placate him herself by her ever-devout prayers so that he would tolerate her troublesome insistence unruffled, for even if she were harassed a thousand times an hour by the assaults of these temptations, every time she would flee to his mercy seeking help, and would always implore his mercy, having firm hope and confidence in him. She had so founded all the strength of her intention on him that she was sure that neither death nor life nor anything afterwards would ever separate her

---

1. 1 Co 10:4

<fidelibus> enarrabat., certam se crederet, quod neque mors
35   neque vita neque cetera que sequuntur, mentem eius ab illius
caritate decetero separarent [1].

143 Videns autem electam suam dominus, immenso certaminis
pondere fatigari., nulloque temptationum impulsu a caritate sua
posse diuelli., quin potius in ea, tanto firmiori quanto magis,
40   fatigata molestijs, eruditiori fiducia, radicari., sue miserationis
oculos ad horam super ipsam aperire dignatus est : ; et quibus
ex causis hoc forte certamen ipsi collatum extiterit., pius dominus
electe sue sub eodem tempore reuelauit. Siquidem, apertis oculis
mentis sue, collatum [2] in munere prefati pondus certaminis a deo
45   sibi, preuidit ; et non vt temptata succumberet., sed vt, erudita
certamine, fortius conuersationis sue gressus in via virtutum
decetero figere disceret : ; non vt demereretur aut perderet.,
sed vt diuinam gratiam propensius tali commercio compararet.,
<h>uius diuturnitatem luctaminis indultam sibi diuinitus, cer-
50   tissime recognouit.

144 Quam reuelationem cum oblatam sibi celitus accepisset.,
in maximum // f. 317 c cordis sui gaudium mox prosilijt., et ad
momentum temporis, ab omni tribulatione sua plenissime conso-
lata, in risum vehementem et insuetum erupit. ; et, quasi nichil
55   molestie retroactis temporibus ipsa pertulerit., ita, diuina se
consolante clementia, licet ad modicum temporis., habundantius
tamen, in domino suus spiritus exultauit. Sed post modicum
temporis, abstracta dulcedine gratie quam gustauerat., iterum
in abyssum illius vehementissimi timoris, ad se reuersa, corruit,
60   et, velut a paradiso transiens ad inferna, collatam sibi leticiam
in merorem denuo commutauit.

mind from the love of him, as the Apostle said about himself and his faithful.[2]

143 The Lord, seeing that Beatrice, his chosen one, was weary with the immense weight of the struggle, and could not be torn from love of him by an onslaught of temptation—indeed she became even more firmly rooted in that love as her confidence, wearied by troubles, grew in training and discipline—seeing this, deigned to open the eyes of his mercy on her briefly. Our loving God then revealed to his chosen one why this vigorous struggle had been given to her by God as a gift, not that she should be tempted and succumb, but she should be trained by the struggle and should learn to plant her footsteps more vigorously in the way of virtue in the future. She perceived with greatest certainty that the length of this combat was a divine favor, not given that she might forfeit or lose grace, but that she might acquire divine grace more lavishly by this exchange.

144 Beatrice's heart leapt for joy as soon as she received this revelation offered her from heaven and, fully consoled for the moment about all her troubles, she broke out in loud and unaccustomed laughter. Under the consolation of divine mercy her spirit rejoiced abundantly in her Lord,[3]—though only for a short time—as though she had tasted no annoyances in the past. But after a little while the sweetness of grace she had tasted was taken away, and coming to herself she fell again into the abyss of violent fear, and as though going from paradise to hell she once again exchanged the happiness given her for sorrow.

2. Rm 8:35   3. Lk 1:47

ℂ DE EO QUOD VIDIT CELUM APERTUM
ET IHESIIM STANTEM A DEXTRIS VIRTUTIS DEI
xiiij. capitulum

145 Alio quoque tempore durante predicto certamine contigit vt,
collectis in-simul omnium viciorum agminibus, aduersarius humani
generis super illam, dimicaturus, irrueret :, et fortissimum cor
illius tam crebris temptationum insultibus, quam sunt varia viciorum genera nimis atrociter impugnaret. Videns ergo miles christi
se, velut, in medio maris positam, vndique procellosis impulsionum
fluctibus obrui., et, ex omni parte, grauissima tempestate ponde-
rosi certaminis infestari :, timore fortissimo mox resoluta contabuit. ; et, virium suarum industriam ad tantam viciorum multitudinem debellandam sufficere posse non estimans :, quid ageret
aut quorsum se verteret ignorauit. Nullius quidem noxialis delicti
singulare certamen extimuit ; nec enim alicuius illorum importunitate, si solum insurgeret., se succumbere posse formidauit : ; sed,
omnibus ın-simul irruentibus et pariter iniquitatis sue negotium
exercentibus, tanta resistendi necessitas ex omni parte se obtulit ;,
vt, lacessitis viribus, et tota pene deficiente fiducia :, propemodum de dei misericordia desperarit.

146 Videns ergo virtutum omnium constantissimas, id est fidem et
spem, intra se pene deficiendo succumbere., nichilque // f. 317 d
virtutis, quo se iam defenderet in tanto discrimine, superesse.,
iamque non presumens amplius ad congressionem tanti certaminis,
affecta dolore simul et tedio, se parare : surgens ad ecclesiam,
ocius fugiendo se contulit., et cum graui lacrimarum imbre, cum
amaris gemitibus, cum suspirijs et fletibus, vt sui misereretur in tam
periculoso discrimine, diuinam clementiam sic inquiens exorauit. :
' O domine iuste et misericors, terribilis et fortissime., si quidem
beneplacitum est in conspectu tuo, quod ego, famularum tuarum
miserrima, gratis demergar in profundum inferni., vel sine causa
rugientis subiciar potestati inimici., beneplacito quidem tuo sponte
consentio : ; sed eternaliter a te separari, super omnia tormentorum infernalium horrenda supplicia, grauissime tolerabo. Et si
quidem hoc necessarium fuerit :, numquam tamen hanc misera-
bilem animam meam, ad ymaginem et similitudinem tuam condi-

HOW SHE SAW HEAVEN OPENED
AND JESUS STANDING AT THE RIGHT HAND
OF THE POWER OF GOD
Chapter Fourteen

145 At another time during the aforementioned struggle it happened that the adversary of the human race, with all the vices as-
sembled in their bands, rushed in upon her ready to fight, and
cruelly attacked her valiant heart with as many assaults of temptation as there are different kinds of vices. Christ's soldier, seeing
herself in the midst of the sea, rocked and overwhelmed by stormy
waves, and harassed on all sides with heavy storms and weighty
struggles, began to waste away, unnerved by great fear. She did
not know what to do or where to turn, thinking that her own exer-
tion could not be enough to suppress such a throng of vices. She
did not fear single combat with any one of them, if it reared up
alone, but with all of them rushing in together and each of them
exercising its own wicked activity, such a need for resistance on
all sides arose that, her strength worn out and confidence all but
collapsing, she nearly despaired of God's mercy.
146 Beatrice, seeing that faith and hope, that most constant of
virtues, were almost on the point of perishing within her, and that
no virtue remained with which to defend herself in such a crisis,
no longer presumed to enter such a struggle; grief-stricken and
worn-out she prepared herself, and rising up fled quickly to the
church, and with a great storm of tears, with bitter groans, sighs,
and weeping she besought the divine clemency to have mercy on
her in such a dangerous crisis, saying: 'O just and merciful Lord,
terrible and very strong, if it is pleasing in your sight that I, the
most wretched of your handmaids, should sink for no reason into
the depth of hell, or be subjected without cause to the power of the
roaring enemy, I willingly consent to your good-pleasure, but I
shall bear the eternal separation from you most grievously, more
than all the hideous tortures of hell. Even if this is necessary, yet
shall I never stain with the foulness of any mortal sin this wretched

tam, alicuius teditate peccati mortalis inficiam ; etiam si ad dirup-
tionem cordis vsque, dimicare necessarium habeam : ; sed in die
iudicij, cum veneris iudicare viuos et mortuos, mundam et immaculatam eam, tua fauente gratia, tibi offeram. Et si tunc quidem
iudicaueris eternaliter puniendam : , tuo iudicio parendo, consentiens humiliter acquiescam. '

147 Hijs ergo, pre nimia cordis amaritudine sic digestis. , ad
orationis solacium mox confugit : , et diuine miserationis clementiam tali verborum ordine deinceps inuocauit.

' O benignissime, inquit, ihesu domine, fili dei viui unigenite,
plene totius consolationis et gratie ; , quamdiu patieris humilem
ancillam tuam in tam laborioso certamine permanere ? Tu quidem,
domine, pro me nascendo de virgine, mundi discrimina suffe-
rendo. , precipueque mortis crudele supplicium et amarissima
iudeorum obprobria tolerando. , tue mihi caritatis indicia demonstrare dignatus es : , qua maior esse non valuit nec valebit. //
f. 318 a At vero, quo pacto me, tanto redemptam precio, tantoque
commercio reparatam. , nunc inter hostiles cateruas solam dese-
ris ; , et dimicantem absque consolationis auxilio derelinquis ?
Peto ergo, domine clemens et pijssime, quatenus me, famularum
tuarum vltimam, quam inter ceteras humani generis creaturas
huius redemptionis participem fieri voluisti. , solam a sinu vni-
versalis misericordie non excludas : , sed consolationis beneficium,
quod nemini, puro corde petenti te, denegas. , in hoc necessitatis
tempore a me, desolatissima, non abscondas. '

148 Oratione vero completa, quam dolor et amaritudo cordis, hijs
verbis alijsque similibus, in longum vsque protraxerant : , inuicta
christi tyro, compositis membris, ad pausandum se contulit, et sic,
reclinata deorsum quasi dormiens, donec, repausatis viribus, ad
certamen, iterum modice recreata, consurgeret, accubauit. At vero
pius et misericors dominus. , qui de sua misericordia confidentes
numquam deserit. , qui iuxta est hijs qui tribulato sunt corde et
humiles spiritu saluare non desinit. , amator hominum, sponsus
animarum, merces laborum, curator infirmantium et consolatio
turbatorum. , dominus ihesus christus, oculos sue miserationis ad
electam sponsam suam in necessitatis tempore conuertere non
despexit : ; sed fidelissime dimicantem aspiciens. , et sub certa-

soul of mine, created to your image and likeness, even if I have to fight till my heart breaks. But in the day of judgment when you come to judge the living and the dead,[1] I shall offer it to you clean and immaculate, by your grace. And if even then you condemn it to be eternally punished, I shall obey your judgment, humbly consenting and acquiescing'.

147 When Beatrice had poured these words forth from the great bitterness of her heart, she quickly fled to the solace of prayer, and she called upon the divine mercy in this way:

'O most kind Lord Jesus, only-begotten Son of the living God, full of all consolation and grace, how long will you allow your humble handmaid to remain in so laborious a struggle? Lord, you deigned to show me the signs of your love for me by being born of a virgin, by suffering the hardships of the world, and especially by bearing the cruel torment of death and the harsh insults of the Jews. Nothing was or will be greater than this love. Yet now that I am redeemed at such a price, restored by such an exchange, why do you leave me alone among the crowds of enemies, and abandon me to fight without the help of consolation? I ask you therefore, most loving and merciful Lord, not to exclude from the bosom of your universal mercy me alone, the least of your handmaids, whom you have chosen to share in this redemption with the other members of the human race. In this time of necessity do not hide from me, your most desolate servant, the benefit of the consolation that you do not deny to anyone who asks you for it with a pure heart'.

148 When Beatrice had completed her prayer, protracted by sorrow and bitterness of heart, in these and similar words, Christ's unconquered recruit pulled herself together and went to bed, lying down, as it were, to sleep until, somewhat refreshed, she should rise to struggle again. But the loving and merciful Lord, who never deserts those who trust in his mercy , who is close to the troubled of heart[2] and always saves the humble in spirit, the lover of men and spouse of souls, the reward of labors, the healer of the sick and consolation of the troubled, the Lord Jesus Christ, did not refuse to turn the eyes of his mercy on his chosen spouse in the time of her need. Regarding his faithful fighter and understanding that

1. *1 P 4:5*   2. Ps 33:19

minis pondere laborantem intelligens., ad consolandum eam
75 misericordie sue manum apposuit., et aerearum potestatum insultibus cunctisque viciorum importunitatibus effugatis., ad portum tranquillitatis illam, ineffabili pietatis sue clementia, reuocauit.
149 Siquidem, cum pausandi gratia, sicut diximus, acclinis iacens,
a turbine procellarum ad tempus semet abscondere iam cepisset :,
80 rapta supra se, vidit in extasi mentis sue., vidit, inquam, non
carnalibus sed mentalibus oculis, apertos celos ;, et jhesum stantem a dextris virtutis dei, se iuuare paratum :, et ad erigendum,
consolandum <et> eruendum a contrariarum potestatum incursibus., // f. *318 b* ad se misericorditer inclinatum. Quem cum
85 desiderabilibus oculis, <omnis> iam ignara tribulationis, pre
multitudine dulcedinis sue virgo domini conspexisset., duo quedam, id est misericordiam et dilectionem, ex se radiare <se
versus> intelligens., quid hec ipsa portenderent illuminata
mentis intelligentia continuo recognouit. Siquidem, in radio mise-
90 ricordie quem aspexit., eo quod tam perturbata fuerit in certamine, tamque grauata timore pariter et dolore :, presertim cum se
tam paratum ad succurrendum, tam potentem ad <eripiendum>
aspiceret., a domino reprehendi meruit. In dilectionis vero radio
dominum sibi propitium et misericordem agnoscens., illius se
95 iuuante clementia, non se vincendam aut huius pretextu certaminis a diuina se <misericordia> separandam :, sed potius
exaltandam, erigendam et in virtutum culmine subleuandam, clara
mentis acie recognouit.

150 Hac ergo celesti visione prospecta confestim ad se redijt :,
100 et se, sub eodem tempore, releuatam ab omni timoris et inquietu-
dinis pondere, mox inuenit. Recogitans autem vbi fuerit aut quid
viderit., simulque diuinam in se clementiam apertissime recognoscens :, cum exultatione cordis omnipotenti deo gratiarum actiones
exhibuit ; et, licet eo tempore <penitus> a predicto certamine
105 liberata non fuerit :, ex tunc tamen et deinceps in fide firmior.,
in spe constantior., in tribulatione <potentior> et contra virtutes
contrarias animosior, adiuuante se domino perdurauit.

she was laboring in a weighty struggle, he put forth his merciful hand to console her, and putting to flight the insults of the demonic powers and all the troubles caused by the vices, he with his unspeakable kindness and mercy called her back into the harbor of tranquillity.

149 While Beatrice was lying down to rest, as we have said, and had begun to shelter herself temporarily from the storm and whirlwind, she was caught up beyond herself and saw in ecstasy of mind—with the eyes of the mind, not of the flesh,—the heavens opened and Jesus standing at the right hand of the power of God,[3] prepared to help her, leaning over mercifully toward her to raise her up, console, and snatch her from the attacks of the opposing powers. When the Lord's virgin, now free from all tribulation because of his overwhelming sweetness, had gazed on him with longing eyes, she perceived two things, mercy and love, radiating from him toward her, and immediately with an enlightened mind she recognized what they meant. In the ray of mercy she saw, she deserved to be rebuked by the Lord for being so disturbed in the struggle, so weighed down with fear and sorrow, especially once she had seen him so prepared to help, so powerful to rescue. In the ray of love she recognized clearly that the Lord was propitious and merciful toward her, that his kindness was helping her, not beating her down or casting her off from the divine mercy under the pretext of this struggle, but rather exalting her, raising her up and lifting her to the summit of the virtues.

150 Having perceived this heavenly vision, she quickly returned to herself, and soon found she had at the same time been relieved of all burdensome fear and anxiety. She gave thanks to Almighty God with exultation of heart, perceiving where she had been and what she had seen, recognizing clearly the divine mercy toward her. Although at that time she was not wholly freed from the forementioned struggle, with the Lord's help she henceforth remained stronger in faith, more constant in hope, more valiant in tribulation, and more spiritual against the opposing powers.

3. Ac 7:56

ℂ DE EO QUOD IN TEMPTATIONUM TEMPORE SACRAMENTUM ALTARIS FREQUENTAUIT

xv. capitulum

151 Fuit autem huic sancte femine, per omne tempus huius labo-
riosi certaminis, summum remedium ac speciale refugium., illud
saluberrimum et viuificum dominici corporis sacramentum. Illud
siquidem, in omni tribulatione sua, quasi singulare patrocinium
amauit, exquisiuit et coluit : ; et frequentissime consolationis gratiam, quam querebat, in huius perceptione degustans., ad resistendum contrarijs viciorum incursibus decetero non // f. 318 c
solum fortior, sed et animosior assurrexit. Quanto vero maiori
pondere certaminis onerari se sensit., tanto feruentiori desiderio
pariter et affectu, huius deifici sacramenti perceptionem exercuit ;
illam dominicam exhortationem in memoria retinens., qua suis
electis dominus huius participationem indulsit :, virtutemque
viuificatiuam in eo consistere demonstrauit. [1]

152 Videns autem humani generis aduersarium, ex omni parte
sibi pertinacissime resistentem, timensque [2] ne ad hoc saluberrimum desiderium, quod in percipiendo viuifico sacramento, domino
largiente, susceperat, tandem aliquando, per torporis ignauiam,
a corde suo, versipellis, excuteret : modis omnibus hoc ignauie
pondus [3], a cervice mentis sue, crebris reluctationibus, abicere
studuit ; et ne tantum in se bonum sua negligentia deperiret.,
et sic demum, illo medicinali destituta suffragio, dyabolicis sua-
sionibus etiam in ceteris temptationibus, male cauta, succumberet :
hoc ipsum [4], deliberatione prouida, non solum ob virtutis illius
effectum., verum etiam ob negligentie quoque vicium euitandum.,
studioso iugiter exercitio frequentauit [5].

153 Nec defuit illi maligni seductoris astutia,: ne se, ad tanti
perceptionem sacramenti velut indignam, et pluribus malarum
cogitationum sordibus inuolutam, irreuerenter ingereret, venenoso
susurrio creberrime suggerentis : ; sed virgo domini, licet indigni-
tatem quidem suam agnosceret., quia tamen nullius mortalis

SHE FREQUENTLY RECEIVED THE SACRAMENT OF THE ALTAR IN THE TIME OF TEMPTATIONS
Chapter Fifteen

151 The saving and life-giving Sacrament of the Lord's Body was this blessed woman's supreme remedy and special refuge throughout this laborious struggle. In all her trouble Beatrice loved, sought and worshipped it as her singular protection, and very often tasting it in the sought-for grace of consolation, she arose from it not only stronger but also more spirited in her resistance against the hostile attacks of the vices. The greater the weight of the struggle with which she felt burdened, the more fervent were the desire and love she exercised in the reception of this deifying Sacrament, remembering the Lord's exhortation by which he shared it with his elect and showed that a life-giving power dwelt in it.[1]

152 Beatrice saw that the adversary of the human race resisted her obstinately at every point, and she feared that in his subtlety he might finally shake from her heart through torpor and cowardice the healthy desire for this life-giving Sacrament received from the Lord. Therefore she strove frequently and in every way to cast off from her neck, so to speak, the weight of this cowardice. Lest so great a good perish by her negligence, and thus being deprived of this medicinal support and poorly on her guard, she should succumb to the devil's argument in other persuasions, she frequently and deliberately received this Sacrament not only for its own effects but also to avoid the vice of negligence.

153 The malicious seducer did not lack cunning, for he very often suggested with poisonous whispers that Beatrice should not irreverently intrude into the reception of so great a Sacrament, unworthy as she was and involved in many sordid evil thoughts. But the Lord's virgin, although recognizing her unworthiness, constantly set her claim to immunity and innocence against this wicked suggestor because she judged herself not guilty of any mortal sin for

1. *Jn 6:51*

piaculi, propter quod ab illius communione foret arcenda, se
35 consciam estimabat., <h>uius immunitatis et innocentie sue
tytulum ipsi malignissimo suggestori constanter obiecit : ; et,
illius ven<en>osas immissiones ad nichilum redigens, immobilis
in suo proposito perdurauit.

154 Frequentissime quoque sancte femine contigit, quod, in
40 perceptione salutaris pabuli, multum consolationis et spiritualis
recreationis inuenit., quibus, in omni virtutum exercitio copio-
sissime renouata., futuris temptationum insidijs, cautiori decetero
diligentia, se obiecit : ; et quas, paulo ante, non sine graui //
f. 318 d molestia tolerare potuerat., velut umbram ad solis ra-
45 dium euanescentem, ita viciorum cateruas, accedens deuotionis
feruor ocius effugauit.

Quociens tamen ad hoc consolationis beneficium, impediente se
sathana, peruenire non potuit : , totiens ad consolatorium sacre
scripture sinum, auxilium quesitura, confugit : ; ibique, dulcissima
50 verba diuine consolationis inueniens., ex hijs suo pro tempore
desiderio satisfecit. Ibi quippe de saluatoris infantia seu puericia,
de christi miraculorum efficacia., de passione, resurrectione vel
ascensione dominica., de gentium electione, de fidelium eterna
predestinatione, consolatoria multa reperiens., confestim, deuo-
55 tionis igne vehementer accensa recanduit : ; et sic iterum, celesti
quodammodo pabulo recreata., consuetis temptationum assultibus,
auxiliante se christi gratia, constantior simul et fortior obuiauit.

155 Sic ergo duplici, sicut prediximus, necessitate constricta : ,
sacramenti huius perceptionem frequentare consueuit. Nam spiri-
60 tualis affectio, qua speciali hoc ipsum deuotione dilexit, ab illo
prorsus abstinere se vetuit : ; et timor, quem ex continuis bellorum
incursibus in mente conceperat, ab hoc, e regione, semetipsam
abstrahere non permisit. Talibus itaque consolationum auxilijs,
per omne tempus huius periculosi certaminis, contra dyabolicos
65 assultus armata processit : ; et licet, multa laboris instantia, fatigata restiterit., diuino tamen adiutorio preualens, ipsum tandem,
vt premisimus, inimicum cum angelis suis apostaticis omniumque
viciorum suorum turmis ad nichilum redigens., procul de cordis
et conscientie sue finibus effugauit.

which she should be kept away from this Communion. She re-
duced his poisonous suggestions to nothing and remained immov-
able in her resolve.

154 The holy woman very often found great consolation and spiritual relief in the reception of this salutary food. Abundantly
renewed in the exercise of all the virtues, she set herself with more
care and caution against the future ambushes of temptations. The
multitude of vices which slightly earlier she could scarcely stand
without grave trouble, were quickly put to flight like shadows
vanishing in the sun's rays by her new fervor and devotion.

Whenever Satan prevented her from attaining this beneficial
consolation, she fled for help to the consoling bosom of Sacred
Scripture, and there found the ever-sweet words of divine consolation, satisfying her desire on them for the time being. There she
found many consolations in the infancy and boyhood of the
Saviour, the election of the gentiles and the eternal predestination
of the faithful, and immediately she was greatly rekindled by the
fire of devotion. Thus she was, in a way, again refreshed with
heavenly food and with the help of Christ's grace she went to meet
the usual assaults of temptations with greater constancy and
bravery.

155 Thus Beatrice was accustomed to receive this Sacrament frequently, constrained by two needs, as we have said. The spiritual
affection and special loving devotion she felt for it forbade her
abstinence from it, and the fear conceived in her mind because of
the continuous attacks of the enemy did not let her withdraw from
it. Armed and aided by such consolations during the whole of this
dangerous struggle, she proceeded against the devil's assaults.
Although she struggled with great fatigue caused by the great intensity of her labor, she did prevail with the divine help, as we
said, and brought to nought the enemy with his apostate angels and
all his crowds of vices, driving them far from her heart and
conscience.

❡ DE GRAUI INCOMMODO
QUOD EX TEDIO PRESENTIS VITE SUSTINUIT
xvj. capitulum

156 Cum autem in predicto certamine virgo christi, continuo
ferme triennio, fidelissime perdurasset, nec ·vmquam ad dextram
vel <ad> sinistram, // f. *319 a* alicuius fatigationis impellente
proteruia, declinando. , victorie triumphum e certamine repor-
tasset ; , hostiles quidem <insidias> aduersantes sibi, decetero,
cum soliti timoris et laboris dispendio, non sustinuit. , nec tamen
ad plenarie quietis <et pacis> fruitionem interim assurgere
potuit : ; sed ab eo statu quem hucusque descripsimus. , rursus
in alium, plenum vtique laboris et erumpnis. , plenum doloris et
miserie declinauit.

Siquidem ex predictis passionibus, hanc mortalem vitam breuem
quidem tempore. , sed infinitis miserijs a prima natiuitatis hora
donec per mortis amaritudinem in puluerem homo resoluatur et
cinerem. , vndique. circum<s>eptam intelligens. , hanc ipsam
magno cepit abhorrere fastidio : , et tamquam in tenebroso carceris
inclusa teneretur ergastulo. , ita se relegatam doluit in hoc mundo.
Hunc quippe nichil aliud quam carcerem tenebrosum et plenum
squaloribus estimans, quanto se grauius huius miserijs et erumpnis, quasi cathenarum nexibus, indesinenter oneratam aspexit : ,
tanto feruentius, ad libertatem patrie celestis aspirans, hinc, tedio
grauata, contabuit. , illinc vero, cum apostolo dissolui cupiens et
esse cum christo pre maximo cordis desiderio. , illud quoque
apostolicum. : 'infelix ego homo, quis me liberabit de corpore
mortis huius'. , per illud tempus repetitione creberrima frequentauit.

157 Creuerat quidem hoc feruens desiderium ab olim in corde
sancte femine : ; verumtamen, istis temporibus, in tantum conua-
lescendo cepit assurgere ; , quod non [1], diebus aut noctibus, ad
aliud quippiam memoriam applicare valuerit. , sed et oculos

THE GRAVE INCONVENIENCE SHE SUFFERED FROM
WEARINESS OF THE PRESENT LIFE
Chapter Sixteen

156 When Christ's virgin Beatrice had very faithfully persevered in the forementioned struggle for almost three continuous years and had carried off the triumph and victory, never deviating either to right or to left through any weariness, she no longer endured the hostile ambushes against her with her usual outlay of fear and labor, but neither could she rise to the enjoyment of full quiet and peace. Instead, she turned from the state we described to another one, full of labor and hardship, sorrow and misery.

From the forementioned sufferings she understood that this mortal life is short[1] in span and everywhere hedged about with unlimited miseries from the first hour of man's birth till he is dissolved into dust and ashes through the bitterness of death, and she began to be weary of it and to abhor it. She grieved at being assigned to this world as if she were held in a gloomy prison. Thinking the world indeed nothing but a gloomy prison, the more she saw herself constantly and heavily burdened with its miseries and hardships as with the links of a chain, the more fervently she sighed for the freedom of the heavenly fatherland. On one hand, she pined away, weighed down with weariness; on the other, wanting with the apostle to be dissolved and to be with Christ,[2] she frequently repeated his words: 'Unhappy man that I am, who will free me from the body of this death?'.[3]

157 This fervent desire had been growing a long time in Beatrice's heart, but now it began to increase so strongly that not only could she not apply her memory to anything else day or night, but scarcely ever could she recall her bodily eyes from looking

---

1. 1 Co 7:29   2. Ph 1:23   3. *Rm 7:24*

corporales vix umquam potuerit ab aspectu supernorum ad hec
infima, sursum erecto desiderio suo nimirum, obsequentes [2] offi-
35 cio reuocare. Unde frequenter accidit, vt ab alijs, modo simili
non affectis., ob hoc, subsannationis iniuriam virgo domini sustineret impune : ; quippe fatuitatem estimantibus, erectis sursum
obtutibus illam, tamquam // f. 319 b deliram, celos <indesi-
nenter> aspicere. Sed mens, cuius erat in celestibus conuersatio,
40 nichil horum aduertens que gerebantur extra se :, nec prouocata
molestijs., nec subsannationibus lacessita., tanto quidem diffi-
cilius ab intentione sua reuocari potuit :, quanto nimirum expeditius ad christum, caput suum, per hec confidebat iniuriarum
vestigia propinquare.
45 In tantum autem huius feruor desiderij mentem eius accenderat :,
ut quotiens hinc exilij sui miserias., illinc vero immarcessibiles patrie celestis opulentias in memoriam reuersabat., totiens suspirantis
palpebre lacrimarum ymbre madescerent ; et plerumque cor illius,
per multum temporis spacium, ex desiderio patefactum, hiantesque
50 simul arterie frequenter illi mortis horrorem incuterent., cum ad
naturalem situm, impediente desiderio, sese reducere non valerent [3].
158 Quid, proch dolor ! hic dicturi sumus nos tepidi et remissi ? Nos, inquam,
peccatorum sordibus et terrenis voluptatibus inuoluti., quorum omnis delectatio
versatur in transitorijs ; quorum requies est in corporalibus immundicijs : ;
55 quorum denique cessat et deficit apperitus, dum vel modicum quid ingeritus
de eternis ? Quid, inquam, dicturi sumus, inertes et stolidi., cum hec de
beatrice nostris auribus insonuerint., quorum non solum non patefiunt corda
pre celestium desiderio, non aperiuntur arterie pre celestium appetitu fame-
lico., non mortem minatur excedens modum, amara simul et dulcis eternorum
60 affectio., sed nec modicum quidem excitatur, ad illorum recordationem, a
terrenis voluptatibus captiuata deuotio. ; quorum mundanis suffocata delicijs
voluntas et intentio, nec monitis nec promissionibus ad meliora proficiunt :,
nec flagellis aut correptionibus erudite, celestium gaudiorum exquirendo delicias, a voluptatis miserabili appetitu, omni bruto stolidiores, omnique duriores
65 // f. 319 c cilice, resipiscunt.
159 Profecto [4] non talis erat huius sancte mulieris, ita celestium

upward to attend to these lower duties, so much was her desire raised on high. Therefore it often happened that others not similarly affected, carelessly hurt the Lord's virgin by making fun of her, thinking it silliness and calling her crazy for constantly looking at the sky with upturned gaze. But her mind's conversation was in heaven[4] and she noticed nothing of what was taking place around her. Neither provoked by annoyances nor exasperated by mockery, she was harder to recall from her intention as she became the more confident she was approaching Christ, her head, through this path of insults.

So much did this fervent desire enkindle her mind that her eyelids would be wet with floods of tears as often as she remembered the miseries of this exile and the unfading riches of the heavenly fatherland. Through desire her heart was often dilated for long periods of time; and this, together with her enlarged arteries would strike her with the shudder of death since her desire prevented them from returning to their natural state and position.

158 Alas, what shall we slack tepid people say? We are wrapped around with the filth of sin and earthly pleasures. All our delight is in passing things, and we take our relaxation in bodily impurities. Our appetite falls off and fails as soon as anything about eternity is introduced. What, I repeat, shall we inert, stolid people say when these things about our Beatrice ring in our ears? Our hearts do not dilate with heavenly desires; our arteries do not open with a famished appetite for heavenly things; an excessive bitter-sweet affection for eternity does not threaten us with death. Our devotion, held captive by earthly pleasures is not even mildly excited by the remembrance of them. Our will and intention, smothered by worldly delights, make no progress under either threats or promises. Being more stolid than any brute and harder than any flint, we are not taught either by blows or corrections to repent and to turn from a miserable appetite for pleasure to seek the delights of heavenly joys.

159 Certainly not such as this was this holy woman's devotion, so

4. Ph 3:20

desiderio gaudiorum <sauciata> deuotio :, <sic> ad eterna
suspirans, vvlnerata simul et amore languens, affectio., vt ex
eius ore, vel e naribus, copiosi sanguinis riuos frequenter, desi-
70 derij <nimij> feruore, eduxerit ;, et sic demum exterioris hominis fragile domicilium, violentia sue correptionis affecerit :, vt
in languorum illud validissimum precipitando deiecerit ; qui tunc
quidem eius in corpore grassando conualuit :, sed, per annorum
multa curricula, quibus postea deguit in hac vita, indiuiduo sibi
75 <colligatus> vinculo passionis⁵, ab eo decetero non recessit.
Sic denique vehementissimum hoc desiderium illius, in mente
continue succrescendo preualuit :, vt aliquotiens, etiam corporalium sensuum obsequio destituta, quid extra se fiebat horum
officio non discerneret ; sed, freneticorum instar et amentium,
80 ad omnia que sustentando corpori agnoscuntur accomoda : nonnisi coacta, vel ab alijs increpata, sensum et animum applicaret.
160 Unum tamen et magnum repperit, in hoc statu nimis erump-
noso, solacium. : viuificum scilicet et consolatorium dominici corporis et sanguinis sacramentum : ; quod nimirum eo tempore tanto
85 frequentauit instantius ;, quantum per hoc ipsis celestibus ad
que iugiter aspirabat, (cum hoc sacramentum nichil aliud quam
ipsum verum natum de virgine christi corpus existat) :, et-si
nondum sempiterne fruitionis copia., saltem crebre participationis
et communionis frequentia, propinquabat. Hoc interim beate
90 femine summum solacium. ; hoc, contra cunctas condicionis humane miserias, vnicum fuit et singulare refugium ; hoc illi simul
et sustentationis pabulum., et in via presentis exilij salutare
viaticum :, et in oppressionibus et erumpnis, medicinale de se⁶,
prebuit alimentum. Fuit etiam in hoc statu per annum fere
95 continuum; in quo, quales et quantas molestias ex hoc vehementissimo // f. 319 d pertulerit desiderio :, quo sublimius
quisque nostrum ad idem assurgere poterit., eo sibi, docente
nimirum experientia, manifestius apparebit.

smitten by the desire of heavenly joys. So much did her affection
sigh for eternal things, so wounded and languishing with love was
it that its vehement desire caused frequent and copious streams of
blood to flow from her mouth and nose. In short, the violence of
its assaults so affected the frail dwelling of the outer man that it
cast her into very grave languor. This languor increased its hold on
her body, and during the many remaining years of her life fastened
itself to her as her own passion. Thus this very vehement desire of
hers waxed increasingly strong in her mind until sometimes she
was deprived of the use of her bodily senses, and did not know by
them what went on around her. Like the mad and insane she would
apply her sense and mind only under external coercion or rebuke
to what is recognized as useful to sustaining the body.

160 The one great solace that Beatrice found in this excessively
distressful state was the life-giving, consoling Sacrament of the
Lord's body and blood. At this time she visited it more insistently
as by it she approached, if not with the abundance of eternal enjoyment, at least by frequent sharing and communion, the
heavenly things to which she forever aspired. For this Sacrament
is nothing else than the true body of Christ, born of the virgin.
This was the blessed woman's greatest solace during this time;
this was her unique and singular refuge against all the miseries of
the human condition. This was both the food that sustained her,
and her wholesome *viaticum* on the road of the present exile. It
provided her with intrinsically medicinal nourishment in her oppression and hardship. Beatrice was in this state for almost a
whole year. The more that any of us can rise to the same degree of
sublimity, the more clearly he will know by experience what kind
of hardships and what great hardships Beatrice suffered from this
vehement desire.

❡ DE EO QUOD A MOLESTIJS CORDIS SUI LIBERARI.,
ET A DOMINO CONSOLARI MERUIT

xvij. capitulum

161 Cum autem complacuit ei qui in electam <sibi> sponsam
hanc euocare dignatus est., vt ab hoc quoque, doloroso nimis
incommodo mentem illius efficacissimo miserationis sue solacio
releuaret;, accidit vna dierum, vt ad sermonem, qui ad edificationem animarum declamatorio proponebatur predicatoris officio,
simul cum ceteris ipsius loci monialibus assideret. Quem cum
virgo domini, multo deuotionis affectu, iam auscultare cepisset.,
et illius optima queque, tenaci retractationis studio, memorie
commendasset:, repente, predicto sermone pro parte media vix
completo., cepit illius spiritus intrinsecus a diuino spiritu constringi mirabiliter et artari. Cuius connexionis tam valida fuit et
indissolubilis vnio:, quod in omni parte corporis vigens anima,
confestim hunc interne complexionis sensum per corporalia quoque membra diffuderit;, et omnis illius humanitas, extrinsecus
huius vnitionis virtutem experiri cepit:, quam, in ipsa sui visita-
tione, suus ille spiritus, intrinsecus degustauit.

162 Cuius insolite nouitatis gratiam, cum electa domini mirando
cepisset aduertere., et quid portenderet hec diuini spiritus, illius
in anima, tam repentina simul et inconsueta diffusio, cum totis
intelligentie sue viribus conaretur indagare;, confestim diuinam
vocem, interius ad animam suam influentem audiuit:, et leui
susurrio per hec verba loquentem sibi dominum intellexit. 'Consolari, inquit, te iam oportet, dilectissima filia:, quia nimias afflic-
tionum tuarum molestias, quibus, huius exilij tui deplorando miserias, fatigari te conspicio, sub tanti laboris dispendio diutius
tolerare te nullatenus // f. 320 a acquiesco. Verum in hoc potius
assentiendo me tibi finaliter obligo., quod ab inuicem non dis-
iungemur decetero, sed ex nunc insimul uniamur., inter nos
confirmato perpetue caritatis et fidei munimento.'

163 Quam <diuine> consolationis vocem cum auido cordis auditu

HOW SHE DESERVED TO BE FREED
FROM THE VEXATIONS OF HER HEART
AND TO BE CONSOLED BY THE LORD
Chapter Seventeen

161 Yet since he who had deigned to arouse this distress in his chosen bride was pleased to relieve her mind of this painful inconvenience by his own very effective solace, it happened one day that Beatrice was sitting with the other nuns of the place, listening to the sermon being given in public for the edification of souls by the preacher in office. The Lord's virgin began to listen to the sermon with great devotion and tenaciously committed its best points to memory. Suddenly, when the sermon was less than half finished, her inner spirit began to be marvellously constricted and compressed by the divine spirit. The union and connection were so strong and so indissoluble that her soul, active in every part of the body, immediately diffused this sense of internal embrace throughout the members of her body. Her whole humanity began to experience outwardly the power of this united action which her spirit tasted inwardly in the visitation itself.

162 When the Lord's chosen began to be aware in amazement of this new and unusual grace and to attempt to investigate with all her strength of mind what this sudden unaccustomed diffusion of the divine spirit in her soul portended, suddenly she heard the divine voice speaking to her soul, and she understood the Lord speaking these words to her in a soft whisper: 'It is right for you to be consoled now, most beloved daughter, for in no way do I consent to you bearing any longer so great an outlay of labor, the excessive vexations and afflictions with which I see you exhausted by your laments over the miseries of this exile. In assenting to this, finally, I pledge to you that we shall never be separated from each other but shall from now on be united, love and faithfulness being perpetually confirmed and ratified between us.'

163 When the servant of God, Beatrice, heard with avid heart this

dei famula suscepisset :, tam delectabili, tamque superfluenti
³⁵ consolationis dulcedine spiritus illius inebriari cepit intrinsecus ;,
vt, sopita totius sensualitatis humanitatisque molestia., nichil
horum que gerebantur exterius, ad fruendum spiritualis dulcedinis adepto beneficio, tractis introrsus ipsis quoque corporalibus
sensibus, eo tempore discernere vel considerare valuerit :; sed,
⁴⁰ pre nimia iocunditatis affluentia sese diutius sustinere non pre-
ualens., in gremio cuiusdam ex monialibus, vicina sibi sessione
coniuncte, deorsum inclinata mox corruit ;, et per totum residui
sermonis spacium, solis interioribus occupata delicijs, ac si corporali sompno detenta iacuerit :, ita, totius corporis membris ab
⁴⁵ omni motu consueto vacantibus., inter brachia socie monialis,
immobilis perdurauit.
Finito vero sermone, sanctimonialis, in cuius gremio paulo ante
reclinata cubauerat., illam, a contemplationis sompno iam aliquantulum excitatam, ab infirmitatis cuiusquam incommodo re-
⁵⁰ pentine correptam existimans., ad stratum suum illam, gratia
repausationis, adduxit :, et in eo, non corporali grauatam incommodo., sed celestis dulcedinis inebriatam poculo, fideli deuotionis obsequio collocauit.
Ibi dei electissima, fruens ineffabilis quiete delectationis, immota
⁵⁵ permansit : quippe cuius animam, vt sibi sentire concessum est.,
lux claritatis diuine perfudit, et eternitatis <radijs>, absque
reuerberationis obstaculo, perlustrauit.
164 Sub eodem siquidem tempore, sancte trinitatis ineffabile
misterium, ad exercitandum in eo deuote meditationis officium.
⁶⁰ illius considerationis <adspectui> crebra repetitione se obtulit :;
vbi nimirum eternaliter a patre nascentem filium., et ab vtroque
procedentem spiritum ; vbi etiam distinctio- // f. 320 b -nem
personarum., vnitatem essentie deitatis simul et potentie., cetera
quoque trinitatis ipsius sacrosancta misteria, tanto viuaciori quanto
⁶⁵ clariori purificate mentis intelligentia peragrare promeruit :; in
quorum recordatione dulcissima, per multa post hec horarum
spacia delectabiliter immorans., in pace mentis et cordis iubilo,
requieuit. Ab eo quoque tempore, molestias presentis exilij, pro-

word of divine consolation, her spirit began to be inwardly inebriated with such a delightful, overflowing sweet consolation that
all the vexations of her human sensuality were lulled to sleep and
she could not discern or consider anything happening around her,
since her physical senses withdrew inside to enjoy the spiritual
sweetness of the favor obtained. For excessive joy she could no
longer hold herself erect, but soon slumped down on the lap of one
of the nuns sitting next to her. For the rest of the sermon Beatrice
remained motionless in the arms of her nun-companion, wholly
occupied in interior delights as if asleep, with all her bodily members quite still.

When the sermon was over, the nun in whose lap she had been
lying, took Beatrice, now somewhat awakened from her contemplative sleep, to her bed for a rest, thinking she had suddenly
been taken ill. The nun obligingly put in bed someone not smitten
by bodily sickness but drunken on the cup of heavenly sweetness.

There God's chosen one remained motionless, enjoying a rest of
unspeakable delight. She was allowed to sense that the light of
divine glory was poured over her soul, illuminating it with the rays
of eternity without hindrance or backlash.

164 At the same time the unspeakable mystery of the Holy Trinity
frequently offered itself to her consideration, to arouse her devout
meditation on it. With the lively clear understanding of her
purified mind she deserved to investigate the Son eternally born of
the Father, the Spirit proceeding from them both, the distinction of
persons, the unity of the divine essence and power, and the other
holy mysteries of the Trinity. Remembering these sweet things,
Beatrice rested in peace of mind and jubilation of heart, dwelling
on them with delight for a long time afterwards. From then on she

tegente se diuina clementia, sentire non potuit :; sed, in diuina
70 promissione[1] spem totam et fiduciam collocans., omne cordis
sui desiderium ipsius beneplacito de cetero conformauit.

ℭ DE FEDERE PERPETUE DILECTIONIS
CONFIRMATO INTER CHRISTUM ET ANIMAM <SUAM>
xviij. capitulum

165 Alio quoque tempore, cum in choro missarum celebritati
5 simul cum alijs interesset., et, multo deuotionis affectu sursum
eleuato corde, soli supernorum contemplationi meditando vaca-
ret., accidit, vt repentino quodam hyatu cor illius, in momento,
in ictu oculi, patefieret, et, citissime reclusum, in situ se solito
relocaret[1]. Cuius rei misterium ignorans, virgo beatissima do-
10 minum exorare cepit attentius., vt causam illi tam momentanee
visitationis ostenderet, et quid super <hoc> iuberet fieri, certa
reuelatione sibi nichilominus indicaret. Cui per hec eadem verba,
non vvlgari sed latino prolata sermone[2]., pius dominus mox
respondit.: 'Fedus, inquit, ineamus., pactum pangamus:, vt
15 decetero non diuidamur, sed veraciter vniamur.' Ad quam vocem
nimis exhilarata., tale continuo responsum domino reddidit:,
 per quod ad obseruationem tam saluberrimi federis, pactione
volontaria se protinus obligauit. 'Paratum, inquit, domine, cor
meum ad exequendum omnia quecumque mandaueris., presertim
20 ad obligandum memet ad obseruationem tanti federis:, per quod
mihi, fidem integram seruaturum te., stipulatione tam liberrima
repromittis'.
166 Qua vix responsione peracta, visum est ei continuo, quod
ipse totius consolationis et misericordie dominus, illius animam,
25 amplexu suauissimo, sibimetipsi totam imprimeret:, et sicut,
impressa sigillo mollis cere materies, illius in se karacterem representat., sic ad ymaginem suam // f. 320 c illam effigiatam,

was protected by divine mercy and could not feel the vexations of the present exile, but placing all her hope and confidence in the divine promise, she thereafter conformed the whole desire of her heart to God's good pleasure.

A PACT OF EVERLASTING LOVE BETWEEN
CHRIST AND HER SOUL IS CONFIRMED
Chapter Eighteen

165 At another time when she was present in choir with the others for the celebration of Mass, and was dwelling in meditating only on heavenly things with heart uplifted in great devotion, it happened in a moment, in the twinkling of an eye,[1] that in a suddenly appearing cleft [in his breast], Christ's heart momentarily appeared, then quickly closed again and the heart restored itself to its usual position. The holy virgin, not knowing what to make of this mystery, began to exhort the Lord more intently to show her the cause of such a momentary visitation, and to give her a clear revelation of what he would order done about it. The loving Lord quickly answered her in these very words, spoken not in the vernacular but in Latin: *'Fedus, inquit, ineamus; pactum pangamus; vt decetero non dividamur, sed veraciter vniamur.'* [Let us enter into a covenant; let us make a pact, that in the future we may be not divided but truly united]. Overjoyed at hearing this, Beatrice immediately gave the Lord this answer by pledging herself willingly to keep such a salutary covenant: 'O Lord', she said, 'my heart is ready[2] to do whatever you command, especially to oblige myself to keep such a covenant by which you promise so freely to keep total faith with me'.

166 Scarcely was the answer out of her mouth when it seemed to her that he, the Lord of all consolation and mercy,[3] pressed her soul wholly to himself in the sweetest embrace; and just as soft wax, pressed with a seal, displays the seal's character in itself, so

1. 1 Co 15:52   2. Ps 65:8   3. 2 Co 1:3

diuinus spiritus redderet : , et, ad similitudinem suam decentissime figuratam, quadam sibi <proportionali> conformaret consonancia.
30 In illa quoque diuini amplexus vnione, rursus dominice sponsionis, de seruanda sibi fide, pignus accipere meruit ; quam et ipsa se firmiter seruaturam, et numquam fore a se decetero violandam iterata stipulatione promisit : ; et, ne, diuine voluntati contrarium quid appetendo. , fidem quam se domino seruare spoponderat
35 irritare presumeret. , illi totum quod potuit, id est corpus simul et animam, loco pignoris obligauit.

Ex tunc vero, perpetua fidei sponsione christo se desponsatam intelligens. , in cordis quiete simul et spiritus libertate, promissa fidelitatis debita iugiter exsoluendo, permansit : , et ad exequen-
40 dum dei beneplacitum, obliuiscendo cum apostolo que retro fuerant. , in anteriora, continuato virtutum exercitio, se extendit. 167 Nec defuit illi diuina probatio qua, veraciter-ne diligeret deum, agnosceret. , et, <utrum> hanc fidelitatis pactionem, etiam in temptationis tempore commendatam haberet : , per fla-
45 gellum correptionis interroganti se domino responderet.

Sub eodem siquidem tempore, festo sanctorum omnium immi- nente [3], graui cotidiane vel acute febris incommodo fatigata : , dolores quidem corporales importunos admodum, vt ipsa vis febrium exigebat, per quot [4] dies illa sustinuit ; sed quanto cru-
50 delius interim vexabatur in corpore. , tanto firmius, in hoc tempta- tionis procelloso turbine, gratiarum actionis et patientie tabulas [5] amplexando, diuine <desponsationis> se dignam exhibuit : , et fidem quam seruare promiserat. , eo firmiori quo magis necessa- rio, presertim in necessitatis tempore, stabilitatis proposito, con-
55 seruauit.

168 Cum autem, annuente superna clementia. , mitigato partim estu febris acutissime, conualescere iam cepisset : , assueuit illud vvlgare prouerbium ad memoriam reuocare quo dicitur : ab egri- tudinis estu conualescentes, ex quadam obseruata consuetudine,
60 vel // f. 320 d meliores solito, vel deteriores fieri. Quapropter, vt,

the divine Spirit modeled her soul according to his own image, and conformed it very appropriately to his own likeness with some proportional harmony. In that divine embrace and union she again deserved to receive the Lord's pledge and promise about keeping faith with her, and she, on her part, again promised firmly to keep the same faith, which she would never again violate in the future. And she bound everything she could, that is, body and soul, as a pledge that she would not withdraw the faithfulness she had promised to the Lord, by seeking anything contrary to the divine will.

From then on Beatrice understood that she was betrothed to Christ forever, and she remained in quietness of heart and freedom of spirit, constantly paying her promised debts of fidelity. Forgetting the things that were behind,[4] she with the Apostle reached out to those that were ahead by the steady exercise of virtues, to achieve divine good-pleasure.

167 There was no lack of divine testing, by which it could be known whether she would truthfully love God and respect this covenant of fidelity even in times of temptation, and how she would answer the Lord who was questioning her by the rod of correction.

About this same time, just before the feast of All Saints, she was grievously fatigued every day by high fevers and for some days suffered recurring bodily pains caused by the violence of the fever; but the more cruelly she was harassed in body, the more firmly she embraced the stipulated demands for thanksgiving and patience in this stormy whirlwind of temptation, thus proving herself worthy of the divine betrothal. She kept the faith she had promised with a resolve of stability that was the firmer for being more necessary especially in this time of distress.

168 When, by heaven's mercy, the very high fever partly abated and she began to improve, she remembered the commonplace proverb which says: it is an observed fact that those convalescing from dire sickness become either better or worse. Now that she

4. Ph 3:13

in huius pytagorice nunc littere biuio constituta., ramum illius
dexterum, id est viam meliorationis apprehendere valuisset:, in
omni tam affectionum quam actionum studio solito, curabat vigilantior inueniri.

65 Spiritus quidem timoris domini mentem illius in tantum affe-
cerat:, vt nullis gratiarum donis quibus a deo locupletari mere-
batur assidue, semetipsam, ne dicam in arrogantiam., sed nec
in modicam meritorum suorum confidentiam, eleuare presumeret;
sed quanto potiora gratiarum in se munera deprehendit:, tanto
70 se firmius obligatam in gratiarum actionibus, eorumdemque donorum virtuosis prouectibus, illi presertim a quo gratis oblata
susceperat, instructa diuini timoris spiritu, certissime recognouit.
169 In tantum etiam ipse timoris spiritus, illius in corde preualuit:, quod, etsi nullo, presenti tempore, de cuiuslibet generis
75 perpetratione peccati, lesam intra se conscienciam inueniret.,
adeo tamen futurorum temporum incertos casus extimuit, vt,
propter nimiam sensuum prauitatem voluntatisque instabilem
firmitatem, in cuiuscumque peccati consensum incidere pertimes-
cens, temporalem hanc mortem ex desiderio frequenter optaret;,
80 et qualiscumque supplicij penas libenter exsolueret;, dum, per
mortis compendium, ad eum statum in quo decetero peccatum
<commissura> non fuerat, absque peccati macula pertingere
valuisset.

Aduertebat <quidem>, limpidissimo discretionis intuitu, timorem
85 hunc, vtpote de quadam pusillanimitatis aut diffidentie radice
nascentem, non satis honori diuino competere:; quapropter et
viuaci zelo rectitudinis hunc, per crebram sui correptionem con-
fessionemque, satagebat a ceruice cordis sui frequenter excutere., Sed quantumcumque, reluctando, se conabatur aduersus
90 illum erigere., ipsum tamen superare vel effugare non potuit:;
donec⁶, ad hunc statum laboris et doloris compassiuo miserationis sue respectu, dominus in alium dignatus est, effugato
predicti timoris offendiculo, commutare.

was placed at the crossroad of this pythagorean saying, she took pains to be more watchful than usual in each effort of her affections and actions so that she might take, with her usual zeal, the right-hand way, that is, the way of improvement.

The spirit of the fear of the Lord took such hold of Beatrice's mind that she did not only presume to rise up in arrogance because of the gifts of grace with which the Lord had steadily enriched her, but she did not even have a moderate confidence in her own merits. Instructed by the spirit of the fear of the Lord, she certainly realized that, the more gifts of grace she saw in herself, the more firmly obligated she was to thank him from whom she had freely received them and to make progress in the virtues and the gifts received.

169 The spirit of fear so prevailed in Beatrice's heart that, even if at the present time she found in herself no wound of conscience regarding some sin, she so feared possible future falls and consent to sins of some kind or other (because of the excessive depravity of the senses and the instability of the will) that she frequently wished for this temporal death, and would willingly have paid the penalties of any punishment as long as she might, without stain of sin, by this shortcut of death arrive at that state where she would no longer commit any sin. With utterly clear discernment Beatrice noticed that this fear, which sprang from a certain pusillanimity and distrust, scarcely honored God, and therefore with a lively zeal for rectitude she frequently worked at shaking it from her heart through frequent self-rebuke and confession. But however much she fought back and tried to rise against it, she could not conquer it or put it to flight, until the Lord, looking with compassion and mercy on this state of labor and sorrow, deigned to raise her to another state, putting to flight this barrier of fear.

// f. 321 a

⟪ DE EO QUOD RAPTA FUERIT IN CHORO SERAPHIN
Decimum nonum capitulum

170 Cum igitur, releuata ab egritudinis lectulo[1], necdum plene
sospitatis virgo christi medelam adepta fuisset : , accidit vna
dierum, vt ante fores oratorij, loco scilicet infirmis debilibusque
specialiter deputato, secum residens, et missale, quod in choro
celebrabatur, officium reuerenter auscultans, totisque nisibus animum ad celestia subleuando quiesceret : , et solis spiritualibus
delicijs occupata, mentem in eternorum contemplatione delectabiliter exerceret. Vbi cum aliquantulo iam temporis spacio, donec
videlicet ad ⟨alleluia⟩ psallendo peruentum est, sic in pace
cordis animique dulcedine recubasset ; , ipse benignissimus misericordiarum dominus, illius animam igne sui amoris, velut ignito
iaculo, repente perfodit : , et vehementissimo quodam impetus sui
mucrone, quasi flammanti gladio, valide penetrauit. In qua per-
cussione, domini vox clamantis al illius animam vsque peruenit. ,
et quod, ex omnibus quos vita mortalis in hoc seculo retinebat,
eam specialiter elegisset, et cum electioribus quos, aut in celesti
patria ⟨iam⟩ regnantes eterna beatitudine recreabat. , vel quos
in presenti seculo pressuris adhuc et tribulationibus exercebat. ,
illius nomen in libro vite, manu sue clementie, conscripsisset :
certis ei demonstrationis indicijs eodem in tempore reuelauit.

171 Ad quam vocem dominice consolationis. , confestim in statu
cognitionis proprie sese recolligens : , humiliato corde dominum
interrogare cepit et querere. , quam ob causam, ad tam sublime
electionis ⟨culmen⟩, illam ⟨adscripserit⟩ ; cum, nullis suis
meritis precedentibus, tam excelse prerogatiuam gratie promereri
valuerit : , quantam illi, gratuite pietatis sue clementia, sub eodem
temporis spacio demonstrauit.

Cui, super hoc sciscitanti, pius dominus sic respondit. : 'Propter

HOW SHE WAS CAUGHT UP
INTO THE CHOIR OF THE SERAPHIM
Chapter Nineteen

170 When Christ's virgin had risen from her sick bed, but had not yet fully recovered her health, it happened one day that she was sitting by herself in front of the doors of the oratory, in the place assigned to the weak and infirm. She was reverently listening to Mass being celebrated in choir, and was quietly resting, lifting her mind to heavenly things, with all her effort. Occupied with spiritual delight alone, she was exercising her mind in delightedly contemplating things eternal. When she had rested there in peace of heart and sweetness of mind for some little time, up to the singing of the Alleluia, the ever-kind Lord of mercies suddenly pierced her soul with the fire of his love as with a fiery javelin, and with the mighty cutting-edge of his thrust penetrated it as with a flaming sword. The voice of the Lord calling out to her reached her soul in this blow, and he made known to her by sure indications that he had especially chosen her from among all those whom mortal life still held in this world. He had written her name with his own merciful hand in the book of life among those chosen ones already reigning in eternal bliss whom he was refreshing, or those whom he was still exercising with pressures and troubles in the present world.

171 At the voice of divine consolation, Beatrice immediately recollected herself in her self-knowledge and began to ask the Lord with humbled heart why he had chosen her for so lofty a summit, when by no antecedent merits of her own could she gain so lofty a prerogative of grace as he had at that moment shown her by his free mercy and kindness.

The loving Lord answered thus his inquirer: 'Remember that

me, inquit, et propter nomen sanctum meum hanc me tibi gratiarum affluentiam infu- // f. 321 b -disse memineris.; nec aliam
huius rei causam inuestigare curaueris., preterquam ipsius rei
35 simplicem euidentiam, procedentem ex mee beneplacito voluntatis.
At si de premissis fortasse dubitans hesitaueris :, ad mee confirmationem assertionis, hec tria tibi profero testimonia veritatis.
Quorum primum est, quod ab omnis criminalis peccati perpetratione mortifera, toto vite tempore te protexi. Secundum vero,
40 quod a diebus ortus tui, per viam compendij., donec in statum
vite perfectioris excresceres, te semper et vbique mea protectione
conseruando perduxi. Porro tercium est, ipsa vehemens attractio.,
qua te, per dulcia pariter et suauia, per dura simul et aspera,
continuis virtutum passibus incedentem., ad me sequendum,
45 infatigabili quadam vehementia spiritusque violentia prouocaui.'
172 Quam responsionem dominicam, illa protinus ad se factam
intelligens, et prefata <specialis> gratie beneficia, pro veritatis
testimonio sibi diuinitus intimata, certissime recognoscens ;, omnipotenti domino copiosas gratiarum actiones exhibuit :, et de
50 tanto electionis sue priuilegio, munificam diuine clementie largitatem, deuotissimo cordis affectu magnifice collaudauit.
Nec mora, cum hijs aliquantulum iam <occupata> fuisset..
repente, carnis sensibus exuta, per contemplationis excessum in
celestia rapitur² :, et in sublimem illum, diuineque presentie
55 vicinissimum chorum seraphin, beatrix, dei famula, diuino spiritu
mente rapta, non corpore., nec carne transuecta, sed anima,
collocatur.
173 Ibi, mirum in modum, et se seraphicum spiritum effectam esse
cognouit :, et ad idem cum illis exequendum laudis et gratiarum
60 actionis officium, ipsis conformata per omnia, diuina reuelatione
se destinatam ad liquidum intellexit.
Ibi beatissimos illos superne patrie spiritus, nouem distinctos
choris et lucidis diuina sapientia mansionibus ordinatos, aspexit :,
et cum illis vna, nouum laudis // f. 321 c canticum, incessabili
65 voce, regi regum domino decantauit. Ibi diuinam essentiam in

for my sake and for the sake of my holy name I have poured this
flood of graces out on you, and do not try to see any other cause for
this matter besides the simple evidence proceeding from my good
will. And if perhaps you doubt and hesitate at what I have said, I
produce for you these three testimonies of truth to confirm my
assertion. The first is that I have protected you all your life from
committing any mortal sin. The second is that I have always and
everywhere led you by shortcuts, keeping you in my protection from
your birth until you grew into the state of a more perfect life. The
third is the vehement attraction by which I have provoked you to
follow me with a certain unflagging vehemence and violence of
spirit, making you walk with steady steps of virtue through things
both sweet and bitter, harsh and smooth.'

172 Beatrice immediately understood this godly answer and recognized with full certainty the benefits of the forementioned special
grace divinely intimated to her with proof. For the great privilege of
her election she thanked the almighty Lord copiously, praising with
magnificent devotion of heart the divine munificence and mercy.

Without delay, when she had been occupied in these matters for a
very little while, she was suddenly caught up to heaven through the
ecstasy of contemplation, stripped of her fleshly senses. Beatrice,
the handmaid of God, was transported to that sublime choir of the
Seraphim, the closest to the divine presence, caught up there by the
divine spirit, in mind, not in body, with her soul, not her flesh.

173 There in a wonderful way she knew she had been made a
seraphic spirit, and by divine revelation she clearly understood that
she was destined to discharge with the Seraphim the same service of
praise and thanksgiving, being conformed to them in everything.

There she gazed upon the blessed spirits of the heavenly fatherland, distinct in nine choirs and assigned by divine wisdom to
bright dwelling places, and together with them she sang with unceasing voice the new song of praise to the Lord, the King of
Kings.[1] There, if it is right to say so, she deserved by the clear

---

1. 1 Tm 6:15

plenitudine glorie sue., perfectissimeque maiestatis sue potentia,
continentem omnia., gubernantem vniuersa., disponentem singula, clara contemplationis acie, si fas est dicere, videre promeruit : ;
et creatorem suum illum intelligens., inexcogitabili delectationis
⁷⁰ amplexu sibi firmiter inherendo., laudans et ardens, in summa
quadam, et humanis sensibus incomprehensibili beatitudine, requieuit.

174 Et licet in omnibus que sibi videre concessa sunt, infinitam
et ineffabilem felicitatis copiam inuenisset :, in nullo tamen,
⁷⁵ preterquam in diuine contemplatione presentie, delectando <spe-
cialiter> immorari potuit ; ; quippe quam presentia summe deitatis sic intra se totam absorbuit :, vt, pre omnibus celestium
gaudiorum effluentijs, hanc solam expeteret., cui se, per caritatis
nexum, vnitam artius et adiunctam vicinius, intellexit.

⁸⁰ Cum autem in hac contemplationis inestimabili beatitudine modico
tempore permansisset :, sancto sibi reuelante spiritu cognouit,
quod in illa celestis gaudij fruitione dulcissima, in qua necdum
eternaliter permanere meruerat, immorari diutius, ad carnis habi-
taculum reducenda, non valeret continuo ; sed cum, excurso pre-
⁸⁵ sentis vite stadio, virtutibus consummata, perfectionis fastigium
ascendere meruisset :, tunc demum ad eundem beatitudinis locum,
a deo sibi perpetualiter ab initio preparatum, secum sine fine
regnatura., perpetuis fruitura gaudijs, in celestibus emigraret.

175 Attende, lector, magna esse valde que dicimus :, et eo nostris temporibus
⁹⁰ vtique rariora., quo pauciores ad apostolice iam perfectionis apicem conscendere videamus. Quid enim, nisi ad apostolice sanctitatis culmen beatricem
nostram ascendisse dixerimus ;, que celestibus gaudijs, in hoc seculo corpore
constituta, recreari pro tempore meruit. ; et priusquam, deposito carnis onere,
debitum humane condi- // f. *321 d* cionis exsoluit;, illius eterne beatitudinis
⁹⁵ premia, momentanee quadam experientia degustauit.

Legimus quippe doctorem gentium paulum, necdum ab hoc ergastulo totaliter
absolutum, siue in corpore siue extra corpus, raptum vsque <in> tercium
celum., et audisse archana verba que non licet homini loqui : ; quod ab hac
visione non multum discrepare coniciet :, si fuerit qui ad plenum, apostolice
¹⁰⁰ visionis modum et ordinem inuestiget.

176 Ille quippe raptus in tercium celum fuisse describitur : ; hec in choro
seraphin a diuino spiritu spiritualiter eleuatur. Quid enim tercium celum esse

light of contemplation to see the divine essence in the fullness of its glory, containing all things, governing everything, disposing each thing by the power of its most perfect Majesty. She understood that he was her creator, and with ardent praise she rested in him in supreme beatitude, incomprehensible to human senses, clinging firmly to him by an embrace of unthinkable delight.

174 Although Beatrice found an infinite and unspeakable profusion of happiness in everything she was allowed to see, she could not tarry especially in delighting on anything but the contemplation of the divine presence. Indeed the presence of the deity so wholly absorbed her within itself that she sought it alone in preference to all this outpouring of heavenly joys, she understood that she was more closely united and joined to it through the bond of love.

When she had remained a short time in this incalculable bliss of contemplation, she realized by revelation of the Holy Spirit that she could no longer dwell in this sweet fruition of heavenly joy, in which she had not yet deserved to remain eternally, but would have to be brought back to her fleshly residence. But when she had finished the course of the present life, and had deserved to mount the summit of perfection, being consummated in virtue, then she would emigrate to heaven, to the same blessed place prepared by God for her perpetually from the beginning, there to reign with him without end and to enjoy everlasting bliss.

175 Notice, reader, that what we are saying is something very great and quite rare in our times, when we see fewer persons ascending now to the pinnacle of apostolic perfection. To what else shall we say our Beatrice ascended if not to the apex of apostolic holiness, since she deserved to be refreshed temporarily with heavenly joys while still in this world according to the body, and she tasted in momentary experience the rewards of eternal beatitude before she had laid down the burden of the flesh and had paid the debt of the human condition.

We read indeed that Paul, the teacher of the Gentiles, not yet wholly freed from this prison, was caught up into the third heaven,[2] either in the body or outside it, and he heard secret words which it is not granted to man to utter. If someone will fully investigate the mode and order of the apostolic vision, he will conjecture that it did not much differ from this vision.

176 Paul is described as caught up to the third heaven: Beatrice is spiritually raised by the divine spirit to the choir of Seraphim. What shall

2. 2 Co 12:2

<dixerimus> ad quod paulus rapitur. , nisi terciam, id est supremam bono-
rum <spirituum> ierarchiam ; , in qua throni cherubin et seraphin conti-
105 nentur ? Et licet merita beatricis illius beatissimi apostolorum prįncipis pauli
<meritis> equiparare non audeam ; quippe qui plus pre omnibus laborauit. ,
et, cum vt persecutor et blasphemus a deo reprobari merito potuisset, repente
vas electionis effectus est , et doctor gentium a domino designatus : alterutrum
tamen visionis modum, <haud> temere sicut puto, non dissimilem alteri
110 dixerim, presertim eodem spiritu operante patratum. , et eodem propemodum
ordine consummatum.

177 Sed erit fortasse qui me temere proferre talia iudicabit : , maxime cum,
et-si paulum apostolum ad tercium celum eleuatum fuisse. , sit nemo qui dubitet. : audisse quidem archana verba que non licet homini loqui ; , non autem dei
115 faciem contemplatus fuisse describitur : ; presertim cum <hoc> a domino
petenti moysi <denegetur>. : ' Faciem, inquit, meam videre non poteris : ,
non enim videbit me homo et viuet. ' Et alibi scriptum legitur. : ' Deum
nemo vidit vmquam.' Quid ergo ad hanc obiectionem validissimam, pauper
ingenio, respondebo ?

120 Illud sane, quod a sanctis patribus eximijsque doctoribus. , augustino videlicet,
haymone, ceterisque sacre scripture dilucidatoribus, ad hoc idem respondisse
legimus : ; qui cum eodem spiritu misteria // f. 322 a scripturarum explanaue-
runt quo constat eas ab initio descriptas et editas extitisse : non temere quod
a talibus assertione veridica declaratum esse cognoscimus. , ad confirmationem
125 responsionis nostre, cum opus fuerit, applicamus.

178 Vnus etenim premissorum, haymo videlicet, vir disertissimus et in ex-
positione sacre pagine non mediocriter approbatus. , cum hec ad chorinthios
pauli verba dissereret : , premissis quibusdam alijs, hec adiecit. : ' Ad intel-
lectualem ' inquit ' visionem, que signatur per tercium celum, raptus et
130 eleuatus est apostolus : ; ibi non solum ea que in spirituali celo sunt intelligendo
vidit, sed etiam ipsam dei substantiam. , verbumque deum per quod facta sunt
omnia in caritate spiritus sancti, non per corpus. , non per similitudinem
corporis ; , sed sicut <est> ipsa veritas, contemplatus est in hac vita. :
videlicet quomodo deus omnipotens trinitas sit in personis et vnitas in sub-
135 stantia : , sicut videndus est ab omnibus sanctis post generalem resurrectionem
in patria. '

179 Hijs quidem de apostolica visione premissis : , ad questionis proposite
solutionem hoc continuo subinfertur. : ' Potest ' inquit ' humana mens, id est
intellectus et rationabilitas anime, diuinitus rapi ex hac vita ad angelicam
140 vitam : , antequam per istam communem mortem carne soluatur : ; sicut
credendum est de beato <Apostolo>, vbi a deo facta est, ab huius vite

we say the third heaven is, to which Paul is caught up, if not the third, that is, the supreme hierarchy of good spirits in which are included the Thrones, the Cherubim and the Seraphim? I dare not make Beatrice's merits equal to those of the most blessed prince of the apostles, Paul, who labored more than all, who was suddenly made a vessel of election[3] and marked out by the Lord as the teacher of the Gentiles, although he could rightly have been rejected by God as a persecutor and blasphemer. But, I would say, and not rashly I think, that the mode of vision was not unlike in each case, especially as achieved by the same Spirit and accomplished in about the same order.

177 Perhaps someone will judge that I have said such things rashly, especially since, although no one doubts that the Apostle was raised to the third heaven and heard secret words which it is not granted man to utter, still he is not described as having contemplated the face of God. The Lord, after all, denied this to Moses who asked for it. 'You cannot see my face and live.'[4] And somewhere else Scripture says: 'No one has ever seen God'.[5] What shall I, who have so poor a mind, answer to so strong an objection?

This, indeed, which we read is the reply made to the same objection by the holy fathers and outstanding teachers, that is, Augustine, Haymo and other interpreters of Sacred Scripture. Since they explained the mysteries of Scripture by the same Spirit with which the Scriptures were written and edited from the beginning, it is not rash for us to apply as confirmation of our answer, when need be, what we know they declared in truthful assertion.

178 One of these men, Haymo, very eloquent and highly esteemed as an expositor of Scripture, said this in conclusion when he was discussing these words of Paul to the Corinthians. 'The Apostle was caught and raised up to intellectual vision, signified by the third heaven. There he saw intellectually not only those things which exist in the spiritual heaven, but also the substance of God, and God the Word by which all things were made in the love of the Holy Spirit. In this life, not through the body or through a bodily likeness, but just as truth itself is, so did he contemplate how almighty God is a Trinity of persons and a Unity of substance, just as all the saints will see this after the general resurrection in the fatherland.'

179 After having said this about the Apostle's vision, the author immediately adds the following as a solution to the question proposed. He says: 'The human mind, that is, the soul's intellect and reason, can be divinely caught up out of this life to angelic life before it is loosed from the flesh by the ordinary sort of death, just as we should believe about the blessed Apostle, in whom God

3. Ac 9:15   4. *Ex 33:20*   5. *Jn 1:18*

sensibus, quedam intentionis auersio. ' Et post pauca. : ' Ita fit, vt illud
verum sit quod dicitur. : ' Nemo potest faciem meam videre et viuere ' ; ,
quia necesse est ab hac vita mentem siue intellectum abstrahi. , quando in
145 illius ineffabilitatem visionis assumitur : , et [3] non sit incredibile, quibusdam
sanctis etiam istam excellentiam visionis fuisse concessam. , nondum ita ex
toto defunctis vt remanerent sepelienda cadauera. ' Quibus vtique verbis hanc
visionis excellentiam, quam apostolo datam exposuit : , alijs etiam sanctis
conferri posse minime denegauit.
150 Sed hijs, non tam ad eruditionem simplicium quam ad confutationem loqua-
cium, vt puto non superflue, subillatis : ad narrationis ordinem redeamus.

180 Igitur cum dei sponsa, a sompno contemplationis experrecta
// f. 322 b, corporalium iam sensuum officia recepisset ; , surgens
cum reuerentia, que iam inchoabatur lectionem euangelicam aus-
155 cultauit : ; et mox incipiens recogitare que viderat, <inestima-
bilis> caritatis igne succensa. , super ostensa sibi celica visione,
diuine pietatis clementiam ymnis et laudibus <honorauit>.

Ex tunc etiam spiritum fortitudinis et constantie tam robustum
a domino se percepisse cognouit : , quod prefati timoris vehemen-
160 tiam, quam, de futuri temporis incertis casibus, illius in corde
coalisse prediximus, ex eo protinus expulit ; quique [4] tam fortis
et vehemens extitit, quod nec mortem nec gladium extimuit. ,
nec cuiuslibet generis tormentum expauit : ; sed nec hominem
nec demonem formidauit.

165 Illud quoque vehemens desiderium, quo per multa tempora
dudum affecta fuerat. , ex corde suo euaporans protinus. velut
fumus euanuit : ; et que prius mori tam feruide concupiuerat. ,
ex tunc ad honorem dei omnipotentis in hac vita subsistere : ,
diuinisque inuigilare beneplacitis ardentius affectabat. Siquidem
170 et hanc promissionem a domino accipere meruit. , quod nulla
deinceps impetenda foret corporali spiritualive molestia : , propter
quad necessarium haberet mortem affectare decetero ; sed solo
summi boni. , celestiumque gaudiorum desiderio mori quidem
cuperet. , sed hoc aliquanto tempore priusquam decederet ex
175 hac vita.

181 Videns ergo spiritum illum fortitudinis intra se magno conatu
vehementer insurgere. , magnorumque executionem operum vigi-

worked a certain turning away of resolve from the senses of this life'. And a little later he says: 'And so it happens that it is truly said: No one can see my face and live, because the mind or intellect must be withdrawn from this life when it is taken up into that unspeakable vision, so that it is not incredible that even so excellent a vision was granted to some saints without their being so wholly dead that their cadavers were left behind to be buried'. By these words he by no means denied that the excellent vision which he explained was granted to the Apostle, could be granted also to other saints.

But now that we have added those things—not superfluously, I think— not so much for the erudition of the simple as the refutation of the talkative, let us return to the sequence of our story.

180 When God's bride, Beatrice, awoke from the sleep of contemplation and received back the use of her bodily senses, she rose with reverence and listened to the reading of the Gospel which had already begun. Soon she began to think over what she had seen, and burning with the fire of immeasurable love she honored the divine mercy and kindness with hymns and praises for the things shown her in celestial vision.

She realized she had received from the Lord at that moment so great a spirit of fortitude and constancy that it had forthwith expelled from her heart that vehement fear of uncertain future slips that we mentioned earlier. This spirit was so strong and vehement that Beatrice feared neither death nor sword,[6] nor any kind of torment, nor any man or demon. That vehement desire which had affected her for so long also evaporated forthwith from her heart and vanished like smoke. She who previously had so fervently desired to die, now willed to live on in this world for the honor of Almighty God, and to be more ardently vigilant for the divine good-pleasure. Indeed she deserved to receive this promise from the Lord that henceforth she would not be assaulted by any bodily or spiritual vexations which would make her long to die, but she would wish to die only out of desire for the supreme good and heavenly joys, and this only a short time before she departed this life.

181 Beatrice, seeing this spirit of fortitude rising up mightily within her and seeking eagerly the accomplishment of great works which she

6. Rm 8:35

lanter expetere :, que non solum proprijs., sed nec quibuslibet
humanis viribus ad plenum valuisset efficere ;, cepit angustiari
180 mirabiliter intra se., parua reputans et exigua que preteritis
temporibus eatenus ipsa patrauerat :; sed et illa fore nimis exilia,
que, suffragante virium corporalium imbecilli subsidio, futuris
temporibus habuit exercere. Fecit tamen quod potuit :, et licet
nimis impares vires // f. 322 c corporis desiderio cordis inuenerit.,
185 ita tamen omnes actus pariter et affectus consilio rationis interius simul exteriusque disposuit, vt nulla sui pars otio vacare
potuerit; sed mentem sanctis affectionibus., os diuinis laudibus.,
manus pijs operibus, ceteraque corporalia membra suis queque
ministerijs deputata, sine qualibet intermissione creatori suo
190 seruire coegit :; et sic, licet ad modicum., illo suo tamen insatiabili desiderio studiosissime satisfecit.

182 Prefate quoque memoria visionis., eque recens, duobus fere
mensibus illius in corde permansit :; quibus omnia que sibi
videre concessa fuerant, iugi speculatione, non vere sicut primi-
195 tus., sed quasi per speculum in enigmate, mirabili gratitudinis
affluentia, peragrauit.

Ab eo quoque tempore sublimes illos spiritus, quos, ob maximam
amoris diuini plenitudinem, seraphin, id est ardentes scriptura
sacra cognominat, et diuine presentie ceteris vicinius inherere
200 pronunciat., in quorum collegio raptam se paulo ante memi-
nerat., <speciali> quadam reuerentia colebat decetero :, et
amoris precipui obsequio diligebat; sicque deinceps impressos
affectui cordis habebat :, vt facile, pre nimia gratitudine, resol-
ueretur in lacrimas, quotiens, aut legendo seu audiendo vel etiam
205 colloquendo, nomen illud seraphin ad memoriam reducebat.

Sed hijs de statu proficiendi nostre virginis satis, vt estimo,
plene, pro modulo nostre paruitatis, hactenus euolutis :, sub-
sistendum est paululum, vt et nos, interim pausando, modice
respiremus, et que sequuntur de statu perfectionis eiusdem [5],
210 alteri libro simul et principio [6] reseruemus.

Explicit liber secundus.

could not bring about fully by her own strength or by any human strength, began to be wonderfully distressed within herself, reckoning as small and scanty whatever she had suffered previously, and also thinking that no matter what she had to do in the future with her weak bodily strength, it would also be too meager. Yet she did what she could. Although she found her bodily strength quite unequal to her heart's desire, she so disposed all her actions and affections interiorly and exteriorly according to reason that no part of her might be empty and idle. She ceaselessly forced her mind to serve its creator with holy affections, her mouth to serve him in divine praises, her hands in loving works, and the other members of her body in their proper actions. Thus, at least to some degree, she zealously satisfied her insatiable desire.

182 The memory of the above mentioned, equally recent, vision remained fresh in her heart for about two months. During this time she reviewed with an abundance of wonderful gratitude and continual exploration everything she had been granted to see, not exactly as she had first seen it, but as though through a mirror in a dim reflection.[7]

From then on she honored with special reverence and cultivated with a particular love those sublime spirits which Sacred Scripture calls Seraphim, that is, the fiery, because of their supreme fullness of divine love, and who, it says, cling more closely than the others to the divine presence, and into whose company Beatrice remembered having been caught up shortly before. She had them thereafter so impressed in the affections of her heart that she easily melted into tears out of great gratitude as often as she recalled the name 'Seraphim' to memory either in reading or hearing or even in speaking.

But now that we have according to our small ability, treated our virgin's state of proficiency adequately, I think, we must stop a little while. In the meantime, we too by taking some rest can breathe a little, keeping for the next and culminating book what follows in regard to Beatrice's state of perfection.

HERE ENDS THE SECOND BOOK

---

7. 1 Co 13:12

183 a INCIPIUNT CAPITULA LIBRI TERCIJ

Sequitur liber tercius. Et primo :

183a   THE CHAPTERS OF BOOK THREE

The end of the Chapters.

The third book follows. And first:

⟨ DE EO QUOD AB OMNIBUS PECCATIS
SUIS EMUNDARI MERUIT
Primum capitulum

183 b Cum igitur in eo statu cuius in precedentis libri finali
⁵ capitulo mentionem fecimus[1], a festiuitate sancti martini ad aduentum vsque[2] continuo laboris exercitio perdurasset., illam
celestem et admirabilem visionem denuo cepit ad memoriam redu-
cendo reuoluere:, et inuenit omnia que vel corporali vel mentali
industria patrare valebat ad promerendam illam seraphicam a
¹⁰ domino sibi promissam beatitudinem, nequaquam posse sufficere.,
licet tantum laboris onus sibimet imposuerit quod sue condi-
// fol. 323 a tionis humana fragilitas nec maius potuisset nec
grauius sustinere.
Quid ergo <faceret> in tanta spiritualis affectus et corporalis
¹⁵ imbecillitatis discrepantia?
Hic[3], fortissimo robore, per maxima virtutum opera promisse
felicitatis gaudia vendicare[4] volebat:, sed sub impositi laboris
onere caro fragilis et tenera neccessario succumbebat. Diuersis
igitur intra se consilijs exquisitis., hanc demum compendiosiorem
²⁰ ad illam felicitatem peruieniendo viam repperit:, vt scilicet,
omnium peccatorum labe mundata, mentem ad sola celestia
desideria suspenderet., et tanto gratiori deuotionis obsequio.,
quanto purificatiori mentis oculo celestibus gaudijs decetero per
mere contemplationis officium inhereret.
²⁵ **187** Mox ergo consurgens, intra se spiritus ille fortitudinis[5] cum
ingenti desiderio postulare cepit a domino, quatenus omnem
vindictam, peccatis atque defectibus suis debitam corpori suo
dignaretur imponere:, et quidquid eatenus dignum expiatione quocumque peccandi modo patrauerat, in se non differret vlciscendo
³⁰ comprimere, seseque tantis penalibus tormentis addicere;, quanta
peccatis suis expiandis presciebat iam iusticia diuina posse suffi-

SHE DESERVED TO BE CLEANSED FROM ALL HER SINS
Chapter One

183b When Beatrice had remained, from the feast of Saint Martin[1] until Advent, laboring in that state which we mentioned in the last chapter of the preceding book, she tried to recall that wonderful heavenly vision again to memory. She found that all she could do by bodily or mental effort to deserve that seraphic blessedness promised her by the Lord could never suffice, even though she imposed so much labor on herself that the human frailty of her condition could bear nothing more. What, therefore, should she do with such a discrepancy between spiritual affection and bodily weakness?

Her spiritual affection wanted to claim the happy joys promised her with great vigor by means of the greatest acts of virtue, but the frail and tender flesh necessarily succumbed under the burden of the labor imposed. Beatrice considered various counsels within herself and finally found this shortcut for arriving at that happiness: cleansed from the stain of every sin, she would let her mind dwell only on heavenly desires, and henceforth she would cling through pure contemplation to heavenly joys by more gracious service of devotion corresponding to the purity of her mind's eye.

184 That spirit of fortitude rising up quickly inside Beatrice began to entreat the Lord with intense desire to impose on her body all the punishment her sins and defects deserved and for anything she had done until then that demanded expiation. She asked that he deliver her to such penal torments for her sins as he foreknew

---

1. 11 November

cere : ; quatenus, ab hijs omnibus expedita, libero corde decetero creatori suo mundam et immaculatam de se valeret hostiam et acceptabile sacrificium immolare.

35 **185** Hoc illius desiderium tam feruens eodem tempore fuit et validum :, quod, vt sibi videbatur, <omnis> eius humanitas, voluntati sue consentiens, idipsum expeteret ; et non tam arden- tissimo voluntatis affectu., quam ipso quoque corporis et mem- brorum gestu desiderium cordis sui promoueri quamcitius a

40 domino postularet. Quod cum successu temporis in tantam vesa- niam excreuisset quod ad perferendum illud vires cordis vix vltra sufficerent :, confestim ad omnipotentis dei clementiam se suppli- catura conuertit ; et mirabilem quidem plenam caritate deo precem obtulit :, in qua, cunctis tormentorum generibus vniuersisque in-

45 firmitatum corporaliumve molestiarum // *fol. 323 b* enumeratis incommodis, vt harum singulis vel electis ex illarum numero quibuscumque, prouot diuine iustitie complaceret., illam, donec a cunctis peccatorum sordibus elimata, clara luce consciencie nitesceret, <per> quantumcumque liberet temporis spacium

50 affligi permitteret :, instantissimo cordis desiderio domino suppli- cauit.

186 "O iustissime, inquit., o potentissime deus, cuius aspectui patent omnia., cui etiam notum est desiderium cordis mei :, tu scis, domine, quante sint iniquitates mee., et peccatorum meorum

55 numerus a te non est absconditus ; peto ergo, vt, iuxta qualitatem et numerum illorum., onus penitentie corpori meo, quod tue ius- titie, quantumcumque libet et expedit, hijs tormentorum generibus flagellandum offero., non dedigneris imponere : ; cum non solum hec enumerata., verum etiam ignes purgatorij, sed et ipsos

60 cruciatus gehennalis incendij parata sim te teste suscipere., donec ad omnimodam cordis et conscientie puritatem, peccatorum om- nium expurgata rubigine, tua fauente clementia merear peruenire. Quod si forte minus quam debueram obtuli, solum tormentis <exponendo> corpusculum :, addo nichilominus et spiritum.,

65 quantumcumque tibi libuerit temptationum et spiritualium moles- tiarum genere cruciandum ; certa quod, iuxta sponsionem aposto- licam, me, supra facultatem virium oneratam, non patieris in

would be adequate for divine justice, so that, unencumbered by all these things, she could immolate herself to her Creator in the future with a free heart as a clean and spotless victim and an acceptable sacrifice.²

185 This desire of hers was so fervent and strong then that, as it seemed to her, her whole humanity consented to her will and sought the same thing. She asked the Lord not only with ardent affection of will but also with the bearing of her body and all its members that her heart's desire might be accomplished as quickly as possible. When with the passage of time this desire had increased to such madness that her strength of heart could hardly bear it any longer, she quickly turned in prayer to the mercy of Almighty God, and offered God this wonderful prayer in love. In it she enumerated every sort of torment and every vexation of sickness and bodily trouble, and with urgent desire of the heart she begged the Lord to permit her to be afflicted for any length of time by each of these or by any combination of them, as it should please divine justice, until she was polished clean of every sin and shone with the clear light of conscience.

186 'O most just, most powerful God', she said, 'all things lie open to your gaze, and the desire of my heart is also known to you. You know, Lord, how many are my iniquities, and the number of my sins is not hidden from you.³ According to their quality and number, I beg you therefore not to disdain to impose the burden of penance on my body which I offer to your justice to be scourged by these torments, as much as it may please you and help me. You are my witness that I am prepared to receive not only these things I have listed, but also the fires of purgatory and even the torments of hell-fire until by the favor of your clemency I deserve to arrive at entire purity of heart and conscience, with the rust of every sin purged away. But if I have perhaps offered less than I ought by exposing only my poor body to torments, I add my spirit no less to be afflicted, as much as it shall please you, by various kinds of temptations and spiritual troubles, certain as I am that, according to the apostle's pledge, you will not let me be burdened beyond

2. Lv 22:21   3. *Ps 68:6*

temptationis pressura deficere :, sed cum temptatione prouentum
facies., vt illius, quamuis graue, pondus valeam sustinere." [6]

70 **187** Cum ergo crebrius hanc orationem in auribus domini sabaoth
cum suspirijs et gemitibus importasset :, super illius exauditionem
quodam tempore consolari meruit a domino. Ad quam exhilarata
professionem [seu promissionem], omnipotentis dei clementie
deuotas gratiarum actiones exhibuit., et per talem verborum
75 ordinem ipsi domino respondit. :
"Nunc igitur, inquit, domine, quoniam ancille tue deprecationem
exaudire dignatus es., hoc humilitatis mee negocium sic exequendum admittas. : // f. 323 c vt iuxta peccatorum meorum
exigentium plus minusve qualicumque tribulatione me punias ;,
80 sciens quod, ex hoc tempore nullam de commissis meis rationem
tibi viuens reddam aut moriens ;, ex quo, libere mentis affectu,
cunctorum peccatorum meorum sordes et maculas pro tue voluntatis arbitrio tibi obtulerim abrogandas".

188 Post hec ergo, cum feruentissimo desiderio visitationis domi-
85 nice per quindenam ferme presentiam expectasset ;, accidit vt ex
spiritualium amicarum suarum numero due deuotissime persone.,
quarum vna fuit illa venerabilis Yda nyvellensis cuius superius
mentionem fecimus, impositum vniuerse carni tributum mortis
exsoluerent :, et ad immortalitatis statum per mortis communem
90 transitum emigrarent [7]. Quo rumore per-culsa, beatrix, dei famula, magnum quidem ex illa temporali amissione dolorem in
corde sustinuit :, sed resumptis nichilominus patientie viribus.,
super illarum <felici vocatione> diuine pietatis clementiam, ex-
cusso doloris stimulo, magnifice collaudauit.

95 **189** Hijs ergo de medio sic sublatis, cepit intra se meditando
reuoluere ne forte dolor hic, quem ex illarum ablatione sustinuit,

the capacity of my strength and so fail under the pressure of temptation. But with temptation you will also provide a way out so that I can bear its weight, however great'.[4]

187 After Beatrice had frequently plied the ears of the Lord of Hosts[5] with this prayer with sighs and groans, she deserved to one day be consoled by the Lord's granting this petition. Exhilarated by this promise, she gave devout thanks to the mercy of Almighty God, and replied to him in these words: 'Lord, now that you have granted your handmaid's prayer,[6] allow this bargain of my humility to take effect: that you punish me with any kind of trouble, more or less according to what my sins demand, knowing that from now on, whether living or dead, I will not render any account of my transgressions. From now on, with the affection of a free mind I shall offer you the filthiness and stains of all my sins to be utterly abolished according to the judgment of your will'.

188 After this, when with the most fervent desire for the Lord's visit she had been awaiting his presence for almost two weeks, it happened that two very devout persons among her spiritual friends—one of them was the venerable Ida of Nivelles mentioned above— paid the price of mortality laid upon all flesh, and migrated to the state of immortality through the common passageway of death. Dejected by this report, the servant of God, Beatrice, bore great pain in her heart for this temporal loss, but she nevertheless recovered the strength of her patience and magnificently praised the divine kindness and mercy for their happy summons, rejecting the sting of her pain.

189 With these two thus removed from her midst, Beatrice began to wonder whether perhaps this pain which she bore because of

4. 1 Co 10:13   5. Jm 5:4   6. Ps 6:10

in vltionem peccatorum suorum a domino sibi collatus exstiterit;
quem cum ad illorum expurgationem omnimodam, vtpote nimis
leuem et exiguum, nequaquam sufficere posse putauerit., non
hoc aliquatenus esse contenta voluit:; sed vt maiorem vel in
corpore vel in anima vindictam acciperet, incessanter diuine
maiestatis <iustitiam> implorauit.

Vix itaque quartus dies allabitur:, cum ecce grauissima febre,
quam acutam dicunt[8], illius corpus omne peruaditur., et non
solum in interioribus, vt assolet interdum., sed in qualibet sui
particula, grauissimo nimis incendio tormentatur. Tunc ergo
primum videres illius spiritum, mirabiliter exultantem:, deuotas
omnipotenti deo laudes exsoluere;, cum tamen adeo iaceret cru-
ciata in corpore:, quod totus eiusdem loci conuentus nichil aliud
quam ipsam mortem estimaret ineuitabiliter imminere.

Hac igitur corporali molestia, iuxta cordis sui desiderium, a domino // f. 323 d visitata:, frequenter in diuina laude labia resol-
uens,. et ineffabili gratitudine dominum alloquens, sic dicebat.:
"O deus, inquit, dulcedo cordis mei., percute me quantum vis:
tue iustitie me flagellandum obtuli:; nec cesset virga correctionis
ab ictibus et flagellis., donec ad plenum elimata fuerint omnia
que deliqui".

190 In hoc vero multipliciter apud se consolabatur eodem tempore., quod, per talia verba deum cordis sui frequenter inuocans,
a ceteris putabatur, iuxta vvlgaris eloquij consonantiam, infir-
mitatem cordis sui per talem formulam inclamare[9].

Tanta vero fuit huius doloris vehemens insolentia:, quod, nullo
temporis spacio vel momento., requietionis vel modicum quid in
aliqua corporis sui parte gustauerit., nisi cum, impresso capite
suo puluinari, dei beneficia sibi collata, forensium rerum strepitu
quiescente, meditando reuoluere licuit. Nam tunc, quasi dormiens,
ad lectulum inclinata facie, domini dei sui clementiam[10], qui
deprecationem suam exaudire dignatus fuerat., eo deuotiori cordis
affectu quo liberiore, ministrantium tunc quiescente tumultu,
gratiarum et laudum actionibus honorabat. Nam instar aque

their removal was given her as a punishment for her sins. But she refused in any way to be content with this, since she thought the pain far too light and paltry to suffice for the complete purgation of her sins. Rather she incessantly implored the justice of divine Majesty so that she would receive a greater retribution either in body or soul.

Hardly four days had passed when, behold, a very severe fever, which they call 'acute', invades her whole body, and she is tormented by an intense burning not only in her inner organs, as sometimes happens, but in every minute part. Then for the first time you could see her spirit wonderfully exulting and praising almighty God devoutly, although she lay so tormented in body that the whole convent thought death was hanging inescapably over her.

Now that she was visited by the Lord with this bodily torment according to her heart's desire, she frequently unleashed divine praises, and addressed the Lord with ineffable gratitude, saying: 'O God, the sweetness of my heart, strike me as much as you will. I have offered myself to your justice to be scourged. Let the rod of correction not cease its blows and scourges until all my failings have been fully cleansed'.

190 At this time Beatrice was doubly consoled within, because while she was often invoking the God of her heart in such words, she was thought by the others to be rebuking some disorder in her heart because of some similar sounding phrase in the vulgar idiom.

Such was the unusual vehemence of this pain that at no moment or instant of time did she taste the slightest rest in any part of her body except when she pressed her head on the pillow and, while the noise of outer things was stilled, could meditate on God's benefit to her. For then, when the commotion of those attending her was stilled, she lay face down on the bed, as though sleeping, and with acts of praise and thanksgiving she honored the mercy of the Lord her God, who had deigned to hear her request; her heart's affection was more devout as it was more free. For as water

sordes abluentis et maculas corporales :, sic animam suam interius
illius doloris incommodo mundari sensit et ablui ;, nec quidquam
sordis in ea remansisse noxialisve piaculi :, quod postmodum ignis
purgatorij necesse foret incendijs emundari.

135 **191** Quanto vero corpusculum acrius infestabatur exterius. , tanto
spirituali consolatione mens iocundius reficiebatur interius : ; et
mirum in modum, nec illius dulcedinem extrinsecus corpus per
sensus suos experiri potuit. , nec exteriores molestias, repleta
spiritualibus delicijs, intrinsecus anima degustauit ; sed mirabili
140 quodam et inconsueto modo, quasi corporalis infirmitas anime
delectatio fuerit :, ita, per id tempus ampliori solito dulcedine
recreata, beatricis anima laudans et exul- // f. 324 a tans in
domino requieuit. Nam cum hijs diebus officium quatuor temporum, iuxta morem in ecclesia, celebriter ageretur[11]. , corpore
145 quidem infirmissima, sed mente sanissima, per totum illud missale
tempus, vna cum conuentu, quecumque spectabant ad idem officium clara voce concinuit :, et, in lectulo decubans, si non corpore
corde tamen et animo psallentium se collegio sociauit. Quinta
vero die postquam a febre correpta fuerat[12], diuina clementia
150 prouidente conualuit ; et velut aurum quod, igne probatum, fulgo-
rem naturalem ex incendio recepit :, ita, recuperata cordis omnimoda puritate. , per ignes et estus febrium transeunte corpusculo,
iam omni auro obriso purior omnique cristallo fulgidior. , in
libertatem filiorum dei, velut in quoddam delectabile refrigerium,
155 emigrauit.

washes away bodily filth and stains, so she felt her soul being cleansed and washed interiorly by the grievousness of the pain. Neither would any filth or hurtful sin remain in her which would have to be purified later by the fires of purgatory.

191 The more sharply her frail body was attacked outwardly, the more happily was her mind inwardly refreshed with spiritual consolations. In a wonderful way her body could neither experience that sweetness outwardly through its senses, nor did her soul, filled with spiritual delights, inwardly taste the outer troubles. Indeed it was as if, in a certain wonderful and unusual way, the body's sickness was the soul's delight. So during that time, Beatrice's soul, refreshed with more than usual sweetness, rested in the Lord in praise and exultation. When at the time the Ember days were celebrated[7] according to church custom, throughout the Mass, very weak in body but very healthy in mind, she sang with a clear voice with the community whatever pertained to this service. Lying in bed she joined the group of singers in heart and soul, if not in body. On the fifth day after being seized with fever, she recovered by the providence of divine mercy, and like gold proved in the fire[8] receiving its natural sheen from the blaze, so with her heart's recovery of total purity and her frail body's passing through the fire and heat of fever, Beatrice moved into the liberty of the children of God[9] as into some delightful refreshment, being made purer than the purest gold and more resplendent than any crystal.

7. mid-December   8. *Pr 17:3*   9. Rm 8:21

⟨ DE EO QUOD IN PERCEPTIONE DOMINICI
SACRAMENTI DIUINUS SPIRITUS
INTRA SE SPIRITUM EIUS ABSORBUIT
Secundum capitulum

5   **192** Die vero secundo epyphanie domini[1], postquam videlicet
ab infirmitate sua iam aliquantulum conualuerat :, ad sacramentum dominici corporis, a quo, posteaquam sanitati restitui cepit,
eatenus abstinuerat., accedere christi virgo proposuit. At vbi
perceptionis tempus appropinquare iam cepit :, incidit in mentem
10   illius vehemens desiderium intelligendi videlicet et sciendi qualiter in anima sua domino complaceret. Quod et votis expetijt :,
et, effusa prece, ipsius diuine complacentie sibi dari noticiam
super hoc, humiliter exorauit.
Sed quid electe sue superna clementia denegasset ?
15   **193** Vix oratione completa, in excessum mentis erepta, vidit illum
dulcissimum anime sue sponsum, dominum ihesum, in altari
stantem., expansis brachijs in eius accessum ineffabili desiderio
prestolantem :, illius quoque vinculo caritatis que cunctis humanis
sensibus supereminet, illam adeo fortiter attrahentem :, quod vix
20   ad consuetum vsque communicandi tempus expectare potuit :;
sed aperto // f. 324 b corde, venisque patefactis, ac si demens
<nimio> desiderio facta fuerit., ita mirabili quodam gestu ad
salutiferam perceptionem dominici corporis aspirauit. Cuius salu-
berrima iam communione refecta, miro quodam ipsius deitatis
25   amplexu totam repente sentiebat animam, per omnia membra
corporalia diffusam, adeo vehementer astringi :, quod ipsum
corpusculum se sentiret in singulis membris suis hoc amplexu
fortissimo colligari.
In illa vero dulcis amplexus vnione, cor electe sue dominus ad
30   cor suum applicuit :, et illius spiritum intra se totum absorbuit ;
ibique celestem illam caritatis affluentiam quam oculus non vidit
nec auris audiuit nec in cor hominis ascendit[2]., iam aliquatenus
celestis vt sic dicam effecta :, beatricis anima degustauit.

IN THE RECEPTION OF THE LORD'S SACRAMENT
THE DIVINE SPIRIT ABSORBED HER SPIRIT INTO ITSELF
Chapter Two

192 On the day after the Epiphany, when Beatrice had somewhat recovered from her sickness, Christ's virgin proposed to approach the Sacrament of the Lord's Body from which she had thus far abstained since beginning to recover her health. When the time of reception began to approach, a vehement desire came to her mind to understand and know in what way the Lord was pleased with her soul.[1] She longed for this, and humbly asked that knowledge of the divine good-pleasure be given to her in this matter.

And indeed, what had heavenly mercy ever denied its chosen one?

193 Scarcely had she completed her prayer when she was caught up into an ecstasy of mind and saw the ever-sweet spouse of her soul, the Lord Jesus, standing and waiting at the altar with arms outstretched in an inexpressible desire for her approach. He was so strongly attracting her with the bond of that love which surpasses all human understanding[2] that she could scarcely wait for the usual time for Communion, but with open heart and enlarged veins, as if she were mad with excessive desire, she aspired in a certain wonderful gesture to receive the Lord's saving Body. Refreshed by this health-giving Communion, Beatrice suddenly felt her whole soul, diffused through all her bodily members, so vehemently drawn together in such a wonderful embrace of the Godhead that even her frail body in each of its members seemed gathered up by this mighty embrace.

In the union of this sweet embrace the Lord applied his chosen maid's heart to his own heart, and absorbed her spirit wholly into himself. There Beatrice's soul, having become in some measure heavenly, so to speak, tasted the heavenly abundance of love which eye has not seen, nor ear heard, and which has not entered into the heart of man.[3]

1. Ph 4:7   2. Eph 3:19   3. 1 Co 2:9

194 Ad cuius gustum cum, deficiente sensuum corporalium vsu,
iam propemodum ad terram caderet. , et pedum officio sustentari
vel subsistere seu vlterius procedere non valeret ; , monialis que
sibi custos in infirmitate sua iuxta morem adheserat. , illi procedens obuia, brachijs suis, ne corrueret, eam sustinuit : et sic
per chorum ducens. , cum ad eius medium procedendo peruentum
est, illam, vtpote iam omnium corporalium sensuum officio destitutam, diutius sustinere non preualens. , donec sibi redderetur, in
terra iam <toto> prostratam corpore, dereliquit. Quam postmodum, ad se reuersam, et in infirmitorium ducens, in lectulo suo
constituit : ; vbi per totum illum diem, inestimabili mentis inebriata
dulcedine, iubilans et exultans. , in tranquilla pace conscientie,
cum domino requieuit.

195 Ab illo quoque tempore fuit omnis eius delectatio summum
bonum appetere : , totaque mentis intentio summe trinitatis essentie, <laudando> pariter et <amando>, de receptisque beneficijs gratias agendo ; , sed et purificato mentis intellectu dei
mirabilia contemplando, iugiter quidem sed humiliter, inherere :
ab omnibus siquidem peccatorum sordibus expurgata, // *f. 324 c*
et celestium iam secretorum gaudijs innouata. , nihil aliud quam
celestia mente concipere potuit. Quibus etiam eo iocundiori mentis
affectu decetero per frequens contemplationis exercitium immorari
libuit : , quo se, remoto carnis obstaculo, nulla penalium tormentorum impediente molestia, peruenturam ad hoc ipsa sperauit ;
nec id frustra quidem, vt ex precedentibus in parte iam patuit : ,
et in hijs que sequuntur manifestius apparebit.

Quanto vero puriorem ab omni se peccatorum sorde cognouit : ,
tanto magis, omnem viciorum labem abhorrens. , in ea semper
voluntate permansit : , vt si quid dignum correctione committeret. ,
non hoc ipsum impune deus ignosceret. , sed iuxta culpe modum. ,
idipsum temporali flagello, suam in hoc exercendo vindictam,
diuina seueritas expurgaret.

194 At the taste of it, Beatrice's bodily senses failed and she almost fell to the ground. Her feet could not support her, or keep her standing or let her advance further. The nun who was usually her nurse in illness, went to her and held her up in her arms lest she fall. She guided her through the choir, but when she had arrived half way, she could no longer hold Beatrice up, for she was bereft of all her bodily senses, and so she left Beatrice prostrate full length on the ground until she returned to herself. When she did return to herself, the nun led her to the infirmary and put her to bed. There she rested with the Lord all day in tranquil peace of conscience, in exultant jubilation, drunk with inestimable sweetness of mind.

195 From then on, all Beatrice's delight was in seeking the Supreme Good, and the whole intention of her mind was to cling constantly but humbly to the essence of the Supreme Trinity, both praising and loving it, giving thanks for benefits received, and contemplating God's marvels with a purified understanding of mind. Since she was purged from all filth of sin and was renewed by the joys of heavenly secrets, she could conceive only heavenly things in her mind. Through the frequent exercise of contemplation she was pleased to dwell on these heavenly things all the happier in affection of mind for hoping to arrive at them, once the obstacle of the flesh had been removed and penal torments no longer stood in the way. Nor was this hope in vain as was partly clear from the foregoing, and will be made clearer still in what follows.

Abhorring every stain of vice, the more Beatrice knew herself to be cleansed from every filth of sin, the more she constantly willed that, if she committed something worthy of correction, God would not ignore it, but divine severity would purge the fault away with temporal affliction according to the mode of the fault, exercising this revenge on it.

❡ DE <PIETATE> CORDIS EIUS
Tercium capitulum

196 Uidens igitur electissima domini nullo se peccatorum impedimento constringi., quo minus in via virtutum absque quolibet
valuisset obstaculo decetero proficisci;, repente semetipsam ex
toto cepit obsequio caritatis exponere.: solum esuriendo sitien-
doque caritatis gustum appetere., solum caritatis beneplacitum
tum actu simul et moribus exercere. Quid enim nisi caritatem
sapere poterat;, que totiens in cellam vinariam introducta, totiens
caritatis nectare debriari celestibusque delitijs satiari meruerat.,
que totiens caritatis gustum in gaudio de saluatoris fontibus
hauriebat? Pennis siquidem quas sibi caritas mater aptauerat,
non solum semetipsam., sed et omnem creaturam humanam
angelicamque trancenderat;, et ad increatum bonum ipsa duce
caritate peruenerat:, vbi, sine repulsa qualibet in sponsi thalamum
introgrediens, ipsum pascentem, // f. 324 d ipsum cubantem in
meridie requirebat; vbi nimirum tanto festiuius ab eo celestibus
gaudijs honorari meruit:, quanto puriori mentis intellectu pariter
et affectu, nulla iam peccatorum impediente molestia, ad dili-
gentis et dilecti sui dulce secretarium euolauit. Nec fas erat ipsum
datorem bonorum omnium electam suam a se vacuam, velut
extraneam quandam, emittere:, sed, celestibus honoratam <xe-
nijs>, quotiens in illud sublime triclinium irrumpere potuit., ad
sua fecit cum gaudio remeare.

197 Hinc enim illud vehemens cordis desiderium quod ab appe-
tendis celestibus numquam reuocari <valuit>; <hinc> illum
feruentissimum anime zelum quo numquam celestis sponsi copia
plene satiari potuit; hinc etiam illam spiritus sui dulcedinem
equanimiter sufferentem omnia., patienterque tam aduersa tole-
rantem quam prospera, reportauit.

Hec ergo tota mentis illius occupatio, tota cordis fuit intentio:
vacare scilicet et videre quam suauis est dominus., et mundam
illi beneplacitamque semper et acceptabilem hostiam exhibere.

THE PIETY OF HER HEART
Chapter Three

196 The Lord's highly chosen one, seeing herself unconstrained by any sinful impediment from progressing further without obstacle in the way of virtue, suddenly began to place herself totally at the service of love, only hungering and thirsting for the taste of love, only carrying out in act and in conduct the good-pleasure of love. What else could she relish except love, she who had been brought so often into the wine cellar, who had been inebriated so often with the nectar of love and satisfied with heavenly delights, she who had so often drawn the taste of love joyously from the Saviour's fountains.[1] With the wings which love, like a mother, had fitted for her, Beatrice transcended not only herself but every human and angelic creature, and arrived under the guidance of love at the uncreated Good. There, entering without any repulse whatever into the Bridegroom's chamber, she sought him as he was feeding and resting at noon.[2] Here she deserved to be more festively honored by him with heavenly joys, according to the greater purity of the mental understanding and affection with which she flew to the sweet secret chamber of her lover and beloved, with no more vexing hindrance of sin. Nor was it right for the giver of all good to send his chosen one away from him empty, like some foreigner, but as often as she could break into that sublime banquet room, he made her return to herself with joy, honored with heavenly presents.

197 From there Beatrice brought back that vehement desire of heart which could never manage to be recalled from seeking heavenly things; from there, that fervent zeal in which she could never be fully satisfied with any abundance of the heavenly Bridegroom's presence; from there, that sweetness of her spirit, bearing everything with an even temper, patiently tolerating both the adverse and the prosperous.

This was the whole occupation of her mind and the whole intention of her heart: to be attentive and see how sweet the Lord is; and always to offer him a clean, pleasing, and acceptable sacrifice.[3]

1. Is 12:3   2. *Sg 1:6*   3. Ps 45:11

Quid enim nisi, de virtûte proficiens in virtutem, expedito gressu
35 ad anteriora se iugiter extendendo procederet :, que sic igne
purgatorio decocta fuerat., vt nullum impuritatis intra se vesti-
gium appareret ? Ab eo siquidem tempore quo febribus hijs de
quibus antea mentionem fecimus estuauerat., in tanta se puritate
cordis subsistere sentiebat :, quantam, ablutus ab omnis peccati
40 contagio, quilibet in baptismi lauachro recipit ; vel quantam in
sua creatione deus anime puritatis gratiam, cum ad suam illam
format ymaginem, imprimit et infundit·

198 Sed ipsum corpusculum in suo modo tanta constabat soliditate
subnixum :, vt in toto vite sue tempore numquam experiendo
45 didicerit quid mala voluntas, quid carna- // fol. 325 a lis affectio
vel commotio seu mundana delectatio fuerit ; sed licet in omnibus
spiritui voluntarie semper obediens et subiectus extiterit., in hoc
solo tamen impedimento sibi fuit., quod, illius obstaculo impe-
ditus affectus, quod desiderabat assequi minime potuit :, et illius
50 mortalitate retentus., ad perpetuam summi boni fruitionem non
valebat attingere quam quesiuit. Instar quippe tenuis membrane
que cito dirumpitur., vel nubis lucidissime que solis claro iubare
facillime penetratur., illius corpus spiritui, sursum iugiter aspi-
ranti, videbatur obsistere :, que sola dirupta, non erat quod illum,
55 ab eterno sole perpetualiter illustrandum, decetero posset alicuius
generis obstacula remouere. Quapropter, vt tenuis illa membrana
citius dirumperetur votis expetijt :, et vt leuis illa nubecula
sempiterni solis radio pelleretur, feruentissimo cordis desiderio
pertinaciter affectauit.

60 **199** At quoniam requietionis tempus necdum aduenerat., hyems-
que peregrinationis huius adhuc pluuiosus et rigidus imminebat.,
totam cordis intentionem ad exequendum dei beneplacitum interim applicare non distulit :; et quid eam vellet facere cum apostolo dominum frequenter interrogans., nouas vite normas, in
65 quarum obseruantia maiestati diuine complacuit., nunc occultis
immissionibus., nunc etiam nocturnis reuelationibus, diuinis illi
spiritus intimauit. Quanto vero sublimius ad montem virtutum post
christum ascenderat et in scola caritatis ceteris magis ipsa profecerat :, tanto profundius in humilitatis conualle sese recipiens,
70 et, iuxta datam a deo sibi gratiam, exemplo pariter et verbo

Since she had been stewed in the fire of purgatory until no trace of impurity appeared within her, what should she do but proceed from virtue to virtue,[4] always reaching out with unimpeded step to what lay ahead? From that time when she so burned with the forementioned fever, she felt herself abiding in the same purity of heart as someone receives when washed free from the infection of all sin in the baptismal font, or when at its creation God impresses and infuses the grace of purity on the soul, forming it to his own image.

198 Beatrice's frail body, however, stood so firm in its own way that never in her whole life did she learn by experience what bad will or carnal affection or excitement or worldly delight was. Although her body was always and in everything obedient and subject to the spirit, in this one matter her body was an impediment: that her affection, impeded by this obstacle, could barely attain what it desired. Restrained by its mortality, her affection could not attain the everlasting fruition of the supreme Good which it sought. Her body, like a thin membrane which is easily broken or like a shining cloud which is easily penetrated by the clear radiance of the sun, seemed still to obstruct her spirit which was always aspiring upward. Once this cloud was dispelled there was nothing by which an obstacle of any sort could keep her spirit from being perpetually illuminated by the eternal sun. Therefore she implored in prayer that this thin membrane be speedily broken, and with fervent desire of the heart she persistently longed for the light little cloud to be driven away by the ray of the eternal sun.

199 But since the time for rest had not yet come, and the rainy, harsh winter of this pilgrimage still hung over her, Beatrice did not meantime delay applying the whole intention of her heart to following the divine good-pleasure. With the apostle, she frequently asked the Lord what he would have her do,[5] and the divine spirit intimated to her, now by secret suggestions, now also by nightly revelations, new forms of life by which to please the divine Majesty. Having more sublimely ascended the mount of virtues after Christ and progressed further than others in the school of love, she entered more profoundly into the valley of humility and by example and word managed

4. Ps 83:8   5. Ac 9:6

cunctis indigentibus talentum sibi creditum administrans :, conuersationem inter homines bonam et optimam, sibi prudens,
vtilis proximo, placens deo, inoffensis passibus, ad destinatum
currens brauium, exercebat.

❡ DE SPIRITUALI LETITIA CORDIS EIUS
iiij. capitulum

200 Super omnia vero bona que deus omnipotens // f. 325 b
electe sue, tam interius infundendo quam exterius applicando,
⁵   contulerat :, spiritualem consolationis et exultationis gratiam sibi
per singulos dies adiciens :, nouis eam gaudijs cotidie recreabat.
Interdum siquidem cum, sanctis meditationibus occupata, dei
mirabilia contemplationis oculo prudenter inspiceret :, interdum
etiam absque meditationis officio, cum mentem quieti forsan ad
¹⁰   modicum tempus indulgeret¹ :, affuit repente diuine gratie consolatio., cor illius ineffabili gaudio quodam sic inebrians et per-
fundens :, vt non solum eius interiora nectareus ille sapor suaui
dulcedine recrearet :, sed foras etiam, ad corporis officinas ebul-
liens., ipsa quoque corporalia membra gestu concutiens ad spiri-
¹⁵   tuale tripudium incitaret.
Interdum etiam ita se sensit affectam interius, quasi nec viuere
diutius nec mori potuerit ; sed velut in momento spiritus illius
se foras excuteret :, et, spreto corporalis claustri retinaculo, libere
ad superna conscendere voluisset, ita virtute sua totum corporis
²⁰   vasculum importune concutiens : spiritualis gaudij <quo> per-
fundebatur impatiens, insaniuit.
201 Quotiens autem in hoc statu se subsistere deprehendit :,
confestim ad secretum, et ab hominum remotum frequentia, locum
fugiendo secessit. ; vbi, tanto quietiori quanto liberiori studio
²⁵   vacans sibi, infusam sibi diuinitus refectionem celestis gratie degustauit. Timebat <quippe>, non solum ab alijs, quo-minus sua
perfrueretur delectandi copia, molestari forsan aut impeti :, verum
etiam id quod sentiebat interius, per alicuius forte gestus indi-
cium, verebatur ne contingeret a ceteris indagari.

the talent entrusted to her for all those in need, according to her God-givengrace. Running without stumbling after the prize appointed for her,[6] she led a good and excellent life among human beings, prudent toward herself, useful to her neighbor, and pleasing to God.

THE SPIRITUAL JOY OF HER HEART
Chapter Four

200 In addition to all the good things almighty God conferred on his elect both by inner infusion and outer application, he daily refreshed her with new joys, increasing in her every day the grace of consolation and exultation. Sometimes when Beatrice was occupied in holy meditations, prudently inspecting the divine wonders with the eye of contemplation, and sometimes when she was giving her mind a little rest and was not meditating, the consolation of divine grace would suddenly present itself, so inebriating and flooding her heart with an ineffable joy that not only would the nectar-like taste refresh her inwardly with much delight, but, also outwardly effervescing into bodily form, it would stir her up to a spiritual dance, in which she would excitedly strike parts of her body.

Sometimes Beatrice felt herself so affected inwardly that she seemed unable either to live longer or to die. It seemed that her spirit would at any moment shake itself out of her body and, spurning the narrow restraints of the body, would willingly go up on high. Thus her spirit grievously shook the whole vessel of her body by its own power, and Beatrice, unable to stand the spiritual joy which flooded her, raved madly.

201 As often as Beatrice realized she was in this state, she quickly withdrew to a secret place removed from human frequentation. There she had the leisure to taste more quietly, because more freely, the divinely infused nourishment of heavenly grace. For she feared not only being sought out and troubled perhaps by others, thus being kept from enjoying her abundant delight, but she also feared that what she felt within might be investigated by others through some sign or gesture of hers.

6. 1 Co 9:24

30 Cum vero diutius hec spiritualis iocunditas illius in corde permansit., deficiente subsidio corporalis adminiculi, frequenter in
infirmitatis lecto decumbere necesse habuit:, quia nec virtus
humanitatis hec que sentiebat in spiritu tolerare preualuit., sed
nec ipse quidem spiritus illud idem ex toto concipere // fol. 325 c
35 potuit quod de celestibus gaudijs intra se cotidie diuina gratia
propinauit.
202 Quodam itaque tempore, cum vltra virium humanarum sufferentiam conquassatus potius et obrutus quam refectus illius spiritus extitisset;, ne decetero sub nimia celestium deliciarum mole
40 deficeret., imbecillitatem suam miseratus, altissimus oportunum
ei consilium inspirauit : vt frequenter videlicet ad dominici corporis communionem accederet :; in qua, quotiens vltra virium tolerantiam a diuino spiritu tacta succumberet., hijs continuo reparatis, in robur virtutis erecta resurgeret;, et, mirum in modum,
45 quam diuina virtus opprimendo <deiceret> :, hec ipsa rursus,
oppressam ab oppressionis pondere, releuaret. Hoc ergo diuino
consilio salubriter aquiescens., multam, illius affectu, cordis simul
et corporis fortitudinem, ad supportandum equanimius onus celestium deliciarum, accepit ; et salutaris alimonie pabulo recreata.,
50 sub quo prius, toto corpore lassata, defecerat :, post, ad baiulan-
dum pondus diuine visitationis, omni corporali sensui importabile.,
non solum fortior., verum etiam alacrior assurgere consueuit.
203 Aliquotiens etenim tam <ineffabili> cordis iubilo tangebatur
interius;, vt nec solum quidem membrum mouere., nec os ad
55 loquendum aperire valuerit :; sed velut amens iacens, vt mortua,
ab omni videbatur exteriorum sensuum officio derelicta.
Interdum etiam, quasi validissima febre, paralisi-ve, correpta
fuerit :, ita, celestium gaudiorum affecta dulcedine, tremens et
pallens toto corpore creticauit· Nec immerito, cum incomprehensi-
60 bilis desiderij febribus estuauerit :, et, amoris perfossa iaculo,
vvlnus inflictum occultare nequiuerit quod in interioribus, sola
teste conscientia, <tolerauit>. Amoris siquidem filia, solum
amoris gustum sapere potuit :; cuius odore mellifluo quanto magis
inebriabatur interius, tanto sitiuit ardentius. Et quanto reficiebatur

When this spiritual happiness lasted in her heart for rather a long time, she often had to take to her sick bed for lack of bodily support, because her human nature could not stand what she felt in her spirit, nor could her spirit itself fully understand the heavenly joys that divine grace was daily giving her to drink within herself.

202 One time when Beatrice's spirit, rather than being refreshed, was crushed and overwhelmed beyond human endurance, the Almighty had mercy on her weakness and inspired her with opportune counsel, lest she be overwhelmed by the excessive mass of heavenly delights. [He inspired her] to approach the Lord's Body in Holy Communion frequently. By means of it, as often as she was being overcome, touched by the divine spirit beyond what she could endure, her strength would be repaired immediately and she would rise up in vigor, erect again. In a wonderful way divine power would raise up again, her whom it had cast down and ejected, relieving her whom it had oppressed from the weight of her oppression. Beatrice acquiesced wholesomely to this divine counsel and received from it effectively much strength of heart and body to support more evenly the burden of heavenly delights. Formerly she had failed under this wholesome food, totally wearied in body by it, but afterwards, refreshed by it, she used to arise not only stronger to carry the weight of divine visitation, which is insupportable by bodily senses, but also more lively and brisk.

203 Sometimes Beatrice was inwardly so touched by unutterable jubilation of heart that not only could she not move a member, but she could not even open her mouth to speak. Rather, lying as if mindless, as though dead, she seemed bereft of any use of the outer senses.

Occasionally, too, affected by the sweetness of heavenly joys she became pale and trembled in her whole body as though at the crisis of a strong fever or paralysis. Not without reason either, since she was burning with the fever of incomprehensible desire. Pierced by love's dart, she could not hide the wound she bore within, with her conscience only as witness. As the daughter of love, she could only relish what tasted of love, and the more inebriated she was within by its honeysweet scent, the more ardently she thirsted for it. The more magnificently refreshed

65 illius dulcedine lautius., tanto fortiori desiderio conualescens insatiabilis appetitus, cum in pre- // *fol. 325 d* sentiarum quod
affectabat ad votum inuenire non potuit :, eterne refectionis satie-
tatem, semper esuriens et famelicus, appetiuit.

204 Intellexit enim amore vehementissimo sese preuentam a
70 domino :; quapropter et ad reddendam amoris vicem se teneri
certa ratione cognouit. Quod cum iuxta desiderij sui latitudinem
efficere non preualuit., eo quod, vt predictum est, ad hoc humanarum virium imbecillitas non suffecit ;, amoris incommodo necessario languit :; et sic, mirabili quadam vicissitudine, commo-
75 dum simul et incommodum., dulce pariter et amarum, ex uno
caritatis fonte manauit. Dulce videlicet in eo quod celestis affluentia delectationis interdum illi copiose propinata non defuit :;
amarum autem ex eo quod amanti sponso, iuxta sui cordis insatiabile desiderium, amando condignam vicissitudinem redibere non
80 potuit. Vel etiam in eo quod ab eternis gaudijs, interim dum
manebat in corpore, sequestrata, presentis exilij molestias cum
afflictione simul et tedio supportabat.

205 Sic ergo viuebat, et in talibus vita spiritus sui : nunc quidem,
amoris igne succensa., feruens et estuans ; nunc celestium deli-
85 ciarum affecta dulcedine, gestiens et tripudians :; nunc in eternorum appetentia sitiens pariter et esuriens ; in omnibus tamen
quieta simul et patiens :, in diuino beneplacito, tam in dulcibus
quam in amaris, tam in aduersis quam in prosperis, per omnia
se conformans. Fuit autem in hoc amoris exercitio multo tempore,
90 sic alternatis vicibus diuersos illius affectus, nunc pariter nunc
si<n>gillatim, experiens :; ex quo demum omnis virtus humanitatis illius adeo lassata succubuit ;, quod in lectum egritudinis
corruens,. toto pene corpore conquassata defecerit :; in qua[2]
etiam per multa annorum curricula, solo languens amoris incendio,
95 perdurauit.

she was by this sweetness, the more her insatiable appetite increased in its desire. Since she could not find what she desired in present things, her appetite, continually hungry and famished, sought the satiety of eternal refection.

204 Beatrice understood that the Lord was anticipating her with his ever vehement love, and therefore she knew for certain that she was bound to accord him the return of her love. And because she could not do this as fully as she desired, the weakness of human nature being incapable of this as we have said, she necessarily languished in a rough patch caused by love.

Thus by a certain marvellous alternation both the smooth and the rough, the sweet and the bitter, flowed from the same spring of love. The sweet, because the abundance of heavenly delight was often copiously poured forth for her; yet bitter, because she could not make the worthy return of love due to her loving Bridegroom according to her heart's insatiable desire. And because, being separated from the eternal joys as long as she lived in the body, she bore the troubles of the present exile with pain and tedium.

205 Thus she lived, and of such things did the life of her spirit consist:[1] at one time burnt up with the fire of love, she would be fervent and bubbling; at another, affected by the sweetness of heavenly delights, she would be gesturing and dancing; again she would hunger and thirst[2] with an appetite for eternal things. In everything, however, she was quiet and patient, conforming herself in all ways to the divine good-pleasure in things both sweet and bitter, adverse and prosperous. For a long time she was in this travail of love, experiencing the different affections in turn, now all together, now one by one. Finally, exhausted by all this, her whole strength gave way and she collapsed on her sick bed, broken and failing in almost every part of her body. She continued in this sickness for many years, languishing under the fire of love alone.

1. Is 38:16   2. Ps 106:5

⊄ DE MENTIS IUBILO
QUEM IN MISSA SENTIRE PROMERUIT
v. capitulum

206 Quodam etiam tempore, cum ex more missarum solempnijs
⁵ interesset, et eleuato corde deı magnalia, pariterque liberalitatis
sue sibi collata beneficia., sed et amoris illius experta // ƒ. *326 a*
sibi totiens in huius valle peregrinationis indicia, mente sedula
pertractaret : accidit vt post eleuationis horam, cum iam in altari
nostre redemptionis precium, natum de virgine corpus dominicum,
¹⁰ presens esset ;, eius anima presentiam illius sentire intra se cum
ingenti feruore deuotionis inciperet : ; ad quam velut ad ignem
validissimum liquefacta, continuo tota simul in illo caritatis pelago
quasi guttula defluens est absorpta.

In qua liquefactione quid, quantumve spiritualis iocunditatis acce-
¹⁵ perit., quid senserit., quid gustauerit, et-si verbis explicari non
valeat :, ex corporalium tamen defectione sensuum extrinsecus
aliquantulum apparebat. Quorum vsus eodem tempore sic defecit :, vt, nichil eorum attendens que tolerabat extrinsecus, ad
terram, prostrato capite, per residuum illud misse spacium deorsum
²⁰ inclinata iacuerit. ; quod tamen, donec expleto missali officio de
loco resurgeret, non aduertit penitus nec attendit.

207 Exurgens tamen a loco, non repente celestis illius refectionis
gustum amisit : ; sed per totum diem illum eius in anima perseue-
rans [1], tam ineffabili dulcedinis affluentia, cordis et mentis ipsius
²⁵ intima penetrauit, quod vix pedibus suis incedere., vix aliquid
operis interim exercere valuerit. Quapropter, ne spiritualis forte delectatio quam experiebatur interius, per aliqua iocunditatis indicia
foras affluens., se prodendo detegeret :, humane societatis fre-
quentiam illo tempore quantum licuit euitauit. Sed id frustra qui-
³⁰ dem. ; nam eodem die, superuenientibus quibusdam amicorum
suorum., ad visitandum illos euocata perrexit : ; quibus cum aliqua iam edificationis colloquia de cordis sui plenitudine propinare
cepisset., ab hijs tam in verbis quam in gestu corporis cum illius
spiritualis fuisset iocunditas aliquantulum deprehensa ;, confestim

THE JUBILATION OF MIND SHE DESERVED
TO FEEL DURING MASS
Chapter Five

206 One time Beatrice was present at Mass as usual, and with uplifted heart was engrossed in pondering the great deeds of God in her mind, and the benefits of his liberality bestowed on her, and the signs of his love she had experienced so often in this valley of exile, it happened that after the elevation, when the price of our redemption, the Lord's Body, born of the Virgin, was present on the altar, her soul began to feel his presence within her with immense fervor and devotion. At his presence she melted as though before an intense fire, and she was immediately and wholly absorbed like a little drop flowing down into the billows of love. Even if she could not explain in words what and how much spiritual delight she received, or what she sensed and tasted in this melting, it was to some extent apparent outwardly by the fainting of her bodily senses. They so failed then that for the rest of the Mass she lay, head on the ground, noticing and attending to nothing around her. Yet she did not notice this fact until she rose from the floor after Mass had ended.

207 When she got up, Beatrice did not immediately lose the taste of this heavenly refreshment, but the taste lasted in her soul that whole day and so penetrated the inside of her heart and mind with an abundance of unspeakable sweetness that she could scarcely walk on her feet or scarcely do any work in the meantime. Wherefore, she avoided human company for that time as much as she could, lest the spiritual delight she was experiencing within should perhaps be betrayed and laid bare by some outward-flowing signs of delight. But it was in vain, for that same day she was summoned to visit some of her friends who had arrived. When she began to pour forth from the fullness of her heart some words of edification and her spiritual delight was to some extent grasped by them from her words as well as her bodily gestures, she quickly left

35 confugiens ad secretarium suum, cum festinatione recessit : vbi
liberiori studio dulci se redibens meditationis officio., secretum
suum sibi vendicans, inter dulcia sponsi // f. 326 b sui brachia
sompnum contemplationis simul capiens et oscula requieuit.

¶ DE EO QUOD SEMETIPSAM
INSANAM FINGERE IN DESIDERIO HABUIT
Sextum capitulum

208 Eodem autem anno quo penitentiam suam, per febris incen-
5   dium vt prediximus transeundo, fauente deo peregerat [1] :, incidit illi quodam tempore rursus cogitatio de multiplici gratiarum affluentia quam in vita sua, domino largiente, susceperat :
quam dulciter videlicet in diebus suis illam, affectu materno,
consolationis lacte nutrierat ; quam suauiter ab omni lapsu morti-
10 fero pedem conuersationis sue custodiens, per viam compendij,
ductu sue pietatis, ad eminentiam vsque perfectioris vite <pro-
uexerat>; quamque delectabiliter eam per dies singulos, in copiosa
benedictionum suarum dulcedine, visitabat. Hanc ergo meditationis sue materiam cum ante cordis aspectum crebra repetitione
15 reduceret., et in ea multum nimis gratiarum actionis debitum
inueniret ;, cepit intra se super insufficientie sue defectu, quo
videlicet impediente minus in gratiarum actione profecerat, admodum grauiter estuare : prorsus indignam se reputans ad tantam
gratiarum affluentiam a domino capescendam., quam nullo posset
20 obsequio, nullo quiuisset retributionis commercio compensare.
209 Cogitans igitur et recogitans., et quid gratum diuine complacentie faceret cum apostolo dominum frequenter interrogans [2]
et intra semetipsam instanter diebus et noctibus simul inuestigans : in hoc tandem applicuit et residere fecit consilium cordis
25 sui ;, quod, sicut ipse misericordiarum dominus obprobria passionis, intuitu sue redemptionis, in corpore suo, quieta mentis
affectione, sustinuit : sic, versa vice, pro se contumeliarum ob-

and fled to her private place. There she gave herself up with freer zeal to meditation, claiming her secret for herself, and in the sweet arms and kisses of her Bridegroom she rested in the sleep of contemplation.

SHE INTENDED TO FEIGN MADNESS
Chapter Six

208 In the same year when by God's favor she had done her penitence by passing through the fiery fever, as we have related, the thought of the multiple abundance of graces she had received from the Lord's generosity in her life came again to Beatrice's mind. How sweetly he had nourished her with the milk of consolation and with motherly affection all her days. How gently he had kept her foot from every deadly lapse, leading her by his kindness through a shortcut to the heights of a more perfect life. How delightfully he had visited her every day in the abundant sweetness of his blessings. When her heart had frequently repeated this meditation and found in it a great debt of thanksgiving, Beatrice began to be gravely agitated over the insufficiency of her progress in thanksgiving, thinking herself wholly unworthy of entering into such an abundance of graces from the Lord, which she could not repay by any possible service or exchange.

209 Mulling this over and over again, and frequently asking the Lord, with the apostle, what she should do to please his divine good-pleasure, and investigating the matter with herself day and night,[1] she finally fixed and settled her heart's design, and it was this: just as the Lord of mercies, with a view to her salvation, had suffered the disgraces of the passion in his body with a quiet affection of mind, so in her turn Beatrice would suffer disgrace and

---

1. Ac 9:6

probria sustineret. Sed qualiter ad hanc iniuriarum sufferentiam semetipsam exponeret;, que ab omnibus colebatur vt sancta,
30 venerabatur vt dei famula preelecta? Non valens ergo leuiorem, ad exequendum cordis sui desi- // f. 326 c derium, occasionis semitam inuenire:, demum in hoc totam assensus sui summam constituit., vt semetipsam insanam fingeret;, et sic, ab omnibus eam intuentibus despectui habita:, per omnimodam abiectionis
35 et vilitatis conformitatem, christi vestigiis decetero perfectius in- hereret. In hac itaque cogitatione <corde> suo concepta tandem bene complacuit:; unde frequenter eam examinans et omnes eius circumstantias diligentius inuestigans;, ne forsan ab eo qui se plerumque in angelum lucis transfigurat <immissam> acce-
40 perit:, sagaci discretionis oculo studiose per id temporis exquisiuit. 210 Verum et-si proposito suo satis accommodam hanc[3] inueniret., ex altera tamen parte <quedam>, ipsi suo proposito minus congruencia, deprehendit. Nam et-si per huiusmodi fictionem ad id quod affectabat assequendum, semet extremis et vilibus appli-
45 cando., de facili peruenire potuerit: ex obliquo tamen ad ordinis obseruantiam., ad horarum regularium solutionem debitam, seu ad proximorum instructionem et amonitionem caritatiuam, se deinceps expedire non posse considerans., ab ipso quod conce- perat in mente proposito continuo territa resiliuit.
50 Sic igitur id diuersis temporibus, nunc appetendo., nunc ab eo denuo resiliendo., in non modicam cordis perplexitatem tandem cecidit:; cum ex vtroque latere grauiter anxiata., quid horum eligere, impedito discretionis iudicio, non inuenit.
211 Prius ergo quam ad aggrediendum hoc cordis sui propositum
55 semetipsam animare presumpsit., sapientis vsa consilio, ne post factum male cauta peniteret, alicuius sapientis consilium in hac sua perplexitate perquirere studuit;, et precipue cuiusdam viri venerabilis henrici nomine., viri sanctitate simul et discretione precipui[4]:, ad cuius familiare consilium in arduis agendorum

contumely for him. But how would she expose herself to suffering these injuries when she was revered by everyone as holy, and was venerated as a specially chosen handmaid of God? Not finding an easier way to follow her heart's desire, she finally gave her whole consent to this plan, that she would feign madness, and so, despised by all who would see her, she would more perfectly cling to Christ's footsteps through this total conformity to abjection and worthlessness. Beatrice was quite pleased with this thought in her heart, and therefore frequently at that time examined it and carefully investigated all its circumstances and inquired into it zealously and with the eye of shrewd discretion, for fear she had perhaps received it from him who often changes himself into an angel of light.

210 Yet even though Beatrice found this [idea] well-suited to her purpose, on the other hand she perceived some things less in harmony with her proposal. For even if by this fiction she could easily attain what she desired by applying herself to the lowest and meanest things, still she considered that the indirect effect would be that she could no longer be useful in the observance of the Order, in the due accomplishment of the regular hours or in the charitable instruction and admonition of her neighbors. Frightened by this, she quickly repudiated what she had proposed in mind.

So in the end she fell into no small perplexity of heart, at one time seeking her object and at another repudiating it. Gravely anxious on both counts, with her judgment and discretion impeded, she did not know which to choose.

211 Before she presumed to move toward the accomplishment of her heart's proposal, Beatrice, using wise counsel, was eager to get counsel from some wise man in this perplexity, lest poorly on her guard she should repent after the deed. She was especially anxious to have the advice of a certain venerable man, Henry, a man outstanding in holiness and discretion, in whose intimate counsel she

60 suorum negotijs eatenus ipsa confugere consueuit. Huius ergo
viri, qui thenis eo tempore morabatur, aduentum, a natiuitate
precursoris domini advsque sancte crucis exaltationem [5] cum
insatiabili desiderio prestolata fuisset., et, illius interim absentia
// f. 326 d prepedita, suo potiri voto minime valuisset ;, tandem,
65 importabili victa desiderio simul et tedio, in languorem continuum
incidit : ; quem, donec prefati viri desiderato releuaretur alloquio,
non sine graui corporis sui dispendio tollerauit.

212 Quo tandem ad monasterium accedente, virgo christi beatrix
omne quod mente conceperat illi diligenter exposuit :, et quid,
70 quam ob causam, quanto tempore vel qualiter affectauerit ex ordine patefaciens, vtrum immissione diuina vel suggestione dyabolica
tam vehemens desiderium in corde susceperit., edoceri se cum
instantia postulauit.

Cui ille. : "Non, inquit, vt suspicaris, hanc <abiectionis> viam,
75 per quam redemptoris tui vestigia sequereris., dyabolica suggestione :, sed sola magistra caritate mente concepisse te noueris :
non tamen hoc fictionis propositum in opus diregere, te vel insanam vel fatuam confingendo, si consilijs meis acquieueris,
aliquatenus attemptabis : ; presertim cum ex hoc non modicum
80 profectus tui dispendium incurrere forte potueris ;, et sic, minus
vtili studio pietatis ex vna parte nimis pertinaciter insistendo :,
magis vtile necessario, non tam in tuum quam in proximorum
grauamen et dampnum, omittere cogeris ".

Hijs dictis, virgo domini, prefato consilio reuerenter simul et
85 humiliter acquiescens., mox consensus sui pedem a vetito calle
non cunctata retrahere ; quod mente conceperat ab intimis cordis
sui desiderium [6] festinanter excussit quidem., sed voluntatis
integritas, ex qua tale propositum emanauerat, in exequendo dei
beneplacito semper immobilis et semper vigens in suo robore
90 perdurauit.

had been accustomed to take refuge in difficult affairs. After she
had awaited with insatiable desire from the birth of the Lord's
Precursor[2] until the exaltation of the Holy Cross[3] for the arrival of
this man, who lived in Tienen, and meanwhile, fretted by his ab-
sence, she could hardly obtain her desire. She was finally overcome with intolerable desire and tedium, and fell into a continual
languor which cost her body a great deal until she was relieved by
her desired conversation with him.

212 When Henry came to the monastery, Christ's virgin Beatrice
carefully laid before him everything she had conceived in her
mind. Disclosing to him in an orderly way what she desired, and
why and how long and in what way, she earnestly begged him to
tell her whether the vehement desire conceived in her heart was of
divine origin or diabolical suggestion.

He said to her: 'You should know that this way of abjection by
which you would follow in your Redeemer's footsteps, is not a
diabolical suggestion, as you surmise; love alone taught your mind
to conceive it. But if you acquiesce to my advice, you will certainly not try to put this fiction into effect by pretending to be insane or a fool, chiefly because you might perhaps incur in this way
no small setback in your progress, and so by following too stubbornly a less useful attempt at piety, you would be forced to leave
aside what is more useful, not so much to your own as to your
neighbor's harm and loss'. When she heard this, the Lord's virgin
reverently and humbly acquiesced in this advice, and did not delay
in withdrawing her foot quickly from the forbidden path. Hastily
she rejected from the depths of her heart the desire she had conceived in her mind, but the integrity of her will, from which such a
proposal had flowed, remained always vigorous and firm in following the divine good-pleasure.

2. 24 June 1232   3. 14 September

¶ DE EO QUOD AD <COGNITIONEM> SANCTE
TRINITATIS EX DESIDERIO ASPIRAUIT
Septimum capitulum

213 Non multo post <hec> tempore circa natiuitatem domini [1],
magnum illi desiderium incidit de concipienda cognitione sancte
et indiuidue trinitatis. Que licet omni humano sensu prorsus sit
incom- // f. *327 a* prehensibilis :, ex maxima tamen confidentia,
non temere, more quorumdam altiora se querentium <et> sensu
proprio profundiora scrutantium. , sed humili corde, mente deuota,
caritate quoque feruida, ad assequendum rem inassequibilem
aspirauit. Nec id frustra quidem : nam interdum cum in libris de
sancta trinitate confectis, quorum penes se copiam retinebat [2], id
quod inuestigare querebat ingenij viuacitate diligenter exquireret:,
interdum etiam cum meditationis officio vel orationis studio
sollerter intenderet. , accidit vt, aperto corde, lumen celestis veritatis in illud tamquam fulgur influeret : in quo, sub momento
temporis, id quod querebat apprehendere meruit ; et quod per
sensus vigorem indagare non potuit :, per immissionem celestis
gratie, non ad recondendum in mente, sed ad fruendum illo
breuissimo tempore, diuinus illi spiritus inspirauit [3].
214 Cum ergo totam sensuum suorum viuacitatem ad apprehensionem patefacte sibi veritatis exigeret. , et quod ad momentum, ad ictum oculi, de summe trinitatis cognitione perceperat,
memorie commendare disponeret :, repente, cognitionis subtracto
lumine, quod mente se tenere putauerat a corde resilijt. , et, tamquam fulgur cito pertransiens, non comparauit. ; donec, electe

WITH DESIRE SHE ASPIRED TO KNOWLEDGE
OF THE HOLY TRINITY
Chapter Seven

213 Not long after this, around Christmas, Beatrice conceived a great desire to know the Holy and Undivided Trinity. Although the Trinity is totally incomprehensible to human understanding, she aspired to the unattainable with great confidence, not rashly like some who seek things too high for them and search into what is deeper than their understanding,[1] but with a humble heart, a devout mind and fervent love. Not in vain either, for sometimes when she was diligently and keenly inquiring after what she sought, using books on the Holy Trinity, a supply of which she kept on hand, and sometimes when she was alertly attending to meditation and prayer, it happened that the light of heavenly truth flowed like lightning into her open heart. There in a moment of time she deserved to lay hold of what she sought; what she could not explore by sensory vigor the divine spirit breathed into her by heavenly grace, not to store away in her mind but to enjoy for the briefest moment.

214 When she called on the full keenness of her senses to grasp the truth laid open to her, and was ready to commit to memory what in a moment and in the twinkling of an eye she had perceived of the most high Trinity, the light of knowledge was suddenly withdrawn. What she thought she held in her mind eluded her heart, passing like a flash of lightning. She did not acquire it until the most high God took pity on the fervent desire of his chosen

---

1. *Si 3:22*

sue feruens desiderium miseratus, deus altissimus illius intima,
prefate cognitionis radio, denuo perlustrauit.

Tali ergo magis magisque vicissitudine prouocata., illius desi-
30 derium numquam ab inuestigando cessare, numquam a querendo
se retrahere potuit :; sed semper erectum sursum habens cordis
intuitum, instar sitientis et vinum optimum oculis suis demonstratum apprehendere non valentis, hec ad <comprehensionem>
rei incomprehensibilis oportune simul et importune se intulit.,
35 et velut <gyrando> circuiens, et quod queritabat in medio
constitutum intelligens, ac propemodum illud manu capiens., sic,
eleuato desiderio, cum quesitum summe trinitatis misterium iamiam
apprehendere iamque // fol. 327 b retinere se credidit : mox
illud⁴, instar fulguris non comparens, frustratam suo desiderio
40 querentis intentionem continuo dereliquit.

215 Cum ergo per aliquantum temporis in hoc comprehensionis
desiderio permansisset :, accidit vt, in die sanctissimo natiuitatis
dominice, totam cordis intentionem ad meditationis studium applicando, sacrosanctum incarnationis dominice misterium apud se
45 corde sedulo pertractare cepisset ; cum ecce, per mentis excessum,
in sublimia rapitur :, et ad videndum admirabilem visionem, a
diuino spiritu sursum euectus, eius spiritus protinus eleuatur.

Videbat enim, et ecce pater omnipotens et eternus ex se magnum
emittebat fluuium : ex quo multi simul hinc et inde riui diriua-
50 bantur et riuuli, qui volentibus ad se appropinquare potum aqua-
rum in vitam eternam salientium offerebant. Bibebant ergo quidam
ex fluuio., quidam ex riuis :; nonnulli vero potum ex riuulis
hauriebant. At illa cui hec videre concessa sunt ex omnibus
potare promeruit. In qua potatione, quid hec omnia portendebant
55 clara mentis acie protinus intellexit.

216 Fluuius etenim ipse fuit dei filius, dominus ihesus christus
eternaliter ex patre genitus :, et ex matre pro redemptione salutis
humane temporaliter procreatus. Riui vero signa reparationis
nostre., stigmata scilicet passionis dominice :, que pro nobis
60 peccatoribus dignatus est in suo corpore super lignum sustinere.

one, and again illuminated her interiorly with a ray of the aforesaid knowledge.

More and more provoked by such fluctuations, Beatrice could never stop her desire to investigate, could never withdraw from the search. In season and out she took it upon herself to comprehend the incomprehensible, her heart's gaze always erect, like a thirsty person unable to take hold of the excellent wine shown him. She acted as if she were circling around something, well knowing that the object of her search was nearby and almost grasping it with her hand. Then when her desires were at their height, when she believed she had grasped the mystery of the all-high Trinity and was holding it, immediately the mystery would disappear like lightning, leaving the searcher's intention frustrated of her desire.

215 After Beatrice's desire for this understanding had continued for some time, it happened on Christmas Day that she had begun to apply her whole heart's intention to fervent meditation and to treat carefully in her heart the holy mystery of the Lord's incarnation. Behold, she was rapt on high in ecstasy of mind, and her spirit was raised by the divine spirit to see an admirable vision.

She looked and behold, the all-powerful and eternal Father was emitting from himself a great river from which many brooks and brooklets here and there branched off and offered a drink of water springing up to eternal life[2] to those who willed to approach them. Some drank from the river, some drank from the brooks, but some drank from the brooklets. Beatrice, to whom it was granted to see these things, was allowed to drink from all of them, and in this drinking she quickly and clearly understood what all these things meant.

216 The river itself was the Son of God, the Lord Jesus Christ, eternally born from the Father, and begotten in time from his mother for human redemption and salvation. The brooks were the signs of our reparation, that is the marks of the Lord's passion which he deigned to bear in his body on the wood of the cross for us sinners.

2. Jn 4:14

Porro riuuli dona sunt gratiarum :, que suis fidelibus, ad exequendum ex eis voluntatis sue beneplacitum, per omnium seculorum tempora non cessat largitor bonorum omnium erogare.

Qui itaque bibebant ex flumine, hij nimirum erant qui, per vite

[65] perfectioris eminentiam, indesinenti studio redemptoris sui vestigijs inherebant :; qui vero bibebant ex riuis hij sunt qui, per
compassionis vicem, profectus sui capiunt incrementum in memoria dominice passionis.

At vero qui bibebant ex riuulis., hij sunt qui per pietatis opera

[70] satagebant indulta // f. 327 c sibi gratiarum dona conuertere
in dominice beneplacito voluntatis. Iuxta meritorum ergo dis-
tantiam ordinata fuit et potantium turba potionumque differentia :
nam primos quidem semetipso [5] potabat ; secundos vero memorie
passionis sue dulci poculo recreabat :; reliquos autem mellifluis

[75] gratiarum donis et consolationum suarum celesti dulcedine sa-
turabat.

Videbat etiam quamplurimos bibere dedignantes ;, nec ad fluuium
quidem nec ad riuos., sed nec ad riuulos appropinquare volentes :; sed ieiunos et vacuos in sua pertinacia permanentes.

[80] Hij vero sunt, per sordes criminalium peccatorum et consuetudine
peruersorum operum, semetipsos ab electorum consortio voluntarie separantes : qui, potius contempnentes dominum quam con-
tempti a domino, ieiuni simul et vacui, celestiumque deliciarum
inexeperti., solis permanent terenis voluptatibus et delicijs in-

[85] hiantes.

217 Hijs ergo virgo domini diligenter <inspectis>, adusque
fontem eternitatis, vnde fluuius oriebatur, illius decursum inten-
tissimo contemplationis oculo prosecuta :, quod de misterio sancte
trinitatis intelligere concupiuerat ibidem inuestigare promeruit ;

[90] et <dominum dei> filium eternaliter ex patre <genitum> et
in <fine> temporum ex matre temporaliter procreatum :, spiritum quoque sanctum <equaliter> ex patre procedentem et filio,;

The brooklets are the gifts of grace which the Giver of every good thing never through all ages ceases giving to his faithful so that by them they can do his will.

Those who were drinking from the river were those who were clinging to the path of the Redeemer with ceaseless zeal through an outstandingly perfect life. Those who were drinking from the brooks are those who through reciprocal compassion augment their progress by remembrance of the Lord's passion.

But those who were drinking from the brooklets are those who were laboring by works of piety to turn the gifts of grace received into what pleases the divine will. The crowds of drinkers and the difference in drinks were arranged according to differing merits. For Christ was giving himself as drink for the first; the second he was refreshing with the sweet cup of the remembrance of his passion; the rest he satisfied with honey-like gifts of grace and the heavenly sweetness of his consolations.

Beatrice also saw many disdaining to drink, not wanting to approach either the river or the brooks or the brooklets, but stubbornly remaining fasting and empty. These voluntarily separate themselves from the company of the elect through the filth of their crimes and sins and by the habit of evil deeds. They despise the Lord rather than being despised by him; fasting and empty, without experience of heavenly delights, they keep panting only after earthly pleasures and delights.

217 The Lord's virgin, Beatrice, having carefully inspected these things, followed with the eye of very intent contemplation the downward course of the river from the eternal spring from which it rose, and she deserved to investigate there what she had desired to understand of the mystery of the holy Trinity. What holy Mother Church throughout the world worships with most perfect faith, Beatrice's soul understood more fully at that instant of time, by revelation of the divine spirit, namely: the Lord, the Son of God eternally born from the Father and begotten temporally from his mother at the end of time, the Holy Spirit proceeding equally from the Father and the

personarum etiam differentiam in vna deitatis eternitatis maiestatis essentia consistentem., ac cetera deifice trinitatis sacro-
95 sancta misteria, que per orbem terre credendo veneratur, in fide
perfectissima, sancta mater ecclesia :, diuino reuelante spiritu,
beatricis anima sub eodem tempore plenius intellexit.

In qua contemplationis dulcedine cum modico tempore permansisset., confestim ad se reuersa, quod per solam mentis intelli-
100 gentiam, eterna sapientia reuelante, cognouerat., per sensus
acumen ad intellectum reducere memorieque mandare se credidit ;
sed vt ab hoc casso labore quiesceret a domino monita., reuerenter obediens acquieuit. Quod enim humano sensu minus //
f. 327 d prouide se comprehendere presumebat., non tam sui
105 quam omnium sensuum humanorum intellectum effugere., so-
laque superne gratia reuelationis apprehendi posse diuinum illi
responsum asseruit. Sed in hoc potius creatoris sui consistere
beneplacitum, vt per caritatis affectum ad subueniendum decetero
necessitatibus proximorum intenderet :, et tam orationum quam
110 exhortationum obsequijs illorum indigentie subueniret :, sancto
reuelante spiritu intellexit.

218 Donum itaque caritatis in munere sibi datum accipiens., et
in illius exercicio diuinum consistere beneplacitum euidenter
intelligens :, paratum cor suum ad executionem diuine voluntatis
115 exhibuit : quod pietatis negotium qualiter per residuum vite sue
tempus exercuit ex sequentibus euidentius apparebit.

Hoc ergo caritatis officium cum oblatum sibi diuinitus accep-
tasset,. mox mirum in modum super omnem latitudinem mundi
cor suum dilatari pariter et extendi sibi visum est : quo sic exploso
120 quasi sagena latissima totum genus humanum intrinsecus apprehendit. Quam nimirum apprehensionem nichil aliud reor porten-
dere quam ipsam latitudinem caritatis :, per quam eodem tempore
tam sapientibus quam insipientibus cum apostolo [6] se debitricem
<exhibuit> :, et ad subueniendum necessitatibus singulorum,
125 iuxta concessam sibi gratiam, in omni fidei puritate cordisque
dulcedine semetipsam exposuit : quod pietatis negotium et deuote
suscepit et deuotius consummauit.

Son, also the difference of persons existing in the one essence of the eternal divine Majesty, and the other sacrosanct mysteries of the divine Trinity.

After she had remained a short time in this sweet contemplation, she suddenly came back to herself, and thought to recall to mind and to commit to memory by the sharpness of her interior sense the revelation of divine wisdom which she had learned by purely mental understanding. But warned by the Lord to rest from this vain labor, she reverently acquiesced and obeyed. The divine reply asserted that what she less prudently presumed she understood by human sense, escaped not so much her own as all human understanding, and could be grasped only by the grace of heavenly revelation. She understood by revelation of the Holy Spirit that her Creator's good-pleasure was instead that in the future she should intend to help her neighbors in their needs with loving affection, relieving their privations by both her prayers and her exhortations.

218 Beatrice received the gift of charity given to her, and since she understood clearly that the divine good-pleasure was that she exercise it, she showed her heart prepared to do the divine will. It will be clear from what follows how she exercised this work of loving kindness for the rest of her life.

When she had received this office of charity divinely offered to her, her heart in a marvelous way soon seemed to enlarge and extend over the whole breadth of the world. Her heart spread out like a vast net, catching within it the whole human race. This catch I understand to signify the very breadth of charity through which Beatrice showed herself, with the apostle, a debtor to both the wise and the unwise.[3] In all purity of faith and sweetness of heart she exposed herself to help each one's needs, according to the grace given to her. This work of piety she received with devotion, and still more devoutly she completed it.

3. Rm 1:14

❡ DE EFFRENATA FORTITUDINE
ET VEHEMENTIA SPIRITUS EIUS
viij. capitulum

219 Sequenti vero die quo beati prothomartiris stephani solemp-
⁵ nia celebrantur. , nouam et insolitam spiritus sui vesaniam intra
semetipsam, impetuoso conamine debachando, consurgere <de-
prehendit>. ; cuius inundatio velut maris fluctus omnis cohabi-
tationis impatiens. , et forti nimis impetu terminorum suorum
metas egrediens, ac si totius // ƒ. *328 a* corpusculi vires infrin-
¹⁰ geret:, ita repentino commota turbine valenter nimis et fortiter
ebulliuit. Hanc autem vim fortitudinis ex eternorum desiderio
quorum reuelatione paulo ante refecta fuerat, vt premissum est. ,
illius spiritus eo tempore plus solito valentiorem accepit ; cuius
impetus tam fortis fuit et validus. , quod omnes corporis vires
¹⁵ velut telam consumens aranee. , vel quasi bestia fortis et indomita
claustra perfragilis abrumpens custodie, sic penitus subiugando
deiecit. , quod, illius impetum <sustinere> non preualens, imbecillitas corporalis ex toto pene defecerit :, et in lectum egritudinis ipsam cito deiciens. , non mediocriter illius vires exhauserit,
²⁰ et morbo paralitico singula corporis sui membra trementia simul
et macie nimis obesa reddiderit;, et sic demum totum illius corpusculum violenter affecerit. , vt speciem quamdam frenetice passionis
eius insania pretendere videretur :, quam ex feruentissimo caritatis incendio soloque supernorum desiderio tolerauit.
²⁵ Quanto vero prefate violentie fortiorem assultum sustinuit. ;
et quanto validiorem impetum sui desiderij supportauit :, tanto
puriorem intra se vigere spiritum intellexit ; et quos puritate
spiritus agnouit magis preditos. , hos ad colloquium libenter simul
et hylariter admittere consueuit :; ex quorum dulci colloquio
³⁰ magnum recreationis antidotum et delectationis fructum suauissimum eo tempore frequentissime reportauit. In quibus autem
aliquid impuritatis in verbis aut in moribus deprehendit, hos non
solum inuitissime, sed et molestissime sibi confabulantes audiuit,
aut coram se conuersantes aspexit : eo quod illorum impuritas.
³⁵ sue prorsus puritati contraria, non solum hunc quem sustinuit

THE UNBRIDLED FORTITUDE
AND VEHEMENCE OF HER SPIRIT
Chapter Eight

219 On the following day, when the solemnity of the blessed protomartyr Stephen is being celebrated,[1] Beatrice understood from raging impetuous spiritual struggles that a new and unfamiliar madness was rising within her. Its flooding was like that of an ocean wave impatient of all restraint, passing beyond its bounds by its great impetus; it boiled up strong and hard in a sudden disturbance as if it would wholly break the strength of her frail body. Her spirit then received this stronger than usual vigor from the desire for eternal things, by the revelation of which she had been refreshed shortly before, as we said. Its impetus was so mighty and strong that it consumed all her bodily strength like a spider's web; or like a strong untamed beast breaking through the fragile pen holding it, it cast her down and thoroughly subjugated her until her weak body could not stand the impetus and almost wholly collapsed. It quickly cast her into her sick bed and, exhausting her strength to no small degree, it made every limb of her body tremble with palsy and grow thin and emaciated. Finally, it affected her whole frail body so violently that the disease seemed to simulate a kind of frenzy which she bore out of most fervent fire of love and sheer desire for heavenly things.

Beatrice understood that the spirit within her was thriving with a purity proportionate to the strong assault of the aforementioned violence and the vigorous impetus of the desire she suffered. And those persons whom she recognized as gifted with greater purity of spirit she used to admit to her conversation gladly and cheerfully, and from their sweet conversation she often at that time received a great antidote and refreshment and the sweet fruit of delight. She was not only greatly unwilling but also much annoyed to hear others speaking with one another or conversing in her presence in some impurity of speech or manners. Their impurity, contrary to her purity, not only increased the sickness of her infirmity,

1. 26 December

infirmitatis morbum accendit., verum etiam hunc, ad mortem vsque, eundem propemodum <aggravavit>.

220 Per idem vero tempus quo prefati languoris incommodo la- // f. *328 b* borauit[1]., in quantum licuit a colloquijs hominum semetipsam abstraxit, et cum propheta[2] nonnumquam etiam a bonis abstinuit : pro eo videlicet quod, ex qualitate verborum a cordis habundantia procedentium, illam quam interius tolerauit amoris insaniam deprehendi posse metuerit ; et hoc discrete qui-dem sed frustra precauit :; nam et-si verbum, silens, ex ore non protulit., morum tamen inconsueta suauitas, quid sentiret in-trinsecus, discretioribus et in disciplina caritatis magis exercitatis, extrinsecus apertissime demonstrauit. Quarum etiam alique, quas ceteris copiosius deuotionis ardor accendit, tam inseparabiliter ipsi dei famule, pro releuando quod patiebatur infirmitatis in-commodo, voluntarie diebus simul et noctibus, adheserunt :, vt numquam illarum obsequium egrotanti defuerit ; quam nisi tam verborum quam obsequiorum ministerio confouissent :, pre nimia cordis insania quamcitius in languorem freneticum illam incidere putauerunt. Ceteris vero, quas deuotionis feruor non adeo affe-cerat., quo laboraret incommodo prorsus manebat incognitum : putantibus eis naturalem esse morbum, cuius experiri non con-sueuerant incentiuum.

221 Fuit autem in hoc statu per sex ebdomadarum ferme spa-cium[3] :, quibus, illo sui spiritus impetu a concepta vesania non cessante, caput ab egritudinis lectulo non leuauit ; quibus tandem expletis, hec eadem spiritualis insania in admirabilem caritatis dulcedinem commutata quieuit : et sic denuo conualescens, quod, vt iam premisimus, ad salutem proximorum expendendum acce-perat, reparatis corporalium virium instrumentis, ipsum caritatis bonum, <in communem> profectum omnium, et singulum singu-lorum ad se confluentium, decetero fideliter erogauit.

Numquam tamen a paralitica passione[4], quamdiu postmodum in hac vita permansit, ad plenum expediri potuit :; sed incertis et

but aggravated it almost to death.

220 During the time Beatrice was laboring under this troublesome languor, she withdrew as far as she might from human conversation, and with the prophet she sometimes abstained even from good things,[2] fearing that from the quality of words proceeding from the abundance of her heart, the mad love she sustained within might be detected. She prayed for this discreetly but in vain. For even if she was silent and spoke not a word, the unusual sweetness of her manners openly and outwardly showed to those more discreet and better practised in the discipline of love, what she was feeling within. Some, who were more enkindled with the ardor of devotion than others, voluntarily stayed inseparably close to the servant of God day and night to relieve the distress of her illness so that their service was never lacking to the invalid. They thought that, unless they nursed her with words and services, she might quickly lapse into frenzy because of the excessive insanity of her heart. The disease under which Beatrice labored remained quite unknown to those not so affected by fervor of devotion; they thought it was a natural sickness whose unbridled intensity they were not used to experiencing.

221 Beatrice was in this state about six weeks, during which she did not lift her head from her sick bed, for the impetuous madness she had conceived in her spirit never ceased. After that this spiritual insanity calmed down and changed into a wonderful sweetness of love. Convalescing, with her bodily members restored, she faithfully thereafter expended the wealth of charity she had received, as we said, for the salvation of her neighbors, for the common profit of all and the individual profit of each who came to her.

As long as she lived, she could not be fully freed from the paralyzing passion, but at episodic and irregular times and especially

2. Ps 38:3

interpolatis temporibus., et tunc maxime cum de summo bo- //
⁷⁰ *f. 328c* no cogitando siue loquendo., vel etiam <alias loquentes>
auscultando, viuacissimum illius spiritum excitari contigit :, confestim omnium membrorum infirmi corporis, et precipue capitis
cordis<que> tremorem sustinuit. ; seu etiam cum amoris insatiabilis appetitus, ad eterna suspirans, ad assequendum as-
⁷⁵ surgere non potuit id quod inexplebili desiderio concupiuit.
In hoc tamen infirmitatis incommodo licet oppido fatigaretur.,
eodem hoc solum commodi, hoc solacij repperit :, quod, cum eam
quam sentiebat intrinsecus delectationem spiritus intra se cohibere
non potuit., illius <eruptiones> indomitas ne saltem agnosce-
⁸⁰ rentur ab alijs, satis congruenter per excusationis stropham, sub
infirmitatis pallio, per id temporis occultauit.

❡ DE EO QUOD VOLUNTATE SUA PER ALIQUANTUM
TEMPORIS EX TOTO PRIUATA FUIT
Nonum capitulum

222 Alio quoque tempore ¹, cum, ex nimia sui feruoris insolentia
⁵ celestiumque premiorum a quibus interim arcebatur ineffabili
pregustata dulcedine, magnum et diuturnum languorem interim
incurrisset :, erat ei maximum desiderium, omnipotentis dei beneplacito, per corporalium operum exercitium, gratum obsequium
et acceptabile seruicium incessanter impendere : ; ob hoc videlicet,
¹⁰ vt per hec istum cordis sui feruidum et insatiabilem appetitum
aliquantulum valuisset, ei satisfaciendo, restringere quod, virium
corporalium adminiculo deficiente, non potuit, vt iam prelibauimus, iuxta desiderij sui magnitudinem adimplere. Licet autem
omni vite sue tempore conformatam huic desiderio voluntatem
¹⁵ habuerit :, hoc tamen in tempore solito <fortius> in mente mu-

when she thought or spoke or even heard others speak of the supreme Good, her ever lively spirit would become excited. Immediately she would tremble in all the members of her weak body, and especially in head and heart. Or this would happen also when her insatiable appetite of love, sighing for eternal things, would be unable to get up to attain what she insatiably desired.

Although Beatrice was much wearied by this annoying weakness, she found only this advantage, this relief, that when she could not restrain within herself the spiritual delight she felt interiorly, then at least she concealed it quite suitably by the artifice of excusing herself under the cloak of sickness, lest her ungovernable eruptions be known to others.

FOR SOME TIME SHE WAS
TOTALLY DEPRIVED OF HER WILL
Chapter Nine

222 At another time when Beatrice had fallen into a great and drawn out languor from the excess of her fervor after having tasted the ineffable sweetness of the heavenly rewards which she was meanwhile kept from approaching, she had a great desire constantly to render pleasing homage and acceptable service to almighty God's good-pleasure through corporal works and exercises. She did this so that, by satisfying it through these works, she might be able somewhat to restrict her fervent, insatiable appetite—something she could not achieve to the greatness of her desire by reason of the failure of her bodily forces, as we said earlier. Although she had kept her will conformed to this desire all her life long, at this time the desire was thriving more vigorously than

lieris beate inualuit, et in tantum supra virium humanarum possibilitatem excreuit : , vt ipsas quoque penas infernales pro tempore
libentissime supportasset in corpore. , dum ad expletionem illius
insatiabilis desiderij post infernalia valuisset incendia peruenire.
20 **223** Sub eodem quoque tempore cum iam humani lan- // *f. 328 d*
guoris et doloris pariter, ex infinito cordis desiderio procedentis,
per dies multos insanabilem molestiam tolerasset, accidit vna
dierum, vt post completorium in lecto decubans. , de cognitione
summi et increati boni, fruitione simul et assecutione, per multas
25 cogitationes apud semetipsam subtilissime disputans. , necdum
hac meditatione finita, mente prorsus excederet : et, <tran-
quillatis> omnium predictarum cogitationum motibus. , pax cordis repentina succederet : ; in quo mentis excessu mox in iudiciorum dei sui profundam abissum, raptam semetipsam inuenit ; vbi
30 illa, sensibus humanis incomprehensibilia maiestatis diuine iudicia,
rerum etiam tam visibilium quam inuisibilium ordinem et pro-
gressum, equis passibus irrefragabiliter[2] incedentem, aspicere
meruit : ; ipsas quoque rerum causas ex eterne iusticie fonte
manantes, terrenis quidem intellectibus inassequibiles, numquam
35 tamen a iusticie tramite deuiantes, limpidissimo contemplationis
oculo perlustrauit. Ibi quoque dei patris potentia cuncta creari, .
filij sapientia gubernari. , spiritus sancti vero clementia conseruata
subsistere, diuina luce copiosius illustrata, cognouit ; ibi quamplurima misteriorum archana, duce gratia spiritus sancti. , de
40 terrenis pariter et celestibus indagauit. .
224 <I>n qua luce clarissime contemplationis cum per modicum
temporis admodum delectabiliter immorata fuisset. , ad se rediens,
omni voluntate sua, qua semetipsam eatenus gubernare consueuerat, ex toto se spoliatam inuenit ; et sic omnium iudiciorum
45 suorum discretione, priuatam se repperit. , vt nullam ex eodem
tempore vite spiritualis ordinationem obseruare potuerit : , sed,
voluntate sua prorsus in diuina voluntate beneplacitoque transfusa. , quod eius inspirante gratia sibi gratum agnouit. , hoc

usual in the blessed woman's mind. It grew so far beyond the pos-
sibilities of human strength that Beatrice would most willingly
have supported the very pains of hell in her body for a time so
long as she could have arrived at the fulfilment of this insatiable
desire after the fires of hell.

223 About the same time, when Beatrice had for many days borne
the incurable trouble of both human languor and pain coming from
the infinite desire of her heart, it happened one day that as she was
lying in bed after compline, thinking over and subtly debating
within herself about knowing, enjoying, and attaining the supreme
and uncreated Good, she was rapt in ecstasy of mind, her meditation not yet finished. All the turmoil of her thoughts was stilled,
and peace of heart suddenly succeeded it. In this ecstasy she found
herself immediately rapt into the deep abyss of the judgments of
her God. There she deserved to behold those judgments of the divine Majesty which are incomprehensible to human knowledge,
and also the order and progress of both visible and invisible things
proceeding irresistibly with even steps. With the utterly limpid eye
of contemplation she examined the very causes of things flowing
from the fountain of eternal justice, never deviating from the path
of justice, but unattainable to earthly intellects. Illuminated more
abundantly by divine light, Beatrice knew that all things are created by the power of God the Father, are governed by the wisdom
of the Son, but subsist preserved by the clemency of the Holy
Spirit. There, guided by the grace of the Holy Spirit, she explored
very many secret mysteries concerning earthly and heavenly
things.

224 When she had dwelt in that utterly clear light of contemplation with great delectation for a short time, Beatrice, returning to
herself, found herself totally stripped of the entire will by which
she had thus far been accustomed to govern herself. She found
herself so deprived of the discretion by which she made all her
judgments that she could not then observe any order to her spiritual life, but with her will wholly transferred to the divine will and
good-pleasure, she kept as the norm of her life for a long time

pro vite norma per multa decetero succedentia tempora custodiuit.
50 Fuit enim in hoc statu multo dierum spacio³; quo sic voluntati
diuine suam conformatam // fol. 329 a habuit voluntatem ;, vt
equali trutina voluntatis corporalem sospitatem infirmitatemque
pensaret., tam prospera quam aduersa pari voto sufferre diligeret., diuinam vltionem cum gratia consolationis equa lance simul
55 appenderet., et salutem omnium, tam notorum videlicet quam
eorum quos habebat incognitos, indifferenti statera ponderaret.
225 Sic autem omni humana voluntate, per annum fere quo in
hoc admirabili statu continue permanebat, ex toto caruit., vt
nec eterna nec temporalia iudicio voluntatis eligeret ; cum eterna
60 quidem voluntate sua totaliter in diuina voluntate transfusa.,
non aliter quam secundum beneplacitum ipsius diuine voluntatis
appeteret :, et nullo proprie voluntatis affectu temporalibus quibuscumque, per illud temporis spacium, inhereret. Omnes quoque
quas eodem tempore fundebat orationes ad dominum, ita semper
65 inchoauit et sic eque terminauit :, vt in hijs que orationis officium
in diuine maiestatis presentia recitauit⁴, nichil aliud quam ipsius
fieri beneplacitum exoptaret. Nam et-si plerumque postulandum
quidquam a domino, iudicio rationis, eligeret;, priusquam finiretur
oratio, rursus ab illo supplicandi proposito, mutata simul inten-
70 tione, resilijt :; et vt diuinum fieret beneplacitum decetero supplicans., hoc demum fine, suam quam agebat orationem aptissime
consummauit.
226 Ex eo quoque tempore, maximum illud et feruens desiderium,
quod, vt prediximus⁵, ad magnum vsque languorem omne corpus
75 illius affecerat, ex toto <sedatum> agnouit :; et, reparata
corporea sospitate, vires solito fortiores in singulis membris
accepit, quibus ab eo tempore reparatis, tanto nimirum instantius
quanto valentius, in omnipotentis dei servicio decetero perdurauit.
Tunc etiam illuminato clarius a luce veritatis intellectu, minus
80 discretum illud inexplebile cordis sui desiderium extitisse conspexit : eo quod multo post plus virium in servicio creatoris sui

thereafter what she knew, by the inspiration of his grace, was pleasing to him. Beatrice was in this state for many, many days. Her will was at that time so conformed to the divine will that she would weigh in the equal balance of her will both bodily health and weakness, and would suffer both prosperity and adversity with equal love. On her scales, divine vengeance was of equal weight with the grace of consolation, and she weighed with an impartial balance the salvation of all, both those known to her and those unknown.

225 For about the space of a year, during which she remained continuously in this wonderful state, Beatrice so wholly lacked any human will that she chose neither eternal nor temporal things by the judgment of her will. So entirely transferred to the eternal divine will was her own will that she would not seek other than according to the good-pleasure of the divine will, and she would cling to no affection of her own for any temporal things whatsoever during that time. All the prayers she poured forth then to the Lord she always began and ended in the same way, so that in whatever the divine office recited in the presence of the divine Majesty, Beatrice yearned that nothing be done save what God pleased. Even if she often chose by rational judgment to ask something from the Lord, before her prayer was finished she changed her intention and repudiated her proposed demand, and very appropriately ended her prayer by begging that the divine good-pleasure be carried out in the future.

226 From then on she recognized that the very great desire which, as we said, had caused her whole body to languish, was totally appeased. With her bodily health restored, Beatrice received more vigor than usual in each member, and with them restored, she continued for the future more energetically and valiantly in the service of almighty God. Then her mind was more clearly enlightened by truth, and she saw that the insatiable desire of her heart had been less than discreet because she had desired to devote much more strength to the service of her Creator

desiderasset exponere, multoque fortiori desiderio gratum ei famulatum impendere. , quam omnis creatura mundana suis potuisset viribus adimplere.

85 Per hanc // *fol. 329 b* quoque <renuntiationem> proprie voluntatis ad tantam spiritus cordisque stabilitatem se peruenisse, duce gratia, recognouit : , vt sine grandi labore beneplacitum diuine voluntatis expleret in omnibus, <e>t non solum in corde feruentior, . in conscientia clarior : , verum etiam in corpore quoque

90 robustior appareret. Agnouit autem in hoc statu suo, plures sibi vires corporis attributas quam in eo quo, tam ingenti, de quo prefati sumus, desiderio. , corporales assequi vires optauerat. , ob hoc maxime, quod omnem voluntatem suam in diuino beneplacito transfundere didicisset ; nam quamdiu voluntas propria,

95 quamuis sancta, feruens et vtilis in corde suo regnabat. , ad hanc sublimem tranquillitatis et pacis excellentiam, impedientibus dumtaxat illius voluntatis sue reliquijs, ad plenum pertingere non valebat.

227 Ex tunc etiam illud caritatis indissolubile vinculum quo summo

100 bono iam dudum astricta fuerat, ita consolidatum et confirmatum in vera dilectione permansit : , vt, quanto plus aliqua corporali vel spirituali molestia vexabatur in corpore vel in mente ; , tanto suauius illius summi boni refrigerata dulcedine, non solum patientissime sed et libentissime supportaret omnia tam dura quam

105 aspera : , totius impatientie vel meroris expers penitus et ignara. Sic igitur equanimiter, vt prediximus, omnia perferens, et de magna dei sui bonitate confidens. , opus suum quod dedit ei pater celestis vt faceret. , in fide firmior <et> in spe constantior, in caritate quoque feruentior, auxiliante christi gratia, residuo vite

110 sue tempore consummauit.

and to render him pleasing obedience with a much stronger desire than any worldly creature could by its own powers fulfil. After this renunciation of self-will, Beatrice recognized that she had by God's grace arrived, at such a stability of spirit and heart that she fulfilled the divine good-pleasure in everything without great labor; moreover she appeared not only more fervent in heart and clearer in conscience, but also stronger in health. In this state she knew that more bodily forces had been granted her than she had wished to attain during the time of that huge yearning of which we spoke. The chief reason for this was that she had learned to transfer her whole will over to the divine good-pleasure. For as long as her self-will—however holy, fervent and useful—reigned in her heart, she could not fully attain to this sublime height of tranquillity and peace, since the remnants of self-will impeded her.

227 From then on, too, that indissoluble bond of love by which she had somewhat earlier been bound to the supreme Good was so consolidated and confirmed in true love that, the more vexed she was in body or mind by any corporal or spiritual trouble, the more sweetly refreshed was she by this supreme Good. Thus she would stand all hard, harsh things not only very patiently but also very willingly, without impatience or sorrow, and even ignorant of them. So, bearing everything with equanimity, as we said, and confiding in the great goodness of her God, Beatrice, with the help of Christ's grace, for the rest of her life perfected the work the heavenly Father had given her to do, being firmer in faith, more constant in hope, and more fervent in love.

¶ DE EDIFICATIONE MONASTERIJ NAZARETH
ET DE EO QUOD IN PRIORISSAM ELECTA FUIT
Decimum capitulum

228 Eodem anno quo sic voluntate sua spoliata fuerat., accidit vt, inspirante diuine gratie clementia, venerabilis pater
virginis edificandi tercium illud, de quo prelocuti sumus in
exordio presentis opusculi monasterium, nazareth appellatum,
desiderium atque voluntatem in mente conciperet.; quam[1] tamen
priusquam opere consummaret electe // f. 329 c filie sue beatrici
frequenter examinandam exposuit:, et, illius creberrime consilium
expetens, ad obtinendum diuine voluntatis assensum per orationes assiduas illam sepius animauit. Ipsa vero, reuerendi viri
salubre propositum et votum commendabile prorsus intelligens.,
illi quidem, donec a domino super hoc certum reuelationis indi-
cium accipere mereretur vt quod voluntate conceperat compleret
opere, consulere distulit; orationes tamen interim incessanter ad
dominum, et per se fudit., et ab alijs fundi precibus suis obtinuit:; donec pijssimus consolator et misericors dominus illi
voluntatis sue beneplacitum in huius operis promotione consistere,
certo reuelationis oraculo demonstrauit. Qua demum reuelatione
diuinitus animata, venerabilem patrem ad aggrediendum illud
opus pietatis hortari cepit instantius:, et vt, de superne pietatis
adminiculo certus existens, quod mente conceperat opere complere
satageret, illum constanter admonuit.; et spiritu carneque germa-
num suum, vvicbertum nomine[2], tunc eiusdem loci conuersum, vt
deuoto patri vigilanter assisteret, exhortatione sedula nichilominus excitauit.

229 Quid plura? Parent christi milites hortatui sancte femine,
petitaque licentia tunc vallis virginum abbatisse[3], in ipsa sanctorum omnium sacra solempnitate, confirmati perceptione salutaris
eucharistie, leti simul et alacres versus oppidum cui lyra voca-

THE MONASTERY OF NAZARETH WAS BUILT
AND SHE WAS ELECTED PRIORESS
Chapter Ten

228 In the same year that she was thus deprived of her will, it happened that the virgin's venerable father, under the inspiration of divine grace and mercy, conceived in his mind a desire and will to build that third monastery, called Nazareth, of which we spoke in the preface to this work. Yet he often disclosed his will for examination to his chosen daughter Beatrice before executing it in reality, and seeking her counsel very frequently he often stirred her to obtain the consent of the divine will by her constant prayers. But Beatrice, well understanding the respected man's wholesome proposal and commendable wish, delayed her advice to him until she had received from the Lord a sure signal revealing that he should complete in deed what he had conceived in will. In the meantime she prayed constantly to the Lord, and had others pray also at her request, until the kind Consoler and merciful Lord showed her by a sure oracle and revelation that the good-pleasure of his will lay in the promotion of this work. At last quickened by this divine revelation, Beatrice began insistently to urge her venerable father to undertake this pious work, and she constantly admonished him to be sure of the divine loving help and to busy himself completing in deed what he had conceived in mind. She also diligently stirred and exhorted Wicbert, her brother by blood and in spirit, then a lay-brother of that place, eagerly to help his devout father.

229 Why say more? Christ's soldiers obey the holy woman's exhortation, and asking the permission of the then-abbess of Maagdendaal, on the very solemnity of All Saints,[1] strengthened by the reception of the saving Eucharist they take to the road, happy and

1. 1 November

bulum est iter arripiunt ; , et assignato sibi loco [4], non procul ab
ipso quod prenominauimus oppido, suo proposito satis acco-
modo [5], noui monasterij fundamenta iaciunt. , oratorium cum
35 edificijs construunt, et cetera queque necessaria congerunt : , et
sic, intra sex mensium spacium, singula queque perficiunt, vt
constructum aptissime monasterium cerneres, et, ordinatis congruenter monasterij ipsius officinis varijs. , in loco horroris et
vaste solitudinis ortum florigerum, iuxta sui nominis [6] inter-
40 pretationem etymologicam, infra breuissimum temporis spacium
inuenires. [7] // f. 329 d
230 Elapsis autem predictis sex mensibus [8], in quibus ad opus
noui monasterij conscribendis libris vacabat iugiter dei famula,
cum duabus sororibus cristina [9] scilicet et <Sybilla>, patrem
45 fratremque secuta. , valefaciens vallis virginum monasterio, ad
illud suum nouum <cenobium>, aliquantis sibi <adiunctis>
ex ipsius collegij gremio [10] monialibus indilate se transtulit : ; in
quo postea cursum presentis vite, vt in sequentibus explanabi-
mus, bono fine felicissime consummauit.

eager, toward the town called Lier. The place assigned them, not far from this town, being quite suitable for their purpose, they lay the foundations of the new monastery. They construct the oratory and buildings, and build whatever else is necessary. Within six months they complete everything so that you would behold a very well-constructed monastery together with the various workshops of this monastery all well laid out. In a very short time, instead of a place of horror and of vast wilderness,[2] you would find a flowering garden, according to the etymological interpretation of the name.

230 After the aforesaid six months had passed, during which the servant of God Beatrice gave herself constantly to the work of writing the choir-books for the new monastery, she and her two sisters, Christine and Sibyl, followed their father and brother and, bidding farewell to the monastery of Maagdendaal, they moved without delay to that new monastery, joined by some nuns of the former community. In this place, as we shall subsequently explain, Beatrice later very happily finished the course of the present life to a good end.

2. Dt 32:10

⁵⁰ Peruenientes vero nazareth humiles dei famule, mox ex ipsius
loci vicinia confluentium virginum numerosum conuentum adu-
nare ceperunt ; quibus <virgo Christi> beatrix officio magistrali
prefuit., ipsaque tam regularibus obseruantijs quam bonis moribus ad plenum imbuit :, et in breui sui sequaces illas efficiens.,
⁵⁵ hunc primiciarum suarum fructum gratissimum cum gaudio domino consecrauit.

231 Anno vero post illarum aduentum expleto ¹¹., iamque cister-
ciensi ordine impetrato ¹²., cristi deuote ad electionem abbatisse,
ceterarumque per quas idem monasterium in spiritualibus ac etiam
⁶⁰ temporalibus gubernari debuerat officialium, aspirare ceperunt :;
et, electa, de gremio suo, prima abbatissa ¹³, cunctis assentientibus
electissima dei sponsa beatrix etiam in priorissam eligitur., et,
licet multum renitens et inuita, noui prioratus officio solempniter
honoratur.

⁶⁵ Quod quidem officium, licet aptissime, nimis tamen inuite nimis-
que moleste pertulit :, ob hoc presertim quod a ceteris eam
honorari, iuxta rationis exigentium at obseruantiam monastice
sanxionis, oportuit que, suo iudicio, despectior omnibus et cunctis
inferior extitit :, et omni prorsus indignam honore sese, quantum-
⁷⁰ cumque venerabatur a ceteris, estimauit. Quoniam ergo non sine
graui molestia venerationes aliarum admittere potuit., illas, quantumcumque valebat, ab huiusmodi venerationis obsequio per dies
singulos, nunc exhortatione, nunc precibus, interdum etiam serio-
sis increpationibus compescere consueuit :, tanto // f. 330 a
⁷⁵ profecto viliorem se reputans, quanto magis indigne reuerentie
pondere se grauari potius quam honorari., molestari quam vene-
rari potius se putauit. Sed quo magis honores temporales effugere
studuit., eo magis ab hijs, quasi vim passa, quocumque se
vertebat [quocumque se vertebat], illos se subsequentes inuenit :;
⁸⁰ vnde et tot spirituales cotidie molestias pertulit., quot eam,

Arriving at Nazareth, the humble servants of God soon began to gather a numerous group of virgins from the local neighborhood. Christ's virgin Beatrice was in charge of teaching them, and she fully imbued them both with the regular observances and with good behavior. In a short time she made them followers of herself, and with joy she consecrated to the Lord this very pleasing offering of her first fruits.

231 A year after their arrival, having been accepted into the Cistercian Order, Christ's devoted [sisters] began to look forward to the election of an abbess and the other officials through whom the same monastery should be governed in spiritual and temporal matters. The first abbess was chosen from among the community, and with everyone's consent God's highly-elect bride Beatrice was elected as prioress, and although she was very reluctant and unwilling, she was ceremoniously installed in the office of new prioress.

Although she carried out this office very fittingly, she bore it very unwillingly and with great annoyance, especially because she who as more despicable and inferior to all in her own judgment, and who esteemed herself unworthy of any honor—however much she was revered by others—had to be honored by the others according to the demands of reason and the observance of monastic custom. Because she could not accept other people's veneration without grave annoyance, she used to restrain them every day from these marks of veneration as much as she could, now by exhortation, now by pleading, sometimes also by earnest reproaches. She thought herself so much more vile as she considered herself more burdened than honored, more vexed than venerated by the weight of undue reverence. But the more zealously she avoided temporal honors and restrained herself the more she found them pursuing her wherever she turned, as though she was suffering violence. Therefore, she daily suffered as many spiritual annoyances as the

venerationum obsequijs, illud inuisum sui prioratus officium. ,
per dies singulos acrius impetiuit.

232 Attende, lector, ad quantum perfectionis culmen hec sancta femina pedem
conuersationis prouexerat. , que sic temporalium honorum sordentes venera-
85 tiunculas abhorrebat. Attendant, queso, nostre beatricis exemplum. , qui, [14]
non electionis merito, sed ambitionis vicio gradum dignitatum ecclesiasti-
carum ascendunt : ; qui prece simul et precio sacris honoribus irreuerenter et
importune se ingerunt ; qui contra dominicam admonitionem primos recubitus
in cenis. , et primas in synagogis cathedras ambiunt : , et, cum nullo venera-
90 tionis tytulo decorentur. , ad officia prelationis indigne promoti, subiectos vel
equales quosque despiciunt : , honoris reuerentiam a ceteris extorquere con-
tendunt : , et, cum despectibiles sint ac vilitatiis deformitate notabiles, contra
fas et iura naturalia, sublimiora se querere nullatenus erubescunt. Attendant,
inquam, beatricem nostram in tantum huius vanitatis abhominabile vicium sub
95 pedibus indignationis sue conculcando comprimere : , quod sine graui molestia
venerationes earum quas sibi subiectas habuit non valuit omni prelationis sue
tempore sustinere. Quando vero, more quorumdam, aspirasset ad sublimia
dignitatum officia ; , que sic omnem ambitionis fruticem a cordis sui finibus
explantauerat. , vt nichil penitus terrene prosperitatis in corde saperet. ,
100 cuius sapore nil gustauit amarius, nil molestius pertulit in hac vita ? Videns
tamen, ex huius promotionis sue causa venerationumque exhi-
bitione molesta, paulatim intra se morbum impatientie rebellando
consurgere. , nec se posse // f. 330 b prioratus officium equanimiter eo de causa precipue baiulare : , frequentissime super hoc
105 imperfectionis nevo semetipsam reprehendere consueuit : necdum
ad tranquillum perfectionis statum peruenisse se reputans. , que,
licet ex virtutis gratia profluentem, aliquantulam tamen impatientie <maculam> in corde suo succrescere deprehendit.

233 Fuit tamen multo vite sue tempore permanens in ipso prioratus officio : ;
110 quo tempore, quantis gratiarum donis omnipotens <eam> in benedictionum
suarum dulcedine preuenire dignatus est. , quibus virtutum prerogatiuis eam
insigniuerit. , nec ex eius libro colligimus nec aliorum relatione comperimus ;
et idcirco premissa sub silentio tegimus. , paucis tamen exceptis, que ad
edificationem legentium subnectemus : , quamuis multo plura prioribus succes-
115 sisse per multa post hec succedentia tempora, comitante superna gratia,
minime dubitemus.

marks of veneration with which the hated office of prioress assaulted her daily.

232 Notice, reader, to what heights of perfection this holy woman advanced, someone who so abhorred the sordid little marks of veneration which pertain to temporal honors. Let those who mount the steps of ecclesiastical dignities, not by merit of election but by vice of ambition, notice our Beatrice's example. By begging and bribing they thrust themselves irreverently and rudely into sacred honors. Contrary to the Lord's warning they seek the first places at banquets and the first seats in the synagogues.[1] When, adorned with no claim to veneration, they are unworthily promoted to the rank of prelate, they despise everyone subject to them or equal to them, and they strive to extort honor and reverence from the rest. Although they are despicable and notably deformed and vile, they do not blush at all to seek things higher than themselves, against all behest and natural law. Let them notice, I say, our Beatrice so trampling under her indignant feet and suppressing this abominable vice of vanity that during the whole time she was a superior she could not, without grave annoyance stand the veneration of those subject to her. When would she have aspired to high dignities, as some do, she who had so rooted out of her heart every trace of ambition that no earthly prosperity had any savor for her heart? Instead nothing tasted more bitter to her, nothing in this life was more annoying. But seeing that the disease of rebellious impatience was gradually rising within her because of this promotion of hers and the annoying exhibition of marks of honor, and that she could not carry the office of prioress with equanimity chiefly for this reason, Beatrice used frequently to scold herself over this fault and imperfection. She thought she had not arrived at the tranquil state of perfection because she perceived some stain of impatience growing up in her heart, even though it flowed from the grace of virtue.

233 Beatrice remained in office as prioress for a great part of her life. We have not found in her book or learned from others with what gifts of grace the Almighty deigned to anticipate her in the sweetness of his blessings, or with what prerogatives of virtues he marked her, and therefore we cover these things with silence, with the exception of a few which we add for the edification of readers, though we in no way doubt that many more than the former things happened by heavenly grace during the long time which followed.

1. Mt 23:6

℄ DE EO QUOD TOTUM MUNDUM QUASI ROTAM
PEDIBUS SUIS VIDIT SUPPOSITUM
Undecimum capitulum

234 Cum autem multum iam temporis in prioratus officio con-
summasset., accidit vna dierum vt quandam ex monialibus illud
beati bernardi recitantem audiret <quo dicitur> : multos quidem
esse qui tormenta patiuntur pro christo:, sed paucos existere
qui semetipsos perfecte diligant propter christum. Quod beati
viri verbum memoriter quidem tenuit et per biduum frequentissime
ruminauit:, sed qualiter id sane deberet intelligi sensu proprio
nullatenus indagare preualuit;, admirans hominis dilectionem in
se reciprocatam aliquatenus posse pluris existere., quam passionis
pro christo supplicia sustinere. Cum enim omnis homo, siue bonus
siue reprobus, semetipsum naturaliter diligat., nemo quippe carnem
suam odio habuit:, multum per omnem modum illa breuis additio
que est: 'propter christum' sibi videbatur ad sensum priorum
verborum superaddere:, cuius additionis intellectum sola potest
experientia, non autem subtilitas humanorum sensuum // f. 330 c
explorare.

235 Videns ergo dei famula quod ad inuestigandum huius verbi
profundissimum intellectum meditaticnis studio non proficeret.,
confestim ad orationem, domino supplicatura, se conuertere studuit:, et vt premissorum intelligentiam sibi dignaretur infundere,
deuota prece dominum exorauit. Sed quid benignus dominus
electe sue, presertim in tam pio laboranti negotio tamque fructuoso vacanti studio, denegasset? Non solum ergo rem quam
postulabat, idest prescripti verbi intellectum, diuine pietatis illi
fauor indulsit:, verum etiam amplioribus secretorum suorum
misterijs et copiosioribus eam reuelationibus erudiuit.

236 Siquidem, in mentis excessu confestim erepta, totam huius
mundi machinam in modum rote siue spere pedibus suis vidit
suppositam:, et se desuper astantem., oculosque contemplationis

SHE SAW THE WHOLE WORLD
AS A WHEEL SET UNDER HER FEET
Chapter Eleven

234 When Beatrice had been in the office of prioress for a long time, she happened one day to hear one of the nuns reading that the blessed Bernard said there were many who suffer torments for Christ, but few who love themselves perfectly on account of Christ. She held the blessed man's word in her memory, and for two days ruminated on it very frequently, but in no way could she find how it should be soundly understood in its proper sense. She wondered how a man's love for himself could somehow be of more worth than enduring torture and suffering for Christ. Since everyone, good or reprobate, naturally loves himself, and no one hates his own flesh,[1] it seemed to her that the little addition 'on account of Christ' added a great deal to the meaning of the earlier words. Only experience and not the subtlety of human senses can explore the meaning of this addition.

235 God's handmaid, seeing that by attentive meditation she was not making any progress in her investigation of the deepest meaning of this saying, turned without delay to prayer, begging the Lord and devoutly asking him to pour the understanding of these things into her mind. But what had the kind Lord ever denied his chosen one, especially when she was laboring in such a devout matter and giving herself to such a fruitful endeavor? Not only did the divine loving kindness favorably grant what she asked, namely the understanding of the forementioned saying, but he also taught her more ample mysteries and secrets and more abundant revelation.

236 Indeed, snatched up immediately in ecstasy of mind, Beatrice saw the whole fabric of this world set under her feet like a wheel or a sphere. She found herself standing atop it, fixing her contemplative eyes

---

1. Eph 5:29

in illam incomprehensibilem diuinitatis essentiam infigentem,
ipsumque summum et increatum., eternum et verum deum et dominum in sue substantia maiestatis intellectuali acie mirabiliter in-
tuentem. Erat ergo mediotenus inter deum et hominem tam <aptis-
sime> collocata :, vt, deo quidem inferior, sed toto mundo sublimior, omnia terrena sub pedibus suis conculcata despiceret, summe
vero deitatis essentie per caritatis amplexum inseparabiliter inhereret. In qua nimirum vnione, qua cum deo iam vnus spiritus
effecta fuerat., ad pristinam illam sui spiritus puritatem liberta-
temque, necnon et <claritatem> in qua creata fuerat ab initio.,
se peruenisse cognouit :; et quasi totaliter in diuino spiritu trans-
funderetur illius spiritus., ita se coniunctam altissime deitati,
totamque celestem effectam, ad modicum quidem temporis intellexit.

237 Nam, ad se reuersa continuo, contemplationis <dulcedinem>
in sola memoria, delectando, non autem experiendo retinuit :;
et quid viderit atque comprehenderit reminiscens, ineffabiliter
celesti dulcedine recreata, suauiter inter dilecti brachia, caritatis
flagrans incendio, requieuit. Tunc etiam illorum que premissa
sunt verborum sensum, non tam intelligendo quam experiendo
cognouit :, et, sese perfecte diligens propter christum, quam paucos // f. 330 d existere qui ad hoc perfecte dilectionis culmen
perueniunt., purificato mentis oculo deprehendit.

⁋ DE EO QUOD VISUM EST EI QUOD SANGUIS CHRISTI
EIUS IN ANIMA FUNDERETUR
xij. capitulum

238 Alio quoque tempore¹, cum ad sacramentum dominici corporis accessisset., et de manu sacerdotis in altari nostre redemptionis precium et sustentationis humane viaticum accepisset.,
ipsaque delectabiliter in dominica christi passione, vvlneribus

on the incomprehensible essence of the divinity, wonderfully beholding with her mind's eye the very supreme and uncreated, eternal and true God and Lord in the substance of his Majesty. She was so very fittingly placed midway between God and man that, inferior to God but higher than all the world, she despised and trampled all earthly things under foot, but she was clinging inseparably to the supreme divine essence by the embrace of love. In this union, by which she was now made one spirit with God, she knew she had arrived at that pristine purity and liberty of her spirit, at that clarity, in which she had been created from the beginning. Just as if her spirit had been totally poured into the divine spirit, she understood for a short time that she was joined to the most high Godhead and made wholly celestial.

237 For quickly returning to herself, Beatrice retained the sweetness of the contemplation but only in her memory by delighting in it, not by experiencing it. Remembering what she had seen and understood, she rested sweetly in the arms of the beloved, ablaze with the fire of love, unspeakably refreshed with heavenly sweetness. Then she knew the meaning of those forementioned words, not so much by understanding as by experience, and loving herself perfectly on account of Christ, she grasped with the purified eye of understanding how few there are who arrive at this pinnacle of perfect love.

IT SEEMED TO HER THAT CHRIST'S BLOOD WAS BEING POURED INTO HER SOUL
Chapter Twelve

238 At another time when Beatrice had approached the Sacrament of the Lord's Body and had received from the priest's hand at the altar the price of our redemption and the nourishing support of man's journey, and was resting with delight in the passion of Christ the Lord,

meditando², quiesceret :, visum est ei quod omnis sanguis qui ex
eius vvlneribus emanauit, ipsius in anima funderetur :, omnesque
gutte tam preciosi liquoris <sic> spargerentur in illa, quod ab
hijs abluta penitus ab omni peccatorum puluere perfectissime
mundaretur.

In illa quoque spirituali ablutione, mirabiliter et super humanum
modum, igne dilectionis accensa flagrauit ; et quasi totus illius
spiritus feruore caritatis inuasus <fuerit>, ita super tolerantiam
virium humanarum, mirabili delectationis incendio concremata
defecit : ; et ad summum quemdam amoris apicem peruenisse se
sentiens., etiam ex nimio caritatis ardore presentem hanc vitam
se amittere funditus estimauit.

239 In illo quoque dilectionis incendio quo cremabatur interius,
oblatus est aspectui cordis eius quidam <specialis> amicus
ipsius, in christo sibi dilectissimus. ; quorum <uterque> spiritus
illo caritatis ineffabili glutino. tam fortissime in christo sunt vniti,
quod vnus efficeretur in christo spiritus e duobus. In eleuatione
quoque deifici sacramenti quemdam radium incomprehensibilis
claritatis ab ipso sacratissimo dominico corpore quasi fulgur
egredientem aspexit :, qui suo flammanti iubare cordis eius intima
penetrauit., eiusque spiritum totaliter ad se traxit.³ In qua
connexione sui spiritus cum spiritu care sue delicias suas esse,
sibique delectabiliter complacere, nec adhuc vitam hanc naturalem, quam pre nimio <dilectionis> incendio se prius estimabat
amittere, finiendam esse :, sed ad exercendum dilectionis et caritatis officium adhuc aliquanto tempore protrahendam fore, dilecte
sue dominus, ineffabili reuelationis incendio, demonstrauit.

meditating on his wounds, it seemed to her that all the blood which flowed from his wounds was poured into her soul, and that all the drops of that precious liquid were so sprinkled on it that it was wholly washed by these drops and most perfectly cleansed from all the dust of sin.

In that spiritual washing she was wonderfully and superhumanly kindled and set on fire by love. As though her whole spirit had been invaded by the fervor of love, she was burned with the marvelous fire of delight beyond what human strength can stand, and she was undone. Feeling that she had arrived at some supreme apex of love, she thought she was wholly letting go of this present life because of the excessive fire of love.

239 In that blaze of love with which Beatrice was burning interiorly, a certain special friend of hers, very dear to her in Christ, was presented to the gaze of her heart. Their two spirits, unspeakably joined in love, were so strongly united in Christ that the two were made one spirit in him. At the elevation of the deifying Sacrament Beatrice saw a ray of incomprehensible clarity flashing like lightning from the Lord's sacred body; it penetrated her inmost heart with its flaming brightness and drew her spirit wholly to itself. The Lord showed his beloved by this ineffable blaze of revelation that he took delight in the union of her spirit with that of her friend, that he delightedly approved it; and that Beatrice's natural life, which theretofore she thought she was going to lose because of the excessive fire of love, was not yet going to end. Instead it would still be prolonged for some time in order that she might be exercised in the services of love and charity.

fol. 331 a

❡ DE EO QUOD COR EIUS PRE AMORIS MAGNITUDINE NATURALEM SITUM DESERUIT,. ET EX OCULIS EIUS LUX MIRE CLARITATIS EFFULSIT.

⁵ xiij. capitulum

240 Sed et alio quodam tempore[1], cum ad verbum predicationis in conuentu suo propositum cum alijs assideret :, repente, pre maximo caritatis ardore, cor suum disrumpi pene visum est <sibi> et totaliter conquassari. Siquidem naturalem situm dese-

¹⁰ rens, ad guttur vsque conscendit[2] :, et in eo per multum temporis spacium tremens et palpitans perdurauit., <e>x quo magnum etiam infirmitatis contraxit incommodum :; et sic, amore lan-guens., per totum illius sermonis spacium, corpore quidem egra sed spiritu robustissima, cum dilecto suo delectabiliter spa-

¹⁵ ciando[.] nimirum, inter amplexus et oscula conquieuit.

241 Sed et aliud <quiddam> valde mirabile sub eodem tempore[3] contigit :, quod tanto mirabilius non immerito poterit quis iudi-care quanto rarius id omni retroacto tempore sanctorum cuiquam <reperietur> accidisse. Siquidem ex caritatis incendio quo cre-

²⁰ mabatur intrinsecus, etiam ad corporales oculos ignis spiritualis ascendit :, qui ex vtroque[4] radium mire claritatis ad aspectum omnium circumsedentium foras emisit., et, vt pace sanctorum dixerim, humilem beatricem electo dei famulo moysi, cui locutus est dominus facie ad faciem, pre claritate vvltus sui cornutam

²⁵ faciem pretendenti., quisquis vtriusque mirabilem vvltus clarita-tem inspexerit, quo-ad electionis meritum aptissime comparabit[5].

Sed et ipsi beate femine, per totum illum diem, vix aliquid intuitu corporalium oculorum, ex hijs que suo demonstrabantur aspectui., discernere licuit : sic nimirum, acie pupillarum obtusa, quod per

HER HEART LEFT ITS NATURAL PLACE BECAUSE
OF THE GREATNESS OF ITS LOVE AND A LIGHT
OF MARVELLOUS BRIGHTNESS SHONE
FROM HER EYES
Chapter Thirteen

240 But at another time when Beatrice was sitting with the others hearing the sermon preached to the community, her heart suddenly seemed to her almost broken and wholly shaken by the very great ardor of love. Indeed it left its natural place and rose to her throat. It stayed there a long time trembling and throbbing, and as a result she became quite unwell. Thus languishing with love, sick in body but extremely robust in soul she remained during the whole sermon delightfully refreshing herself with her beloved, resting in his embraces and kisses.

241 But something else very wonderful occurred at the same time, something that can, not undeservedly, be judged as more wonderful, the more rarely it is found to have happened to any of the saints in all times past. From the fire of love with which she was burning inside, a spiritual fire also rose to her physical eyes, and from both her eyes it emitted a ray of wonderful brightness for those sitting around her to see. And to speak with all due reverence for the saints, anyone who was to examine the wonderful brightness shining on the faces of both the humble Beatrice and of Moses, the chosen servant of God to whom the Lord spoke face to face and whose face seemed to have horns because of its brightness, will very rightly compare the two in regard to its merit of election as well. The blessed woman herself, however, could scarcely make anything out within the field of the vision of her bodily eyes all day long. So dulled were the pupils of her eyes that

30 multum illius diei spacium circa res quidem exteriores excecata
permanserit., nichilominus tamen, in illa celesti claritate, tam
visibilia quam inuisibilia, tam corporalia quam spiritualia, mirabili
contemplationis acie penetrauit.

In hac autem accensione spiritus optabat ∥ f. 331 b omnipotenti
35 deo gratam oblationem et acceptabile sacrificium aliquod immolare : et responsum est ei diuinitus quod patri filium, ipsique filio
suam offerret animam., sanctoque spiritui totum sui cordis affectum amoris et dilectionis hostiam consecraret.

242 Quodam etiam die circumcisionis dominice [6], cum post minu-
40 tionem sanguinis debilitata quiesceret et repausandis viribus
pausationis modicum indulgeret :, puerulus quidam mire pulchri-
tudinis et precipui decoris, ad quiescentem accedens, eidem
adiocari cepit et alludere. Sed virgo christi, debilitatis pondere
fatigata, tunc quidem illius plausibus intentionem occupare non
45 valuit :; sed cum post paululum ad prandium resideret., idem
puer ad eam redijt., et tunc ab ea delectabiliter amplexatus,
ibidem cum ea permansit et sua dulci presentia tunc temporis eam
non mediocriter confortauit. Quis autem iste puer extiterit, aut
vnde venerit michi quidem manet incognitum ; puto tamen ali-
50 quam fuisse angelicam visionem, ad se confortandam a domino
destinatam :, aut etiam eo die circumcisum pro nobis ipsum
dominum ihesum christum.

Sed et indomite volucres et siluestres auicule nonnumquam, ad
eam a nemorum latebris aduolantes., in sinu suo mansuetissime
55 consederunt., et ei dulciter applaudentes., omnis expertem im-
mansuetudinis, quam in ceteris hominibus huiusmodi tam bestiole
quam auicule naturaliter expauescunt., nouis et inconsuetis ap-
plausus sui congratulationibus, hanc preelectam dei famulam
ostenderunt.

60 243 Vere tua sunt hec domine ihesu christi mirabilia ;, qui sanctos tuos in
terra ita glorificas [7]., vt ad eorum <visionem> immansueta mansuefacias.,
indomita seruituti sue subicias., diuersa gratiarum dona infundas :, et, paulo-

she remained blinded much of that day in regard to outward things. But in that heavenly clarity she penetrated, with the marvellous keenness of contemplation, things both visible and invisible, corporal and spiritual.

In this kindling of her spirit Beatrice wished to consecrate some pleasing oblation and acceptable sacrifice to almighty God. She was divinely answered that she should offer the Son to the Father, and her own soul to the Son, and that she should consecrate the whole affection of her heart and sacrifice of love to the Holy Spirit.

242 One day on the Lord's Circumcision,[1] while Beatrice, weakened by blood-letting, was resting and recovering her strength by sleeping a little, a small boy of striking beauty and outstanding exactness approached her while resting, and began to caress and play with her. But Christ's virgin, weary and weighed down with weakness, could not manage to pay attention to his hand-clapping. Shortly afterwards, however, when she sat up for lunch, the same boy returned to her and was then embraced by her delightedly. He remained there with her and comforted her not a little by his sweet presence. Who this boy was and whence he came remains unknown to me, but I think he was some angelic vision sent by the Lord to comfort her; or else he was the Lord Jesus Christ himself circumcised that day for us.

Also wild birds and small woodland fowl sometimes flew to her from their hiding places in the groves, and sat in her lap very tamely, fluttering up against her sweetly. By their novel and unusual joy in fluttering up to her they showed that this specially chosen servant of God was wholly lacking that harshness which little animals and birds of this kind naturally fear in other human beings.

243 Truly these are your marvels, O Lord Jesus Christ. Thus you so glorify your saints on earth that by the sight of them you tame the untamed, you subject the unruly to your servitude and you pour out a diversity of gifts and graces;

1. 1 January

minus ab angelis minoratos, celestium etiam secretorum conscios, efficias
<symmistas>.

65 Vere felicem et hanc nostram beatricem dixerim :, que, dum, christi fideliter
inherendo vestigijs, // f. *331 c* per tribulationes et afflictiones varias ipsum
caput suum adusque sublimem perfectionis statum et caritatis fastigium est
secuta., tot tantisque gratiarum donis et tam multiplicibus est virtutum pri-
uilegijs honorata.

70 Mirentur forsan alij a sanctis antiqui temporis, in signis et virtutibus copiose
satis superque patrata miracula ; mirentur ab obsessis corporibus fugata
demonia., et a morte resuscitata cadauera ; necnon et alia quamplurima, vel
hijs maiora vel horum similia :, de quibus loquitur in euangelio dominus
dicens ita. : 'Qui credit in me opera que ergo facio et ipse faciet : et maiora

75 horum faciet [8]. Ego vero, pace sanctorum, beatricis caritatem multis miraculis
et signis prefero ; de quibus alibi dicitur. : 'signa data sunt non fidelibus
sed infidelibus' [9] :, presertim cum absque signis ad regnum celorum multi
perueniunt. Absque caritate vero, que per vestem nuptialem aptissime figu-
ratur., quisquis in extremo discussionis examine repertus fuerit., ligatis

80 manibus et pedibus proiectus in tenebras exteriores vbi erit fletus et stridor
dentium [10], cum dyabolo et angelis eius eterno supplicio subiacebit [11]. Sed et
inter signorum operatores mirificos etiam nonnullos reperiendos existimo
quibus hec vestis nuptialis deerit in futuro. Quibus, de signorum se perpetratione iactantibus et dicentibus. : 'domine nonne in nomine tuo demonia

85 eiecimus et in tuo nomine virtutes multas fecimus' :, a domino responde-
bitur. : 'Amen dico vobis nescio vos., discedite a me maledicti in ignem
eternum' [12] et cetera que sequuntur.

244 Si quis tamen seriem lectionis quam de vita beatricis huius digessimus
diligenter inspexerit et cum generatione praua et peruersa signa quesierit :,

90 et-si non corporalibus forte, que pauci estimanda sunt., spiritualibus tamen
redundare miraculis hanc ipsam <apertissime> comprobabit.

Quid enim mirabilius estimari possit in hoc seculo quam in celo rapi cum
apostolo., celestibus interesse misterijs., et diuino cum beatis spiritibus imbui
sacramento ? Idem quoque beatus apostolus, // f. *331 d* in abyssum iudiciorum

95 dei raptus, in clamorem erumpit. : 'O, inquiens, altitudo diuitiarum sapientie
et scientie dei : quam incomprehensibilia sunt iudicia eius, et inuestigabiles vie
eius'.[13] Et dauid sanctus. : 'Justitia tua, inquit, sicut montes dei :, et iudicia
tua abyssus multa'.[14] Nimirum in hanc ipsam dei iudiciorum abyssum illorum
vterque diuersus [15] :, et ex eorum indagatione mirabiliter ad proferendum talia

those who have been made a little lower than the angels,[2] you make confidants of heavenly secrets and initiates in mysteries.

I would call this Beatrice of ours truly blessed. She followed Christ her head, clinging faithfully to his footsteps through various troubles and afflictions up to sublime perfection and the summit of love, and she was honored by so many and such great gifts of grace and privileges of virtue.

Others may perhaps wonder at the miracles worked by signs and acts of power so copiously and superabundantly by the saints of old. They may wonder at the demons chased out of those possessed, the corpses raised to life, and many other things like these or greater than these. The Lord said of these in the Gospel: 'He that believes in me shall also do the works I do, and greater than these shall he do'.[3] Yet, with all due reverence to the saints, I prefer Beatrice's love to many miracles and signs, of which it is said elsewhere: 'Signs are given not to believers, but to unbelievers',[4] especially since many arrive at the kingdom of heaven without signs. But anyone who is caught at the last judgment without love, which is very aptly symbolized by the wedding garment, will be bound hand and foot and thrown into the outer darkness where there will be weeping and gnashing of teeth,[5] and will be subject to eternal punishment with the devil and his angels.[6] But among the workers of signs I think, will be found some who will lack this wedding garment[7] in the future. While they are boasting about their wonder-working and saying: 'Lord, did we not cast out devils in your name and work many miracles in your name',[8] the Lord will answer: 'Amen, I say to you, I know you not.[9] Depart from me, you cursed, into everlasting fire', and the rest which follows.[10]

244 If anyone has looked carefully at this account of our Beatrice's life which we have composed, and like a wicked and perverse generation has sought for signs,[11] even if he does not perhaps find corporal miracles, which are to be esteemed of little worth, he will plainly find that Beatrice abounded in spiritual miracles.

What can be esteemed more highly in this world than to be caught up into heaven with the apostle, to be present among heavenly mysteries, and with the blessed spirits to be saturated in divine mystery? The same blessed apostle, caught up in the abyss of God's judgments, cried out, saying: 'O depth of the riches of the wisdom and of the knowledge of God! How incomprehensible are his judgments, and how unsearchable his ways'.[12] And holy David said: 'Your justice is as the mountains of God, your judgments are a great deep'.[13] No doubt each of these two was led differently into this abyss of God's judgments, and by their searchings they were wonderfully incited to utter such

2. Heb 2:9   3. *Jn 14:12*   4. *1 Co 14:22*   5. Mt 22:13

6. Rv 12:9   7. Mt 22:11   8. *Mt 7:22*   9. *Mt 25:12*

10. *Mt 25:41*   11. *Dt 32:5*   12. *Rm 11:33*   13. *Ps 35:7*

100 prouocatus. Sed nec beatricem, quo-ad hunc statum, inferiorem dixerim : , que, duce gratia sancti spiritus, interdum purificate mentis intellectu in eandem abyssi latitudinem erepta prosilijt, et archana dei sui misteria, de ipso fonte sapientie reportauit.

Ysaie labia calculo tanguntur. , et a peccatis suis propheta diluitur [16] : beatrix
105 vero typo febris acute quinquennio [17] tangitur. , et ad plenum a peccatorum sordibus emundatur. Ezechiel propheta, dum in visione dei iuxta fluuium chobar in spiritu rapitur, quatuor animalium et rotarum totidem misteria contemplatur [18] : et beatricis spiritus, dum ad alta sustollitur. , quasi rotam totum hunc mundum suis subiectum pedibus admiratur.
110 Helyas thesbites a coruis iussu omnipotentis dei in deserto pascitur [19] : sed et beatrix nostra non minus ab indomitis et siluestribus auiculis in monasterio frequentatur. Multipharie multisque modis olim deus loquebatur patribus in prophetis [20] : et beatrici frequentissime reuelatum est celitus de celestibus misterijs et secretis.
115 **245** Longum esset ire $<$per$>$ singula : , sed studiosi lectoris iudicio, cui cure fuerit hec diligentius indagare, relinquimus. An forte nostri temporis hanc sanctam feminam, priscorum sanctis temporum $<$in$>$ spiritualium miraculorum merito comparemus ? Cum enim vnus sit deus omnium diues in omnes qui inuocant illum : , quis miretur quod in gratiarum collatione multiplici,
120 beatrici sue deus omnipotens liberalis et munificus extiterit. , que, sicut ex pre- // f. 332 a missis aperte colligitur. , ipsum redemptorem suum incessanter diebus et noctibus inuocauit [21] ? Sed iam, hijs pretermissis, ad propositum reuertamur : , ne, finem operi imponere festinantes, dispendioso prolixioris disputationis obstaculo retrahamur.

❡ DE CARITATE DEI ET . vij . EIUS GRADIBUS
xiiij. capitulum

246 Nunc igitur, antequam finem dictis stiloque silentium indi- camus : , opere precium est vt de caritate beate femine pauca sub
5 compendio premittamus. At quoniam in dei proximique dilectione

things. But I would not say Beatrice was inferior in this regard. Under the grace and guidance of the Holy Spirit and by the purification of her mental understanding she was sometimes caught up into the same broad abyss, and she brought back from the very fountainhead of wisdom the hidden mysteries of her God.

Isaiah's lips are touched by a pebble, and the prophet is washed from his sins;[14] Beatrice is touched by five days of really acute fever, and she is fully cleansed from the stains of sins. When the prophet Ezechiel is caught up in spirit in the vision of God by the river Chebar,[15] he contemplates the mysteries of the four animals and the four wheels.[16] While Beatrice's spirit is raised on high, she marvels at this whole world lying under her feet like a wheel.

Elijah the Tishbite is fed by ravens in the desert at Almighty God's order;[17] but our Beatrice is no less visited in the monastery by wild woodland birds. God at many times and in different ways spoke in times past to the fathers by the prophets;[18] heavenly mysteries and secrets were very often divinely revealed to Beatrice.

245 It would take too long to go into the details, but we leave this to the judgment of the attentive reader who cares to investigate these things more diligently. Would we rightly compare this holy woman of our times to the saints of former times in terms of spiritual miracles? Since the one God of all is rich to all who call upon him,[19] who would wonder if Almighty God was liberal and munificent in granting many graces to his Beatrice, who, as is plainly seen from the foregoing, incessantly, day and night called upon her Redeemer. But now passing over these things, let us return to our purpose lest, hastening to finish this work, we be held back by the obstacle of a wordy wasteful disputation.

THE LOVE OF GOD AND ITS SEVEN DEGREES
Chapter Fourteen

246 Now before we end our story and silence our pen, it is worthwhile to set forth a few things in summary about the blessed woman's charity. But since charity consists in the love of God and

---

14. Is 6:6   15. Ezk 1:1   16. Ezk 1:5
17. 1 Ch 17:6   18. *Heb 1:1*   19. Rm 10:12

consistit caritas., ad primum eius membrum, id est caritatem dei,
narrationem interim applicemus :, et quibus caritatis gradibus ad
statum perfectionis hec sancta femina peruenerit., vt breuius
poterimus, enarremus. [1]

10　Sunt igitur hij dilectionis gradus siue status septem numero:,
per quos ad dilectum suum,
non equalibus quidem passibus., sed nunc vt pedibus in-
15　cedendo., nunc cursu velocis-
simo properando., nonnumquam
etiam, sumptis agilitatis pennis,
pernicius euolando, peruenire
promeruit:, et quod quesiuit
20　ipsum summum et increatum
bonum, per speculum dumtaxat
<et> in enigmate cum in hac
vita substitit [2]., et presentia-

DE SEPTEM
MODIS SANCTI AMORIS

Septem sunt amoris modi ex
altissimo loco venientes et ad
summum redeuntes.

neighbor, let us apply ourselves now to the first part, the love of God, and let us relate as briefly as we can, by what degrees of love this blessed woman Beatrice arrived at the state of perfection.

THE SEVEN MANNERS OF HOLY LOVE

Text of the *Vita*   Vernacular Text
                                              Latinized by Reypens

These then are the seven degrees or stages of love, seven in number, through which she deserved to come to her beloved, not at an even pace, but now as if walking on foot, now running swiftly, and sometimes even flying nimbly on agile wings. After passing through the exile of this mortal life she grasped by actual presence the supreme and uncreated good, which she sought only as in a mirror and in a dim reflexion[1] while she was in this life.

There are seven manners of loving which come down from the highest place and which return again to the summit from which they came.

1. 1 Co 13:12

liter post excursum huius mor-
²⁵ talitatis exilium apprehendit.
247 Horum autem graduum

Primus extitit magnum et feruens quoddam desiderium per-
ueniendi ad illam libertatem,
³⁰ puritatem et nobilitatem spiritus., in qua creata fuerat ad
ymaginem et similitudinem creatoris. In hac autem animi puritate dies suos ob hoc <prae-
³⁵ sertim> ducere cupiebat., vt
per hanc viam compendiosam
expeditius ad statum vite perfectioris ascenderet:, et quem
querebat fructum ordinate cari-
⁴⁰ tatis, hoc studioso conamine facilius apprehendere <valuisset>.
Fuit autem in hoc statu multo
tempore, semper illam quam
aspirabat vite puritatem queri-
⁴⁵ tans:, et omne quodcumque //
ƒ. *332 b* sibi nociuum et in exe-
cutione voti sui contrarium estimabat a se procul abiciens, et
sic e contrario quodcumque
⁵⁰ sibi proficuum et vtile iudicabat
totis desiderij sui conatibus ap-
prehendens. Quantum autem,
pro hac de qua mentionem
fecimus libertate spiritus obti-
⁵⁵ nenda, votis et desiderijs ac

Primus est desiderium ac-
tive oriens ex amore. Diu
regnare debet in corde antequam omnes adversarios bene
expellere valeat, et fortiter et
sollerter operari debet, et in
hoc animose progredi.
Hic modus desiderium est
certe proveniens ex amore, id
est quod bona anima Domino
nostro fideliter deservire, forti
animo eum sequi et veraciter
amare cupiens, in studium trahitur ut eam puritatem, libertatem et nobilitatem consequatur et in eis maneat, in
quibus a suo Creatore facta
est ad eius imaginem et similitudinem: quod valde amandum est et servandum.
In quo studio totam vitam
suam ducere cupit, et cum eo
operari, crescere et ascendere
in maiorem altitudinem amoris et in propinquiorem cognitionem Dei, usque ad hanc
perfectionem ad quam ad plenum a Deo facta est et vo-
cata.

247 Of these degrees:

The first is a certain great and fervent longing to arrive at that liberty, purity, and nobility of spirit in which she had been created according to the image and likeness of the Creator. She especially desired to spend her days in this purity of soul in order to ascend more quickly by this shortcut to the more perfect state of life, and to be able to grasp more easily by this attentive effort the fruit of orderly love which she was seeking. She was in this state a long time, always seeking that purity of life to which she aspired, casting far from her everything she thought harmful to her and contrary to the attainment of her desire, but grasping with all avid efforts whatever she judged profitable and useful. It is beyond human capacity to tell how much Beatrice continually aroused her heart's intention day and night by desires

The first manner is an active longing which proceeds from love. It must rule a long time in the heart before it can thoroughly expel all opposition and it should act strongly and skillfully, and progress eagerly in this.

This manner is surely a longing arising from love: that is, the pious soul desiring to serve our Lord faithfully, to follow him vigorously and to love him truly, is actively drawn into the zeal to attain and to remain in that purity, liberty and nobility in which it was made by its Creator according to his image and likeness; something which the soul must intensely love and preserve.

The soul desires to lead its whole life so as to work, grow, and ascend to a greater height of love and a closer knowledge of God, until it reaches that perfection for which it is fully made and called by God.

etiam corporalibus exercitijs
intentionem cordis sui per dies
et noctes iugiter excitauerit, .
non est humane possibilitatis
⁶⁰ euoluere :.; nam et supra virium
possibilitatem naturalium erat
hoc feruentissimum desiderium
in fragili cordis vasculo continue sustinere.

⁶⁵ **248** In hoc siquidem statu erat
beate femine circa sui cognitionem, quam sibi in hoc
<suo> negocio necessariam
estimabat, permaxima conside-
⁷⁰ rationis occupatio ; : qualis scilicet erat apud se, qualis esse
debuerit. , vbi vel quantum proficiebat. , vel etiam contrarijs
defectibus subiacebat, diligenter
⁷⁵ examinando cognoscere : ; quatenus, effugatis defectibus, ad
puritatis gratiam quam optabat
expedito valuisset incessu facilius peruenire. Quos cum inter-
⁸⁰ dum sibi rebellantes aspiceret. ,
et ad votum illos expugnando
repellere non valeret:, tunc, pre
nimio feruore desiderij, corporales etiam languores solebat in-
⁸⁵ currere.; quibus aliquotiens adeo
grauabatur in corpore, quod mortem sibi <crederet> imminere.
In hoc quoque statu quanto
magis in assecutione rei quesite
⁹⁰ proficiebat illius spiritus:, tanto
viuacius ad progrediendum ex-
citabatur interius ; et quanto

Ad hoc mane et vespere nititur, et sic tota seipsam tradit.
Et haec est petitio sua et studium et flagitatio apud Deum,
haec est cogitatio sua : quomodo huc pervenire queat, et
quomodo obtinere valeat pro-
ximam ad amorem conformi-
tatem, in omni virtutum or-
natu et in omni puritate altis-
simae nobilitatis amoris.
Haec anima saepe serio scru-
tatur quid sit ipsa, quid esse
debeat, quidnam habeat et
quidnam desiderio suo desit.
Et tota cum diligentia sua,
magnaque cum appetitione et
cum tota qua valet sollertia,
conititur cavere et vitare quidquid sibi ad tale negotium
impedimento et nocumento
esse potest; nec umquam cor
suum quiescit ab inquirendo
et flagitando et discendo et
sibi attrahendo et retinendo
quidquid ad amorem eam
adiuvare et promovere potest.
Hoc est maximum studium
animae in hoc modo positae;
in quo operari et multum laborare debet, donec diligentia
et fidelitate sua a Deo obtinuerit, ut in posterum sine impedimento praeteritarum no-
xarum, amori inservire valeat
cum libera conscientia, pura
mente et clara intelligentia.

and also corporal exercises, in order to obtain that liberty of spirit we mentioned. It was beyond the possibility of natural forces to bear uninterruptedly this most fervent desire in the frail vessel of the heart.

248 In this stage the blessed woman was immensely occupied by the consideration of self-knowledge which she held to be necessary in this matter of hers: carefully to know by examination what she was in herself, what she should be, where and how much she was progressing, or was subject to the opposite defects, so that she could arrive with a quicker step and more easily at the grace of purity she desired, putting to flight her defects. When she saw her defects sometimes rebelling against her and she could not fight them off and repel them as she would like to, then she even used to fall into bodily languors because of the great fervor of her desire. Sometimes she was so weighed down by them that she thought death was near. In this stage the more her spirit progressed in attaining what it sought, the more vivaciously was she excited inwardly to make progress; and the closer

Morning and evening the soul strives for this, and surrenders itself thus totally. This is its request, its zeal, and its supplication made to God. Its thought is: how can it arrive at this point, and how can it attain a close conformity to love, with all the adornment of the virtues and with all the purity of the highest nobility of love.

Such a soul often seriously scrutinizes what it is, what it should be, what is possesses, and what is lacking to its desire. With all its diligence, with great longing and all possible ingenuity it strives to beware and avoid whatever can impede or harm it in this matter. Its heart never rests from inquiring and entreating and learning and drawing to itself and retaining whatever can help or bring the soul toward love. This is the soul's greatest concern when it is established in this manner, and in it the soul should work and labor much until, by its diligence and fidelity, it obtains from God that henceforth without impediment from its past misdeeds it can serve love with a free conscience, a pure spirit and a clear intelligence.

summe puritati vicinior apparebat :, tanto magis insatiabili
95 desiderio gressum intentionis in
anteriora proficiens extendebat.

Talis modus desiderii, tam
magnae puritatis et nobilitatis,
certe ex amore non ex timore
oritur. Nam timor efficit ut
operetur et patiatur, faciat et
omittat ex metu irae Domini
nostri et iudicii iusti Iudicis,
aut aeternae vindictae aut af-
flictionum temporalium. Sed
amor solum operatur et nititur
ad puritatem et altitudinem et
ad supremam nobilitatem, sicut ipse est in se in essentia,
possessione et fruitione. Et
talem activitatem docet eos
qui eum colunt.

249 Secundus modus dilectionis
erat quidam status in quo, non
ob recompensationem mercedis
100 cuiuslibet siue presentis gratie
siue glorie post future, sed sim-
pliciter propter se., non vt
mercenaria domino., sed vt
sponsa sponso, feruentissimo
105 cordis affectu // f. 332 c tam in
se, pure dilectionis officio,
quam in membris suis, humili
deuotionis obsequio, seruiebat.
Quanto vero sublimior erat
110 huius seruitutis intentio., tanto
feruentior existebat humillima
seruientis affectio :; nec laboris
grauitas cuiuscumque, deuotam
mentem a sancto proposito re-
115 trahere potuit, quam, ad minis-
trandi studium, increati boni
sola nobilitas incitauit.

Secundus modus amo-
ris. Quandoque amor habet
et alium modum, scilicet ut
adoriatur Domino nostro gratuito servire ex solo amore,
sine quocumque alio motivo,
et absque quacumque mercede
gratiae vel gloriae. Et sicut
nobilis domicella quae domino
suo ex magno amore et absque remuneratione inservit, et
cui sufficit ei servire et dominum pati ut ei serviat; sic
amorose cupit servire amori
absque modo et supra modum
et humanum sensum et rationem, cum omni fidelitatis ministerio.
Cum sic afficitur, tam ardens
est in desiderio, tam parata
in ministerio, tam agilis in

she seemed to supreme purity, the more did she stretch forth the foot of her intention with more insatiable desire to what lay ahead.

249 The second manner of loving was a certain stage in which she served, not like a hired woman serving her lord for any recompense either of present grace or of future glory, but simply for himself, as a bride serving the bridegroom, using with fervent affection of heart both herself and her members with pure love and humble devotion. The more sublime the aim of this servitude, the more fervent was the very humble affection of the server; neither could the weight of any labor whatever withdraw the devout spirit from this holy undertaking, for the spirit was stirred up to this zealous ministry only by the nobility of the uncreated good.

A desire of such great purity and nobility certainly arises from love and not from fear. For fear makes one work and suffer, act and desist from acting, for fear of our Lord's anger and the judgment of the just judge, either eternal punishment or temporal afflictions. But love works and strives only for purity and sublimity and for the supreme nobility as love itself is in its very nature, possession and fruition. And love teaches such activity to those who cultivate love.

The second manner of loving. Sometimes the soul has also another manner, that it sets itself the task to serve our Lord freely out of love alone, without any other motive and without any reward of grace or glory. As a noble maiden serves her lord out of great love and without remuneration, so to her it is enough that she serves him and that the lord allows her to serve lovingly, without measure, beyond measure and beyond human sense and reason, faithfully performing every service.

When the soul attains this state, it becomes so ardent in desire, so ready to serve, so nimble in

250 Erat ergo videre beatam
feminam in hoc statu cunctis
120 se per humillime subiectionis
officium inclinantem,. cunctis
fideliter obsequentem,. in aduersis patientem,. in tribulationibus exultantem,. et totum
125 cordis affectum, communiter
omnium et singulariter singu-
lorum,. maiorum scilicet et
minorum obsequijs equanimiter
exponentem. Nec frustra qui-
130 dem has pietatis operas ipsi
dilecto suo, tam in se quam
in alijs, exhibuit :; sed quo
plus caritatiue seruitutis im-
pendit., eo nimirum amplius
135 de bonis domjni recipere meruit ; et quod nullo retributionis
intuitu sed solo caritatis affectu in diuinis erogauit obsequijs :, hoc multiplicibus gra-
140 tiarum donis et varijs celestium
premiorum recompensatum habuit incrementis.

Quid enim irremuneratum a
dilecta sua suscipere potuit
145 benignus largitor bonorum omnium :, apud quem est omnis
merces laborantium et copia
premiorum.

Super qua tamen retributionis
150 impensa cum interdum virgo
domini causaretur, et quod gratis impenderat lucroso se recipere commercio quereretur :,
mox, radio superne gratie il-
155 lustrata, diuinum in hoc esse

opere, tam mitis in molestia,
tam laeta in tribulatione ! Et
cum toto quod est, cupit pla-
cere Domino, et amoenum ei
est invenire aliquid faciendum
vel patiendum in amoris mi-
nisterium et honorem.

250 The blessed woman was therefore to be seen in this stage bowing down before everyone faithfully. She was patient in adversity, exultant in tribulations, with an even temper showing her whole heart's affection in the service of everyone commonly, and to each one singly, both great and small. It was not in vain that she showed her beloved these kindly works both in herself and towards others. The more loving service she showed, the more she deserved to receive from the Lord's goods; and she received in recompense many gifts and graces and various increases of heavenly rewards for what she had paid out in the divine service from loving affection alone, with no eye to the reward.

What could the kindly giver of every good thing receive from this beloved without rewarding her? With him is the whole recompense of those who labor, and the abundance of rewards. When the Lord's virgin was once disputing about this repayment and was complaining that she was receiving a lucrative return for what she had paid out freely, she was quickly illuminated by a ray of heavenly grace and understood that this was the divine good-pleasure.

work, so meek in annoyance, so joyful in trouble! With its whole being it desires to please the Lord, and it is pleasant for it to find something to do or to suffer for the service and honor of love.

beneplacitum intellexit. ; et sic
demum, humiliter acquiescens, .
etiam cum laudibus et gratiarum
actionibus idipsum quod accepe-
160   rat, interne negotiationis exercitio multipliciter ampliauit.

251 Tercius modus siue gradus
erat alius quidam conuersationis status in quo, sicut in
165   plerisque locis digessimus, //
f. 332 d ipsi caritati que deus
est per <acceptum> caritatis
<obsequium> plenam dilec-
tionis vicem redibendo satis-
170   facere concupiuit.
Ad hoc autem efficaciter adimplendum non solum internas
affectiones. , sed et omnes
corporales vires exposuit, : et
175   quod viribus deerat, feruentissimo cordis desiderio compen-
sauit. Et licet hoc arduum caritatis negotium viribus humanis
inexplebile, docente ratione,
180   cognosceret. , et, attemptata
multotiens experientia testante,
nullatenus ignoraret;, cum ipsa
que deus est caritas nullis sit
inclusa terminis., nullo <loci>
185   vel temporis spacio circum-
scripta. , virium autem humanarum breuissima sit et angusta
nimis industria : non tamen,
hoc sano rationis concilio,

Tertius modus amoris.
Quandoque bona anima alium
amoris modum tenet, multos
dolores habentem annexos,
scilicet cum cupit amori satisfacere et obsequi in omni ministerio et in omni obedientia
et in omni amoris submissione.
Quod desiderium interdum in
anima valde agitatur, ita ut
forti impetu moliatur omnia
aggredi, omnem virtutem sequi, omnia pati et sufferre et
omnia opera sua non parcendo
et sine modo in amore adimplere.
In quo modo valde parata est
in omni ministerio, et prompta
et intrepida in labore et dolore; attamen non satisfacta
manet et impacata in omnibus
operibus suis. Sed supra omnia haec est maximus ei dolor :
non posse secundum magnum
desiderium suum amori satisfacere, et tam multum sibi in
amore necessario deesse.
Bene novit hanc adimpletio-

Then finally she humbly acquiesced, and even with praise and
thanksgiving she multiplied many-
fold by her interior exercises the
things she received.

251 The third manner or degree
was another stage of conduct, in
which as we have often narrated,
she desired to satisfy and fully
repay, through loving service, the
love which God is.

To fulfill this desire effica-
ciously, she put forth not only her
interior affections but all her bodily
forces, and she compensated with
the most fervent desire of her heart
what was lacking to these forces.
She could not withdraw her mind
from this undertaking by rational
counsel, although she knew by
reason— and was certainly not
unaware of it through the many
experiments she had attempt-
ed—, that this arduous work of
love could not be fulfilled by
human strength, since the love
which God is is unlimited, un-
circumscribed by any space of
time, while the energy of human
forces is very short and narrow.

The third manner of loving.
Sometimes the good soul has
another manner of loving, which
has many sorrows connected
with it, namely when it desires
to satisfy and yield to love in all
service and all obedience and all
loving submission. Sometimes
this desire so greatly agitates the
soul that it strives vigorously to
undertake everything, to follow
after every virtue, to suffer and
endure everything, to fulfill all
its work in love, withholding
nothing and without measure.

In this state the soul is very
ready for every service, and is
eager and unafraid in labor and
sorrow; yet it remains unsatis-
fied and unappeased in all its
works. But aside from all this its
greatest sorrow is that it cannot
satisfy love according to its own
great desire, and that it is, necessarily so, lacking in love. It
knows well that such fulfillment

190 mentem a cepto proposito
retrahere potuit. Idipsum siquidem quod impossibilitatem
suam obstantem sibi repperit :, interdum vires desiderij
195 fortius, vt assolet, augmen-
tauit.

252 In hoc ergo statu grauissi-
simis plerumque molestijs arta-
batur et opprimebatur angus-
200 tijs :; nam cum, deficiente virium adminiculo, nil superesset
quod in caritatis obsequium ex-
pendere potuisset., et voluntatis intentio non solum a suo
205 proposito non quiesceret :, verum etiam vltra totius humane
virtutis tolerantiam ad peragendum quod ceperat inexplebili quodam desiderio festina-
210 ret :, non minimos plerumque
languores incurrit., et, vt ipsa
fatetur, infernalem quodammodo vitam agens, et mortem vi-
uendo sustinens, in multa tribu-
215 latione cordis, et corporis imbe-
cillitate permansit, donec hunc
nimis importabilem in alium
leuiorem statum, solita pietatis
sue clementia, superna dignatio
220 commutauit.

nem superare omnem huma-
nam sufficientiam omnemque
virtutem propriam. Nam quod
cupit omnibus creaturis impossibile et inane est, scilicet
ut in obsequio et amore et
observantia iuxta dignitatem
amoris, sola tam multa adimplere possit et innumerabiliter
plura quam omnes in terra
homines et omnes in coelo
spiritus et omnis creatura supra et infra. Et quod in hoc
praestando in operibus tam
multo modo sibi deest, sup-
plere cupit cum plena voluntate et forti desiderio. Quod
tamen ei satisfacere nequit.

Bene novit huius desiderii
adimpletionem vires suas, humanam rationem et omnes
sensus multum excedere; attamen non potest sibi mensuram imponere neque sese con-
tinere neque sedare.

Facit quod potest : laudans
gratias agit Amori; operatur
et laborat propter Amorem;
suspirat et cupit Amorem;
tradit seipsam totam Amori,
et omne quod facit adimpletur
in amore. Totum hoc non dat
ei quietem, quodque desiderare debet quod non potest
consequi, magno dolori ei est.
Quapropter in cordis cruciatu
manere necesse est et habitare
in moerore. Et sic ei est ac si

The very fact that she found her own incapacity obstructing her, sometimes increased the vigor of her desire, as usually happens.

252 In this stage she was straitened and oppressed by much trouble and anguish. For when nothing was left that could be spent in the service of love, because her strength has failed, and when not only the intention of her will did not slacken from its proposal but even hastened with insatiable desire beyond all human endurance, to do what it had undertaken, then she underwent many and grave sicknesses. As she herself said, she was, in a way leading the life of hell, undergoing death while living, dragging along in much trouble of heart and weakness of body, until heavenly mercy with its usual kindness changed this intolerable state for a lighter one.

surpasses all human capacity and all her own strength. For what the soul desires is impossible and improper for any creature, namely that the soul alone could serve, love, and honor Love in accordance with Love's dignity and moreover do this as much as, and innumerably more than, all human beings on earth and all spirits in heaven and all creatures above and below. With full will and strong desire the soul wills to supply what is so greatly lacking to its works, but it cannot satisfy this desire.

The soul well knows that fulfilling this desire much exceeds its own strength and human reason and all understanding, and yet it cannot moderate, contain, or calm itself.

It does what it can; it praises and thanks Love; it works and labors for Love; it desires and sighs for Love; it gives itself wholly to Love, and it perfects in love everything it does. All this gives the soul no rest; what it ought to desire but cannot attain is a great pain to it. Therefore the soul must remain in agony of heart and dwell in grief. Thus it seems to the soul

vivens moreretur et moriens
dolorem inferni sentiret, totaque vita eius infernalis est et
infortunium et afflictio ex horrore formidolosi desiderii cui
satisfacere, quodque placare
aut sedare non potest.

In quo cruciatu manere debet
usque ad hanc horam in qua
Dominus noster eam conso-
letur et in alium amoris et
desiderii modum ponat et in
propinquiorem ad Eum cognitionem. Et tunc agere debet
secundum quod ei datur a
Domino nostro.

253 Quartus modus dilectionis
erat status quidam delectabilis
et quietus in quo <dominus>
omnipotens nectareum quemdam amoris gustum absque
quolibet additamento corporalis
vel etiam spiritualis industrie,
de quo[3] // f. *333 a* paulo ante
premisimus, in corde dilecte sue
gratuita benignitatis sue clementia velut in vase purissimo
propinauit.

In hoc siquidem statu fortissi-
mus quidam amoris affectus,
intra cor suum diuinitus exci-
tatus, idipsum tam valenter
<adstrinxit>., tam delectabi-
liter inuasit., tam fortiter alli-
gauit :, vt, pre nimia spiritualis

Quartus modus amo-
ris. Solet etiam Dominus
noster alios dare modos amoris, nunc in magna voluptate,
nunc autem in magno moe-
rore. De quo nunc volo loqui.
Quandoque fit ut amor sua-
viter excitetur in anima et
cum gaudio surgat et in corde
sese moveat nulla collaborante
actione humana. Et tunc cor
tam tenero amore tangitur, et
tanto desiderio in amorem trahitur, et tam cordialiter amore
complectitur et tam valide
amore subigitur et tam amabiliter in amplexu amoris te-
netur, ut amore tota vincatur.
In quo experitur magnam

as if it lives while dying and dies while it feels the pain of hell. All its life is hellish, misfortune and affliction because of the horror of this dreadful desire which it can neither satisfy, nor appease nor calm.

The soul must remain in this torment until the hour when our Lord consoles it and places it in a different manner of love and desire, and in a closer knowledge of himself. Then the soul should do as our Lord allows it. The fourth manner of loving. Our Lord is also accustomed to give other manners of loving, at one time with great pleasure, but at another with great sorrow. I wish to speak of this now. Sometimes it happens that love is sweetly awakened in the soul, rising up with joy, and flows in the heart without any human collaboration. And then the heart is so touched with tender love, is drawn towards love with such desire, is embraced so cordially by love, is subjected by love so strongly, and is held in love's embrace so lovingly, that it is wholly conquered by love. In this the heart

253 The fourth manner of loving was a certain delightful quiet stage in which the almighty Lord of his free kindness and mercy poured into his beloved's heart as into a most pure vessel a certain nectar-like taste of love without any additional effort of body or of spirit such as we have just been talking about.

In this stage a very strong loving affection, divinely aroused in her heart, bound it so strongly, invaded it so deliciously, and tied it so firmly that Beatrice was, as it were, absorbed

The following pages (305 and 309) contain lines omitted in the Reypen's edition. The additions are marked by acute brackets (< >) in the translation.

240 dulcedinis habundantia, velut
in abissum caritatis absorta,
tota celestis effecta fuerit. , et,
instar guttule decurrentis in
maris amplissimam latitudinem,
245 tota simul affectio cordis eius
in pelagus eternitatis immersa,
celestem quodammodo naturam
induerit.

In quo statu quantum spiritua-
250 lis dulcedinis, beate felicitatis
et felicissime iocunditatis in
mente <gustaverit>. , quantum igne feruentissime caritatis
accensa flagrauerit : , non ver-
255 borum affluentia, sed sola tes-
tis experientia, misterium hoc
indagare volentibus explicabit.
Illa quippe caritatis supereми-
nens pulchritudo, que sensus
260 humanos exsuperat, in tantum
illius mentem allexerat, sibique
totam cum suis affectibus at-
trahens et amplexans intra sinum incircumscripte profundi-
265 tatis sue glutiuerat : , vt nichil
preter caritatem saperet. , nichil
aduerteret nichil in ore sonaret
nisi caritas. , nichil in opere
preter caritatem demonstraret.
270 **254** Fuit etiam in hoc statu
tam delicatus sancte mulieris
affectus : , vt, liquefacto corde,
frequentissime lacrimarum imbre madesceret. , et, pre nimia
275 spiritualis copia delectationis,

proximitatem ad Deum, et
substantialem claritatem, et
miram voluptatem, et nobilem
libertatem, et beatam dulcedinem. Et tunc sentit omnes
sensus suos sanctificatos in
amore, et voluntatem suam
amorem factam et tam alte
demersam et absorptam in
abyssum amoris ut ipsa tota
amor facta sit.

Amoris pulchritudo consump-
sit eam; fortitudo amoris con-
fecit eam; dulcedo amoris im-
mersit eam; magnitudo amoris
absorpsit eam et altitudo
amoris sustulit eam et sic sibi
univit, ut tota amori esse debeat nec aliud amare possit.

Quando sic se sentit in hac
superabundantia deliciarum et
in hac magna plenitudine cordis, mens eius in amorem tota
demergitur et corpus ei sub-
trahitur, cor eius liquescit et
tota potentia eius absumitur,
et in tantum amore vincitur,
ut vix sustentare se possit et
saepe membris et sensibus iam
non potitur.

Et sicut vas plenum cum movetur subito effluit et exun-
dat, sic valde cito, ex magna
plenitudine cordis movetur et
tota devincitur, ita ut saepe
invita erumpat necesse sit.

in the abyss of charity and made wholly celestial because of the excessive abundance of spiritual sweetness. All the affection of her heart took on, in some way, a celestial nature like a little drop of water running down into the vast expanse of the sea and immersed in the ocean of eternity.

Not a flood of words but only personal experience will explain, to those who want to know, what spiritual sweetness, what blessed happiness and happy delight Beatrice tasted in her mind and with what a fire of ever fervent love she glowed in this stage. That supreme beauty of love which surpasses human understanding, so allured her mind, so attracted her with all her affections to itself, so embraced and swallowed her into the bosom of its unlimited depths that she relished nothing but love, she noticed nothing but love, she spoke of nothing but love, and in her works she showed forth nothing but love.

254 In this stage the holy woman's affection was so tender that she was often soaked with the flood of tears from her melted heart, and sometimes because of the excessive abundance of spiritual delight,

feels a great closeness to God, a substantial clarity, a wonderful delight, a noble liberty and a ravishing sweetness, <and a great impulse of a stronger love and an abundant fullness of greater delights>. Then it feels all its senses sanctified in love, its will turned into love and so deeply immersed and absorbed in the abyss of love that it [the soul] is made wholly into love.

Love's beauty has consumed it. Love's strength has eaten it up. Love's sweetness has immersed it. Love's greatness has absorbed it. Love's exaltedness has raised it up and so united it to itself that the soul must wholly belong to Love, nor should it love anything else. When the soul feels itself in the superabundance of delights and in this great fullness of heart, its mind is wholly immersed in love and its body is withdrawn from itself; the heart melts away and all its power is consumed. So conquered is it by love that it can scarcely sustain itself, and loses its power over its members and senses.

And just as a full vessel overflows and spills when it is suddenly moved, so at times the soul is very quickly moved and totally overcome by the great fullness of heart so that in spite of itself it must often spill over.

interdum, virium deficiente pre-
sidio, languens et egrotans
in lectulo decubaret. Quotiens
<tamen> hoc amoris typo
280 vexabatur interius:, permaxima
fuit illi sollicitudo quod sentiebat intra semetipsam, ne a ceteris deprehenderetur, occulere ;
sed nec de deo loquentem ali-
285 quem, ne videlicet illam amoris
sui superfluentem habundantiam per aliqua forsan indicia
foras emanare contingeret, //
f. 333 b mirum dictu, per id
290 temporis aut voluit aut potuit
auscultare. Nam id quotiens
fieri contingebat., tunc videlicet cum aut sermonibus aut
collationibus interesset., vel
295 etiam cum edificatorium quippiam ipsa dissereret :, frequenter accidit vt, ad vasis similitudinem quod, cum plenum liquoris fuerit., impulsum vel mo-
300 dice, mox quod continet ei-
ciendo refundit ;, et ipsa, per
plurima sancti amoris indicia,
quod sentiebat intrinsecus, velut impulsa, refunderet :; aut
305 certe paraliticum quodammodo
tremorem incurreret., aut alia
queque languoris incommoda
sustineret.

she lay languishing and sick in bed, deprived of all her strength. As often as she was interiorly troubled by this kind of love, she was greatly concerned to conceal what she felt inside, lest it be noticed by others. During that time, wonderful to say, she willed not to listen or could not listen to anyone speaking about God, lest that superabundance of his love should perhaps become known through some signs. How often this used to happen when she attended sermons or conferences, or also when she herself spoke of something edifying. Just as a vessel filled with liquid spills what it contains when it is only slightly pushed, so it happened frequently that Beatrice, pushed as it were, would let spill out by many signs of holy love what she felt inside; or else she would undergo a kind of paralyzed trembling, or would be burdened with some other discomfort of languor.

255 Quintus modus erat insania quedam sancti desiderij
et amoris, <quam> interdum
intra se tam fortiter grassantem
agnouit :, vt, instar belue rugientis et indomite, totum illud
singulare domicilium corporis
sui debachando concuteret., et
sic intra ediculam cordis illius
insaniret;, ac si, foras erumpere
gestiens, illud quod tantopere
queritabat, violenter apprehendere voluisset.

In hoc autem statu nichil de
interioribus., nichil vel de exterioribus ociosum vel quietum
esse potuit ; et, quamuis corporalis debilitas vires ad. supportandum onus, tam humanis viribus importabile, denegaret,.
non tamen vel sensus exterior
vel affectus interior a sancto
proposito quiescere potuit:; sed
quo magis imbecillitatem corporis vis amoris et desiderij sibi
resistentem in intentionis itinere
repperit., eo fortius in mente,
velut in arto conclusa meatu,
feruens et estuans, impetuoso
turbine cuncta sibi repugnantia
penetrans et inuoluens, per vias
interiorum affectuum ad exteriores vsque sensus corporeos
inundauit. Siquidem ipsum cor,
ad illius inuasionem viribus
destitutum, frequenter, ipsa sen-
tiente simul et a foris audiente,

Quintus modus amoris.
Interdum fit etiam ut amor in
anima vehementer excitetur
et sicut procella surgit, cum
magno strepitu et magna cum
rabie, quasi per vim cor con-
fracturus et animam extra se
et supra se tracturus in exercitium amoris et in deficien-
tiam amoris. Vel cupit quiescere in dulci amplexu amoris
et in desiderabili beatitudine
et in deliciis possessionis, ita
ut cor et sensus eius hoc desi-
derant et diligenter quaerant
et ex animo intendant.

Cum in hoc versatur, tam
strenua est in spiritu et tam
multa meditans in corde, corpore tam robustior et in ope-
rando alacrior, tam negotiosa
exterius et interius, ut sibi
videatur omnia quae in ea
sunt operari et occupari, eti-
amsi ad extra tota quiescit.

Simul interius experitur vali-
dam attractionem et propen-
sionem ad amorem, et multas
impatientias in desiderio mul-
tiformemque dolorem ex magna molestia. Vel sine ulla
causa cruciatum experitur ex
ipso magno sensu amoris vel
ex eo quod desiderio suo pe-
culiariter exposcit in amore,
vel ex cruciatu deficientis
fruitionis amoris.

255 The fifth manner was a certain madness of holy desire and love which she recognized sometimes as rioting so strongly within her that, raving like some roaring, untamed beast, it struck the whole framework of her body and acted like a madman within the house of her heart as if it wished to break out of it and grab with violence that which it so much desired.

In this condition nothing could be leisurely or quiet within or without, and although bodily weakness denied her the strength to support the humanly insupportable burden, still neither the exterior sense nor the exterior affection could rest from the holy desire. Rather, the more the force of her love and desire found the weakness of her body resisting it on its intended journey, the more vigorously did this force, hot and agitated, act in the mind like a flood enclosed in some narrow channel, penetrating and enveloping every obstacle with its impetuous swirl, proceeding through the paths of the interior affections and reaching to the exterior bodily senses. Indeed her heart, deprived of strength by this invasion, often gave off a sound like that of a shattering vessel, while

The fifth manner of loving. Sometimes it also happens that love is vehemently excited in the soul and it rises like a storm with a great uproar and a great frenzy, as though it would draw the soul outside itself into the exercise of love and into the exhaustion of love. <And strongly is the soul also pulled into the longing of love to accomplish the great and pure deeds of love>. Or else it desires to rest in the sweet embrace of love, in desirable happiness and in the delights of possession, so that its heart and sense desire this, diligently seek it and heartily intend it.

When the soul is in this state, it is so vigorous in spirit, so mindful of many things in its heart, so much stronger in body and keen in operation, so active in exterior and interior business that it seems to itself to be universally operative and occupied, even if outwardly it is wholly at rest.

The soul experiences interiorly a strong attraction and at the same time propensity for love, and much impatient desire for love, and many kinds of sorrow from a great dissatisfaction. Or else the soul experiences suffering without any cause from the great sense of love, or it may be from what it has specially requested by its longing for love, or because it suffers from having no fruition of love.

quasi vas quod // f. 333 c con-
fringitur <sonitum> fractionis
emisit : ; ipse quoque sanguis,
per corporalia membra diffu-
350 sus, apertis venis exiliens.,
ebulliuit ;, ossibusque contrac-
tis ipsa quoque medulla disparuit :, pectoris siccitas ipsius
gutturis raucitatem induxit:, et,
355 vt paucis multa concludam.,
ipse feruor sancti desiderij et
amoris omnia membra corporea,
mirum in modum sensibiliter
estuanti., incendio conflagrauit.
360 Interdum, quasi sagitta, fulgur
quoddam, ex sancti amoris igne
prosiliens, cor illius <ac>
pectus et <ad> cerebrum vsque, cuncta gutturis et capitis
356 organa penetrauit : ; nonnumquam vero, quasi flammam
ignis omnia deuorantis, ipsum
amoris incendium intra se se-
uiendo consurgere deprehendit.
370 **256** Talibus igitur violentijs
interdum cor sancte mulieris
conquassatum, amoris incommodo necessario languit : ; et ad
ipsa quoque corporalia membra
375 languor egrediens, ab egritudinis lectulo consurgere, vel sospitatis frui beneficio, non permisit.
Nec estimet quis electissimam
dei sponsam in tanto discrimine
380 a domino derelictam ; sed qui
caritatis iaculo vvlnus inflixit.,

Interea amor, cum tam vehementer et tumultuose sese
movet in corde, fit immodicus
et tam exundans in anima, ut
putet cor suum multipliciter
valde vulnerari, haecque vul-
nera quotidie renovari et ag-
gravari in magis amaris doloribus et in nova semper actua-
litate. Et sic videntur ei venae
suae aperiri et sanguis effer-
vescere, medulla marcessere,
crura debilitari, pectus uri et
guttur exsiccari, ita ut facies
eius et omnia membra calorem
internum percipiant et amoris
tumultum experiantur. Quo
tempore etiam sentit sagittam
transfigere cor suum usque
ad guttur, et ulterius usque
ad cerebrum, quasi sensum
amissura esset. Et sicut ignis
devorans, cuncta in se attra-
hens et consumens quo potiri
potest, sic sentit amorem tumultuose intra se operari, nulli
rei parcendo et sine modo
omnia in se corripiens et consumens. His omnibus multum
vulneratur, et cor eius valde
laeditur et tota virtus eius
deficit. Verum anima eius
nutritur, et amor eius alitur,
et mens eius suspenditur.
Nam amor alte omni intellec-
tui supereminet, ut ad nullam

she both felt the same and heard it exteriorly. Also the blood diffused through her bodily members boiled over through her open veins. Her bones contracted and the marrow disappeared; the dryness of her chest produced hoarseness of throat. And to make a long story short, the very fervor of her holy longing and love blazed up as a fire in all her bodily members, making her perceptibly hot in a wondrous way. Sometimes a kind of lightning, like an arrow, springing forth from the fire of holy love, pierced her heart and breast and penetrating through all the organs of her throat and head, reached even to her brain. But sometimes she found the fire of love rising and raging within her, like a flame of fire which devours everything.

256 The heart of the holy woman, assaulted by such violence, sometimes necessarily languished in a discomfort caused by love, and the languor proceeding to her bodily members did not allow her to rise from her sick bed or to enjoy the benefit of good health. Let no one think that God's elect bride was abandoned in such straits by the Lord, but he who wounded her with the dart of love, also

Meantime, when love acts in the heart so vehemently and riotously, it becomes so excessive and exuberant in the soul that the soul thinks its heart has been wounded in many and grave ways, and that these wounds are daily renewed and aggravated by more bitter sorrows and each time actualized anew. So it seems that its veins are opened and its blood is boiling out, its marrow is withered and its legs are weak, its chest burns and its throat is dry, so that its face and all its members perceive the inner heat and experience the tumult that love is making. At this time she also feels an arrow piercing through her heart all the way to the throat and beyond, even to the brain, as if she would lose her mind. And the soul thus feels love acting riotously within it, sparing nothing, uncontrollably seizing and consuming everything within the soul like a devouring fire which draws to itself and consumes everything it can get hold of. By all these things the soul is much wounded and its heart much damaged and all its strength fails. Yet the soul is nourished, its love is fed and its mind is lifted up and suspended. For Love so greatly surpasses all understanding that

ipse languorem vvlneris <eius-
dem> caritatis antydoto rep-
pulit : , et, cum illi placuit, hunc
385   statum in alium commutando,
tam in corpore quam in mente
virium adminicula celesti medi-
camine reparauit.

eius fruitionem anima attingere valeat; unde ex dolore
interdum cupit vinculum rum-
pere ne unitas amoris fran-
gatur. Sed hoc vinculo tam
arcte adstringitur, et excessu
amoris ita devincitur, ut modum rationemque tenere ne-
queat, nec cum sensu rationem
exercere, nec mensuram tenere parcendo, nec secundum
discretionem quieta manere.
Quanto amplius ei datur desuper, tanto plus exigit, et
quanto maiora ei ostenduntur,
eo maiori desiderio suspenditur propius accedendi ad lumen veritatis et puritatis et
nobilitatis et fruitionis amoris.
Et semper magis ac magis excitatur et trahitur, at non sa-
turatur neque satiatur. Hoc
ipsum quod magis eam cruciat
atque vulnerat, idipsum magis
integrat et lenit, et quod eam
profundius vulnerat, hoc solum dat ei sanitatem.

257 Sextus gradus amoris erat
390   ille status vite sublimis, in quo
caritatem ipsam que deus est,
intra domicilium cordis sui quiete regnantem et secure domi-
nantem accepit : , ac <sic>,
395   effugatis omnium contrarieta-
tum obstaculis, in medio cordis

Sextus amor. Cum sponsa
Domini longius processit et
altius ascendit in maiore robore, experitur et alium modum amoris in eminentiore
habitu et altiore intellectu.
Sentit amorem intra se vicisse
omnes adversarios suos, defec-

repulsed the languor of the wound with an antidote of the same love, and when it pleased him, he repaired with the help of heavenly medicine her strength in both body and mind by changing this state into another one.

257 The sixth degree of love was that sublime state of life in which she accepted within the dwelling place of her heart that love which is God, accepting it as reigning quietly and dominating securely. Thus she kept it in the midst of her heart

the soul can attain to no fruition of it. Therefore, out of pain the soul sometimes desires to break the bond without breaking the unity of love. But the soul is so closely throttled by this bond and is so overcome by the excess of love that it cannot maintain measure and reason, or maintain moderation by restraint, or remain quiet according to good judgment.

The more the soul is given from above, the more it demands, and the greater the things shown to it, by greater desire is it drawn up to approach closer to the light of truth and purity and nobility and the fruition of love. The soul is always more and more stirred up and drawn along but it is not satisfied or satiated. What most afflicts and wounds it, also heals and soothes it; what wounds it most deeply is the only thing that gives it health.

The sixth love. When the Lord's bride has proceeded further and mounted higher with greater strength, she experiences another manner of loving loftier in hearing and higher in understanding. She feels that love has conquered all her adversaries

sui, tranquillo potientem domi-
nio, conseruauit.

In hoc siquidem statu, velut
materfamilias omnem domus
sue familiam gubernans prouide, sapienter ordinans et potenter dirigens et conseruans:,
ipsa caritas in alto mentis solio
residens., imperiosa virtutis
sue freta potentia., tam affectionum quam sensuum nume-
rosam familiam rexit prouide,
sapienter instruxit // f. 333 d
ac sine quolibet recalcitrationis
offendiculo, potens et imperans
in suo queque ministerio conseruauit.

Nec erat valde laborandum in
hoc sancto regimine:, cum ad
votum obsequerentur omnia,
summe tranquillitatis et pacis
requiem indicente matre virtutum ordinatissima, caritate.
Quid amore sublimius;, quid
caritate potentius? 'Caritas
enim, vt ait apostolus, omnia
suffert, omnia sustinet':, et
cetera que ad laudem caritatis
plenissime subsequuntur.

258 Verum et-si nobilis et imperiosa caritas ad hunc perfectionis statum, mentem beate
mulieris extulerit:, in quo sen-
sualitatum motus sub quieto
silentio pacifice gubernauit,.
<n>on tamen ad hoc culmen
perfectionis hanc repente vel

tus correxisse et sensus sub-
iecisse, naturam ornavisse ani-
maeque statum ampliasse et
exaltasse, et sibi ipsi absque
contradictione sic dominatum
esse, ut cor possederit in se-
curitate, et frui possit in pace,
et liberum exercitium habere
necesse sit.

Cum in hoc statu est, omnia
animae videntur parva esse,
et omne quod ad dignitatem
amoris pertinet facile ad faciendum et omittendum, tole-
randum et ferendum; et sic
dulce ei est exercere se in
amore. Tunc experitur divi-
nam quandam potentiam et
claram puritatem et spiritualem dulcedinem et desidera-
bilem libertatem et discernen-
tem sapientiam et dulcem
aditum ad Dominum nostrum
et intimam cognitionem Dei.
Tunc est sicut materfamilias
quae domum suam bene rexit,
et sapienter, discrete et pulchre
ordinavit, et providenter tue-
tur et prudenter custodit, et
cum discretione operatur. Et
introducit et educit, et ut vult
facit et omittit. Ita fit cum
tali anima: amor est, et amor
intra eam fortiter regnat et
potenter; ad voluntatem eius
quiescens, faciens et omittens,
ad extra et ad intra.

in its tranquil enjoyment of dominion with all obstacles and contradictions put to flight.

In this state, like a housewife governing the whole family and household prudently, wisely setting it in order and powerfully directing and preserving it,—love herself sitting on the high dais of the mind— [Beatrice] relying on the mighty power of her virtue, prudently ruled and wisely instructed the numerous family of affections and senses, and she preserved each in its own ministry by her power and might, without any hindrance or rebellion.

Nor was there much need for effort in this holy regime, since everything obeyed her vow; and love, the supremely well-ordered mother of virtues, enjoined the repose of great tranquillity and peace. What is more sublime than love; what is more powerful than love? For, as the apostle says, 'love bears all things, endures all things'[2] and so on, in abundance to the praise of love.

258 But even if noble and commanding love raised the blessed woman's mind to this state of perfection in which the movements of sensuality were governed quietly, silently and peacefully, it should not be thought that Beatrice arrived at this peak of perfection suddenly

within her, has corrected her defects and subdued her senses, has adorned her nature, has amplified and exalted her state of soul and gained dominion over herself without contradiction that she, the bride, possesses her heart in security, can delight in it in peace and must have the free exercise of it.

When the soul is in this state, all things seem small, and everything which pertains to love's dignity seems easy to do and to refrain from doing to tolerate and to bear, and so it is pleasing for the soul to exercise itself in love. Then it experiences some hint of divine power and clear purity and spiritual sweetness and desirable liberty, a discerning wisdom, a gentle drawing near to our Lord and an intimate knowledge of God. Then the soul is like a housewife who governs her house well, and orders it wisely, discreetly, and beautifully; providently she watches and prudently she keeps guard, and she acts with discretion. She brings in and takes away, she acts and she refrains from acting, as she wills. So it is with such a soul. It is love, and love within it rules strongly and powerfully. The soul rests, acts and refrains from acting, without and within to Love's will.

2. *2 Co 13:7*

subito venisse putandum est ; :
sed post multos agones quos
pertulit. , post plurimos perfectionis gradus quos paulatim ascendit. , tandem ad hunc tranquillitatis et pacis apicem peruenire promeruit ; in quo, tota
quodammodo celestis effecta,
suam in celis conuersationem
esse cum apostolo dicere potuit : ; presertim cum solum
corpusculi sui parietem ab eternis gaudijs spiritum arcentem,
iam, <vt> prediximus[4], in
eterne fruitionis eleuatum confinio, tolerans[5], in sublimi quodam perfectionis vertice constituta, viuens in corpore vitam
angelicam in terris ageret. , et
celestibus gaudijs innouata, in
quodam future vite confinio
arto resideret.

Ad tantam quoque libertatem
spiritus, cordis constantiam et
conscientie puritatem in hoc
statu mens sancta peruenerat. ,
vt non hominem vereretur, non
demonem, non angelicum etiam
vel diuinum iudicium in omni
facto siue cogitatu suo per-
timesceret : ; presertim cum ip-

Et ad instar piscis qui natat
in latitudine fluvii et quiescit
in profundo; et sicut avis qui
audacter volat in aeris amplitudine et celsitudine, ita sentit
spiritum suum libere sese mo-
ventem in latitudine et pro-
funditate et in amplitudine et
altitudine amoris.

Vis amoris animam traxit et
duxit, tutata est et protexit, et
dedit ei prudentiam et sapientiam, dulcedinem et fortitudinem
amoris. Attamen vehementiam
suam animae celavit donec in
altiora ascenderit et a seipsa
penitus libera facta sit, et amor
intra eam potenter regnet.

Tunc amor tam audacem et li-
beram eam facit, ut in omni sua
actione vel omissione, in opere
et quiete, nec homines perti-
mescat nec daemonem, nec
angelum, nec sanctos, neque
ipsum Deum; et bene sentit
amorem intra se tam alacrem
et operosum in quiete corporis
quam in multis actionibus;
bene novit et sentit amorem in
eis in quibus regnat non consistere in labore neque dolore.

and unexpectedly. Rather she deserved to arrive eventually at this summit of tranquillity and peace after many struggles borne out, after many steps of perfection which she ascended little by little. In this state she became in a way entirely celestial and could say with the apostle that her conversation was in heaven,[3] especially since, tolerating the partition of her frail body as the only thing holding back from eternal joy her spirit already raised to the frontier of eternal enjoyment (as we said previously); and established in a sublime summit of perfection, yet living in the body, she led an angelic life on earth and dwelt on the threshold of the future life, renewed by heavenly joys.

In this state her holy mind had arrived at such liberty of spirit, constancy of heart and purity of conscience that she feared neither man nor demon, not the angelic or even the divine judgment, since that divine Love which dominates

Like a fish swimming in a broad river and resting in the depths, and like a bird flying boldly in the vastness and the height of the sky, so the soul feels its spirit moving freely in the breadth and depth and vastness and height of love.

Love's power has drawn the soul and led it, has watched over and protected it, has given it the prudence and wisdom, the sweetness and strength of love. But love has concealed its own vehemence from the soul until the soul shall have mounted higher and been made wholly free from itself and until love reigns powerfully within it.

Then love makes the soul so bold and free that in all its actions and restraints at work and at rest it fears neither men nor the demon, neither angel nor saints, nor God himself, and it truly feels that love is as lively and operative in bodily rest as in great activity. It well knows and feels that love does not consist in labor and sorrow for those in whom it reigns.

3. Ph 3:20

465 sa dominatrix omnium, diuina caritas, hunc timorem foras expelleret., et in omni quod patrabat opere, conscientie libertatem, immotam et sta-
470 bilem in suo robore conseruaret.

Sed omnes qui ad amorem pervenire volunt, debent eum timentes quaerere, fideliter obsequi, desideranter exercere; quod non possunt si parcant sibi in magno labore et in multis doloribus, in ferendo incommoda, in contemptum patiendo. Et parvas res omnes ducere debent magnas, donec eo perveniant ut amor intra sese regnet, qui fortia opera amoris operatur, omnem rem minutam facit, omnem laborem dulcem; omnem dolorem mitigat et omne debitum solvit.

Haec est libertas conscientiae et dulcedo cordis et alacritas sensuum et nobilitas animae et sublimitas mentis et initium vitae aeternae. Haec est iam hic vita angelica, post quam sequitur vita aeterna. Quam Deus propter bonitatem suam nobis omnibus dare velit.

259 Sequitur caritatis gradus septimus : . illud scilicet ineffabile desiderium eterna beatitu-
475 dine perfruendi :, quod, sicut nullo lingue plectro valet exprimi., sic a non experiente, // ʃ. *334 a* quantum in se fuerit nullo valet sensu concipi, nulla
480 posset intelligentia comprehendi.

Quis enim vel mente conciperet

Septimus modus amoris. Habet etiam beata anima altioris amoris modum, qui non modicum laboris dat ad intra, scilicet cum in amorem trahitur supra quod humanum est, et supra humanum sensum et rationem, et supra omnia opera cordis nostri ; et per solum Amorem aeternum trahitur in aeternitatem Amo-

everything, expelled this fear[4] and preserved her liberty of conscience, unmoved and strongly stable in every work she performed.

But all who want to attain love must seek it with fear and follow it faithfully, and exercise it longingly, and this they cannot do if they spare themselves in great labors and many pains, in bearing trouble and in suffering contempt. They must reckon all little things great until they arrive at the point where love reigns within them and works its mighty works of love, making everything little, every labor easy, softening every pain and remitting every debt.

This is freedom of conscience, sweetness of heart, animation of the senses, nobility of soul, loftiness of mind and the beginning of eternal life. This is the angelic life already here [on earth], after which comes eternal life: May God in his own goodness deign to grant it to all of us.

259 The seventh degree of love comes next, namely, the unspeakable desire to enjoy eternal beatitude. Just as it cannot be expressed by the plectrum of any tongue, so it cannot be conceived by any sense or comprehended by any mind as it is in itself, unless one has experienced it.

Who might conceive in mind

The seventh manner of love. The blessed soul has also a higher manner of loving which gives it no little labor within, namely when it is drawn into a love beyond what is human, beyond human sense and reason, and beyond all the works of our heart. It is drawn through eternal Love alone into the eternity of

4. 1 Jn 4:18

aut verbis exprimeret quanto
cordis desiderio, quantis lacrimis, quantis singultibus et suspirijs ad illam futuram quietem
beatitudinis aspirauerit. , quantis hec orationibus expetierit
que, sicut paulo ante prediximus, . in terris solo corpore,
mente vero tota in celestibus
habitauit ?

Quis, inquam, digne referat
quam deuotissimo cordis affectu celestem illam beatorum
spirituum patriam cotidie fre-
quentauerit. , cotidie sanctorum angelorum agmina celestiumque virtutum consortia vi-
sitauerit ; , et [in] ea pertransiens, ad dilectum festinauerit
ascendere quam quesiuit ?

Ibi salutabat angelos ; ibi venerabatur archangelos. ; et precipue, sanctorum seraphin spiritus honorandos : , quibus in
excessu mentis aliquando sociata fuerat, et quos speciali
propterea venerationis obsequio
diligebat.

Ibi quoque patriarcharum ac
prophetarum conuentus almi-
fluos. ; ibi beatorum apostolorum cetus gloriosos. ; ibi mar-
tyrum peragrabat triumphos. ;
ibi confessorum circuibat cu-
neos. ; ibi sanctis coniuncta virginibus amoris canticum christo
cecinit : , et cum sanctis omni-

ris et in incomprehensibilita-
tem, in amplitudinem et in-
accessibilem sublimitatem et
in profundam abyssum Divi-
nitatis, quae tota est in omnibus rebus et incomprehensibi-
liter manet supra omnia et
quae est immutabilis, totum
esse, omnipotens, omnia intelligens, cum omni virtute
operans.

In hoc modo beata anima tam
dulciter in amore demersa est
et tam vehementer in desiderio attracta, ut cor eius
valde furens et intolerans fiat
ad intra, anima eius amore
fluens et languens, mens eius
insane suspensa ex vehementi
cupidine; et huc trahunt omnes sensus eius, ut esse velit
in fruitione Amoris. Hoc apud
Deum instantius expetit, et
hoc quaerit ex corde a Deo,
et valde hoc cupiat necesse
est. Nam amor non sinit eam
sedari neque quietari nec pace
frui.

Amor attollit eam et dimittit,
brevi mulcet et postea torquet;
dat mortem et affert vitam;
dat sanitatem et tunc iterum
sauciat : dementem reddit et
sapientem. Sic in altiorem
statum eam trahit. Sic, in spiritu tempus transgressa, in
aeternitatem ascendit et supra

or express in words with what desire
of heart, with what tears, what sobs
and sighs, Beatrice aspired to that
future rest and happiness, and with
what prayers she sought it, since, as
we said shortly before, only with her
body did she dwell on earth, but
with her whole mind she dwelt in
heaven?

Who might worthily tell with what
devout affection of heart she daily
frequented the heavenly homeland
of the blessed spirits, daily visited
the throngs of holy angels, the company of celestial virtues and, passing
through them, hastened to mount to
the beloved whom she sought?

There she greeted the angels, there
she venerated the archangels and
especially the honorable spirits of
the holy seraphim, to whom she had
once been associated in ecstasy and
whom as a result she loved with
special service and veneration.

There she traversed the kind
and bountiful gatherings of the
patriarchs and prophets, the glorious company of the apostles,
and the triumphant assembly of
the martyrs. There she went
around the throngs of confessors;
there in union with the holy virgins she sang to Christ the canticle
of love, and with all the saints

Love, and into the incomprehen-
sibility and vastness and inacces-
sible sublimity and deep abyss of
the Godhead, which is totally present in all things and remains in-
comprehensibly beyond all things,
which is immutable, perfect Being,
all-powerful, all-intelligent, al-
mightily operating.

In this manner the blessed soul
is so sweetly immersed in love
and so vehemently attracted by
desire that its heart rages and
becomes fidgety within; its soul
melts and languishes in love; its
mind is madly lifted up with
vehement desire and all its senses
draw it thither until it wills to be
in the fruition of Love. This it
desires from God insistently, and
seeks it ardently from God, and it
must necessarily desire it intensely. For love does not allow
the soul to rest or relax or enjoy
peace. Love lifts it up and sets it
down, soothes it for a short while
and then torments it; gives it
death and then brings it life;
gives it health and then wounds it
again; makes it first demented
and then wise. So love draws the
soul into a higher state. Thus, in
spirit transcending time, the soul
ascends into eternity and above

520 bus laudum et gratiarum actionibus omnipotenti domino iubi-
labat.

260 Verum quoniam hec per
speculum tantum et in enigmate
525 sancte femine contingebant[6]:
valde necessarium erat vt
quanto iocundius per contem-
plationum exercitium eternis
gaudijs interfuerat. , tanto mo-
530 lestius ab hijs abstracta denuo
sibi redderetur in terris reuo-
cante se nimirum humanitatis
pondere quod gestabat.

Hinc proinde fletus et suspiria
535 numquam illi deesse poterant : ;
hinc, sursum eleuato corde,
<manusque cum> oculis, ac
si et ipsa membra corporis ad
eternam aspirarent patriam,
540 ductu cordis erecta superius ad
celestia, prominebant. Hinc etiam illud apostolicum ' cupio
dissolui et esse cum christo'
semper versabatur in pectore : ;
545 hinc illud propheticum. ' heu
mihi quia incolatus meus pro-
longatus est' audires frequentissime beata labia resonare.

Hec siquidem prolongatio, quam
550 necessario pertulit, tam insana-
bili vvlnere desiderij et amoris cordis eius intima sauciauit :, vt cunctis tormentis //
f. 334 b estimaret grauius, huius

dona Amoris in aeternitatem
Amoris quae absque tempore
est ; et supra humanum modum in Amore sublata est,
et supra propriam naturam in
desiderio eam transgrediendi.
Ibi est totum quod est, tota
voluntas eius, desiderium et
amor eius : in secura veritate
et in pura claritate et in nobili
sublimitate et in pulchritudine
magnifica, et in dulci societate
supernorum spirituum, qui su-
pereffluente amore exundant,
qui sunt in clara cognitione et
in possessione et in fruitione
Amoris eorum.

Tunc superne, inter spiritus
est eius desiderabile commercium, et praesertim inter ardentes Seraphim; in magna
Deitate, et in alta Trinitate
est amabilis eius quies et frui-
tiva habitatio.

Dilectum quaerit in Maiestate
sua, huc prosequitur Eum, et
aspicit Eum corde et mente.
Novit Eum, amat Eum et ita
Eum desiderat, ut nec sanctis
nec hominibus nec angelis nec
creaturis attendere possit nisi
communi in Eo amore quo
omnia amat ; et in amore suo
Eum solum eligit supra omnia, et sub omnibus et inter

she jubilantly praised and thanked the almighty Lord.

260 But because these things happened to the holy woman only as through a mirror and in a dim reflection[5] it necessarily happened that the more pleasantly she took part in the eternal joys through the exercise of contemplation, the more vexed she was to come to herself again, withdrawn from there and returned to earth, recalled by the weight of the humanity she bore.

Hence weeping and sighing must always accompany her. Hence, with her heart lifted up, her hands and eyes too were lifted up to heaven under the impulse of her heart, as if even these bodily members aspired to the everlasting fatherland. Hence those words of the apostle: 'I long to be dissolved and to be with Christ',[6] were constantly present in her heart. Hence you would hear her blessed lips frequently saying with the prophet: 'Alas that my sojourning here is prolonged'.[7] This prolongation which she bore of necessity, caused such an incurable wound of desire and love in her inmost heart that she thought wasting

Love's gifts into Love's eternity, which is without time. It is lifted up above the human mode into Love, and above its own nature in the desire of transcending it. All that the soul is, all its will, its desire, its love are there in that secure truth and pure clarity and noble sublimity and magnificent beauty, and in the sweet society of the heavenly spirits who spill over with superabundant love and who exist in clear knowledge, possession and fruition of their Love.

Then the soul's longed-for dealings are with the heavenly spirits, especially with the ardent seraphim; its delightful rest and enjoyable dwelling is with the great Godhead and the lofty Trinity.

The soul seeks its beloved in his Majesty; it pursues him there, and gazes on him with heart and mind. The soul knows him, loves him, and desires him so much that it cannot pay attention to saints or men or angels or creatures except with that common love in him by which it loves everything; and in its love it chooses him alone above everything and under everything and within

---

5. 1 Co 13:12   6. *Ph 1:23*   7. *Ps 119:5*

555 mundani carcecis exilio con-
tabescere ;, quo solum impediente, quod querebat apprehendere non valuit : ; quod
solum desiderabat non potuit
560 obtinere.

261 Fuit enim huius desiderij
tam vehemens insolentia:, quod,
pre nimia imporunitate <vel
sensum sui> se putaret inter-
565 dum amittere vel etiam vite
sue dies, pre magna lesione vi-
talium et cordis angustia, bre-
uiare. Nam sepe, doloris huius
nimis impatiens, aut huius vite
570 miseriam aut future beatitudinis gloriam nec ipsa meditando
reuoluere, nec aliorum relatione
valebat seu potius audebat attendere :, sed, quantumcumque
575 potuit, idipsum a sinu memorie
conabatur excutere ; quod si
libere grassari, laxis habenis,
intra se sineret :, <instar>
flammantis gladij deuorantis
580 pariter et mactantis, non dubitabat vires corporis et cordis
funditus eneruare.

262 Sed quid hijs diutius immo-
ror ;, que, sicut alias protestatus
585 sum, sola mentis experientia, non
autem verborum affluentia possunt
concipi., et non littera sed spiritu,
non carnali sed spirituali valent intelligentia comprehendi? Proinde licet
590 vix e multis pauca <tetigerimus>,
et copiosam diuine caritatis amplissi-
mamque [verborum] materiam nimia
verborum parcitate, non dico plene,

omnia, ita ut cum tota pro-
pensione cordis, et cum tota
mentis virtute cupiat Eum videre et possidere et Eo frui.
Unde terra est ei magnum exilium, et firmus carcer, et gravis molestia. Mundum despi-
cit ; terra taedet eam et quod
terrae est nequit eam sedare
nec ei satisfacere. Et hoc ei
magnae maestitiae est, quod
tam longinqua esse debet et
tam peregrina videri. Exilium
non potest oblivisci; desiderium eius non potest sedari;
quod cupit misere vexat eam,
et sic cruciatur et torquetur
supra modum et sine remis-
sione.

Quare maxime cupit et fortiter desiderat ex hoc exilio liberari et ab hoc corpore solvi.
Unde tunc corde afflicto sicut
Apostolus dicit : 'Cupio dis-
solvi et esse cum Christo'.
Similiter anima in vehementi
desiderio est et in dolorosa
impatientia ut liberetur et vi-
vat cum Christo. Non ex
maerore praesentis temporis,
nec ex timore futurae tribulationis, sed solummodo ex
sancto et aeterno amore, ar-
denter et languens et magno-
pere cupit in aeternam patriam venire et in gloriam fruitionis.

away in the prison and exile of this world worse than all torments. Only because of it, she could not grasp what she sought, not obtain the only thing she wanted.

261 The vehemence of this desire was so excessive that she sometimes thought she would lose her mind for its grievousness, or would shorten the days of her life because of her anguish of heart and great damage to her vital bodily organs. For often when she was too harassed by this pain, she could not, or rather did not dare, meditate upon or attend to what others said about the misery of this life or the glory of future blessedness, but as much as she could, she tried to shake these thoughts out of the recesses of her memory. If she relaxed the reins and allowed these thoughts free scope within her, she did not doubt that they would thoroughly enervate her strength of body and heart like a flaming sword which devastates and slaughters.

262 But why do I delay more on these matters, which, as I have stated elsewhere, can be conceived only by experience, not by a flood of words, and which can be understood not in the letter but in the spirit, not with carnal but with spiritual understanding? Therefore, although we have touched scarcely a few out of many things, and have not adequately even summarized, much less

everything so that with its whole inclination of heart and total power of the mind it desires to see, possess and have fruition in him. Therefore earth is a great exile, a stout prison and a grave annoyance to the soul. It despises the world; earth wearies it and what belongs to earth cannot calm or satisfy it. The soul's great sadness is to have to be so far away and to seem so alien. It cannot forget its exile; its desire cannot be calmed; what the soul longs for wretchedly vexes it and thus afflicts and torments it beyond measure and without respite.

For this reason the soul greatly longs and strongly desires to be freed from this exile and loosed from the body. With afflicted heart it then says with the apostle: 'I long to be dissolved and to be with Christ'.[8] Similarly, the soul has a vehement desire and a grievous impatience to be freed and to live with Christ. Not for sadness about the present time, not for fear of future trouble, but only for holy and eternal love does the soul ardently and impetuously long and languish to arrive at the eternal land and its glorious fruition.

8. *Ph 1:23*

sed nec sufficienter quidem hucvsque
595 perstrinxerim :, ne tamen fastidiosis
lectoribus onerosus efficiar dum deuotis officio deuotionis inseruio, celestem materiam celestium contempla-
toribus exercendam quam legendam
300 potius derelinquo, secundumque caritatis membrum, quod in dilectione
proximi consistere dictum est., ad
edificationem omnium inserendum
huic operi, priusquam dictis finem
605 faciam, apprehendo.

Quod desiderium in ea ma-
gnum est et vehemens, et impatientia eius gravis et dura,
et quem ex desiderio patitur
dolor nimis magnus. Attamen
in spe vivere debet, et spes
anhelare eam facit et elan-
guescere.

O sancta cupido amoris, quam
valida est virtus tua in anima
amante! Est beata passio, et
acutum tormentum, et diu-
turnum malum, et necans
mors, et vita moriens!

Ad supera pervenire non potest, his in terris quiescere et
durare nequit; Dilecti sui memoriam ob desiderium ferre
non potest, et Eo carere dat
ei ex desiderio languorem. Et
sic vivendum ei est in magno
incommodo.

Hinc est quod nec potest nec
vult consolari, sicut dicit propheta: 'Renuit consolari anima mea'. Quo fit ut tunc
saepe ab ipso Deo et creaturis
eius omnem consolationem
abnuat. Nam omne solamen
quod ei exinde provenire possit amorem eius magis corro-
borat et desiderium eius ad
altiorem statum trahit; et hoc
renovat cupidinem amorem
fovendi, in fruitione Amoris
versandi et absque gaudio in
exilio vivendi. Et sic in omni-

treated fully, the abundant and most ample matter about divine love in my far too few words, nevertheless lest I be burdensome to fastidious readers while I am serving the devout with devoted service, I leave heavenly matters to be exercised, rather than read about, by those who contemplate heavenly things, and I undertake the second branch of love, which is said to consist in the love of neighbor,[9] and insert it in this work before I end, so that everyone may be edified.

This desire in the soul is great and vehement; its impatience is grave and harsh; the pain it suffers from desire is exceedingly great. Yet the soul must live in hope, and hope makes it pant and languish.

O holy desire of love, how strong your power is in a loving soul. It is a blessed passion, a sharp torment, a long-drawn-out evil, a murderous death and a dying life. The soul cannot attain the heights, it cannot rest and remain here on earth. It cannot bear the memory of its beloved out of desire for him; and to be without him makes it languish with desire. And so the soul must live in great discomfort.

Thus it is that the soul cannot and does not wish to be consoled. As the prophet says: 'My soul refused to be consoled'.[10] Therefore it happens then that the soul often refuses all consolation from God himself and from his creatures, for every consolation that could come from them, strengthen its love still more and draws its desire to a higher state, and this renews the soul's desire to foster love, and to remain in the fruition of love, and to live in exile without joy. And thus in

9. Mt 22:39

10. *Ps 76:3*

bus donis manet insatiata et
impacata, donec obtinuerit
quod tam incessanter quaerit.
Haec est laboriosa vita, nam
hic solatio levari non vult,
nisi obtinuerit quod tam incessanter quaerit.

Amor traxit eam et duxit eam,
et vias suas ire docuit, quas
fideliter secuta est. Saepe in
magno labore et in multiplici
opere, in magna cupidine et
vehementi desiderio, in multi-
moda impatientia et in magno
maerore; in afflictione et pros-
peritate et in multo dolore;
in quaerendo et in poscendo,
in carendo et in habendo; in
ascendendo et suspensa ma-
nendo, in sequendo et coni-
tendo; in necessitate et sollicitudine, in timore et in curis,
in languore et deperitione;
in magna fidelitate et in multa
infidelitate; in gratis et mo-
lestis: sic ad patiendum parata est. In morte et vita amare vult, et in sensu cordis
multos patitur dolores, et
propter Amorem patriam adi-
pisci cupit.

Et postquam in hoc exilio
omnia ei obvenerunt, in gloria est totum eius refugium.
Nam hoc est revera opus
amoris, ut quod supremum est
cupiat, et hunc statum prose-
quatur in quo plurimum amare
possit. Unde semper vult
Amorem sequi, Amorem nosse

all these gifts the soul remains un-
satisfied and unpacified until it obtains what it so incessantly seeks.
This is a laborious life, because the
soul does not wish to be lifted up by
consolation here, unless it has obtained what it so incessantly seeks.

Love has tugged it and led it; love
has taught the soul to travel Love's
paths, and the soul has followed
them faithfully, often in great labor
and with many kinds of work, in
much longing and vehement desire,
in many kinds of impatience and
great sadness, in weal and woe and
in much pain, in seeking and in
asking, in lacking and possessing, in
climbing and remaining suspended,
in following and striving, in need
and distress, in fear and in cares, in
languor and in ruin, in great faithfulness and much unfaithfulness, in
joys and in sorrows, and thus the
soul is prepared to suffer. It wills to
love both in life and in death; it suffers many pains in its heart, and it
longs to attain the fatherland for the
sake of Love.

After all these things have befallen
the soul in this exile, its whole
refuge lies in glory. For this is
truly love's work, to desire what
is supremely best, and to pursue
that state in which it can love the
most. Therefore the soul always
wills to follow Love, to know Love,

et Amore frui, quod in hoc
exilio ei contingere non potest. Propterea vult pergere
ad patriam, ubi domum suam
fundavit et totum desiderium
direxit et ubi amorose quiescit. Nam bene novit : ibi omne
impedimentum ei aufertur et
amabiliter a Dilecto recipitur.
Ibi cupide aspiciet quod tam
tenere amavit, et Eum possi-
debit ad suam beatitudinem,
cui fideliter inservivit ; et Eo
fruetur cum plena delectatione, quem saepe in anima cum
amore amplexa est.

Et ibi intrabit in gaudium Domini sui, sicut dicit sanctus
Augustinus : ' Qui in te intrat,
intrat in gaudium Domini sui '
etc. , et non timebit sed se
habebit optime in Optimo.

Illic anima unitur Sponso suo,
et tota unus spiritus cum Eo
efficitur, in inseparabili fidelitate et in amore aeterno. Et
qui Eum coluit in tempore
gratiae, Eo fruetur in aeterna
gloria, ubi nihil aliud facient
quam laudare et amare. Quo
Deus nos omnes perducat !
Amen.

and to have fruition of Love—
something which cannot happen
to it in exile. Therefore the soul
wants to proceed to the fatherland where it has built its home
and directed its whole desire,
and where it rests in love, for it
well knows that there every impediment will be removed from
it and that it will be received
with love by its beloved. There it
will gaze with eagerness upon
what it has so tenderly loved,
and it will possess for its own
blessedness Him whom it has
faithfully served, and it will with
full delight have fruition of him
whom it has often embraced in
the soul with love.

There it will enter into the joy
of its Lord, as Saint Augustine
says: 'He who enters into you,
enters into the joy of his Lord'
etc., and he will not fear. In him
who is all perfection he shall
have all perfection.

There the soul is united to its
bridegroom, and is wholly made
one spirit with him in inseparable faithfulness and eternal love. Having worshipped
him in the time of grace, it will
have fruition of him in eternal
glory where there will be no activity save praising and loving.
May God lead us all there.
Amen.

ℂ DE CARITATE PROXIMI
xv. capitulum

263 Quoniam <igitur> in precedentibus ,qualiter hec sancta
dei famula caritatis donum ad excitandum circa proximorum
salutem[1], a deo collatum acceperit, paucis expressimus:, nunc,
qualiter idipsum exercuerit, etiam sub breuitatis modulo per-
stringamus.

At quoniam in cellam vinariam introducta, sicut sponsa [sicut]
electissima, fuerat, vbi rex ipse celestis in ea caritatem ordi-
nauerat[2] opere precium erat // f. 334 c vt illum caritatis gustum
nectareum ad vsum proximorum partiendo refunderet:, et, celestis
talenti largissima dispensatrix, caritatis <donum> quod acceperat ad lucrum alijs erogaret. Hoc est ordinate caritatis officium.,
vt proximorum saluti studio deuotionis inseruiat:, et <sicut>
deum, omnium creatorem, amplissime dilectionis brachijs incessanter amplectitur., ita quoque, rerum creatarum necessitatibus inclinata, bonos simul et malos diligat., et ad ipsas etiam
irrationabiles creaturas, dilatato sinu clementie, se extendat. Si
enim tantum eos diligeret qui se diligunt:, quam mercedem acciperet.,[3] aut quid retributionis acquireret si se salutantes solummodo salutaret[4]?

264 Proinde beatrix nostra quam diligenter hanc caritatis normam
exercuit., quam indigentibus in omni necessitate compatiens
fuerit., etsi non sit qui plenius enarrare sufficiat:, ex eo tamen
quasi ex quodam rationabili argumento, conicere quis valebit,
quod, in caritate dei sui firmissime radicata, numquam ab eius
beneplacito discrepando recedere potuit; sed potius illius magisterio mancipata velut magistram discipula, vel sicut ancilla do-
min<am>, necessaria quadam, vt sic dixerim benevolentia
coluit:, et ei, tamquam matrifamilias, in cuncto voluntatis sue
proposito fideliter obediuit.

THE LOVE OF NEIGHBOR
Chapter Fifteen

263 We have already briefly told how this holy servant of God Beatrice received from God the gift of charity to be stirred up in regard to her neighbor's salvation, and so now let us also tell briefly how she exercised the same gift.

Because like a chosen bride she had been brought into the wine cellar where the heavenly king himself had set charity in order in her,[1] it was fitting that she pour that nectar-like taste of charity back out in sharing it for her neighbors' use, and that she, as an abundant dispenser of the heavenly talent, should pay out for the profit of others the gift of charity which she had received. It is the duty of well-ordered charity to serve a neighbor's salvation with attention and devotion. Just as love unceasingly embraces God, the creator of all, with outstretched arms, so it should incline to the needs of creatures, loving good and bad alike, and should extend itself with a generous merciful bosom even to irrational creatures. If charity only loved those who loved it, what reward should it have,[2] or what recompense should it have if it only greeted those who greet it?[3]

264 Consequently, even if no one may be qualified to tell fully how diligently our Beatrice exercised this norm of charity or how compassionate she was with those suffering any need, one can conjecture by a kind of rational argument that she who was firmly rooted in the love of her God could never draw back or diverge from what pleased him. Rather, delivered over to his teaching, she revered him with a certain necessary benevolence, so to speak, as a pupil does her teacher, or a servant her mistress; and like a housewife she obeyed him faithfully in every intention of her will.

1. Sg 2:4   2. *Mt 5:46*   3. Mt 5:47

Hinc etiam, apostolicam sequens regulam [5], cum infirmantibus
infirmabatur et cum scandalizatis vrebatur cotidie : ; hinc, omnem
aliene tolerantie seruitutem necessariam in se transferens, a compassionis affectu non potuit, in quocumque necessitatis articulo,
viscera misericordie cohibere. Quanto namque per caritatis affectum ipsi creatori cunctarum rerum artius inherebat : , tanto
profecto fidelius, non tam voluntarium quam etiam necessarium
ipsis creaturis adepte caritatis obsequium impendebat.

265 Erat ergo videre diuersarum etatum conditionum et profes-
sionum homines ad beatam feminam tamquam ad singularem pa-
tronam in suarum necessitatum articulo cotidie confluentes ; hic
se vexari temptationibus. , ille se grauari potentum querebatur
oppressionibus : ; hic spirituales, ille se corporales sufferre molestias causabatur. ; hic se gratie lacrimarum querebatur expertem. ,
ille vero ad vacandum orationum studio se referebat, aut // f. *334d*
cordis aut corporis debilitatis viribus, impotentem. Alter fraternum
odium a corde suo non posse se profitebatur expellere : , alter vero
seu inuidie seu iracundie passionibus. , aut aliorum quorumcumque
viciorum importunis se <narrabat> infestationibus subiacere.
Quibus omnibus a venerabili christi famula patrocinium implo-
tantibus. , et, pro qualitate vel corporalium vel spiritualium in-
commodorum, aut consiliorum aut orationum ab ea beneficia
postulantibus, virgo domini, patefacto sinu clementie, mox oc-
currere consueuit : ; et hijs doctrine pabulum, illis salubre consilium impendendo. , vel orationum suarum deuota subsidia pro-
mittendo. , frequentissime sanatos [6], aut in magna parte consolatos
reddidit, superna cooperante clementia, que, per merita sancte
femine, talium innumerosam multitudinem a varijs tribulationibus
et <oppressione> seruitutis dyabolice liberauit. ; **266** <Q>uos
autem in peccatorum sorde <demersos>, aut, perniciosa consuetudine delinquendi, per suggestiones demoniacas adeo repperit
induratos vt non facile salutaribus monitis acquiescerent : hos
omni sollicitudine qua potuit, nunc arguendo vel increpando

For this reason, following the apostle's rule, she was weak with the weak, and she burned daily with those who were scandalized.[4] For this reason also she necessarily took upon herself whatever servitude the other person was suffering, not being able to withhold her mercy and compassion in any grievous situation. The more closely she clung to the creator of all things through the affection of love, the more faithfully she gave to his creatures a charitable service that was not so much voluntary as necessary.

265 Therefore persons of various ages, conditions, and professions were to be seen daily coming with their needs to the blessed woman Beatrice as to a special patroness. This one complained of being vexed with temptations, that one, that he was grieviously oppressed by the powerful; one pleaded that he suffered spiritual troubles, and another that he suffered bodily troubles; this one complained that he lacked the grace of tears, and that one said he was unable to apply himself attentively to prayer through some weakness of heart or body. This one would confess that he could not drive fraternal hatred from his heart; another would tell how subject he was to the passions of envy or anger or the troublesome attacks of all kinds of other vices. To all these who were imploring the protection of Christ's venerable servant, and asking the benefits of her counsels and prayers according to their bodily or spiritual ailments, the Lord's virgin Beatrice opened the bosom of her compassion and quickly came to their help. She sent them away very often healed or in great measure consoled by giving to some the food of her teaching, to others healthy counsel, or by promising the devout help of her prayers. Divine mercy cooperated and through the merits of the holy woman freed an innumerable multitude of such persons from various troubles and the oppression of servitude to the devil.

266 Those whom she found so sunk in the filth of sin or so hardened by the devil's suggestions in the deadly habit of transgressing that they would not easily agree to her salutary advice, such persons Beatrice would strive to snatch from the snare of sin, at one time censuring and

4. 2 Co 11:29

⁶⁵ verbis, aut minis etiam deterrendo., nunc autem, cum oportunum
erat, blandis obsecrationibus humiliter erigendo iuxta regulam
apostolicam, a laqueo peccatorum eripere studuit ; et hijs paterne
correptionis stimulum, illis materne consolationis proferens blan-
dimentum, in omni patientia et doctrina cunctorum necessitatibus
⁷⁰ obuiare non distulit :, et, omnibus omnia cum apostolo facta
vt omnes lucrifaceret ⁷, omni residuo vite sue tempore, per hec
vel hijs similia caritatis obsequia, celestia lucra thesaurizando
profecit., et ipsi rerum omnium creatori, qui est omnium princi-
pium caput et origo bonorum, tam in se, per affectum sancti
⁷⁵ amoris, quam in membris suis, per virtutum animarumque profectum, fidelissimo seruitutis officio decetero ministrauit.
267 Tantam quoque gratiam electe sue dominus in hoc pio caritatis obsequio dederat exequendo :, quod multotiens, antequam
hominum causas apud supernum iudicem susciperet promouendas,
⁸⁰ ipsa totam causarum originem et processum, nemine reuelante,
cognosceret., et penam peccatis hominum debitam, ∥ ƒ. 335·a
diuineque seueritatis indignationem contra peccatores accensam.,
ex sola reuelatione sancti spiritus ad liquidum indagaret.
Quorum vtique miseranda negotia quanto videbantur ex immani-
⁸⁵ tate scelerum grauiora., tanto fortiori compassionis affectu fra-
ternam miseriam in se transferens et proximorum inedie condescendens, ad miserorum subuentionem totam cordis intentionem
apposuit :, et velut aduocata ⁸ fidelis, non orationibus preces aut
fletibus, <sed> miserorum causas allegatione deuota coram dis-
⁹⁰ stricto iudice <portauit>. Verum quoniam ipsa scelerum immanis
enormitas interdum oranti viam exauditionis obstruere videbatur :,
quotiens id contingebat, erat videre deuotam feminam, nimio doloris incommodo fatigatam ac si propria fuissent crimina que plan-
gebat, eiulando merendoque tabescere, cuius anima profecto conso-
⁹⁵ lari renuit :, donec orationum illius ac lacrimarum euictus instantia,
pius dominus quod petebatur dignatus est misericorditer indulgere.

reproving them by words with all possible care, or also restraining them with threats. At another time, when it was opportune, she humbly lifted them up with enticing entreaties, according to the apostolic rule.[5] She promptly faced everyone's needs with all patience and teaching,[6] providing the goad of paternal rebuke to some and the enticement of maternal consolation to others. All the rest of her life she progressed in storing up heavenly treasures[7] through these and other, similar works of charity, making herself, with the apostle, all things to all men that she might gain all.[8] With ever faithful and dutiful service she continued to minister to the Creator of all things, the beginning, head and origin of all that is good. This she did to the Creator himself through the affection of holy love, and to his members through progress in virtue and through the advancement of souls.

267 The Lord had given Beatrice, his chosen one, such grace in pursuing this charitable duty that often, before she had undertaken the advocacy of men's cases before the heavenly judge, she knew without disclosure the whole origin and process of the case, and by revelation of the Holy Spirit alone she clearly searched into the punishment due men's sins and the severe divine anger kindled against sinners.

She applied the whole intention of her heart to help the misery of those whose pitiable troubles seemed indeed to be frightfully more serious crimes, transferring to herself with much stronger affective compassion her brother's wretchedness and condescending to her neighbors' extreme penury. Like a faithful advocate, she did not forward the cases of the wretched merely by prayers and weeping but she devoutly commissioned herself to bring them before the strict judge. As often as it happened that the huge enormity of the crimes seemed to bar the way to a successful hearing of the prayer, the devout woman was then to be seen wearied with excessive pain and trouble as if she were bewailing her own crimes, and she would waste away, lamenting and grieving, her soul refusing to be consoled[9] until the loving Lord, conquered by the persistence of her prayers and tears, deigned mercifully to grant what she asked.

5. Eph 4:1   6. 2 Tm 4:2   7. 1 Co 9:22
8. *1 Co 9:19*   9. Ps 76:3

268 Sic ergo, quod pro <speciali> munere dudum acceperat,
officium caritatis erga proximorum salutem, diebus multis exercuit :, sic per suorum suffragia meritorum peccatoribus viam
100   diuine clementie patefecit. Sic a laqueo dyabolice seruitutis peccatorum animas, auxiliante deo, potenter eripuit :, sic leuiathan
serpentem tortuosum [9], humani generis crudelissimum inimicum,
eneruatis potentie sue viribus, ab antiquis ditionis sue sedibus
effugauit. Tantam quoque compassionis affluentiam in eius sancto
105   pectore diuina gratia propinauerat :, vt non solum hominibus,
sed ipsis brutis animalibus quoque in suis necessitatibus plenissimo compateretur affectu ; et sic minutissimis quoque bestiolis
aut auiculis in <suarum> sufferentia passionum affectuose
condescenderet :, vt illorum aliquid a quocumque ledi vel occidi
110   homine sine multo compassionis affectu conspicere non valeret.
269 Sed quia iam tempus instat vt finem dictis facere debeam., et amicum
silentij portum, iam lassis eloquentie viribus, apprehendam, narrationi mee,
quam de moribus et vita venerabilis beatricis, et-si non ad plenum vt debueram., ad mediocrem tamen vt credo sufficientiam, hucvsque protraxi,
115   metam statuo :; nunc autem qualiter ex hac luce migrauerit., et per optatum
mortis transitum ad celestem patriam // f. 335 b euolauerit., quod non ex
libro vite sue sed ex fidelium narratione comperi., maxime venerabilis
christine sororis sue, sibi in prioratus regimine succedentis, vt competentiorem
huic operi finem faciam, verbis breuibus <hic> adiungo.

❡ DE TRANSITU EIUS
xvi. capitulum

270 Cum ergo tempus instare cepisset vt, consummato presentis vite cursu,
pius dominus electam suam <eterne> felicitatis brauio remunerare dispone-
5   ret ;, et, quem in terris messuerat., in celis fructum perpetue felicitatis sibi
centupliciter restauraret :, virgo domini, prout ab olim acceperat in promisso. :
quod aliquanto videlicet tempore priusquam ex hac vita decederet, amoris
incendio ardens mori cuperet ;, <sic quod> pre nimio celestium desiderio,
corporalibus exhaustis viribus, egrotaret [1] : circa celeberrimam natiuitatis
10   dominice solempnitatem [2] amoris febre corripi., et feruentissimo caritatis typo

268 Thus for many days Beatrice exercised the duty of charity toward her neighbors' salvation, which she had formerly taken up as a special task. In this way by her suffrages and merits she opened the way of divine mercy for sinners; in this way by God's help she powerfully snatched the souls of sinners from the snare of the devil's slavery; in this way she expelled from the seat of his ancient power Leviathan, the crooked serpent,[10] the cruel enemy of the human race, and his powers were weakened. Divine grace had poured out in her holy breast such an abundance of compassion that she had the fullest compassionate affection not only for men but also for the very brute animals in their needs, and she would so affectionately condescend to the smallest little animals and birds in their sufferings that she could not see any of them wounded or killed by anyone without great affectionate compassion.

269 But now the time has come when I put an end to my speaking, and land in the friendly harbor of silence, my forces of eloquence being exhausted. I finish my story which I have drawn out thus far about the life and character of the venerable Beatrice; even if it is not as complete as I should have made it, still I think it tolerably sufficient. In a few words I now add how she left this life and flew off to the heavenly fatherland through the longed-for-passage of death. I have learned of this not from the book of her own life but from what reliable people told me, especially her venerable sister Christine, who succeeded her as prioress, and thus I end this work in a quite fitting way.

HER PASSAGE
Chapter Sixteen

270 The time began to draw near that the loving Lord should reward his chosen handmaid with the prize of eternal happiness[1] at the close of this present life, and should restore a hundredfold to her in heaven the fruit of eternal happiness which she had reaped on earth.[2] This was in accordance with the promise formerly received by the Lord's virgin, namely that a short time before she would depart this life, burning with the fire of love, she would ardently desire to die, and that, her bodily strength spent, she would grow sick because of her excessive desire for heaven. So Beatrice began to be seized with the fever of love

10. Is 27:1   1. 2 Tm 4:7   2. Mt 19:29

tam vehementer cepit et acriter infestari ; , quod, virium, vt dictum est, officio destituta, caput ab infirmitatis strato releuare nequiuerit : ; sed per dies aliquos quibus superuixit, infinito cordis desiderio vocationis sue tempus ala-criter expectauit.

15 **271** Cum igitur, a predicta solempnitate natiuitatis dominice ad augusti terminum vsque[3], iacens in lectulo grauiter egrotasset. , et, debilitato natu-ralium virium adminiculo, morti iam propinquare cepisset ; , extreme vnctionis oleo peruncta et viuifici sacramenti viatico premunita, in medio iuuencularum tympanistriarum[4], letantibus angelis et beatorum omnium sanctis agminibus,
20 inter sponsi sui brachia, quem affuisse neminem dubitare presumimus, astan-tibus tam eiusdem loci monialibus quam vtriusque sexus ex vicinis locis congregatis secularibus[5], ipsius patrocinijs se iuuari firmiter confidentibus. , beatum spiritum leta reddidit, et ad chorum seraphin, vbi locus perpetue requietionis ab olim sibi deputatus extiterat[6], cum hymnidicis canticis et
25 tripudio, christi sine fine fruitura solacio, feliciter emigrauit. Et vere feliciter : quippe que, sicut quibusdam religiosis et fide dignis certa reuelatione mon-stratum est, omnibus in eius transitu tunc presentibus, vt in // fol. 335 c statu saluandorum et in electorum asscriberentur numero, suis meritis impe-trauit. [7]
30 **272** Facta est autem eius sanctissima depositio dominice incarnationis anno m°. cc°. lx viij°, iiij° kalendas augusti[8] ; et sepulta est inter ecclesiam et capitulum, in claustri ambulatorio, loco scilicet honestissimo : ; regnante domino nostro ihesu christo. , cui cum patre et spiritu sancto est honor et imperium in secula seculorum. Amen.

❡ SEQUITUR CONCLUSIO <HUIUS OPERIS>
xvij. capitulum

273 Nunc igitur, o dilecte domine[1] in christo et sorores[2], hoc, quod a vobis iniunctum acceperam, huius translationis opere per dei gratiam executo. ,
5 deuotionem vestram ego, conseruus et confrater vester, hortor et admoneo : ,

and to be strongly attacked by the most fervent type of love around the great feast of the Lord's birth. Deprived of all strength, as we said, she could not raise her head from her sick bed, but during the days remaining to her, she eagerly awaited the time of her call with unlimited desire of the heart.

271 Therefore when she had lain gravely sick in bed from the aforesaid solemnity of the Lord's birth until the end of August, and had begun to come close to death by the weakening of her natural strength, then, anointed with the oil of Extreme Unction and fortified beforehand with the viaticum of the life-giving Sacrament, Beatrice gladly surrendered her blessed spirit into the arms of her spouse whom we presume no one doubts to have been present, in the midst of the maidens sounding their timbrels,[3] with the rejoicing angels and the holy throngs of all the blessed, with the nuns of the same place standing around together with seculars of both sexes, gathered from neighboring places, persons who trusted firmly that they would be helped by her patronage. Thus happily she migrated with hymns, canticles and dancing into the choir of Seraphs where her place of perpetual rest had previously been assigned to her, there to enjoy without end the consolation of Christ. And truly happily, because as was revealed with certitude to some religious persons worthy of belief, she obtained by her merits that all those who were then present at her passing would be registered in the state of those to be saved and in the number of the elect.

272 Her holy burial took place on the fourth of the calends of August in the year one thousand two hundred and sixty-eight of the Lord's Incarnation; she was buried in the ambulatory of the cloister between the church and the chapter, a place of great honor under the reign of Our Lord Jesus Christ, to whom is honor and dominion together with the Father and the Holy Spirit forever and ever. Amen.

CONCLUSION OF THIS WORK
Chapter Seventeen

273 Therefore, beloved Ladies and Sisters in Christ, now that I have, by the grace of God, completed by this work of translation what I undertook from you, I, your fellow-servant and brother, exhort and admonish your

---

3. Ps 67:26

quatenus vos que beatam hanc in carne presentem habere meruistis. , et illa
caritatis opera, tanto vobis tempore demonstrata, perpetue memorie, sicut fas
est credere, commendastis ; , illa virtutum exempla sic vestris quoque moribus
imprimere studeatis : , vt <eius> vos sequaces, eius vos discipulas, rec-
tissime conuersationis operibus, ostendatis : et vestris quoque sequacibus ac-
ceptam ab ea viuendi normam, exercendam olim post futuro tempore relin-
quatis : ; gratias agentes omnipotenti domino. , qui vobis, in beatrice sua, tam
perfectam <conuersandi> formam exhibuit. , et, vt sic dixerim, oculata fide
viam celestis patrie vobis aspiciendam obtulit. , et, perhennis stilo memorie
vestris <inscriptam> mentibus, inculcauit.

274 Vobis etiam que venerabilem hanc dei famulam corporalibus oculis, in
carnis degentem ergastulo, non vidistis [3], fraterno caritatis affectu supplico,
quatenus imitabilem sue conuersationis ymaginem, quam vestris subtractam
doletis aspectibus, tam ex libro vite sue quam ex maiorum vestrarum conuersatione collectam [4]. , sic vestris mentibus imprimatis et in tabulis cordis
carnalibus tam firmiter inscribatis : , vt et vos quoque venerabilis beatricis
discipulas. , ymmo christi, qui solus in celo pariter et in terra <perfecto>
magisterij nomine et officio fungitur, ostendatis ; quatenus et vos ad electionis
tytulum, cum hijs quibus depositioni sancte virginis interesse superna con-
cessit gratia, deo propicio, pertingere valeatis : et me, conseruum vestrum in
christo, simul in vnum // f. 335 d omnes vos alloquor, orationum vestrarum
participem [me] faciatis.

275 Et te quoque, lector [5], admoneo, rogans et deprecans vt sic presentis
opusculi lectionem transcurras. , vt edificationis fructum, quem in eo quesieris,
efficaciter apprehendas : , non michi sed domino gratias referens si quid in eo
profeceris ; , qui scribentis stilum ad finem vsque perduxit : , et quod ad
edificationem tuam <insererem>, vbi et quomodo voluit, inspirauit [6]. Nec
tibi longa narrationis<mee>protractio fastidium generet. , cum, sicut protestatus sum ab initio, non mea sed aliena protulerim : ; quamquam non
modicam partem, in <plerisque> locis, omiserim eorum que sui nimia pro-
funditate lectoris sensum effugere potuissent ; que quidem, et-si perfectioribus
intelligibilia : , minus tamen exercitatos in huiusmodi habentibus intellectus,

kindness: that you who have deserved to have this blessed woman Beatrice present in the flesh and who have impressed on your memories forever, as it is right to believe, those works of charity manifested to you for so long a time, I exhort you to impress these examples of the virtues on your conduct as well, so that you show yourselves her followers and disciples by the works of a most upright life, and that you leave to those who follow you the pattern of life formerly received from her, to be carried out for the time to come. Thank the almighty Lord who has shown you in his Beatrice such a perfect form of living, and who has shown you by an eye-witness, so to speak, how to behold the way to heaven, and who has inscribed it on your minds with the stylus of everlasting memory.

274 With the affection of brotherly charity I also beg those who have not seen this venerable servant of God with bodily eyes while she was living in the prison of the flesh. May you firmly imprint on your minds and inscribe on the fleshy tablets of your heart the imitable image of her life which you grieve to have been withdrawn from your eyes. But you have gathered from the book of her life and from the words of your elders so much that you too may show yourselves to be the disciples of the venerable Beatrice, indeed of Christ who alone in heaven and on earth exercises perfectly the name and office of teacher.[1] Thus may you also attain, by God's favor, the title of election with those whom divine grace allowed to be present at the burial of the holy virgin. Speaking to all of you together I say, make me, your fellow-servant in Christ, a sharer in your prayers.

275 I also admonish you, the reader, asking and begging that you so peruse the reading of this present work as to grasp effectively the fruit of edification that you seek in it, thanking not me but the Lord if you in any way profit by it. He has brought the writer's pen through to the end, and whatever I might have inserted for your edification, he has inspired where and as he willed. Do not let my long-drawn-out narrative account beget weariness in you, since, as I protested from the beginning, I was not putting forth my own but someone else's cause. Yet in many places I have omitted no small part of those things which might have evaded the reader's understanding by their excessive depth. Even if they were intelligible to the more perfect, they would have been more tedious than edifying, would have done more harm than good to those with minds less practiced in these matters.

1. Jn 13:13

magis tedio quam edificationi. , magis dampno quam lucro forsitan extitissent.
276 Ne ergo multa que in libro suo beatrix sancta de dei proximique caritate
40 subtilissima ratione disseruit, omnino pretermisisse viderer. , et sic magnam
partem voluminis dicerer detruncasse ; vel, econtrario, cuncta, prout ea
susceperam oblata, describens, superfluis viderer quam necessarijs potius
insudasse : mediam quamdam viam eligens, <feci> quod potui. , et latissi-
mam, interminabilemque materiam ita sub verborum breuitate perstrinxi. ,
45 quod sapientibus, quibus pauca tetigisse satis est, in paucitate verborum occa-
sionem inuestigandi potiora caritatis misteria prebui. , et fastidiosis, amico
breuitatis compendio satisfeci.
277 Sed et te, venerabilis christi sponsa simul et filia, beatrix sancta, cui in
hoc opere mei <pauperis> merito pariter et ingenio, vt potui deseruiuit
50 industria, te, inquam, deprecor, o beata, quatenus hunc studij mei laborem
recommendatum habeas : , et ihesu christi, sponsi tui, gratiam, quam huius
laboris mei premium et mercedem fore desidero, tuis sanctis meritis preci-
busque michi, cum omnibus huius operis tui lectoribus et deuotis tuis, obti-
neas. , et in extremo nostre vocationis termino, ne nos antiqui seductoris
55 infestet astutia, protegas ac defendas ; et ad illa superna gaudia quibus
frueris, annuente christi misericordia, prouehas et perducas: ; qui cum <deo>
patre et spiritu sancto viuit et regnat deus per omnia secula seculorum. Amen.

276 I have chosen a certain middle way, doing what I could, lest I seem altogether to have omitted the many things that the holy Beatrice discussed in her book with very subtle reasoning about the love of God and neighbor, (and so I might be said to have thus truncated a large part of her volume), or lest, on the other hand, I should describe everything I received and so should seem to have sweated over what is superfluous, rather than what is necessary. I have touched briefly on the very extensive and interminable material so that in a few words I have given to the wise—for whom it suffices to have touched a few points—the occasion of investigating the greater mysteries of charity, and I have satisfied the fastidious with a kindly short compendium.

277 But you, holy Beatrice, Christ's venerable bride and daughter, whom my efforts have served as best I could in this work of mine, poor both in merit and skill, I beseech you, O blessed one, to accept this, my zealous labor. By your holy merits and prayers obtain for me, and for all the readers of this work of yours and for your devoted ones, the grace of Jesus Christ, your bridegroom, which I desire as the prize and reward of my labor. Protect and defend us to the last moment of our summoning, lest the cunningness of the old seducer attack us. Convey and lead us to those heavenly joys which you enjoy, by the mercy of Christ who lives and reigns with God the Father and the Holy Spirit, God forever and ever. Amen.

BIBLIOGRAPHY

Berlière, Ursmer. 'Ecoles claustrales au Moyen Age', *Académie royale de la Belgique. Bulletin de la Classe des Lettres et des Sciences morales et politiques*. Brussels 12 (1921) 550-71.

Bets, P.V. 'Preface inédite de la B. Béatrice de Tirlemont', *AHEB* 7 (1954) 77-82.

Brett, Edward. Tr. *Humbert of Romans. His Life and Views of Thirteenth Century Society.* Toronto, 1984. *Opusculum Tripartitum,* 176-194.

Canivez, Joseph. *Statuta Capitulorum Generalium Cisterciensis Ordinis Ordinis 16-1786.* 8 vols. Leuven, 1933-41.

Ceglar, Stanislas. *William of St. Thierry. The Chronology of His Life...* Dissertation. Washington D.C. 1971.

De Bruin, Cebus C. 'De prologen van de eerste Historiebijbels geplaatst in het raam van hun tijd'. *The Bible and Medieval Culture.* W. Lourdaux and D. Verhelst, eds. Leuven, 1979.

De Ganck, Roger. 'Over de benoeming van een nieuwe rector te Nazareth in 1448'. *Citeaux* 5 (1954) 45-54.

———— . 'Chronological Data in the Lives of Ida of Nivelles and Beatrice of Nazareth'. *OGE* 57 (1983) 14-27.

Despy, George. Les débuts de l'Inquisition dans les anciens Pays-Bas au XIIIe siècle. *Problèmes du Christianisme* 9. Brussels, 1980: 71-104.

Duggan, Charles. 'Equity and Compassion in Papal Marriage Decretals in England'. *Love and Marriage in the Twelfth Century.* W. Van Hoecke and A. Welkenhuysen, eds. Leuven, 1981.

Fredericq, Paul. *Corpus documentorum Inquisitionis pravitatis Neerlandicae.* 2 vols. Ghent-Den Hague, 1889.

Grundmann, Herbert. *Religiöse Bewegungen im Mittelalter.* Berlin 1935, rpt Hildesheim, 1961.

Hart, Colomba. 'Consecratio Virginum: Thirteenth-Century Witnesses'. *The American Benedictine Review* 23 (1972) 267-87.

Häring, Nicolas M. 'Der Lieraturkatalog im Affligem'. *RBén* 80 (1949) 64-96.

Haskins, Charles Homer. *Studies in Medieval Culture,* 2nd ed. New York, 1965.

Hautcoeur, Edouard. *Histoire de l'abbaye de Flines,* 2nd ed. Lille, 1909.

Hendrix, Guido. 'Cistercian Sympathies in the 14th Century Catalogus virorum illustriorum'. *Citeaux* 27 (1976) 267-87.

———. 'Primitive Versions of Thomas of Cantimpré's *Vita Lutgardis'.* *Citeaux* 29 (1978) 153-206.

Henriquez, Chrysostom. *Quinque prudentes virgines.* Antwerp, 1630.

Herlihy, David. *The Social History of Italy and Western Europe, 700-1500.* London, 1979.

Hilka, Alfons. 'Altfranzösische Mystik und Beguinentum'. *Zeitschrift für romanische Philologie* 47 (1927) 121-70.

Hoste, Anselme. 'Het Levensboek van Beatrijs van Nazareth'. *Librije.* July-September, 1966. 81-93.

Huyghe, Gérard. La clôture des moniales des origines à la fin du XIIIe siècle. Roubaix, 1947.

Lambrecht, Daniel. *De synode in het oude bisdom Doornik gesitueerd in de Europese Ontwikkeling.* Dissertation. Ghent, 1976: 263-427.

Lerner, Robert E. *The Heresy of the Free Spirit in the Later Middle Ages.* Berkeley-Los Angeles-London, 1972.

Lynch, J.H. 'The Cistercians and Underage Novices'. *Citeaux* 24 (1973) 283-97.

Marchal, Jean. *Le 'droit d'oblat'. Essai sur une variété de pensionnés monastiques.* Archives de la France monastique 49. Ligugé-Paris, 1955.

McDonnell, Ernest. *The Beguines and Beghards in Medieval Culture.* With Special Emphasis on the Belgian Scene. New Brunswick, N.J., 1954.

Metz, René. *La consécration des vierges dans l'Eglise romaine. Étude d'histoire et de liturgie.* Rome, 1954.

Milis, Ludo. 'William de St. Thierry. Son origine, sa formation et ses premières expériences monastiques'. *Saint-Thierry. Une abbaye du VIe au XXe siècle,* 1979.

Noonan, John T. *Contraception.* Harvard, MA, 1966.

Oppenheimer, Philipp. *Die Consecratio Virginum as geistesges-chichtliches Problem. Eine Studie zu ihrem Aufbau, ihren Wert und ihrer Geschichte.* Rome, 1943.

Paris, Julien. *Nomasticon Cisterciense.* Paris, 1664.

Pirenne, Henri. 'L'Instruction des marchands au Moyen Age.' Rpt in *Histoire de l'Occident Médiéval.* Bruges, 1951: 551-70.

Reypens, Léonce and Joseph Van Mierlo. *Beatrijs van Nazareth. Seven Manieren van Minne.* Leuven, 1926.

————. 'Nog een dertiendeeuwse Mystieke Cisterciësernon'. *OGE* 23 (1949) 225-46.

————. 'Een derde Beatrijs in onze dertiendeeuwse Letterkunde? Beatrijs van Dendermonde'. *OGE* 37 (1963) 419-22.

Roisin, Simone. *L'Hagiographie cistercienne dans le diocèse de Liége au XIIIe siècle.* Leuven-Brussels, 1947.

Séjalon, Hugo. *Nomasticon Cisterciense.* Solesmes, 1892.

Stroick, Autpert. 'Der Verfasser und Quellen der *Collectio de scandalis ecclesiae'. Archivum Franciscanum Historicum* 23 (1930) 3-41; 273-99; 433-66.

————. 'Ausgabe der *Collectio'. Archivum Franciscanum Historicum* 24 (1931) 33-62.

Van Schoors, Jo. *Ida van Leuven.* Dissertation. Leuven, 1982.

Van Doninck, Benedikt. *Obituarium monasterii Loci Sancti Bernardi.* Lérins, 1901.

Vekeman, H.W.J. 'Vita Beatricis en Seven Manieren van Minne. Een vergelijkende studie'. *OGE* 46 (1972) 3-54.

————. and J.J. Th.M. Tersteeg. *Van Seuen Manieren van Heiliger Minnen.* Zutphen, 1970.

See also the fuller Bibliography in *Towards Unification with God. Beatrice of Nazareth in Her Context. Part III.* Cistercian Studies Series, Number 122.

BIBLICAL REFERENCES

Scriptural citations are located by the paragraph number and line of the latin edition. Direct quotations of Scripture appear in italic type: paraphrases in roman type.

1,7	*Mt 25:7*	33,75	*Mt 24:12; 1 Jn 5:19*
2,12	Lk 14:30	33,78	Jn 6:61
4,40	1 Co 2:11	34,7	Ac 14:21
4,43	*Si 1:21*	34,12	Jb 2:7
4,47	*Mt 13:44*	34,13	Jb 2:8
6,63	Mt 6:1	34,16	Jb 2:10
6,65	Mt 5:16	36,11	*Mt 5:3*
6,68	Ep 6:11	39,56	*Ph 3:13*
6,71	*Mt 5:15*	41,71	*2 Co 4:10*
8,17	1 Tm 3:4	42,9	*Pr 4:23*
9,21	1 Tm 3:4	42,17	Sg 2:14
10,32	Ep 6:12	42,20	1 Tm 2:5
12,76	Lk 10:42	48,78	Mt 11:30
12,88	*Mt 13:44*	50,41	*Mt 13:24*
14,128	1 Ch 23:1	52,87	*Lk 1:46*
14,129	Mt 25:21	55,32	Ps 150:3
17,26	Is 8:4	59,122	*Sg 2:4*
18,45	Mt 10:37	62,48	*Mt 10:16*
18,54	Lm 3:28	62,60	Mt 28:20
24,23	*Mt 15:27; Jn 6:12*	62,72	*I Co 1:3*
24,27	Ps 131:4	64,94	*2 Co 1:3*
24,28	*Sg 1:12*	68,47	Jm 1:5
25,31	*Ps 77:26*	68,56	2 Co 6:1
25,32	Is 58:11	69,79	*Ex 16:16*
25,34	Ps 18:11	72,33	Eph 6:12
27,73	*Ac 4:32*	76,10	*Mt 25:6*
29,110	*Is 14:13*	77,54	Gn 29:18
29,111	*Jb 40:18*	78,58	Sg 5:6
29,117	*Ep 6:12*	80,27	*Ps 67:3*
30,9	Jb 2:7	80,28	Dt 4:24, Heb 12:29

INDEX

1 . Index of Persons

2. Index of Places and Subjects